Anthropology and the New C

ASA Monographs

ISSN 0066-9679

Anthropology and the New Cosmopolitanism

Rooted, Feminist and Vernacular Perspectives

**Edited by
Pnina Werbner**

Oxford • New York

First published in 2008 by
Berg
Editorial offices:
1st Floor, Angel Court, 81 St Clements Street, Oxford, OX4 1AW, UK
175 Fifth Avenue, New York, NY 10010, USA

Berg is the imprint of Oxford International Publishers Ltd.

Library of Congress Cataloguing-in-Publication Data

Anthropology and the new cosmopolitanism : rooted, feminist and vernacular
perspectives / edited by Pnina Werbner.
   p. cm.
   Includes bibliographical references and index.
   ISBN-13: 978-1-84788-197-7 (cloth)
   ISBN-10: 1-84788-197-1 (cloth)
   ISBN-13: 978-1-84788-198-4 (pbk.)
   ISBN-10: 1-84788-198-X (pbk.)
  1. Anthropology. 2. Cosmopolitanism. 3. Globalization—Social aspects.
I. Werbner, Pnina.

GN25.A64 2008
301—dc22

2008005171

British Library Cataloguing-in-Publication Data

A catalogue record for this book is available from the British Library.

ISBN 978 184788 197 7 (Cloth)
ISBN 978 184788 198 4 (Paper)

Typeset by JS Typesetting Ltd, Porthcawl, Mid Glamorgan
Printed in the United Kingdom by Biddles Ltd, King's Lynn

www.bergpublishers.com

Contents

Contents

Contributors

Aref Abu-Rabia is Chair of the Department of Middle Eastern Studies and teaches anthropology at Ben-Gurion University of the Negev, Beer-Sheva, Israel. He is author of four books, including *The Negev Bedouin and Livestock Rearing: Social, Economic and Political Aspects* (Berg 1994), and *A Bedouin Century: Education and Development Among the Negev Tribes in the Twentieth Century* (Berghahn 2002). He has published numerous scholarly articles across a range of subjects, including traditional medicine, ethno-botany, family customs, holy saints, education, violence, and abuse of children in the Middle East.

Elizabeth Colson is Professor Emeritus in the Department of Anthropology, University of California, Berkeley. She is author of *The Makah* (Manchester 1953), *Three Pomo Women* (California 1966), *Marriage and the Family among the Plateau Tonga* (Manchester 1958) *Social Organization of the Gwembe Tonga* (Manchester 1962), *Social Consequences of Resettlement* (Manchester 1973), *Tradition and Contract* (Aldine 1975), and most recently, *Tonga Religious Life in the 20th Century* (Bookworld Publishers 2006). She continues to do fieldwork among the Tonga of Zambia.

Richard Fardon is Professor and Head of the Department of Anthropology and Sociology at SOAS, University of London, where he teaches anthropological theory and the ethnography of West Africa. His most recent book, *Lela in Bali: History Through Ceremony in Cameroon* (Berghahn 2006), traces 200 years of change in a 'national' event across precolonial, colonial and postcolonial regimes. Other authored books include *Mary Douglas: an Intellectual Biography* (Routledge 1999) and a long-term project comparing the masquerades of the Nigerian Middle Belt, *Fusions: Masquerades and Thought-Style East of the Niger-Benue* (London, Saffron 2007). His edited books include *From Prague Poet to Oxford Anthropologist: Franz Baermann Steiner Celebrated* (with J. Alder and C. Tully, Munich 2003), *African Broadcast Cultures: Radio in Transition* (with Graham Furness, Praeger 2000), and *Modernity on a Shoestring: Dimensions of Globalization, Consumption and Development in Africa and Beyond* (Leiden 1999). He was editor of *Africa* until 2007.

David Graeber is Lecturer in Anthropology at Goldsmiths College, and the author of *Toward an Anthropological Theory of Value* (Palgrave 2002) and *Fragments of an Anarchist Anthropology* (Chicago 2004). His most recent books are *Lost People: Magic and the Legacy of Slavery in Madagascar* (Indiana 2007). Two books – *Possibilities: Essays on Hierarchy, Rebellion, and Desire*, and *Direct Action: An Ethnography*, are both forthcoming. He co-authored with Stevphen Shukaitis *Constituent Imagination: Militant Investigation, Collective Theorization* (AK Press 2007).

Stuart Hall is currently Professor Emeritus at the Open University and Visiting Professor, Goldsmiths College. He was born in Kingston, Jamaica, and was educated in Jamaica and at Merton College, Oxford, where he was Rhodes Scholar. A socialist, he joined forces in the 1950s with E.P. Thompson, Raymond Williams and others to launch two radical journals, *The New Reasoner* and the *New Left Review*, of which he was the editor (1959–61). In 1957 he joined the Campaign for Nuclear Disarmament with many other leading activists. He was Director of the Centre for Contemporary Cultural Studies at Birmingham University (1968–79) before becoming Professor of Sociology at the Open University. Among his many books are *Situating Marx* (1972), *Policing the Crisis* (1978), *The Hard Road to Renewal: Thatcherism and the Crisis of the Left* (1988), *New Times (1989), Resistance through Rituals* (1989), *Gramsci's Political Thought* (1990), *Formations of Modernity* (1991), *Questions of Cultural Identity* (1996), *Cultural Representations and Signifying Practices* (1997), *Visual Culture* (1999) and *Critical Dialogues in Cultural Studies (2004)*.

Chris Hann is Director of the Max Planck Institute for Social Anthropology, Halle, Germany. Prior to moving to Germany in 1999 he taught social anthropology in Britain at the Universities of Kent and Cambridge. He has published extensively in economic and political anthropology. Recent books include *'Not the Horse We Wanted!' Postsocialism, Neoliberalism and Eurasia*, and (with the 'Civil Religion' Group) *The Postsocialist Religious Question; Faith and Power in Central Asia and East-Central Europe*, (both volumes published by LIT Verlag 2006).

Eric Hirsch is Reader in Social Anthropology at Brunel University, West London. He has a long-standing interest in the ethnography and history of Melanesia and has also conducted anthropological research in Greater London. He recently co-edited *Transactions and Creations: Property Debates and the Stimulus of Melanesia* (Berghahn 2004), and a special edition of the journal *History and Anthropology* on the theme of 'Ethnographies of Historicity' (2005).

Dorothy L. Hodgson is Professor of Anthropology and Director of the Institute for Research on Women at Rutgers University, New Brunswick. She is the author of *The Church of Women: Gendered Encounters between Maasai and Missionaries* (Indiana 2005) and *Once Intrepid Warriors: Gender, Ethnicity and the Cultural Politics of Maasai Development* (Indiana 2001); editor of *Gendered Modernities: Ethnographic Perspectives* (Palgrave 2001) and *Rethinking Pastoralism in Africa: Gender, Culture and the Myth of the Patriarchal Pastoralist* (James Currey 2000), and co-editor with Sheryl McCurdy of *'Wicked' Women and the Reconfiguration of Gender in Africa* (Heinemann 2001). Her current work explores the historical and contemporary dynamics of pastoralist organisations, transnational advocacy and the state in Tanzania, forms of collective action among women in Africa, and tensions between the culture of rights and the rights of culture.

Joel S. Kahn, currently Professor of Anthropology at Melbourne's La Trobe University, has been carrying out anthropological research in Malaysia, Singapore and Indonesia for three decades. His publications include *Minangkabau Social Formations: Indonesian Peasants and the World Economy* (Cambridge 1980), *Constituting the Minangkabau: Peasants, Culture and Modernity in Colonial Indonesia* (Berg 1993), *Culture, Multiculture, Postculture* (Sage 1995) and *Modernity and Exclusion* (Sage 2001). His latest book is *Other Malays: Nationalism and Cosmopolitanism in the Modern Malay World* (NIAS and University of Hawaii Press 2006). He is currently researching 'Translocal Identities in the Modern Malay World', a project funded by the Australian Research Council.

Jonathan Parry is Professor of Anthropology at the London School of Economics and Political Science. He has done field research in various parts of north and central India on various topics. His publications include *Caste and Kinship in Kangra* (Routledge 1979), *Death in Banaras* (Cambridge 1994), *Death and the Regeneration of Life* (co-edited with M. Bloch, Cambridge 1982), *Money and the Morality of Exchange* (co-edited with M. Bloch, Cambridge 1989), *The Worlds of Indian Industrial Labour* (co-edited with J. Breman and K. Kapadia, Sage 1999), *Institutions and Inequalities* (co-edited with R. Guha, Oxford University Press 1999) and *Questions of Anthropology* (co-edited with R. Astuti and C. Stafford, Berg 2007).

Kalpana Ram is Senior Lecturer in Anthropology at Macquarie University where she is currently the Head of Department. Her main ethnography is *Mukkuvar Women: Gender, Hegemony and Capitalist Transformations in a South Indian Fishing Community* (Allen and Unwin 1991, Kali for Women Press 1992). Her edited collections include *Maternities and Modernities: Colonial and Post Colonial Experiences in Asia and the Pacific* (co-edited with M. Jolly, Cambridge

1998) and *Borders of Being: Citizenship, Sexuality and Reproduction in Asia and the Pacific* (co-edited with M. Jolly, Michigan 2001). She is currently working on a book that attempts to re-figure the terms of statist and intellectualist versions of modernity in India from the perspective of embodied experiences of fertility and spirit possession among rural poor women. She also writes on Indian dance, diaspora, gender and modernity.

Kathryn Robinson is Professor of Anthropology in the Research School of Pacific and Asian Studies, Australian National University. A significant strand of her research, focused on South Sulawesi, Indonesia, has been on aspects of contemporary women's social participation in Indonesia, including women's political activism, Islam, and international female labour migration. Her major publications include *Asian and Pacific Cosmopolitans: Self and Subject in Motion* (editor, Palgrave 2007), *Stepchildren of Progress: The Political Economy of Development in an Indonesian Mining Town* (SUNY 1986), *Living Through Histories: Culture, History and Social Life in South Sulawesi* (co-edited with Mukhlis Paini, ANU 1998), and *Women in Indonesia: Gender Equity and Development* (co-edited with Sharon Besell, Singapore ISEAS 2002). She is editor of the *Asia Pacific Journal of Anthropology.*

Owen B. Sichone is Senior Lecturer in the Department of Social Anthropology, University of Cape Town. He is a graduate of the University of Zambia, obtained his MA from Sussex University and PhD at Cambridge. He has taught social anthropology at Wits University and the University of Cape Town in South Africa. He has written extensively on Zambian politics and urban culture, and his most recent book is *South Africa's Diverse Peoples: A Reference Sourcebook* (ABC-Clio 2005). He is currently writing a study of xenophobia and xenophilia in Cape Town.

Maila Stivens is Director of Gender Studies at the University of Melbourne. She has carried out research on middle-class kinship in Sydney; in Malaysia on 'matrilineal' Negeri Sembilan; on modernity, work and family among the new Malay middle classes; on 'public' and 'private' in Southeast Asia; on the 'Asian Family'; on Family Values East and West, and is currently working on an Australian Research Council project on New Asian Childhoods. Previously a Lecturer in Anthropology at University College London, she has also been a visiting fellow at the Asia Research Institute, NUS, Singapore in 2004. Her main publications include: *Why Gender Matters in Southeast Asian Politics* (editor, Monash 1991), *Malay Peasant Women and the Land* (with Jomo Sundaram and Cecilia Ng, Zed 1994), *Matriliny and Modernity: Sexual Politics and Social Change in Rural Malaysia* (Allen and Unwin 1996), and two co-edited volumes

Gender and Power in Affluent Asia (with Krishna Sen, Routledge 1998) and *Human Rights and Gender Politics: Asia-Pacific Perspectives* (with Anne-Marie Hilsdon, Martha Macintyre and Vera Mackie, Routledge 2000).

Pnina Werbner is Professor of Social Anthropology at Keele University. She is the author of 'The Manchester Migration Trilogy' which includes *The Migration Process: Capital, Gifts and Offerings among British Pakistanis* (Berg 1990 and 2002), *Imagined Diasporas among Manchester Muslims: The Public Performance of Transnational Identity Politics* (James Currey, and School of American Research 2002) and *Pilgrims of Love: The Anthropology of a Global Sufi Cult* (Hurst and Indiana 2003). Edited collections include *Debating Cultural Hybridity* and *The Politics of Multiculturalism in the New Europe*, both co-edited with Tariq Modood (Zed Books 1997), *Embodying Charisma: Modernity, Locality and the Performance of Emotion in Sufi Cults* (co-edited with Helene Basu, Routledge 1998), *Women, Citizenship and Difference* (co-edited with Nira Yuval-Davis, Zed Books 1999), and a special issue of the journal *Diaspora* on the topic of 'The Materiality of Diaspora', co-edited with Karen Leonard (2000). Her fieldwork has included research in Britain, Pakistan and Botswana, where she studied Women and the Changing Public Sphere, the Manual Workers Union and Aids activists. Recent awards include an ESRC large grant to study 'New African Migrants in the Gateway City' and a comparative study of the Filipino diaspora in Israel and Saudi Arabia, supported by a large grant from the AHRC.

Richard Werbner is Emeritus Professor in African Anthropology and Honorary Research Professor in Visual Anthropology at the University of Manchester. Among his books are *Reasonable Radicals and Citizenship in Botswana* (Indiana 2004), *Ritual Passage, Sacred Journey* (Smithsonian 1989), *Postcolonial Identities in Africa* (editor, Zed Books 1996), *Memory and the Postcolony* (editor, Zed Books1998), *Postcolonial Subjectivities in Africa* (editor, Zed Books 2002) and *Tears of the Dead: The Social Biography of an African Family* (Edinburgh and Smithsonian 1991), for which he received the Amaury Talbot Prize of the Royal Anthropological Institute. He has directed and produced two ethnographic films, *Séance Reflections with Richard Werbner* (2004) and *Shade Seekers and the Mixer* (2007), and is currently working on a third *Eloyi*. He has carried out long-term research in Zimbabwe and Botswana. He is a member of the editorial boards of *Journal of Southern African Studies, Cultural Dynamics* and *Social Analysis*.

Preface

This book is the outcome of the ASA Diamond Jubilee conference on 'Cosmopolitanism and Anthropology', convened with Sean McLoughlin from Leeds University and held at Keele University in April 2006. In addition to the articles included here, the conference was the occasion for many other outstanding papers and attested to the wide interest of anthropologists in this topic. Several collections have come out of the conference: a special issue of *Nature and Culture* (2008) on cosmopolitanism and the environment, edited by Ben Campbell; a volume on *Cosmopolitanism in Practice*, edited by Magdalena Nowicka and Maria Rovisco (Ashgate 2007); *Sharing the Sacra: the Politics and Pragmatics of Inter-communal Relations around Holy Places*, edited by Glenn Bowman (Berghahn 2008), and *Cosmopolitanism, Morality and Existentialism*, edited by Lisette Josephides and Alex Hall (forthcoming). In addition to five plenary sessions and several keynote speakers, the meeting included twenty other workshops on diverse themes: Cosmopolitanism and Youth, Museums, Diaspora, the Indian Ocean, Health, Cities, Morality, Landscape, Material Culture, Popular Music, Practice, and Elites; Interpretive and Discrepant Cosmopolitanisms; Syncretism, and Religious Frameworks.

Many people helped make the conference, and this book, a success. In particular, I would like to thank Richard Fardon, then Chair of the ASA, for his unstinting faith and support throughout. The conversation with the contributors and the other keynote and plenary speakers, which started at the conference, has made the book, I believe, an intellectual journey for all of us. Elizabeth Colson and André Beteille travelled great distances to be with us. As ever, my husband, Dick Werbner, gave of his time and immense knowledge in the subject.

Pnina Werbner
April 2007

Introduction: Towards a New Cosmopolitan Anthropology[1]

Pnina Werbner

In the Beginning...

Ten people met in July 1946 to found the professional Association of Social Anthropologists, joined by a score of other anthropologists the following year. In many ways, Elizabeth Colson (who was there) tells us,

> those who came to London, as well as the absent members, were a cosmopolitan group. They had crossed disciplinary and territorial boundaries in becoming anthropologists... They came out of history, law, geography, psychology, economics, biology, and engineering. They drew on their reading in other fields as they dealt with what they regarded as anthropological questions. Those born in Great Britain were in the minority. The remainder of that first group of perhaps 30 members were born in South Africa, Australia, New Zealand, and India, of parents some of whom had never visited Great Britain, while Nadel came from Austria and Peristiany from Cyprus. A cosmopolitan cohort, yet their subject matter was far removed from the cosmopolitan metropolis in which they gathered.

The New Cosmopolitanism(s)

Sixty years after the founding of the Association of Social Anthropologists of the UK and the Commonwealth, the aim of this book is to reposition social anthropology in relation to an evolving new cosmopolitanism, theorised in political philosophy, sociology of globalisation and postcolonial cultural studies. Words like cosmopolitanism may seem remote from anthropology's subjects, embedded in European liberal elitist ideas of world consciousness artificially imposed on the out-of-the-way locales that anthropologists mostly study. Yet it is remarkable that anthropologists have made significant contributions since the 1990s, and even before that, to contemporary debates on cosmopolitanism. In inaugurating a new anthropology of cosmopolitanism, we argue in this book that both in practice and substantive terms a *situated* cosmopolitanism, broadly defined, may indeed today be at the heart of the discipline.

Cosmopolitanism, derived from the Greek conjunction of 'world' (*cosmos*) and 'city' (*polis*), describes a 'citizen of the world', member in a 'universal circle of belonging that involves the transcendence of the particular and blindly given ties of kinship and country' (Cheah 2006: 487). Against 'globalisation', a term implying the free movement of capital and the global (mainly Western) spread of ideas and practices, cosmopolitanism is a word used by the new cosmopolitans to emphasise empathy, toleration and respect for other cultures and values. Thus, at its most basic, cosmopolitanism is about reaching out across cultural differences through dialogue, aesthetic enjoyment, and respect; of living together with difference. It is also about the cosmopolitan right to abode and hospitality in strange lands and, alongside that, the urgent need to devise ways of living together in peace in the international community. Against the slur that cosmopolitans are rootless, with no commitments to place or nation, the new post-1990s cosmopolitanism attempts to theorise the complex ways in which cosmopolitans juggle particular and trans-cendent loyalties – morally, and inevitably also, politically.

Whatever the definition, and whether we are talking of rooted, vernacular or elite interpretations of the term, cosmopolitanism has to be grasped as an ethical horizon – an aspirational outlook and mode of practice. Cosmopolitans insist on the human capacity to imagine the world from an Other's perspective, and to imagine the possibility of a borderless world of cultural plurality. We often label as cosmopolitan individuals with a certain subjective capacity to enjoy cultural diversity and travel; but because cosmopolitanism is itself a product of creativity and communication in the context of diversity, it must ultimately be understood not merely as individual, but as collective, relational and thus historically located.

The New 'Normative' Cosmopolitanism

The year 1990 was a watershed one for the new cosmopolitanism scholarship. The fall of the Berlin Wall, signalling the end of the cold war, coincided with an awareness of a 'speeded up' economic globalisation, the spectacular rise of extra-terrestrial media during the 1992 first Gulf War, and increasing consciousness of the perils of a looming ecological planetary disaster. The new normative cosmopolitanism, heralded by David Held's *Democracy and the Global Order* (1995), took up the vision of Immanuel Kant's 'Perpetual Peace' to argue for the apparently utopian possibility of cosmopolitan citizenship. Kant, it will be recalled, proposed that only a confederation of republics could guarantee peace and the cosmopolitan right of individuals to venture out as strangers and sojourn in other territories.

There were, originally, three discernible strands to this new normative cosmo-politanism. These have increasingly converged as empirical research reveals the complexity of the contemporary global public sphere. All three strands respond to the demise of the so-called Westphalian order, the sacralised, inviolable sovereignty of the nation-state. This inviolability was first questioned by the post-World War II Nurenberg Tribunal and UN 1948 Universal Declaration of Human Rights, followed by a subsequent series of international rights conventions. National boundaries were also increasingly undermined by neoliberal economic globalisation and the lowering of trade barriers. Issues of rights and accountability within and among states, and limitations on state sovereignty, came however to dominate international policy in the aftermath of the cold war (Held 1995: 101–7).

The first strand in the new normative cosmopolitan relates to global governance. Daniele Archibugi, while acknowledging its critics and sceptics, phrases it optimistically as an 'endless process' of globalising democracy or democratising globalisation (2004: 438). The idea is that 'democracy cannot be understood in static terms' (ibid.: 439) and that the move is from local democracy to democratising the international arena, underpinned by treaties, alliances and binding international conventions. The basic Kantian assumption is that democracy within states favours peace between states (ibid.: 441–2).

Perhaps the horizons of democracy are even greater than Archibugi suggests. David Graeber (Chapter 14) traces the provenance of concepts associated with 'Western freedoms' like democracy, and demonstrates that they are the product of 'endless entanglements' within and beyond the West, to the extent that, ironically, '[o]pposition to European expansion in much of the world, even quite early on, appears to have been carried out in the name of "Western values" *that the Europeans in question did not yet even have.*' Put simply, notions of rights to popular self-governance and autonomy have been widespread in many quite separated societies. The US constitution, particularly its federal structure, Graeber reminds us, was inspired in part by the Iroquois Six Nation Confederacy. Democracy could be and was invented in widely separated places: from pirate ships to African assemblies. Democratic *practice*, whether defined as procedures of egalitarian decision-making, or government by public discussion, tends, Graeber argues, to emerge from situations in which communities of one sort or another manage their own affairs outside the purview of the state, while democratic innovation, and the emergence of what might be called democratic values, has a tendency to spring from what he calls 'zones of cultural improvisation ... in which diverse sorts of people with different traditions and experiences are obliged to figure out some way to get on with one another.' He concludes that in the contemporary world 'the endless elaboration of new cosmopolitan spaces, and the retreat of states in so many parts of the globe, suggests that there is the potential at least for a vast outpouring of new democratic creativity.'

Perhaps surprisingly, Graeber's suspicion of the coercive aspects of democracy is one that was shared by Immanuel Kant. In *Perpetual Peace* Kant rejects a world superstate as inevitably 'despotic'. A state, Kant says,

> [is] not, like the ground which it occupies, a piece of property (*patrimonium*). It is a society of men whom no one else has any right to command or to dispose except the state itself. It is a trunk with its own roots. ... to incorporate it into another state, like a graft, is to destroy its existence as a moral person, reducing it to a thing (Principle 2).

With this organic image of nations and cultures Kant attacks the senseless 'plunder' by the 'civilised' of the remote corners of the earth. 'The injustice which they show to lands and peoples they visit (which is equivalent to conquering them) is carried by them to terrifying lengths,' he says,

> [u]nder the pretence of establishing economic undertakings, they brought in foreign soldiers and used them to oppress the natives, excited widespread wars among the various states, spread famine, rebellion, perfidy, and the whole litany of evils which afflict mankind.

In the face of this violence, he maintains,

> [s]ince the narrower or wider community of the peoples of the earth has developed so far that a violation of rights in one place is felt throughout the world, the idea of a law of world citizenship is no high-flown or exaggerated notion (Third Definitive Article).

What distinguishes the 'league of peace', then, is not the obliteration of difference, but *procedural* universalism: the rule of law, the separation of the executive from the legislative and judicial (which he terms republicanism), the rights of citizens (in a 'kingdom of ends'), and the right of strangers to temporary abode.

Reflecting on the popular roots of democracy and cosmopolitanism, Hall (Chapter 17) says:

> I don't think we can march around the world and make people cosmopolitan. On the other hand, the more people can begin to hope and aspire in a cosmopolitan way, the less we will be driven to ethnically cleanse people who are not like us, to murder people who won't convert to us, people who won't subscribe to the western way of life, etc.

Terms like cosmopolitan, he confesses, make him uneasy, evoking for him colonial claims to bring enlightenment to the natives. At the same time, he admits,

> I am a child of the Enlightenment. I think the one good thing the Enlightenment did understand was, it required a big argument, it required a row, it required a lot of talking...

Not stabbing them in the street... It is quarrels that created the enfranchisement of women. Or that gave the majority of people the vote.

Hence, if the first strand in the new normative cosmopolitan is to theorise the democratisation of a new international order, the second strand is often attributed to Habermas's revisioning of Kant's *Perpetual Peace,* Habermas argues that international non-governmental organisations have created an alternative 'global public sphere' of debate and advocacy (Habermas 1999: 176). Listing UN-sponsored world conferences on global issues which took place in the 1990s – human rights (Vienna), ecology (Rio), women (Beijing), population (Cairo), poverty (Copenhagen), global warning (Berlin),[2] Habermas points to the central role played by non-governmental actors which 'confront states from within the network of an international civil society' (ibid.: 177). Nevertheless, he also recognises that the possibility of global peace is undercut by international inequalities, leading to civil wars and autocratic regimes in the developing world. In the post-cold war period ethnic conflicts – in the former Yugoslavia, Chechnya, several African countries (Ruanda, Sierra Leone, Liberia, Democratic Republic of Congo, Sudan, Somalia), South East Asia (Indonesia, Philippines, Thailand) and the Middle East (Afghanistan and Iraq) – and the apparently inviolable persistence of autocratic regimes, like Robert Mugabe's in Zimbabwe, threaten world peace and expose as hollow claims of international human rights.

The third strand in the new normative cosmopolitanism is perhaps best defined by Ulrich Beck when he distinguishes between globalisation, on the one hand, and cosmopolitanism as an emerging ethical response ('vision') to it on the other. Beck's 'banal' or 'latent' cosmopolitanism is, arguably, very close to what we normally call globalisation. Against that, the interest in his work lies in his theorisation of what may be termed 'reflexive' globalisation;[3] his insight that 'What is new is not forced mixing but awareness of it, its self-conscious political affirmation, its reflection and recognition before a global public via the mass media, in the news and in the global social movements of blacks, women and minorities' (2006: 21). For Beck this constitutes a new process – cosmopolitanisation. It involves a move from globalisation, to consciousness, to institutionalised normative cosmopolitanism, from principle to practice. 'Under what conditions', he asks, 'subject to what limits and by which actors are certain cosmopolitan principles nevertheless translated into practice, and thereby acquire an enduring reality?' Conscious recognition creates the grounds for 'cosmopolitan solutions' (ibid.: 22).

While Beck's stress on consciousness makes a critical advance, his argument has to be qualified in the light of anthropological analyses of rooted or vernacular forms of cosmopolitanism. In these, the salient move is from cosmopolitan *practice* to cosmopolitan consciousness or *conviction*. Whereas Beck posits a simple denial of nationalism, for anthropologists, cosmopolitanism is as much a local engagement *within* postcolonial states – with cultural pluralism, global rights movements, ideas about democracy and the right to dissent – as beyond their borders. Consciousness of cosmopolitan values may emerge where in the past a taken-for-granted *de facto* cosmopolitanism flourished, as in Sarajebo, in response to violent internal ethnic or religious conflicts and civil wars within states.

In a far-reaching critical evaluation of Beck's work, Parry argues against the view that cosmopolitanism is necessarily antithetical to the 'national outlook' or that it is entirely value-neutral, accepting all cultures on their own terms, as equal in their difference. Nor is it true in the context of Indian caste, religious and cultural hierarchies and divisions, he contends, that the 'salad bowl' mixing without an implicit universalism, advocated by some Indian scholars, can lead to toleration and egalitarianism. The hidden assumptions on value behind cosmopolitan theorisations are here exposed by Parry through a subtle analysis of steel workers' demotic cosmopolitanism, in contrast to a sons-of-the-earth local movement. He highlights the role of the Nehruvian state in promoting universal values of equity and merit, and providing the structural conditions of work in which these can thrive. The experimental worldliness and enthusiasms of workers and their ever-more-sophisticated children, as they socialise across previously unbridgeable social chasms, are described by Parry with an eye to the wonderfully humorous intimate details of contemporary Indian cosmopolitanisms. Equally remarkable is the communal harmony maintained in the town, in the face of religious rioting and violence elsewhere.

Beck's critique of so-called 'methodological nationalism' in sociology – the conflation of 'society' with the nation-state – has never been applicable to anthropology – the study of part-societies and social fields (see my Chapter 3). While the discipline is perennially accused of a tendency to reify the little community or 'culture' contained within or straddling international borders, arguably a major advance in anthropology has been the recognition of the need to theorise the engagement of the people we study with the colonial and postcolonial state (Asad 1973; Werbner and Ranger 1996).

Even for sociology, Bryan Turner argues against Beck that it began as a study of the 'social', not of 'society' (2006: 135). Because the social is a 'moral field', he says, it can contribute directly to 'the study and promotion of cosmopolitanism which must also reflect on the ethical dimensions of the social, especially in developing a hermeneutics of Otherness' (ibid.: 134). Durkheim espoused 'world patriotism', an anti-nationalist cosmopolitan sociology, so that

[w]hile anthropology was the study of Man, its exploration of difference produced a science of men, or the local in the global. Sociology, as a science of the social, has

retained a stronger sense of the universality of its moral field, of the global in the local. In this sense, sociology points towards a cosmopolitan epistemology of a shared reality (ibid.: 140–1).

Thus, Turner says, in 'equating what he called "true patriotism" with cosmopolitanism, Durkheim anticipated the modern debate about republicanism, patriotism and cosmopolitanism by almost a century' (ibid.: 141).

Despite the optimism, the new normative cosmopolitanism has thrown up painful dilemmas. Beck remarks that the 'concepts of emancipatory and political cosmopolitanism are interwoven with *despotic* cosmopolitanism' (2006: 154). The ambivalence at the heart of normative cosmopolitanism has been driven home by the war in Iraq, fought against 'terror' in the name of liberty and democracy. In a world of unequal power relations cosmopolitan intervention in the affairs of other states, however lofty its stated ideals, continuously risks being construed as Western hegemonic expansion in disguise. The same accusation of false (hegemonic) cosmopolitanism has been applied to anthropology's claims as a discipline, a matter I return to below.

Rather than being autonomous, Held argues, the no-longer-sovereign state lies 'at the crossroads of a vast array of networks and organisations that have been established to regulate and manage diverse areas of international and transnational activity' (2004: 366). Transnationally networked NGOs are often the 'wild cards' of normative cosmopolitanism, DeMars's penetrating analysis discloses (2005). Held demonstrates the plurality of these actors and stakeholders; the complexity, overlap and often conflicting or competing mandates they hold; the fragmentation, incoherence, paralysis and 'accountability deficit' of global decision-makers vis-à-vis relevant constituencies; the inequalities and responsibility gaps, all of which plague the international arena. It is precisely these factors, it may be argued, that point to the continued importance of the nation-state as the most accountable political community for mediating and implementing decisions taken in international forums. But this itself discloses, as Sally Engle Merry proposes, a central conundrum:

> In the aftermath of the Holocaust, states are no longer trusted by the international community to govern their own citizens without international oversight. On the other hand, the focus of much human rights activism is the state. Sometimes the state is the human rights violator, when it subjects its citizens to torture or extrajudicial killings, for example. Ironically it is also the agent for carrying out human rights reforms in many cases. Social and economic rights, such as the right to development or the right to adequate housing, require state action, as does the provision of many civil and political rights... Thus, human rights activism ends up demanding more state regulation and service. (Merry 2006: 5)

The relationship between the local and the cosmopolitan is even more complex, Merry proposes, since for cosmopolitan ideas such as human rights to be effective, they 'need to be remade in the vernacular', to be interpreted, reframed and translated by local activists (ibid.: 1–2). This process of translation and negotiation points also to the central preoccupation of the present book: not to focus solely on cosmopolitan travellers outside their own milieus, but on the way individual and collective actors in the postcolonial world make that world by engaging with each other and with cosmopolitan ideas and movements beyond their immediate locales.

In her study of the Maasai indigenous rights movement, Dorothy Hodgson (Chapter 11) portrays the dialectics and dilemmas of this engagement among a new generation of Maasai intellectuals and civic-cum-global activists. These activists have mobilised to defend the rights of pastoralists in the face of predatory land expropriations, legitimised by a state neoliberalism that endorses private ownership and market-oriented economic development. From being stigmatised as 'primitive', Maasai intellectuals and NGOs have worked, first in the international arena and subsequently in Tanzanian civil society, to create cross-ethnic alliances, lobbies and advocacy groups to protect their pastoral citizenship rights under the umbrella of a global rights movement. Starting with the biography of a single local-turned-global activist, Hodgson traces the historical development of this movement in the context of a liberalising post-socialist Tanzania. Her analysis discloses the emergence of a kind of rooted, pragmatic cosmopolitanism which recognises the crucial need to redefine 'indigeneity' (a label the government rejects) as the basis for universalist claims, by creating a broad, cross-ethnic alliance in which claims as Tanzanian citizens to both economic and cultural rights can be legitimately made in the newly emergent democratic, post-socialist public sphere and civil society.

The New Anthropological Cosmopolitanism

The mobilisation of the Maasai in Tanzania to claim their rights within this newly emergent democracy points to the contours of the new anthropological cosmopolitanism, which theorises the cosmopolitics of increasingly democratising postcolonies. 'Third wave' democratisation has 'swept' Latin America, parts of Asia and Africa, Central Europe and some former Soviet republics (DeMars 2005: 115). Archibugi reports that there were in 2004, 120 states with elected governments compared to 41 in 1974 and 76 in 1990, an indication of how much democracy — albeit often in imperfect forms — has expanded worldwide (Archibugi 2004: 442). In Africa there is talk of a Second Liberation Movement. Although often still an aspirational horizon bogged down by past failures, imposed neoliberal policies and incompetent or corrupt elites (Osaghae 2005), it nevertheless signals a radical departure. Unlike the first liberation that led to independence from colonial rule and was hijacked by kleptomaniac, intolerant and often violent authoritarian regimes, the second liberation signals the (patriotic) right to dissent, demand accountability and claim the rights of minorities to legitimate cultural and religious recognition within the nation. Richard Werbner speaks of this movement as 'post-liberalism', a 'ferment of ideas and debate on the just balance between different rights, group and individual ... open-ended enough to be heuristic for ... the renewed debate in Africa marking a second postcolonial era, after nearly all the early nation-building tyrants have had their all too long day' (R. Werbner 2004a: 263).[4]

Such post-liberal ideas about multicultural, feminist and indigenous rights, the contributors to this volume disclose, are taking root not only throughout Africa (Hodgson, Chapter 14, Werbner, Chapter 9, Fardon, Chapter 12, Sichone, Chapter 15) but in post-Suharto Indonesia (Robinson, Chapter 6), India (Parry, Chapter 16, Ram, Chapter 7), among progressive Islamists in Malaysia (Stivens, Chapter 5) or Zapatista in Mexico (Graeber, Chapter 14). While it may be true, however, that 'in the cosmopolitan paradigm of the second modernity' as Beck says, 'non-Western societies share the same time and space horizon as the West' (2004: 70), and that the 'idea' of cosmopolitanism 'can find fertile soil in many cultures and many contexts ... though the language, idiom and form in which it is expressed may differ' (Vertovec and Cohen 2002: 16), the urgent need remains to theorise the distinctive historical trajectories which make the post-1990s, new postcolonial cosmopolitanism so important, and so vulnerable. (On this distinctiveness, see Parry 1991: 41).

One scholarly pitfall denied by the new anthropological cosmopolitanism is the idea that all postcolonial elites are rootless – endemically corrupt and hence anti-cosmopolitan. Cosmopolitanism does not imply rootlessness. Rooted cosmopolitanism is a salient feature of many in the postcolonial elite, whether they are organic intellectuals leading indigenous and minoritarian rights movements or privileged, affluent minority elites in the capital (R. Werbner, Chapter 9). Mitchell Cohen, who coined the term, speaks of multiple patriotisms and 'multicultural exchange', while recognising that these are 'not easily harmonised' (Cohen 1992: 483).

> What is needed is the fashioning of a dialectical concept of *rooted* cosmopolitanism, which accepts a multiplicity of roots and branches and that rests on the legitimacy of plural loyalties, of standing in many circles, but with common ground. (ibid.)

This belonging to multiple circles of sentimental loyalty, having a 'multiplicity of roots', 'layers of identification' – despite the xenophobic separations generated by the Middle East conflict, is analysed reflectively by Aref Abu-Rabia (Chapter

8), recalling a trip he made with his family from Palestine-Israel across the Jordanian border and back again, in which he was painfully reminded of his Israeliness, but also more pleasurably of his Bedouin and Palestinian roots and connections. Abu-Rabia criticises as parochial Ghassan Hage's definition of white elite Australian 'cosmopolites' who 'consume' ethnic commodities and espouse multiculturalism, but whose declared tolerance 'obscures an underlying racism.' Instead, he argues,

> Within the university and anthropological community in Israel there are some who document the Palestinian minority's predicament, and this is true of some members of the Jewish and Jewish-Palestinian peace movement. Not all are 'false' cosmopolites. In this respect, I do not feel that I am alone. But we rooted cosmopolitans are weak politically and marginalised socially.
>
> Despite all this, I am not a stranger. I live in my own land and want its long-term welfare, the welfare of my people, Israel, Palestine and the whole Middle East. In this sense, perhaps, I am a 'rooted' cosmopolitan, or cosmopolitan patriot.

To be a rooted cosmopolitan in an intolerant environment requires enormous courage and faith, Abu-Rabia discloses, and this is signalled also in the biographies of Maasai and Kalanga activists in modern Africa (Hodgson, Chapter 11, Werbner, Chapter 9). Against that, there has been a tendency among some on the left to expose metropolitan postcolonial intellectuals as mere 'cosmopolite' pretenders. Timothy Brennan (1997: 37–41), for example, has argued that Third World novels in English by diasporic writers such as Salman Rushdie, while admittedly promoting genuine aesthetic novelty or 'hybridity' within the English novel, are celebrated because they fit a Western liberal aesthetics and novelty-dominated consumer market. By contrast, politically committed Third World novelists like the Egyptian Naguib Mahfouz, who write from within richly layered indigenous aesthetic traditions and address Arab audiences beyond the English-speaking metropolis, are marginalised (ibid.: 42–3). Jonathan Friedman, rejecting the postmodernist celebration of cultural multiplicity and hybridity, argues in somewhat similar vein that 'Today's cosmopolitans are cosmopolitans without modernism.' Unlike the old, progressive 'rationalist universalist' cosmopolitans, 'whose identity was defined in terms of the abstract, the rights of man, not of cultures', they lack rootedness in the 'street', i.e. in the plight of the underprivileged (1997: 74, 75). Elite intellectuals from the Third World living in the First, he argues, have quite different life experiences from immigrants in the ghetto yet they invoke their cosmopolitan sensibility as the only morality and truth against so-called reactionary ethnics, as though hybridity was not itself just another identity (ibid.: 78 *passim*).

We see in Friedman's denunciation the swan song of the 'old' cosmopolitanism that refuses to acknowledge that the politics of difference is a genuine politics – that postcolonial and diasporic intellectuals today grapple with intractable political challenges arising from essentialising racisms, religious communalisms, fundamentalisms and castism, the tyranny of culture. The politics of recognition and of cultural dignity must tread the fine line among individual and social rights, essentialising identities and hegemonic cultural homogenisation. In embedding their writing in rich and varied non-European literary and mythological traditions, the best of these cosmopolitan writers, like Salman Rushdie, rewrite their own histories as world histories even as they enrich the English novel. Nevertheless, Brennan in particular rightly points to the urgent need to focus on the predicaments faced by organic intellectuals and activists in contemporary postcolonies. This is the theoretical challenge the new anthropological cosmopolitanism must address.

Global Movements, Counter-Cosmopolitans

The fear of essentialising identitarian movements points to the fact that cosmopolitanism is threatened on two fronts: on one front is xenophobia, a fear and rejection of strangers; on the other, hegemonic cultural universalisation which is homogenising and intolerant of difference. Both have dire consequences from a cosmopolitan point of view. As Stuart Hall warns (Chapter 17), an attempt to 'homogenise the world globally ... look like us, learn our languages, learn our histories, become like us' can lead to a defensive retreat into essentialised identities. The homogenising version of Enlightenment cosmopolitanism would make it, as Joel Kahn points out (Chapter 13), no different from new universalising, culturally effacing, homogenising global Islamic 'reform' movements. By contrast, the Malay world of migratory movements and cultural interchange that he describes, although grounded (in postcolonial Malaysia) in self-conscious ethnic and religious categorisations, is nevertheless characterised by ethnic co-responsibility, mutual exchange and cosmopolitan practice.

Not all boundary-crossing, globally oriented groups are cosmopolitan. Anthony Appiah labels religiously exclusivist global movements such as Al Qaida, that appear to espouse a singular truth and demonise the other, at times violently, as 'counter' cosmopolitan, despite these movements' transnational networks and global moral aspirations (Appiah 2006). One needs to avoid, however, lumping all global 'fundamentalist' movements together. Some strands of global Islamism play a critical, dissenting, advocacy role, as Stivens (Chapter 5) highlights in her analysis of Islamic feminism in Malaysia. In Indonesia, women in the '*Islam pribumi*' movement position themselves in opposition both to global Islamism and a generic traditional Islam originating in the Middle East. Robinson (Chapter 6) compares this movement's cosmopolitan religious hermeneutics to the counter-cosmopolitan position of radical Muslim women's 'global fundamentalist thinking', which nevertheless stresses the evils of poverty and inequality. Like in Malaysia, Islam has thus opened up possibilities for women's activism and progressive interpretations of the scriptures in the context of broader alliances for women's rights, struggling to overturn centuries of traditional paternalism. For Tamil Christian Dalit women in India, Kalpana Ram shows (Chapter 7) emancipatory politics necessarily involves a rejection of custom and tradition in favour of universalist, modernist notions of rights.

Such nuanced observations highlight the complexity of analysing situated cosmopolitanisms in the postcolonial world, and particularly so in relation to contemporary feminism or Christianity's and Islam's global reach. As a great ethical religion with a universal moral message, many cosmopolitan civilisations have repeatedly flourished in the realm of Islam, from Andalusia in Spain through the Near East to Mughal India, Indonesia and China, well before so-called Western democracy took root.

Demotic Cosmopolitans, Cosmopolitan National Spaces

Elite cosmopolitan literary intellectuals are not the only cosmopolitans in a globalising world. Along with the view that postcolonial elites are necessarily rootless and corrupt, a second false assumption the new anthropological cosmopolitanism rejects is the idea that cosmopolitanism is only and singularly elitist. Cosmopolitanism can equally be working class, as Jonathan Parry shows in his study of Indian workers (Chapter 16). Indian factory workers deny and transcend divisions of caste and ethnicity entrenched elsewhere in India, and mobilise consciously as part of a global trade union movement. Proletarian cosmopolitanism, rooted in Marx's exhortation to workers of the world to unite, was undermined by popular nationalism (Cheah 2006), but in the post-liberal postcolonies of today, worker cosmopolitan consciousness of rights is a growing reality, underpinned by ILO conventions and international trade unions.

In a rapidly industrialising India, the experience of working together has created its own historical trajectory, Parry argues, and this is echoed by Richard Fardon's study of Nigeria (Chapter 12), a large linguistically and religiously plural state that some would contend may be conceived of as cosmopolitan from its inception. Fardon argues in relation to the Chamba, a small peripheral group by Nigerian standards who historically have struggled to resist domination from the neighbouring Fulani, that 'Particularly if you belong to a minority ethnic group nationally, a cosmopolitan sensibility, in so far as the term is understood to apply to a capacity to reach beyond cultural difference – and not only the cultural differences of people outside your own nation – is necessary to feel any sense of belonging to your own nationalist project.' Patriotism in multi-ethnic nations, at least for minorities, as Richard Werbner too argues (Chapter 9), is by definition cosmopolitan. Indeed, it is minorities, Werbner proposes, who extend notions of citizenship by insisting on universal rights for all, while also insisting on their entitlement to public recognition. For the Chamba in Nigeria, the nation is, in a sense, internally, a 'cosmopolitan nation', a space of myriad cosmopolitan encounters and dialogues. The same may be said of India (Parry, Chapter 16), Malaysia (Kahn, Chapter 13, Stivens, Chapter 4) Indonesia (Robinson, Chapter 5) South Africa (Sichone, Chapter 15) and the Caribbean (Hall, Chapter 17). But even smaller nations like Papua New Guinea, Tanzania, Botswana and Israel are ethnically plural (Hirsch, Chapter 10, Hodgson, Chapter 11, Werbner, Chapter 9, Abu-Rabia, Chapter 8). Within ethnically plural nations the social contract guiding relations among the multitude of ethnic, religious and linguistic groups is historically produced and continuously renegotiated culturally and politically in different spaces and arenas. Hence, for example, in non-secular but democratic Malaysia, Kahn shows, an appearance of rigid religio-ethnic separations, defined constitutionally, disguises a long history of regional migrations, and with it a more fluid and hybridised sense of Malayness, so that the achievement and preservation of a 'relative peace' relies 'on the presence not of a single, culturally neutral public space but of a myriad of spaces and language games that together may be labeled *peranakan* [creole] Malay.' Despite nationalist narratives of Malay indigeneity and purity, Kahn argues then, all Malays are to some extent *peranakan* (Chapter 13, Kahn 2006). Rooted cosmopolitan practice thus emanates, against the grain, from a uniquely Malaysian social contract among ethno-religious groups.

This points, as we have seen, to the fact that cosmopolitanism's fundamental values are not necessarily 'Western' – a feature, we saw, Graeber documents in a wide-ranging comparative analysis (Chapter 14). Indeed, it may be said that cosmopolitanism is always, in some sense at least, vernacular, historically and spatially positioned, and hence also necessarily political, contested, dialectical. This is also the point made evocatively by Bruce Robbins (1998a, 1998b) in his discussion of transnational commitments, feelings and loyalties within and beyond the nation. Cosmopolitanism reflects the striving for universal ideals and local multiculturalisms within a particular field of power. Related to this politicised aspect of cosmopolitanism, the final canard rejected in this volume is that anthropology itself, rather than being a comparative cosmopolitan discipline is merely another expression of Western hegemony (Colson, Chapter 2; P.Werbner, Chapter 3; Hann Chapter 4), a point I return to below.

Despite some optimism about the cosmopolitanisation of the postcolonial world, global inequalities still threaten to undermine any genuine sense of universal solidarity across class and wealth, north and south (Cheah 2006). Critical cosmopolitanism engages with these inequalities as well as with the sense that cosmopolitanism remains a term too closely associated with the rhetoric of former imperial colonisers or moralising elites (Hall, Chapter 17), whereas the people anthropologists study, like the Chamba in Nigeria, aspire – more modestly – to autonomy and self-rule within a local context (Fardon, Chapter 12). At the same time it is possible to argue, as Graeber does, that since the values associated with democracy and cosmopolitanism are widespread and not singularly the creation of the 'West', it is indeed questionable whether the West ever existed at all.

Vernacular and Rooted Cosmopolitanisms

This questioning of the 'West' by the new anthropological and postcolonial cosmo-politanism points to the conjunctural dialectics of what might broadly be called vernacular cosmopolitan. Vernacular cosmopolitanism – an apparent oxymoron that seems to join contradictory notions of local specificity and universal enlightenment – is at the crux of current debates on cosmopolitanism. These pose the question first, whether local, parochial, rooted, and culturally specific loyalties may coexist with translocal, transnational, transcendent, elitist, enlightened, universalist and modernist ones; and second, whether boundary-crossing demotic migrations may be compared to the globe-trotting travel, sophisticated cultural knowledge and moral worldview of deracinated intellectuals. Indeed, the question is often reversed to ask whether there can be an enlightened normative cosmopolitanism which is not rooted, in the final analysis, in patriotic and culturally committed loyalties and understandings.

Vernacular cosmopolitanism belongs to a family of concepts all of which combine in similar fashion apparently contradictory opposites: cosmopolitan patriotism, rooted cosmopolitanism, cosmopolitan ethnicity, working-class cosmopolitanism, discrepant cosmopolitanism. Such conjunctions attempt to come to terms with the dialectical elements of postcolonial and precolonial forms of cosmopolitanism and travel, while probing the conceptual boundaries of cosmo-politanism and its usefulness as an analytic concept. Paul Rabinow early on called cosmopolitanism a 'twin valorisation' of 'worldwide macro-interdependency encompassing any local particularity.' He adds that '[we] seem to have trouble with the balancing act, preferring to reify local identities or construct universal ones. We live in-between' (Rabinow 1986: 258).

Vernacular cosmopolitanism is perhaps the most ambiguous of all these conjunctural terms: are we talking about *non-elite* forms of travel and trade in a postcolonial world, as in the case of the Senegalese Mourides described by Diouf (2000) and others, or of *non-European* but nevertheless *high* cultures produced and consumed by non-Western elites, such as those of the Sanskritic, Urdu, Persian or Ottoman worlds? The Sanskritic cosmopolis spanned an area extending from Afghanistan to Java and from Sri Lanka to Nepal, a non-Western but nevertheless cosmopolitan literary world that is contrasted by Pollock (2000) with the vernacular traditions that succeeded it. Are we to define, by analogy, contemporary south-east Asian, Hindi/Urdu or Cantonese mass-consumer and mediatised cultural worlds as cosmopolitan, or as vernacular (Robinson 2007)? So too, how are we to place minority elites in new postcolonial nations, who struggle to defend their vernacular cultures, and seek justice through multicultural citizenship, while being at the same time liberal, tolerant and highly educated world travellers, as Richard Werbner (Chapter 9) highlights in his portrayal of a Kalanga elder statesman? Werbner calls such cosmopolitan practice among Kalanga elites in Botswana 'cosmopolitan ethnicity' (Werbner 2004b; also 2002).

Terms such as cosmopolitan ethnicity or rooted cosmopolitanism, rather than denying the legacy of the 'old' Enlightenment cosmopolitanism of universalism beyond the local, as Friedman (2002) or Hollinger suggest (2002: 228), aim to incorporate the Greek and Kantian ideas which first defined cosmopolitanism into a more complex and subtle understanding of what it means to be a cosmopolitan at the turn of the twenty-first century. The worldview of Kalanga 'reasonable radicals' highlights the conjunctural features of cosmopolitanism, the fact that ethnic rootedness does not negate openness to cultural difference or the fostering of a universalist civic consciousness and a sense of moral responsibility beyond the local. This is also the point made by Kwame Anthony Appiah (1998), who argues that cosmopolitanism is equally an argument *within* postcolonial states about citizenship, equal dignity, cultural rights and the rule of law. Appiah speaks of cosmopolitan 'patriotism', a 'rooted' cosmopolitanism, and proposes that cosmopolitans begin from membership in morally and emotionally significant communities (families, ethnic groups) while espousing notions of toleration and openness to the world, the transcendence of ethnic difference, moral responsibility for the other. Postcolonial traveller elites may and do feel sentimentally attached to several homes in several different countries. In a wide reaching critical appreciation of Appiah's foundational text(s), Richard Werbner (Chapter 9) considers a lack in Appiah's stress on the liberal individual: *public* cosmopolitanism is necessarily, Werbner argues, a socially inclusive political project of creating alliances between like-minded individuals and collectivities. This project is rooted in and involves, he shows, 'first, the restless quest for the further horizon; second, the imperative of moral re-centring; and third, the constructing and transcending of difference.'

Intellectuals in Malaysia (Kahn, Chapter 13), post-civil servants in Botswana (Werbner, Chapter 9; 2004: 27), Muslim feminists in Indonesia or Malaysia (Robinson, Chapter 5; Stivens, Chapter 4), Dalit women in India (Ram, Chapter 6), an Israeli Palestinian Bedouin academic in modern Israel (Abu-Rabia, Chapter 8),

Maasai activists in Tanzania (Hodgson, Chapter 11), a village intellectual in Papua New Guinea (Hirsch, Chapter 10) or Chiapo activists in Mexico (Graeber Chapter 14) are all examples of rooted cosmopolitans who first make parochial interpretations of culture, religion and ethnicity in order to transcend them and assert wider cosmopolitan values. The conjunctural dialectic between particular and universal is never, it seems fully resolved.

Elite and Demotic World Travellers

Our analysis of rooted cosmopolitans expands the horizons of an earlier anthropological debate on the cosmopolitan as world traveller. The debate was initiated by Ulf Hannerz who proposed a set of useful distinctions among such travellers between cosmopolitan afficianados 'willing to engage with the Other' aesthetically (Hannerz, 1990: 239), who consciously foster their knowledge, understanding, appreciation and enjoyment of traditions and cultures other than their own; locals, 'representatives of more circumscribed territorial cultures' (Hannerz, 1992: 252), and transnationals, frequent travellers (usually occupational) who share 'structures of meaning carried by social networks' (ibid.: 248–9). By contrast to foreign correspondents or oil engineers, Hannerz lumps migrants and refugees, the demotic travellers of a global age, with 'tourists' because, he says, they regard involvement with other cultures as a 'necessary cost' (ibid.: 248). They lack, in other words, consciousness and appreciation of the cultural milieu into which they are inserted.

This has led to accusations of elitism and Eurocentrism (Robbins 1998b; P. Werbner, 1999). In my own work I bring a counter-example of a 'working-class cosmopolitan' in the figure of the expanding cosmopolitan subjectivity of a Pakistani migrant working on a building site in the Gulf, a simple man who embraces different cultures and members of diverse ethnic groups, but who nevertheless retains his transnational yet rooted identity as a Sufi.

African migrants display similar competencies, Owen Sichone argues, when they are away from home (Chapter 15). He portrays the complex life history of a certain type of migrant, the sort that travels without passports or visas, without any particular destination, making a new life wherever he or she happens to land. Such itineracy challenges, he argues, the system of global apartheid by claiming the right to move freely in defiance of state border regimes. These migrants also make it possible for others, who belong to the immobile 97 per cent of the human population that never leaves home, to connect with the world in ways that allow cultural and economic transfers between centre and periphery. Sometimes their dramatic and unpredictable impact upon the host population belies their small numbers.

Sichone's chapter celebrates demotic cosmopolitanism – personal mobility in post-apartheid South Africa, and seeks to shift the focus in migration studies from labour migration and refugees to independent 'economic' migrants. Despite the best efforts of postcolonial states to tie Africans' mobility to labour contracts, some migrants have managed to venture beyond the confines of their nation-states, crafts or levels of education in order to 'find a place for themselves' wherever they choose.

The challenge to the idea that cosmopolitans are necessarily members of the elite was first posed by James Clifford who reflects on the status of companion servants, guides and migrant labourers, and the grounds of equivalence between privileged and unprivileged travellers (1992: 106–7; cf. also 1998). Clifford proposes that 'the project of comparing and translating different travelling cultures need not be class- or ethno-centric' (1992: 107). Differential, often violent, displacements that impel locals to travel create, he says, 'discrepant' cosmopolitanisms (ibid.:108). Nevertheless, Clifford accepts the definition of cosmopolitans as individual travellers, exiles or diasporics, which he pitches against an allegedly restricted anthropological focus on the little community or culture. Our volume challenges this historiography of anthropology, as it challenges the idea that cosmopolitans necessarily reside or move permanently beyond their nations and cultures. Not all postcolonial cosmopolitans are travellers – nor are all travellers (as Hannerz reminds us) cosmopolitan. At the present cosmopolitan moment in anthropology there is a temptation to label almost anyone – African labour migrants, urbanites, Pentecostals, traders, diasporics – 'cosmopolitan'. This obscures the ethical grounding of the new cosmopolitan anthropology in ideas of tolerance, inclusiveness, hospitality, personal autonomy, emancipation. For the Nigerian Chamba inhabiting a country torn by bitter animosities between Christians and Muslims, their ethnic identity enables them to transcend divisions among themselves to live in peace, Fardon argues (Chapter 12); so too the Sufi order I studied preached tolerance, inclusiveness and peace (Chapter 3); Muslim feminists in Indonesia were part of a peace alliance with Chinese and other persecuted minorities (Robinson, Chapter 6).

The notion that there are many, different, cosmopolitan practices co-existing in late modernity, with their own historicities and distinctive worldviews, has led nevertheless also to an exploration of marginal cosmopolitanisms. Homi Bhabha, who possibly coined the term 'vernacular cosmopolitanism', is uneasy with Martha Nussbaum's image of the self, following the Greek Stoic Hierocles, as at the centre of a series of concentric circles, with universal liberal values privileged above family, ethnic group or nation (Nussbaum, 1994). The notion of a borderless cosmopolitan community seems inadequate, he proposes, in relation to the millions of refugees and migrants fleeing violence and poverty. Drawing on Appiah's vision, Bhabha proposes a 'cosmopolitan community envisaged in *marginality'*, a border zone which he terms vernacular cosmopolitanism (1996: 195–6).

Such violently dislocated populations differ significantly from settled groups on the margins. Melanesian cultural groups, positioned on the margins of the metropolitan world, Eric Hirsch argues (Chapter 10), nevertheless view themselves as located at the *centre*, managing a vast symbolic world of exchange in which cultural boundaries and horizons were never fixed. So, too, the Stoics' vision of concentricity, Richard Werbner contends (Chapter 9) was not 'static' but 'dynamic': 'to be civic and truly moral ... Stoics demanded active, deliberate change of a certain kind in the light of moral reason and perceived virtue'.

Although Hannerz has revised his earlier position, acknowledging that more people beyond the elite may now be identified as cosmopolitan, he notes that 'bottom-up' cosmopolitans are unlikely to be recognised as such in their own environment (2004: 77). Societies differ culturally in the extent to which they celebrate (or denigrate) familiarity with diverse cultures. Stuart Hall (Chapter 17) says of 'cosmopolitans from below', part of the 'enormous tide of transnational movement', who are driven by civil war, ethnic cleansing, famine, economic disaster, and search for economic benefits, that they 'live a global life' by *necessity*, arising from 'the disjunctures of globalisation'. Despite that, their understanding or knowledge is just as complex, he points out, as that of global entrepreneurs; they too are 'in translation'.

This raises the critical question of cosmopolitan consciousness: in what sense does cosmopolitanism need to be grounded in an open, experimental, inclusive, normative consciousness of the cultural other? Such a consciousness would need to include elements of self-doubt and reflexive self-distantiation, an awareness of the existence and equal validity of other cultures, other values, and other mores. Is travel without such an inclusive consciousness cosmopolitan? Does travel inevitably lead to such openness and reflexivity? Despite their global commercial acumen, Senegalese Mouride traders are said to engage in 'rites of social exclusiveness' so that 'Mouride diasporic culture is homogenised in a way that excludes foreign values' ((Diouf, 2000: 694, 695). Similarly, members of the jet-setting wealthy Chinese overseas trading diaspora studied by Aihwa Ong (e.g. 1998, 1999), with their multiple passports and multiple homes in different countries, appear to lack the kind of cultural openness and sensitivity normally associated with cosmopolitanism. Diasporas, by definition, are heterogeneous, and not all their members are equally cosmopolitan as I show elsewhere, in my analysis of the Pakistani diasporic public sphere (Werbner 2002). Sometimes it is factory workers rather than wealthy merchants who display more openness to their non-diasporic compatriots. So, too, diasporic intellectuals may be alienated from underprivileged members of their community despite their celebration of cultural hybridity. But not all diasporic elites are so alienated. Similarly, not all

Senegalese in Italy are inward looking, even if Mourides regard Italy as a 'polluting' environment. Riccio (2001) reports that Senegalese in Italy are a multi-ethnic and multi-religious community who seek, as one migrant told him, not 'only to look for jobs. To emigrate is to know new things, to broaden one's horizons in such a way that one can bring back home what one discovered and learned.'

Much depends on context. Some environments are more cosmopolitan than others. Zubaida (1999) invokes the 'legendary cosmopolitan enclaves of Cairo, but especially Alexandria, the paradigm case of Middle Eastern cosmopolitanism' – a hub of ideas, religions, goods and people from East and West, protected by an imperial context. Thessalonica was, according to Kenneth Brown (forthcoming), 'a great Balkan cosmopolitan city for centuries, a veritable Babel of languages, religions, cultures and local traditions.' If we take vernacular cosmopolitanism to refer to a multicentred world, beyond the West, in the sense proposed by Arjun Appadurai, it is perhaps among the elites of such cosmopolitan cities that distinctive vernacular cosmopolitanisms are created.

Feminist and Non-Violence Cosmopolitan Movements

Feminism introduces a new kind of 'difference' into the cosmopolitan debate. Despite some attention to women and globalisation, and to the complex relations between First and Third World feminists, cosmopolitanism has been a 'virtually insignificant presence of gender issues in the now voluminous literature on cosmopolitanism' as Maila Stivens (Chapter 4) points out, an absence 'all the more remarkable,' she observes, because 'feminisms have engaged both theoretically and practically with many of the besetting difficulties within the cosmopolitanism debates' – 'universalism, ethnocentricity, neo-imperialism', and have developed 'ideas of transversal politics and versions of what can be seen as grounded cosmopolitanism.' In a wide-ranging review of the literature, Stivens suggests that the hiatus may be linked to 'a long-term disdain in political thought for what is deemed the "private", "domestic" or intimate', the main focus of women's democratisation movements. For Islamic feminists in Malaysia and Indonesia, highly self-conscious translation and interpretation, as well as political activism and lobbying, have been the crux of their cosmopolitan project.

In her richly documented account of the development of Indonesian Muslim feminism, Kathryn Robinson (Chapter 5) shows the extent to which Muslim women scholars and political leaders have engaged with Muslim feminist revisionist thought in the wider Muslim world. Their aim has been to create jointly a gendered revolution in theorising the positioning of women in Islamic societies, based on a new hermeneutics of sacred texts. As in Malaysia, the movement has created alliances with other women's organisations to address a range of issues

– from domestic violence to polygamy, marriage and divorce laws – and mobilised in public protest against paramilitary military and ethnic violence against women, internationally and within Indonesia.

Robinson grounds her analysis in the changing political landscape of Indonesia, the country with the largest Muslim population in the world. She argues that the

> flood of new Islamic feminist literature exemplifies the cosmopolitan character of Islamic social and political thought as a counterpoint and complement to western thinking (in a manner remarkably similar to the development of Indonesian nationalism in the early twentieth century). The principles of gender equity discovered through hermeneutical readings of texts are similar to the principles put forward by proponents of Islam as a basis for democracy, or for a distinctive Islamic form of human rights. For these scholars, feminism (like democracy and human rights) is not exclusive to western cosmopolitan ideals.

The activists have successfully converted a popular women's ritual of joyous singing in praise of the Prophet into one of joyous singing in praise of 'Justice' or 'Jender' equality, as a way of spreading their message among the wider population.

The high level of cosmopolitan consciousness among feminists is thus rooted in the local and political specificities of Indonesian society. In Malaysia, too, a women's coalition has set out a manifesto of women's rights and Agenda for Change, which 'deplores the manipulation of ethnicity and religion and the use of fear and oppressive forces to divide women.' One member organisation, Sisters of Islam, is well known internationally and has been highly active in global NGO forums. As in Indonesia, SIS engages Malaysian society 'in a highly reflexive and participatory process of "cultural" mediation or dialogue,' in which it locates women's (universal) rights, and intellectual and political activism within the evolving state, within culturally particular, communal values, rather than denying these values.

In addition to these highly conscious cosmopolitan elites, other women, more underprivileged and living on the margins, may also engage in cosmopolitan practice. Within a general atmosphere of xenophobia in post-Apartheid South Africa, Owen Sichone says (Chapter 15), local women in the townships in Cape Town, much like the British women who welcomed black American GIs in World War II (Nava 2006), are far more hospitable to strangers from other African countries than are their menfolk; more willing to understand, as Sichone puts it quoting Julius Nyerere, 'greeting strangers with gifts of food and on the third day, giving them the hoe and inviting them to join in the cultivation of land' – in other words, incorporating prior strangers into the community.

In India, Dalit Christian women, Kalpana Ram proposes (Chapter 7), break the bondage of home and village community as they embrace modernist cosmopolitan values which postcolonial writers have critically viewed as merely – and exclusively – defining the middle classes in India. Inspired by these values, the women take on new responsibilities and assert their agency by moving freely between villages. Theirs is a local cosmopolitanism, but it is nevertheless associated with a wider vision of the world and their rights as unbounded citizens. Ram wants to develop the emotional, embodied, phenomenological groundings of cosmopolitanism in the flow of feelings of unboundedness in relation to an Other.

Both Stivens and Robinson draw on Yuval-Davis's notion of transversal dialogue to point to the challenge of bridging divisions between actors, all the more so in the context of violent conflict. Although Appiah rightly points out that in some cosmopolitanism 'conversations', protagonists can only agree to disagree (2006: 78), endemic ethnic conflict, gender inequalities or imposed religious dogma do require a committed and genuine attempt to arrive at agreed strategies for living in amity, without denying differences.

Public Cosmopolitans, Cosmopolitan Subjectivities, Fluid Boundaries

Several of the chapters examine in depth the personal biographies and evolving subjectivities of postcolonial intellectuals or public radicals, from different perspectives. Among the Fuyuge in Papua New Guinea, a world of fluid exchange relations of objects, places and names is premised on the idea of *cosmopolitan centrality*, Eric Hirsch argues (Chapter 10).[5] Each group sees itself as at the centre of this universe of exchange between equals. The 'entification' of territorially demarcated groups by gold-mining companies has divided the indivisible and created relations of inequality and power imbalance between local people and the mining company, the latter supported by the state. In this new context, Hirsch shows, both a travelled public urban intellectual and a local Fuyuge village intellectual perceive a danger of being overwhelmed by an outside culture, in a new kind of fear that did not exist previously in the fluid, constantly re-centering indigenous Melanesian form of cosmopolitanism. Aref Abu-Rabia traces his own intellectual biography and the predicaments Palestinian public intellectuals faced in Palestine-Israel (Chapter 8), while Dorothy Hodgson traces the biography of a Maasai intellectual and activist (Chapter 11). In modern Botswana, Richard Werbner locates the biography of a leading Kalanga public activist in his experiences of ethnic persecution and the changing landscape of racist southern Africa, and traces his subsequent role in nation-building republicanism, and in the formation and defence of civil society in postcolonial Botswana (Chapter 9). A trained lawyer committed to public transparency and the rule of law, he nevertheless remained rooted in his Kalanga identity and the values of the countryside until the end of his life. His funeral was an occasion for memorialising his visionary life history as a maverick and as a rooted public cosmopolitan. In reviewing Anthony Appiah's impressive oevre on cosmopolitanism, Werbner is concerned that perhaps his 'holistic optimism' underestimates the painful social and political contradictions and the price involved in struggling to be both patriotic and cosmopolitan.

Writing Social Anthropology as Cosmopolitan Theory and Practice

In a deeply insightful keynote address analysing the historical phases of anthropology as a cosmopolitan discipline, Elizabeth Colson (Chapter 2) stresses the relative fieldwork isolation of the early generation of modern anthropologists when compared to today's jet-setting, in-and-out-of-the-field generation. This inevitably led, she argues, to a greater 'intensity' of knowledge of a smaller region, to less dialogue with members of other disciplines – who rarely ventured into the hinterland – and to the unlikelihood of being 'bothered by frequent visits from officialdom or missionaries.' The rest of the world seemed very remote by comparison to today's locales of anthropological study.

In the aftermath of World War I, and in the face of the rise of European fascism, anthropologists in the inter-World War period were cosmopolitan in a unique sense, Colson argues: 'The superiority of Western values and Western institutions was not nearly as taken for granted as it was in later prosperous decades', and hence they 'were likely to respect the political economies, ritual orders, and dogmatic beliefs they described as *viable alternative systems* of order, i.e. ideal models of alternative reality from which much of the contention caused by perceptions of inequality and other evils was eliminated.' Sceptical of 'innate European superiority, the long term viability of European institutions' and Western ideas of progress, in some ways the inter- and post-war anthropologists resembled today's postmodernists. But they were not textual deconstructivists: 'They had seen for themselves the importance of economic and political factors in determining the history of their own times, and they gave primacy to such factors in pursuing their own research agendas.'

In my chapter (Chapter 3) I address the deconstructive critique of social anthropology in the mid-1980s that challenged the discipline's claims to be cosmopolitan in practice (doing fieldwork in out-of-the-way places) and in social theory (the comparative study of societies and cultures). The attack focused on the evident power imbalance between predominantly Western researchers and non-Western subjects during the colonial era. In many ways this imbalance has persisted into the present. Beneath the scientific façade of ethnographic objectivity, the critics argued, the hegemonic fieldworker remains invisible and the 'native voices' of the cultural and social other are suppressed.

Of course, although undoubtedly well-intentioned, this denial of anthropology's cosmopolitan claims starts from the distinctly sceptical, un-cosmopolitan assumption that just because one happens to come from a certain society, one is incapable of understanding other societies, empathising with their members' predicaments and joys, learning their language, poetry, myth making or story telling, appreciating their material culture, the challenges of their environment, their mundane everyday lives. In short, celebrating their difference. This identitarian 'nativist' approach, Adam Kuper has argued, sees its salvation in representing the (unedited) voices of the people – the oppressed other (1994: 542–3), buying into the 'gospel' that 'white people could never appreciate what it meant to be black, that men could not understand women ... that only the native could understand the native, only the native has the right to study the native' (ibid.: 544). The alternative view, I argue, is that the gaze of the stranger enables new insights (Chapter 3).

A second strand is that the denial of social anthropology's cosmopolitanism relates to an alleged tendency of the discipline to study 'closed' cultures – to misrecognise cultural openness, fluidity, internal contestation or mobility. Structural functionalism, it was taken for granted, was the study of closed social systems, just as cultural anthropology studied closed cultures. Against that, I argue (Chapter 3) that social anthropologists, especially those in the Durkheimian Radcliffe-Brownian tradition, studied unbounded social fields, much as Bryan Turner, we saw, argued for sociology. Referring to Herder's notion of *volk* culture, Chris Hann (Chapter 4) considers the cosmopolitan impact of central European thought on social anthropologists such Malinowski and Gellner, who came to Britain from Poland and Czechoslovakia, and argues that both were influenced by Herder's ideas, as was Boas in the United States. There is little doubt that Malinowski, originating from the small Polish academic elite of a 'subjugated nation' (Stocking 1991: 34), displayed a Herderian impulse in his theorising and defence of the integrity of pre-contact cultures and his open recognition of the destructiveness of modern 'civilisation' (ibid: 60–1) – despite his faith in enlightenment ideas of science. The same impulse is evident in Herder's romantic nationalism, which evolved in opposition to the imperialist hegemony of French metropolitan culture in Germany, and its civilisational and rationalist message. Against that, Herder insisted that all cultures were equally authentic, rooted, organic, inviolable and constitutive of overarching collective values.

In practice, however, Malinowski's and Gellner's visions of culture were in some ways more sceptical than Herder's. Culture was something individuals or groups manipulated for personal or collective utility; their reach was regional; and they were epiphenomenal: the real truths were environmental, economic, political or psychological.[6] Gellner recognised that Muslim society was riven by political conflicts, ideological divisions and moral disagreements, and he saw national culture as an invented tradition for the sake of capitalist expansion. Like their fellow British social anthropologists, Hann argues, Malinowski and Gellner regarded anthropology as a science, yet both were patriots, hence rooted cosmopolitans. Gellner returned to the Czech Republic after the fall of communism to help establish anthropology in the university. Malinowski, Hann tells us, was engaging himself actively on behalf of Poland when he died in New Haven in 1942. Hann argues that the principle of rooted cosmopolitanism has far-reaching implications for the discipline – specifically, that local folklorists 'at home' should be incorporated into anthropology departments in Eastern Europe.

The intellectual biographies of modern anthropologists such as Radcliffe-Brown or Boas raise the question: how deep have been the differences between British social and American cultural anthropology? Kuper maintains that 'the American project of cultural anthropology ... [was] quite distinct ... from the dominantly European project of social anthropology.' American anthropology was grounded in the German romantic tradition's stress on each society possessing a distinct culture, a 'complete way of life', which created 'distinctive modes of experiencing the world' and 'moulding personality' (Kuper 1994: 539–40). Culture was a 'system of symbols' or 'texts'. Echoing this division, Colson recalls that the early ASA rejected American anthropology (with the exception of Radcliffe-Brown's students at Chicago). Against that, Marshall Sahlins (1999), citing cultural diffusion theories, argues that 'it is astonishing from the perspective of North American cultural anthropology to claim that our intellectual ancestors constructed a notion of cultures as rigidly bounded, separate, unchanging, coherent, uniform, totalized and systemic' (Sahlins 1999: 404). Indeed, they spoke 'of "the fallacy of cultural separation": the mistaken idea that because cultures are distinctive they are closed' (ibid.).

In Chapter 3 I show that social anthropologists from the start analysed transcultural systems of economic exchange, pilgrimage and regional cults. Critiquing the idea of an 'anthropological obsession, exclusively, with self-containment, closed culture, social boundedness', Richard Werbner has argued that the 'transinterest' in anthropology, including 'creolization, hybridity and syncretism is at least as old as the nineteenth century ethnography of the Ghost Dance ... among American Indians ... or the Kula ring' (R. Werbner 2004c: 390). My chapter proposes that such flows and movements are central to understanding regional and pilgrimage cults,.

Following Sahlins, Jonathan Friedman (2002) similarly rejects a currently pervasive trope positing that in the past, anthropologists studied only 'bounded' cultures, localities and communities, while transnational or global encounters necessarily generate hybrid objects (or cultures). This, he argues, stems from a current tendency to individualise and reduce culture to a substance that 'fills' people or objects so they can either 'be pure or mixed' (ibid.: 25). Rejecting attacks on indigenous movements, Friedman defends an earlier 'global systemic anthropology' which argued that '[t]he fact that people occupying a particular place and living and constructing a particular world are *in their entirety* integrated into a *larger* system of relationships does not contradict the fact that they make their world where they are' (ibid.: 31, emphasis added).

It seems, then, that in practice neither British nor American modern anthropology were ever the study of closed cultures. Most anthropologists would agree with Kuper and others (e.g. Kahn 2003) that we are increasingly involved in a collaborative effort, in dialogue with the people we study, with local academics, journalists, public activists and other experts from a range of disciplines, in regional debates (Fardon 1990), and beyond that, in conversation among ourselves and with closely allied disciplines like sociology or social history. Above all, social anthropologists, with their comparative knowledge and cosmopolitan sensibility, can add a less parochial dimension to what are all too often Eurocentric analyses in the social sciences – *even these days when the focus is on globalisation*. To quote Colson, 'the anthropologists of the 1940s encroached upon the realm of the social philosophers, moralists, religious thinkers, and other social critics ... [They] directed attention to the narrowness of vision of economists, psychologists, and humanitarians who unthinkingly adopted western yardsticks and assumed the givenness of western categories.'

Hence, I argue (Chapter 3) that it is not the encounter during fieldwork which makes the anthropologist a cosmopolitan; rather, anthropologists *become* cosmopolitan as a community of scholars engaged in building a comparative subject through argumentation and critical debate. From this perspective, cosmopolitanism is dialogical – a collective, creative endeavour, beyond the individual. But as travellers and strangers, anthropologists rely on the hospitality and welcome of the people they study. Paradoxically, then, it is *they* who, as cosmopolitan hosts, enable the emergence of a shared cosmopolitan dialogue.

Notes

1. I would like to thank Elizabeth Colson and Richard Werbner for their helpful comments on this introduction. Citations from Stuart Hall are from the filmed interview.
2. Habermas misses some of these.
3. Beck speaks instead of 'Reflexive Cosmopolitanism' (2004: 94) as a critique of the 'national outlook'.

4. As I write this, Robert Mugabe is still in power, one of the last irrational tyrants, with the international community and neighbouring African countries apparently helpless to replace him.
5. Anna Tsing, from another perspective, shows the creative re-centring of the Meratus (Tsing 1993: 251–83).
6. On Malinowski see Sahlins (1976), especially Chapter 2. Invoking Gellner, Rapport (2007) has recently advocated an individual 'enlightenment' vision of cosmopolitanism anthropology, while perpetuating the stereotypical myth of the 'closed society' or 'culture' (British and American) – holistic, collectivistic, relativistic – and thus devoid of individual consciousness, agency or moral imperatives, supposedly characterising anthropological theory (ibid.: 262).

References

Appiah, Kwame Anthony (1998), 'Cosmopolitan Patriots', in Pheng Cheah and Bruce Robbins (eds), *Cosmopolitics: Thinking and Feeling Beyond the Nation*, Minneapolis: University of Minnesota Press, pp. 91–116.
—— (2006), *Cosmopolitanism: Ethics in a World of Strangers*, London: Allen Lane.
Archibugi, Daniele (2004), 'Cosmopolitan Democracy and its Critics', *European Journal of International Relations* 10 (3): 437–73.
Asad, Talal (1973), *Anthropology and the Colonial Encounter*, London: Ithaca Press.
Beck, Ulrich (2006) [2004], *The Cosmopolitan Vision*, translated by Ciaran Cronin, Cambridge: Polity Press.
Bhabha, Homi K. (1996), 'Unsatisfied: Notes on Vernacular Cosmopolitanism', in Laura Garcia-Morena and Peter C. Pfeifer (eds), *Text and Nation*, London: Camden House, pp. 191–207.
Brennan, Timothy (1997), *At Home in the World: the Cosmopolitan Now*, Cambridge Mass: Harvard University Press.
Brown, Kenneth (in press), 'Some Aspects of Cosmopolitanism', *Biblioteka of Alexandria*.
Cheah, Pheng (2006), 'Cosmopolitanism', Special Issue 'Problematising Global Knowledge', *Theory Culture & Society* 23 (2–3): 486–96.
Clifford, James (1992), 'Travelling Cultures', in Lawrence Grossberg, Cary Nelson and Paula A. Treichler (eds), *Cultural Studies*, London: Routledge, pp. 96–116.
—— (1998), 'Mixed Feelings', in Pheng Cheah and Bruce Robbins (eds), *Cosmopolitics: Thinking and Feeling Beyond the Nation*, Mineapolis: University of Minnesota Press, pp. 362–70.

Cohen, Mitchell (1992), 'Rooted Cosmopolitanism: Thoughts on the Left, Nationalism, and Multiculturalism', *Dissent* (Fall): 478–83.

DeMars, William (2005), *NGOs and Transnational Networks: Wild Cars in World Politics*, London: Pluto Press.

Diouf, Mamadou (2000), 'The Senegalese Murid Trade Diaspora and the Making of a Vernacular Cosmopolitanism', *Public Culture* 12 (3): 679–702.

Fardon, Richard (1990), *Localising Strategies: Regional Traditions of Ethnographic Writing*, Edinburgh: Scottish Academic Press.

Friedman, Jonathan (1997), 'Global Crises, the Struggle for Cultural Identity and Intellectual Porkbarrelling: Cosmopolitans versus Locals, Ethnics and Nationals in an Era of De-Hegemonisation', in Pnina Werbner and Tariq Modood (eds), *Debating Cultural Hybridity: Multi-Cultural Identities and the Politics of Anti-Racism*, London: Zed Books, pp. 70–89.

—— (2002), 'From Roots to Routes: Tropes for Trippers', *Anthropological Theory* 2 (1): 21–36.

Habermas, Jürgen (1999), *The Inclusion of the Other: Studies in Political Theory*, Edited by Ciaran Cronin and Pablo De Greiff, Cambridge Mass: MIT Press.

Hannerz, Ulf (1990), 'Cosmopolitans and Locals in World Culture', in Mike Featherstone (ed.), Special Issue 'Global Culture', *Theory, Culture & Society* 7 (2): 237–51.

—— (1992), *Cultural Complexity: Studies in the Social Organisation of Meaning*, New York: Columbia University Press.

—— (2004), 'Cosmopolitanism', in David Nugent and Joan Vincent (eds), *A Companion to the Anthropology of Politics*, Oxford: Blackwell, pp. 69–85.

Held, David (1995), *Democracy and the Global Order: from the Modern State to Cosmopolitan Governance*, Cambridge: Polity Press.

—— (2004), 'Democratic Accountability and Political Effectiveness from a Cosmopolitan Perspective', *Government and Opposition* 39 (2): 364–91.

Hollinger, David A. (2002), 'Not Universalists, Not Pluralists: the New Cosmopolitans Find their Own Way', in Steven Vertovec and Robin Cohen (eds), *Conceiving Cosmopolitanism: Theory, Context and Practice*, Oxford: Oxford University Press, pp. 227–39.

Kahn, Joel S. (2003), 'Anthropology as Cosmopolitan Practice?' *Anthropological Theory* 3, 4: 403–15.

—— (2006), *Other Malays: Nationalism and Cosmopolitanism in the Modern Malay World*, Honolulu: University of Hawaii Press.

Kant, Immanuel (1784/1970), 'Perpetual Peace: a Philosophical Sketch', in Hans Reiss (ed.), *Kant's Political Writings*, Cambridge: Cambridge University Press, pp. 93–130 (also available online).

Kuper, Adam (1994), 'Culture, Identity and the Project of a Cosmopolitan Anthropology', *Man* (NS), 29 (3): 537–54.

Merry, Sally Engle (2006), *Human Rights and Gender Violence: Translating International Law into Local Justice*, Chicago: the University of Chicago Press.

Nava, Mica (2006), 'Domestic Cosmopolitanism and Structures of Feeling: the Specificity of London', in Nira Yuval-Davis, Kalpana Kannabiran and Ulrike Vieten (eds), *The Situated Politics of Belonging*, Thousand Oaks, CA: Sage: 42–53.

Nussbaum, Martha (1994), 'Patriotism and Cosmopolitanism', *Boston Review* XIX (5) (Oct/Nov) (internet source: www.soci.niu.edu/~phildept/kapitan/nusbaum1.html).

Ong, Aiwa (1998), 'Flexible Citizenship among Chinese Cosmopolitans', in Pheng Cheah and Bruce Robbins (eds), *Cosmopolitics: Thinking and Feeling Beyond the Nation*, Mineapolis: University of Minnesota Press, pp. 134–62.

—— (1999), *Flexible Citizenship*, Durham NC: Duke University Press.

Osaghae, Eghosa E. (2005), 'The State of Africa's Second Liberation', *Interventions* 7 (1): 1–20.

Parry, Benita (1991), 'The Contradictions of Cultural Studies', *Transition* 53: 37–45.

Pollock, Sheldon (2000), 'Cosmopolitan and Vernacular History', *Public Culture* 12 (3): 591–625.

Rabinow, Paul (1986), 'Representations are Social Facts: Modernity and Post-Modernity in Anthropology', in James Clifford and George E. Marcus (eds), *Writing Culture: The Poetics and Politics of Ethnography*, Berkeley: University of California Press, pp. 234–61.

Rapport, Nigel (2007), 'An Outline for Cosmopolitan Study: Reclaiming the Human through Introspection', *Current Anthropology* 48 (2): 257–83.

Riccio, Bruno (2001), 'From "ethnic group" to "transnational community"? Senegalese migrants' ambivalent experiences and multiple trajectories', *Journal of Ethnic and Migration Studies* 27 (4): 583–600

Robbins, Bruce (1998a), 'Introduction Part I: Actually Existing Cosmopolitanism', in Pheng Cheah and Bruce Robbins (eds), *Cosmopolitics: Thinking and Feeling Beyond the Nation*, Mineapolis: University of Minnesota Press, pp. 1–19.

—— (1998b), 'Comparative Cosmopolitanisms', in Cheah and Robbins (eds), pp. 246–64.

Robinson, Kathryn (ed.) (2007), *Southeast Asian and Pacific Cosmopolitans: Self and Subject in Motion*, London: Palgrave.

Sahlins, Marshall (1976), *Culture and Practical Reason*, Chicago IL: Chicago University Press.

—— (1999), 'Two or Three Things I Know about Culture', *JRAI* (incorporating *Man*), 5 (3): 399–422.

Stocking, George W. (1991), 'Maclay, Kubari, Malinowski: Archetypes from the Dreamtime of Anthropology', in George W. Stocking (ed.), *Colonial Situations: Essays on the Contextualization of Ethnographic Knowledge*, pp. 9–74.

Tsing, Anna Lowenhaupt (1993), *In the Realm of the Diamond Queen*, Princeton NJ: Princeton University Press.

Turner, Bryan S. (2006), 'Classical Sociology and Cosmopolitanism: a Critical Defence of the Social', *British Journal of Sociology* 57 (1): 133–51.

Vertovec Steven and Robin Cohen (2002), 'Introduction: Conceiving Cosmopolitanism', in Steven Vertovec and Robin Cohen (eds), *Conceiving Cosmopolitanism: Theory, Context and Practice*, Oxford: Oxford University Press, pp. 1–22.

Werbner, Pnina (1999), 'Global Pathways: Working Class Cosmopolitans and the Creation of Transnational Ethnic Worlds', *Social Anthropology* 7 (1): 17–35.

—— (2006), 'Vernacular Cosmopolitanism', Special Issue 'Problematising Global Knowledge', *Theory Culture and Society* 23 (2–3): 496–98.

Werbner, Richard (2002), 'Cosmopolitan Ethnicity, Entrepreneurship and the Nation: Minority Elites in Botswana', *Journal of Southern African Studies* 28 (4): 731–53.

—— (2004a), 'Epilogue: the New Dialogue with Post-Liberalism', in Harri Englund and Francis B. Nyamnjoh (eds), *Rights and the Politics of Recognition in Africa*, London: Zed Books, pp. 261–74.

—— (2004b), *Reasonable Radicals and Citizenship in Botswana: the Public Anthropology of Kalanga Elites*, Bloomington: Indiana University Press.

—— (2004c), 'Sacred Centrality and Flows across Town and Country: Sedimo in Botswana's Time of AIDS', in Peter Probst and Gerd Spittler (eds), *Between Resistance and Expansion: Explorations of Local Vitality in Africa*, Munster: Lit Verlag, pp. 389–413.

Werbner, Richard and Terence Ranger (eds) (1996), *Postcolonial Identities in Africa*, London: Zed Books.

Zubaida, Sami (1999), 'Cosmopolitanism and the Middle East', in Roel Meijer (ed.), *Cosmopolitanism, Identity and Authenticity in the Middle East*, London: Curzon, pp. 15–34.

Section I
Anthropology as a Cosmopolitan Discipline

The Founding Moment: Sixty Years Ago[1]
Elizabeth Colson

When I was asked to speak about the early days of the Association of Social Anthropologists at the celebration of the 60th anniversary of its founding, I began to consider what I knew of the founders and speculate about their enduring impact on anthropology. As one way to check on the latter, I had a citation check carried out on ten of them for the period January 2005 to March 2006. Amazingly all ten are still being cited. The majority have been dead these thirty years or more, but what they wrote is still an active part of the intellectual heritage of anthropology. Another legacy is the Association itself even though it has grown out of all knowledge and no longer provides a forum for a small number of people who know each other well and read each other's work.

The Association

Ten people met in July 1946 to discuss the desirability of an association devoted specifically to the furtherance of the interests of social anthropology and social anthropologists. Some months later a committee drew up a list of other potential members, nine of whom, according to David Mills, were based in Great Britain while another 15 to 20 were scattered around the Commonwealth (Mills 2003: 9–10). They all held post-graduate degrees in anthropology, overwhelmingly from LSE. Fifteen years later, in 1961, the Association had grown to include 142 members. Here I am relying on the Ardeners (Ardener and Ardener 1965: 30). By 1990, by my own count, it had 500 members whose advanced degrees had been taken at some 55 different universities, including some outside the Commonwealth (Colson 1991: 50).

The first meeting I attended was held in London in late 1947 or early 1948, a little over a year after the original gathering. I think every member of the Association who was then in Great Britain came, which meant there were about fifteen of us in the room. We fitted easily around a table. I don't remember if anyone gave a paper, but the discussion was collegial and combative. Even then not everyone spoke up. As a young anthropologist newly admitted to the august body and very impressed by the eminence of everyone else, I kept discreetly silent. But as a compulsive notetaker, I recorded what others said. Unfortunately those field notes have long since disappeared. I never expected to write them up. I do remember referring to the occasion as the meeting of the FFs; for down the side of the notebook alternated the names of Firth, Forde, Fortes, and Fortune with only occasional interpolations from Gluckman, Nadel, Richards, and Mair, and even rarer comments by Peristiany, Leach, and Little. The last two seemed to be regarded as neophytes. Evans-Pritchard was characteristically expressively silent.

In some respects those who came to London, as well as the absent members, were a cosmopolitan group. They had crossed disciplinary and territorial boundaries in becoming anthropologists. I doubt that any of them started out to be one: before World War II, anthropology was rarely taught as an undergraduate degree in British universities. They came out of history, law, geography, psychology, economics, biology, and engineering. They drew on their reading in other fields as they dealt with what they regarded as anthropological questions. Those born in Great Britain were in the minority. The remainder of that first group of perhaps 30 members were born in South Africa, Australia, New Zealand, and India, of parents some of whom had never visited Great Britain, while Nadel came from Austria and Peristiany from Cyprus. Oddly enough, that first group contained no Canadians, which suggests that Canadians of that period who became anthropologists looked to the United States. All had travelled outside their home country, and all had at least for a time lived in Great Britain. They were familiar with cities strung around the globe. Their field research had taken them to different ethnographic regions, to Africa, North America, Asia, and the Pacific. I think none had worked in Europe or South America. Anthropological investigation of cities and peasant communities may have already been envisaged. In fact, by the beginning of World War II they had already been undertaken by John Embree in Japan, Robert Redfield at Tepoztlan, Hortense Powermarker in the deep south of the United States, and W. Lloyd Warner and his team in the city of Newburyport, but I think none had been undertaken by the social anthropologists of Britain. Money available to them for field research was largely to finance research elsewhere in the Commonwealth, on the colonised rather than the colonisers. But among the students of 1947 were some who would soon leave to work in Spain, France, Greece, and Turkey.

Besides their cosmopolitan transcending of boundaries, the first members of the Association had another thing in common. All, except myself, Radcliffe-Brown and Brenda Seligman, had sat as students in Malinowski's seminar, and at least the latter two had known Malinowski. Subsequently Malinowski's students may have revolted against him, but they still bore his mark. Whatever else they had read, and in comparison with their American contemporaries most of them had read little ethnography, they had all read Malinowski on the Trobriands. Their seminars would be modelled on Malinowski's seminar, just as was their ethnography in its reliance on participant observation which privileged the contemporary; and their mode of analysis was that of functionalism in that it involved a search for how activities are interrelated and justified in what later came to be called 'cognitive models'. Along with Malinowski, they assumed thinking actors, who might be working from assumptions about reality that could be challenged, but were nevertheless behaving rationally given those assumptions. The Association was thus a descent group as well as a guild.

Its members recognised this, and were quick to differentiate between themselves and others who might claim to be anthropologists. Cosmopolitan sympathies were extended only so far. They had little good to say of American anthropology, except that carried out by Chicago students of Radcliffe-Brown, and were especially dismissive of work labelled culture and personality. They were adamant that various British anthropologists who were not of the Malinowskian elite were unworthy of the name even though they might hold teaching positions in Britain itself and their ethnographic publications, at least to the outsider, compared well with those admitted to the canon. 'He (or she) is not a social anthropologist' were the damning words that consigned such persons to an inferior status.

While criteria for membership were much discussed in the early years, it was difficult to be certain what they were or how they applied. Having a degree and holding a job in Britain or elsewhere in the Commonwealth were said to be essential, but did not guarantee acceptability. Publication cannot have counted or I would never have been admitted when I was, since I had published little or nothing in 1947. My degree was from an American university and I had never laid eyes on Malinowski. I did have a job based in Northern Rhodesia, now Zambia. The selection process was influenced by economic considerations as much as by a desire to maintain an unsullied line of descent. The goods for which anthropologists competed, jobs and research funds, were limited and determined by conditions not of the anthropologists' making. In 1947 there were only four professorships in all of Britain, and perhaps three or four more elsewhere in the Commonwealth. There was an expectation that resources would be more abundant now that the war was over and the Colonial Development and Welfare Fund seemed ready to help finance research institutes and independent fellowships. Those returning to civilian life in 1945, or being released from various government agencies as the war ended, looked upon this as a chance to obtain jobs and research funds for themselves and their future students. In such situations people are likely to operate on what Foster has called a principle of 'limited good' (Foster 1965), and so they tried to limit the number of those who might compete with them for scarce goods.

The social anthropologists of the 1940s were well aware of how easily disciplinary boundaries could be crossed and the likelihood that those with little or no formal training in the discipline would be regarded as anthropologists. Some of the few academic posts for anthropologists in Britain were held by people who had learned their anthropology on the job, as colonial administrators and missionaries; and a further cadre of such people existed, members in good standing of the Royal Anthropological Institute, who might be given consideration as academic posts became available. This gave impetus to the call for a professional association limited to those trained in anthropology in the only schools they saw as capable of providing such training, that of Malinowski and Radcliffe-Brown. The year before, similar concerns had led to the reorganisation of the American Anthropological Association into a two-tiered body of fellows and members, with only fellows entitled to be regarded as fully qualified professional anthropologists. Others might be interested contributors to the subject, but they were refused the imprimatur which would stamp them as qualified craftsmen whose workmanship had been tested against the standards of the profession.

About a decade later, in the 1950s, in Britain and elsewhere in the Commonwealth, academic jobs and research funding increased substantially for a few years, providing funds for the founding of new departments, a large increase in the number of academic jobs, and rather abundant funding for fieldwork. The inevitable happened. Those interested in anthropology were encouraged to regard it as a viable professional choice and emerged as well-trained professionals looking for jobs and other funding in a less expansive universe, subject to the competition of those in other fields. The concern with competition has waxed and waned over the years of the Association, and probably again resonates strongly among Association members in 2006, especially now that boundary jumping is again the order of the day – everyone is an expert on culture, and sometimes all the world seems to claim to do ethnography. One of the expected benefits referred to by Paul Sillitoe, when he urged the adoption of measures aimed at increasing the professional status of anthropology, is the prevention of 'the poorly qualified passing themselves off as anthropologists (2003: 2)'. I am not sure that all of them want to be regarded as anthropologists. Many seem quite happy to be geographers, demographers, historians, political scientists, or workers in public health, education, policy studies, development, crisis management, or cultural studies. It might be more to the point if they could be prevented from passing themselves off as competent ethnographers if they are not. In fact, some are doing very good ethnographic studies and tread firmly on our ground. If people in other fields speak our language and do equally good work, we may need to rethink our own claims to making a distinctive contribution.

Members of the new Association agreed in 1947 that it was important to create a specialised professional identity for social anthropologists that differentiated them from the many who had interests in anthropology. They were in less agreement about what that identity entailed, and about what work was appropriate for social anthropologists. Some thought their skills could and should be used in shaping policy and advising how programmes should be implemented. They shared the old liberal dream that truth is ascertainable and that when truth is made known, right action follows. This, of course, assumes that the system is run by people of good will in the interests of an ascertainable public good. Others urged the exclusive claims of teaching and basic research that would advance theory and disciplinary practice. Here, too, we have continuity; for arguments about the appropriate use of anthropological skills have continued through the years. Today probably more anthropologists hold positions outside academia than in, working as 'practising anthropologists' or 'applied anthropologists', and even those in academic positions do not necessarily sneer at the chance to work as consultants. The Association periodically tells us we must go out and make ourselves useful so that we will be valued by the general public and earn our keep. At the same time, status within the profession may well go to those who turn their attention to specialised esoteric subjects and write for fellow anthropologists or even for a restricted number of like-minded spirits. Probably we will continue to differ, and the centenary meeting of the Association will find its members arguing about what makes an anthropologist as well as what it is that anthropologists should be doing.

Issues and Controversies

The theoretical issues that informed discussions during the early meetings of the Association have proved less lasting: they are no longer divisive nor do they interest many of us. Some of them, of course, no longer interest us because they were explored so comprehensively in the 1940s and 1950s that there is nothing new to be said about them and further research simply confirms what is already known. Thus it was with kinship studies until technological developments made people rethink assumptions about what constitutes kinship. They then found new and interesting questions to pursue, where the answers were not already boringly blatant.

Theoretical continuities between the 1940s and the present are to be found less in the theoretical questions that guide anthropological interests than in the persistence of theoretical battles within the profession, thereby producing a dialectic through which any momentary agreement gives rise to new divisions. In 1947 I found members claiming to disagree about what should constitute the subject matter of social anthropology and appropriate modes of analysis. They formed factions attributed to doctrinal differences, although who belonged to which faction might be in dispute. The major rift at the time could be said to reflect both geography and allegiance to a leader for it pitted Oxford and the LSE against each other, with the structural-functionalism of Radcliffe-Brown dominating the former and the functionalism of Malinowski the latter. Geographical outliers at Cambridge or University College sided with one or the other, or if neutral were likely to be claimed by both. That rift, of course, was soon to be superseded by other and more numerous rifts as former allies drifted apart to found their own schools whose students happily entered the fray and insisted on ever-widening disagreements. The Manchester department came into being in 1949, and soon thereafter there was a Manchester school. Cambridge was won for social anthropology with the appointment of Meyer Fortes to the chair about 1950, and Cambridge quickly acquired its own dogmas and sense of superiority. And so it went. In such ways does the field of anthropology and the history of the Association conform to anthropological theory and illustrate how demographic and geographical factors affect human affairs. For what is factionalism but the playing-out of fission and fusion in group formation and disintegration, the latter hindered and delayed by the existence of cross-cutting ties among contenders.

In 1947, however, people claimed doctrinal issues as the basis for their oppositions. It was battles over the rival merits of structural functionalism and functionalism that enlivened ASA gatherings and sparked a determination to know what rivals might be up to that could be used to undercut their position or suborn their supporters. From time to time it was muttered 'So and so is really one of us', suggesting that the person agreed to the rival doctrine only for tactical reasons associated with jobs and future advancement, while being at heart a follower of the true faith. Or, the practicality of subversion was canvassed. In fact, as in so many factional struggles, in 1947 it was often difficult for an outsider to see why people felt so strongly about what seemed to be minor disagreements. I fell into disgrace by saying that, as someone trained in the United States, I couldn't see why they argued so vehemently and sometimes so intolerantly when they worked in much the same fashion and spoke much the same disciplinary language. For that matter they were too few in number to have developed distinct dialects. In those days, before jet travel became available or international conferences frequent, if they wanted to speak to anyone they had to speak to each other, and for the moment they were particularly loquacious because they had been separated during five years of war and were starved of anthropological talk. The more disputes the better. I should have recognised that 'difference' is all.

Divisiveness, therefore, has been an endemic element of the Association's nature since its beginnings. But then, division is a prerequisite of human social organisation and anthropologists are humans despite being anthropologists. What is surprising is how often they ignore this and seem surprised to discover that what they posit about the nature of social relationships applies to how they themselves interact with their fellows or others they encounter.

In 1947, division did not preclude fellowship. It may now, given the size of the Association so that many meet as unknown strangers. Originally members of the Association formed a single small face-to-face gossipy community, even if some of them might be stationed in the antipodes. They could count on other members of the Association reading what they wrote. This is something present members may envy until they remember this meant only about 30 readers. They met together in a single room and afterwards foregathered at a single pub. In another context, Max Gluckman once criticised the city planners responsible for the laying-out of a new town because they had provided for only one pub whereas anyone with a sense of social dynamics knew that a community needed at least two. Here, he ignored anthropological history, as the gathering in one pub long continued to be the hallmark of the discipline and was lauded for its furtherance of lively discussion, communal solidarity, and the symbolic link to that primal London pub where those attending Malinowski's seminar in the 1920s and 1930s adjourned. There, social anthropology might be said to have been born amidst the arguments of those who were then postgraduate students.

The divisions and rivalries of 1947 have long since become history, vaguely remembered by only a few. They happened well before most of the present members of the ASA were born. What about the intellectual contribution of the founders? If you are dismissive of their work, you need feel no compunction. They were equally dismissive of their predecessors. By 1947, paradigms had shifted and none of them claimed Rivers, Haddon, or Marrett as ancestors. For the most part, they despised what they had written, or grudgingly acknowledged the merit of an article or two while pointing out how these had been surpassed. Even Malinowski was said by some to have lacked understanding of social structure and to have been wrong about some other matters.

Changing Perspectives

Those who planned this conference on 'Cosmopolitanism and Anthropology', have suggested that anthropological training is conducive to the cosmopolitan virtues that transcend 'the parochialism or ethnicism of the nation-state', and thus are prone to give empathetic consideration to so-called others (Anon 2004: 33). We may be able to do so in some circumstances, but I would argue that we find it difficult to extend any such empathetic consideration to our own immediate forebears whose work is there to be transcended. We measure our advance by their short-comings. Writing styles change. Reflexively, too, we project into the past what we take for granted within our own era. That is one of the problems with hindsight: what happened, having led to the present, becomes the inevitable outcome of the past while what once seemed possible alternatives become inauthentic. It is no wonder if each generation of anthropologists sees the work of earlier generations slantwise and finds it difficult to understand why they paid attention to what after all now seem minor matters, slighted what now seems obvious, and seemed oblivious to what now would be foregrounded.

Current members of the Association quite rightly think of themselves as far removed from the anthropology of the 1940s: they ask different questions, conceptualise their subject matter differently, and work in situations where their forerunners did not. Even the seniors among you are of another generation and your interests for the most part are very different from those which preoccupied the men and women who founded the Association. After all you matured in a different world. Though you may sometimes cite them, you find it difficult to read what they wrote knowledgeably, because their vocabulary is now old-fashioned and because you lack contexts they took so much for granted that they did not realise they needed to supply them. In time, your own failures to provide such contexts because you assume your readers know the background against which you write will come back to haunt you when that background disappears.

The truth is that those who founded the Association had experienced a very specific world which moulded what they took for granted and what they challenged. They concentrated on what seemed important in their own time and place. Their research methods were of also of the period. Let me try to provide a context for their work.

Time, Space and the Nature of Fieldwork

All the founders, save Radcliffe-Brown and Brenda Seligman, were students in the years between World War I and World War II. They began fieldwork in the late 1920s or in the 1930s, and they usually went where no other anthropologist had set foot before, which in a way is a rather enviable thing although it had its drawbacks. Given the transportation available at the time, once arrived they were usually confined to an area that could be covered by foot, bicycle, or canoe. In consequence they concentrated on the people who lived in the small region immediately surrounding them, and what they knew about local links to other areas was usually based on what local people told them. They did not have the facilities to follow them in their travels. Nor, usually, were they able to follow them over time, for when access to a place meant travel by ship, then rail, then truck and then foot, once arrived you stayed put until you left and once you left you did not return. One result was that the fieldwork experience was probably more intense than it is today. Friends did not fly in from all over the world to pay a visit; probably nobody within miles was a native speaker of your own language; weekends in town were out of the question; you had no wireless or phone; and even the arrival of mail was occasional and could not be counted upon. You and those you were working among were also unlikely to be bothered by frequent visits from officialdom or missionaries. Perforce you immersed yourself in what was happening locally and rarely came up for air. This had its repercussions on what fieldworkers looked at. If kinship loomed large in their subsequent publications, this is because on the scale at which they were able to work, much of what happened was organised through kinship relationships, whether these were regarded as biological or fictional. While theoretical issues guide the formulation of research questions, feasibility dictates what fieldworkers can do in practice, as does the luck of the draw: that is the sheer serendipity of happening to be there when something happens.

Those engaged in ethnographic research in the 1930s were certainly aware of the impact of colonial governance and international markets, but the conditions of the time made the rest of the world seem remote and not immediately important. Much of the social anthropology written in the late 1940s therefore lacks the global context that we would expect to find today.

Historical context may also have been lacking, although by the 1930s some studies of social change had begun to appear. This, too, is a feature of the time in which their fieldwork was carried out. In the first place, as students of Malinowski and Radcliffe-Brown they were in revolt against the conjectural history of the previous evolutionary and diffusionist anthropology. They were also empiricists. Social anthropology, they thought, should deal with the contemporary, with what they could see with their own eyes and hear with their own ears. Their time span, therefore, was usually as limited as their spatial span, though Evans-Pritchard was working on his historical study of the Sanussi Order. The one-time field visit was the order of the day – long-term research with repeated visits now so taken for granted was a thing of the future, Isaac Schapera being a notable exception here. They usually had no way to check on whether what they observed was representative of other times except from what people told them about the past, and they were leery of such accounts because it was accepted knowledge that myths and other tales of the past are social charters that validate present institutions and hierarchies. They were lucky if any previous visitor to the area or any local person had published an account against which they could measure their own findings. Archives were scattered and access might be closed or given only under stipulations that made it wiser to avoid them. Written histories of a country or region were rare. Historians weren't interested in working where they worked. Historians arrived along with sociologists, political scientists, and economists only in the 1950s and 1960s when living conditions more nearly approached those they were accustomed to at home. Then, also, scholarly work by local historians and social scientists became common as students emerged from newly founded national universities. The lack of global and historical context in much of what was being written when the Association was founded now seems glaringly apparent in a period when we take for granted that our fieldnotes can be supplemented by newspaper and radio reports, and by an abundance of documentation supplied by those in other disciplines, and that we ourselves pay repeated visits, and between visits keep in touch with those we have worked among by post, telephone, and the Internet. Often enough we look over the shoulders of ethnographers who described the area in earlier decades. Whether we like it or not, currently it is hard not to walk in others' footprints or even be provoked by their physical presence in terrain we would like to call our own. Annoying yes, but it all makes for the possibility to do much better work now, and a good many of you are producing work that your predecessors would envy. That is, if they recognised it as anthropology and could understand it.

Experience and Premises

They approached their work with premises that may seem alien to you. They had been moulded under very different circumstances. They had seen for themselves the importance of economic and political factors in determining the history of their own times, and they gave primacy to such factors in pursuing their own research agendas.

With the exception of Radcliffe-Brown and Brenda Seligman, they had grown up in the years after World War I: a war that put paid to nineteenth-century illusions about progress and European rationality. All of them had experienced the Great Depression of the 1930s when the economic collapse beggared many, brought on massive unemployment, and put in question the viability of economic systems based on the market. As fieldworkers in the late 1920s and 1930s, they found themselves among people who relied upon the land or water to supply the majority of their needs. When markets crash, as they did in the 1930s, those who can support themselves off the land are arguably better off than those who have come to depend upon a market economy that betrays them. A certain wariness of technological and economic innovation was therefore characteristic of this generation of anthropologists – as, incidentally, it was of many colonial officials who had no desire to see the people they administered become as poverty-stricken and traumatised as those in their home country who were dependent upon the dole.

The rise of Fascism and Nazism in Europe in the 1920s and 1930s also left them suspicious of the rationality of political and economic systems that provided the seed beds from which these emerged. Several had left European homelands when they became at risk as Hitler rose to power, and others had lived with the knowledge that their lives might well be forfeit if Britain was successfully invaded. The superiority of Western values and Western institutions was not nearly as taken for granted as it was in later prosperous decades when technological advances seemed to promise the end of drudgery and poverty, and there was glib talk of modernisation and the end of poverty throughout the world. In the 1930s and in the 1940s, Marx was taken seriously. Some of them saw Communism as a viable and relatively benign alternative to Nazism or the capitalism which had devastated Western economies, but I don't think that in 1947 any of them wanted to live under such a system. Socialism was more congenial, especially in the terms preached by the British Fabians and the then Labour Party, only recently come to power.

In 1946, they had just emerged from World War II which had dominated their lives for over six years. Some had been on the battle lines. Others were survivors of the London blitz. Their students in 1946 and for some years thereafter were mostly war veterans. Rationing was still on and the food search was a constant reminder of the basic importance of provisioning in determining both what people do and what they think about. All were undergoing something of an identity crisis as they shifted from their familiar wartime roles and statuses. When they turned again to writing up their neglected fieldnotes, usually stemming from the late 1930s, they had much on their own minds that influenced how they analysed what they had recorded.

If they preferred people as they found them, it was because they were not at all certain that those who promised them a better future if they changed could deliver on their promises. Instead, they were likely to respect the political economies, ritual orders, and dogmatic beliefs they described as viable alternative systems of order, i.e. ideal models of alternative reality from which much of the contention caused by perceptions of inequality and other evils was eliminated. This left them open to charges of sentimentality and antiquarianism – or, even worse, paternalism, especially some decades later when newly independent countries wrenched themselves away from colonial domination but chose to adopt institutions which they saw as having led to the empowerment of Europeans. But the 1930s had left those who founded the Association, and many others of their period, sceptical of the long-term viability of European institutions, the superiority of European values, or any innate superiority of Europeans or those of European descent. That scepticism, I suspect, is shared by many of you at the present time, who have new reasons to worry about where the Western trajectory is heading.

Again, whatever their ethnic background, their intellectual stance was one of resistance to creeds that preached racial inferiority or justified the subordination of others on racial grounds. The South Africans among them were particularly vehement in this respect. You may say, 'yes, but they accepted and served colonialism'. This was true but only up to a point. They may not have demanded that Britain immediately dismantle its colonial empire. In the 1930s, that would have meant that other colonial powers would have moved in to take over. They thought some colonial regimes better than others, and they were probably right. They saw their own role as one of providing a body of knowledge that could be used to inform and reform colonial policy in general and the way administrative and technical officers worked at the local level.

Anthropology as Critique

Colonial governments certainly did not regard anthropologists as reliable upholders of the system. Rather they were critics of the colonial order, under suspicion as possible agents of subversion, especially since their fraternisation with local people did not conform to colonial etiquette 'and might give people ideas'. There is a certain irony in this since local people were likely to suspect them of spying for the colonial government. But then suspicion of the fieldworker goes with the role. While working on the Makah Reservation in 1941–42, I was suspected of being a German spy; in Northern Rhodesia during the colonial regime, the administration watched to see if I was preaching subversive communism, while local people thought I was an odd-ball member of the administration, the less dangerous because I was a woman; in independent Zambia, suspicion continued but in a new guise. Any American anthropologist is regarded as a potential worker for the CIA. Anthropological curiosity is rarely seen as an adequate explanation for the presence and persistent questioning of someone alien to the system.

You may say you have solved such problems by carrying out your ethnography at home rather than in places where you would be alien, and so you have obliterated the dichotomy between the us and the other that mars the work of your predecessors. This, of course, subverts the idea that anthropology is cosmopolitan in approach and tries to transcend boundaries to reach an empathetic understanding of others. It is also based on the false assumption that home is a homogenised place where people think and act the same way and share the same traditions, whereas it is likely to be a meeting place of many communities who relate to each other in different ways. Assumptions of homogeneity came to be seen as one of the distorting weaknesses of the social anthropology of the 1940s when attention shifted to the role played by conflicting constructs, situational choices and competing power interests. But even if one could assume homogeneity, returning home does not solve for the anthropologist the problems of alienation caused by the dichotomy between the us and the other. Built into the very nature of anthropology is the necessity for comparison if only to celebrate the unique, and comparison always raises the possibility of alternative standards. It requires one to stand off and look, especially at the familiar, as something that requires explanation and needs justification, as one more alternative human arrangement. One questions what others see as natural and right, the guarantors of their self-worth and even superiority, to foreground it for study. The alien who cannot be expected to know, who needs instruction, may be seen as less subversive than one who should understand and accept the basic premises by which people live. So long as your goals include contributing to the ethnographic record that makes comparisons possible and inevitable, you share with your predecessors, wherever you work, this quality of being other.

A Summing Up

In this chapter, I have written as an old-fashioned social anthropologist and followed the anthropological dictum that one must stand off and critique whatever it is one looks at, including one's own society, but one does so in order to acquire a deeper understanding of the nature of social life. Though my ethnography may be faulty since it relies on undocumented memory, I have tried to do something of an anthropological analysis of the Association and its members at the time of its inception.

The Association was founded by people of a given time who had learned to question their own society because they had so often found it wanting. Their ethnographic work may have dealt with other people, but it contributed to what after all has been the primary role of anthropology: the recording of the spectrum of human ingenuity that, in turn, foregrounds the familiar world of home and so opens it to informed thought. In doing this the anthropologists of the 1940s encroached upon the realm of the social philosophers, moralists, religious thinkers, and other social critics. Their anthropology, and that of those they did not recognise as fellow social anthropologists, influenced Western thought and taught others to think in terms they introduced. It directed attention to the narrowness of vision of economists, psychologists, and humanitarians who unthinkingly adopted Western yardsticks and assumed the givenness of Western categories. One has only to read and listen to catch echoes, in the common parlance of scholarship and popular culture, of what they said and wrote. This has been absorbed into the culture of the cosmopolitan globalised world of the 21st century.

Those who founded the Association left an organisation, which continues to be divisive and productive of new thought. They left an ethnographic tradition built on respect for others. Some other things remain to you, including the way your own thought has been moulded by their impact on Western civilisation and the times that have formed you.

Notes

1. Pnina Werbner is responsible for this article in the sense that she invited me to speak at the 60th anniversary meeting of the ASA and provided me with a

title. Suzanne Calpestre, the John Rowe Research Librarian in the George and Mary Foster Library of Anthropology (University of California, Berkeley), did the citation search. My thanks to both and to members of the Association who patiently listened.

References

Anon (2004), ASA Conferences: 'Cosmopolitanism and Anthropology', *Annals of the Association of Social Anthropologists of the UK and the Commonwealth*, 22: 33–36.

Ardener, Edwin and Shirley Ardener, (1965), 'A Directory Study of Social Anthropologists', *The British Journal of Sociology* 16 (4): 295–314.

Colson, Elizabeth (1991), 'Social/Cultural Anthropology', in Sydel Silverman, (ed.) *Wenner-Gren Foundation, Report for 1990 and 1991*, New York: Wenner-Gren Foundation, pp. 49–61.

Foster, George (1965), 'Peasant Society and the Image of Limited Good', *American Anthropologist* 67: 293–315.

Mills, David (2003), 'Professionalizing or Popularizing Anthropology? A Brief History of Anthropology's Scholarly Associations in the UK', *Anthropology Today* 19 (5): 8–13.

Sillitoe, Paul (2003), 'Time to be Professional', *Anthropology Today* 19 (1): 1–2.

–3–

The Cosmopolitan Encounter: Social Anthropology and the Kindness of Strangers[1]

Pnina Werbner

Anthropology: a Cosmopolitan Discipline?

On the face of it, anthropology is *the* cosmopolitan subject *par excellence*. As a discipline devoted to the study of the diversity of world cultures, it is humanist and comparative. On each side of the Atlantic, the anthropological moieties that emerged in the twentieth century – British Social Anthropology versus American Cultural Anthropology – appeared to be divided by their opposed stress on universalism versus cultural relativism, comparative social science versus a holistic science of 'man'. This division led to exclusive associations, with the British ASA rejecting the four-field encompassment of the American AAA.[2] Nevertheless, on both sides of the Atlantic, modern social and cultural anthropologists since Malinowski and Boas argued mainly for non-evolutionary understandings of human societies across the globe, and hence for their comparability or equal status. They thus shared much in common, including, above all, respect for the integrity and viability of different ways of living. For both social and cultural anthropologists, the fundamental project was that of imagining societies beyond the West in all their social and cultural complexity. The critical difference in approach related to whether 'culture' or 'society', patterns of meaning and consciousness or of social institutions, was to be prioritised. There were also differences of regional focus, and these generated arcane debates and fierce arguments within each moiety about the limits of legitimate comparison: of the vision quest of American Indians, Indian caste, African segmentary systems, Melanesia gift exchange, and so forth. But in reality, anthropologists on both sides of the Atlantic started from an assumption of difference within the broader context of resemblance. They also started from a particular anthropological stance: anthropologists were strangers seeking to understand unfamiliar cultures which were presumed to be as rich and complex as their own. Evans-Pritchard's classic study of Azande witchcraft (1937) was foundational in establishing anthropology as a discipline that takes the stance of the stranger in order to probe beneath the commonsense assumptions of everyday life in another society. The stranger's gaze was a precondition for insight into the social rules and implicit assumptions of another society, and – by implication – of our own society as well.[3]

Anthropologists: Cosmopolitan Subjects

Like the discipline itself, many of the most prominent members of the founding circle of modernist anthropology were immigrants, refugees, exiles or secular Jews, the archetypal cosmopolitans, and often all four. In Britain, they included at the LSE Bronislaw Malinowski (a Pole), and alongside him Isaac Schapera (a South African Jew), and Raymond Firth (a New Zealander); at Cambridge, Meyer Fortes (another South African Jew); at SOAS, Christof von Fürer-Heimendorf (an Austrian), at Manchester, Max Gluckman (yet another South African Jew), Bill Epstein (an Irish Jew) and Clyde Mitchell (a South African); at LSE and at Durham Siegfried Nadel (an Austrian Catholic convert). In the USA – Franz Boaz (a German Jew) was founding father of American cultural and psychological anthropology, and he surrounded himself by first and second-generation German speakers – Kroeber (a non-Jew), Lowie, Sapir, Radin, and Bunzel, the only immigrant woman (all Jews). In France, Claude Levi-Strauss, like Emile Durkheim and Marcel Mauss, was a secular Jew. British anthropologists included at Oxford, E.E. Evans-Pritchard, who was Welsh, and Victor Turner at Manchester who was a Scottish Catholic convert. There were, of course, some English nationals among these early anthropologists: A.A. Radcliffe-Brown, Lucy Mair, Audrey Richards and Edmund Leach. Of these, several, like Radcliffe-Brown, spent many years living and teaching abroad – in Cape Town, Sydney, Chicago, Sao Paulo, and Rhodes University, as well as Oxford (Stocking 1995: 298–366; also 1984: 131–191).

But are anthropologists cosmopolitans? And is cosmopolitanism a quality of *individuals?* In its aesthetic connotation, the word cosmopolitan evokes a certain kind of familiar cultural image or person. A cosmopolitan is someone, the anthropologist Ulf Hannerz has argued, open to and knowledgeable about other cultures. 'Genuine' cosmopolitanism, he claims,

> is first of all an orientation, a willingness to engage with the Other. It entails an intellectual and aesthetic openness towards divergent cultural experiences, a search for contrasts rather than uniformity. To become acquainted with more cultures is to turn into an *aficionado*, to view them as artworks. At the same, however, cosmopolitanism can be a matter of competence, and competence of both a generalised and more specialised kind. There is an aspect of a state of readiness, a personal ability to make one's way into other cultures, through listening, looking, intuiting, reflecting. And there is a cultural

competence in the stricter sense of the term, a built-up skill in manoeuvring more or less expertly with a particular system of meanings.

In short, the cosmopolitan in Hannerz's definition is really an anthropologist! We might say that the anthropologist sees himself in the mirror of cosmopolitanism. But while this may be a fair depiction of anthropological fieldwork practices, does this really make anthropologists into cosmopolitans? Arguably not. Although they do, of course, familiarise themselves with another culture in all its intricacy, the disciplinary aim of many anthropologists is to remain a passive, invisible, fly-on-the-wall observer. Such anthropologists hope that their presence will be disattended to, and that it will not change the culture they study. Their cosmopolitan message is brought back to the metropolitan centre. It is there that anthropologists have forged a cosmopolitan language and discipline. And it is in the metropolis that anthropology has created a cosmopolitan discipline that has incurred postcolonial condemnation for its complicity with Western hegemony.[4] This critique raises the question of whether a cosmopolitan social science is possible at all. But before addressing this question, I want first to consider who the cosmopolitan is, not as an anthropologist or an idealistic sociologist or political scientist theorising on global citizenship and global justice, but as a familiar cultural figure, historically constituted in the popular imagination.

Elite Tastes and Cosmopolitan Worlds

Unlike the intrepid anthropological traveller or the world citizen, cosmopolitans are normally associated with cosmopolitan spaces, and with the creation of a transcendent culture beyond the local. Indeed, they are often accused of disdaining the local. Paris in the early twentieth century was a classic example of a cosmopolitan city. Here, at this historic moment, a pan-European *avant garde* movement in art and literature emerged out of the interaction of writers and artists coming from all over Europe and the United States: Joyce, Beckett, Hemingway, Fitzgerald, Picasso, Modigliani, Lipschitz, Chagall, Rivera, Brancusi. The 'art world' that emerged included creative artists and writers alongside an elite of consumers, publishers, gallery owners and agents on both sides of the Atlantic (indeed, art is essentially a collective endeavour, as Becker 1982 has argued). Local French culture was merely the backdrop to the creative interaction among members of this artistic elite. In 1919 Marcel Duchamp purchased for his American patron a vial of Parisian air. As Jones tells us, "the air of Paris was, for anyone interested in the arts, the most precious substance in the world. It was magical, and redemptive. Paris could make you a genius. It made Gertrude Stein a genius" (2004: 21).

Hence, another reason why anthropology may not be a truly cosmopolitan discipline relates to the fact that cosmopolitanism contains hidden assumptions about the *ranking* of cultures. A cosmopolitan is, historically, an elect member of his or her society, familiar with the languages and high cultural products of European and American literature, art and music, able to converse about world history, philosophy, classical music, ballet, theatre and human rights. Culturally, such a cosmopolitan is an aesthetic consumer, living an elegant lifestyle, a connoisseur of good wine, *haute cuisine* and *haute couture*; a fashionable person with immaculate table manners, a sophisticated conversationalist and *bon vivant*, *au fait* with the latest novels and world current affairs. In other words, the 'true' cosmopolitan – unlike many anthropologists – is a man or woman of the world, but of a very specific world – that of Western, and especially European, elites. He or she is usually also a collector of world art. Indeed, like Levi-Strauss in the passage below, she or he may also have great depth of knowledge about primitive and non-Western art and its incommensurable value.

In what amounts to a manifesto of aesthetic cosmopolitanism, Claude Lévi-Strauss, describes the New York he encountered when he arrived there as a refugee in 1941 – an 'agglomeration' of ethnic villages in which he and fellow French intellectuals Max Ernst, André Breton and Georges Duthuit wandered, as in Ali Baba's cave, inspecting 'exquisite masks from Teotihuacan and the magnificent wood carvings from the northwest Pacific coast... Mochica, Nazca and Chimu vases, gold encrusted jewellery boxes flogged by Russian émigrés, Oriental rugs, Utamaro prints, Peruvian antiques' (1985: 259–61). Later, after the war, he urged the French consulate in vain to acquire pre-Columbian gold jewellery and Indian art. These great valuables ended up in American museums.

Against this image of the aesthetic cosmopolitan may be pitched a more sociological definition of cosmopolitan spaces: they are trans-ethnic, collectively emergent 'worlds', shared discourses that transcend cultural boundaries and parochial lifestyles. According to this definition, a cosmopolitan is a person who actively belongs to, participates in and contributes to the creation of such trans-ethnic cultural and ideological worlds.

Apparent here is a tension between two dominant definitions of cosmopolitanism. At one pole are academic disciplines, political, moral and social philosophy, political theory and sociology of globalisation, which define cosmopolitanism in *normative* terms – as a transcendent worldview about the possibility of creating a global cosmopolitan society in the Kantian sense, a space of peace rather than war, of neighbourly relations, open borders and hospitality to strangers and sojourners; a vision of global justice within a federal 'league of nations' of democratic republics (Kant 1784/1970).[5] At the other pole are *cultural aesthetic* definitions by historians and literary or art critics who define cosmopolitanism as a space of cultural difference and toleration, multiple cultural competences and shared communication across cultures. Both strands in the cosmopolitan debate share cosmopolitan *conviction,* a Kantian faith in the necessity for open borders and the inalienable human right to move beyond one's own society. The question is: can anthropology bridge the chasm between these normative and cultural visions of cosmopolitanism? To begin with, both orientations share a stress on blurred boundaries, whether political, cultural or social, and on the transcendence of social and cultural differences *without their effacement.* Second, and this is a point less often explicitly highlighted, in both the primary stress is on *collective creativity:* rather than a quality of individuals, cosmopolitanism emerges as a joint, transcendent order, ethos and meta-culture, so that individual cosmopolitan actors, whether travellers or stay-at-homes, are the products of this collective ethos and meta-culture. This is not to deny individual consciousness or the capacity for introspection. Kant defined this ethos as a third sphere of cosmopolitan right, in between civil and international rights, applying to individuals and to states who as 'citizens of the earth' 'may be regarded as having the right to hospitality or temporary sojourn' (Kant 1784/1970: 98–9; see also Kleingeld and Brown 2002).

Anthropology and anthropologists forging a language and discourse of comparative world cultures may be said to have collectively created such a cosmopolitan space, ethos and meta-culture. Yet the comparative analysis of cultures in anthropological discourse, refined at the metropolitan centre, has led to an attack against anthropology, as though by objectifying the Other, the discipline is merely asserting – and indeed legitimising – the dominance of the West over the rest. In the postcolonial era, in response particularly to Said's orientalist critique, anthropology has been caught in a predicament that denies its cosmopolitan roots. It is a predicament that it shares with the new, normative cosmopolitans espousing global human rights, world citizenship and governance. They, too, have been accused of being the invisible hand of the new American expansionist imperialism, disguised in a human-rights, utopianist cosmopolitan language.[6]

The Crisis of Representation in Anthropology

Despite much evidence to the contrary, anthropology as a discipline has been subject to a major critique on methodological grounds. The crisis of representation in anthropology was inaugurated, perhaps, by Talal Asad (1973) and culminated in the work of the *Writing Culture* authors (Clifford and Marcus 1986, Marcus and Fischer 1986, Clifford 1988). What appeared to have been a somewhat utopian cosmopolitan project to reach out to a cultural and social Other and create a cross-cultural comparative discipline, was reconstructed in this critique as an act of hegemonic domination. Anthropology was accused of being the handmaiden of colonialism. There were three strands to this challenge to cosmopolitan anthropology.

First, it was argued that anthropologists did not study societies as they presently were, but attempted to reconstruct a lost pristine past. They engaged in 'salvage' anthropology, obsessed by the idea that cultures were disappearing forever and must be recorded before this happened, like species in nature. Cultures were thus defined as bounded and whole. Against this, the critics argued, cultures are changing and inventive, not fixed. But just as this criticism distorted Boas and his followers' understanding of culture, so too it also evaded the – political – question of whether the celebration of cultural inventiveness and hybridity was not merely a celebration of invading Western modernising forces that were indeed destroying the cultural autonomy and social self-sufficiency of vulnerable groups.

Second, the charge was that the impact of the colonial presence in the societies they studied was ignored and disguised by the anthropologists, especially those studying in Africa between the two world wars. So called 'colonial anthropology' constructed societies as pristine when in fact these societies were subject to colonial rule. This was certainly not universally true, as I show below, and the critics disattended to studies of towns and of the colonial encounter.

Finally, and perhaps most saliently, the critics questioned the right of anthropologists to study the Other from a dominant metropolitan position. The ethnographic authority of the cosmopolitan anthropologist was challenged and constructed as a form of domination. We see here the *politicising* of cosmopolitanism as a discourse and disciplinary approach. This politicising of cosmopolitan orientations in the academy is something that anthropology shares with Middle East studies, and with the new normative academic and transnational non-governmental cosmopolitan discourse of human rights, global justice and global governmentality, a predicament I return to below.

In addition to internal deconstructive critiques, postcolonial anthropology and the anthropology of the postcolony also had to contend with the emergence of a third world postcolonial literature and of postcolonial academic scholars. While the new literary works appeared to displace the anthropologist by invoking the images, ambience and experiences of postcolonial subjects, the new postcolonial scholars in the postcolonies (or in Western academia to which many of them migrated) often claimed a disciplinary monopoly over the study of their own societies, and rejected the intrusion and apparently objective claims of anthropologists from the ex-colonial metropolitan centre (see Kuper 1994). Kuper's rebuttal against this 'nativism' is to argue for a vision of social anthropology, not as a more, or less, adequate descriptive account of another 'culture', but as a collective, discursively forged, comparative intellectual project, much as I argued above.

But the argument for a cosmopolitan anthropology is surely much more fundamental. It relates to the Kantian invocation of the natural right of cosmopolitan hospitality. All men, Kant proposes, 'are entitled to present themselves in the society of others by right to communal possession of the earth's surface' (Kant

1784/1970: 106). By 'attempting' to enter into relations with 'native inhabitants', he argues, distant continents may enter into peaceful mutual relations that will bring us 'nearer and nearer' to a 'cosmopolitan constitution' (ibid.). Kant strongly condemns imperial conquest which he defines as quite different from peaceful temporary sojourning (ibid.: 106–7). Often considered a racist, in *Perpetual Peace* he argues that no 'society of men', which 'like a tree has its own roots', can be possessed by another, 'terminating' its 'moral personality' and making it into a 'commodity' (ibid.: 94). He indicts the 'appalling' 'oppression of natives' in the name of trade, so that 'America, the Negro countries, the Spice Islands, the Cape, etc.,' he says, 'were looked upon at the time of their discovery as ownerless territories; for the native inhabitants were counted as nothing' and subjected to a 'whole litany of evil' (106–7; see also Wood 1998: 62–3).

If we recognise the cosmopolitan right to hospitality as a conditional universal moral right this raises the serious question of who is the cosmopolitan – the anthropologist traveller sojourner or the peoples who historically have extended – and continue to extend – hospitality to her or him? Kant's moral sphere of cosmopolitan right includes both, in a dialogic move of mutual respect that enhances human interdependency across borders (Benhabib 2004: 37).

It is still quite rare to find anthropologists in developing countries studying beyond their own society. They prefer to study the internal Other, rather than seeking to study the Other beyond national boundaries. The latter *cosmopolitan* project remains a key feature of anthropology located at the metropolitan centre.[7]

Nevertheless, despite its limitations, the crisis of representation in anthropology had positive as well as negative consequences. On the negative side, the critique has induced an anthropological failure of nerve, as anthropologists have accepted the self-definition imposed upon them by postmodernist anthropologists and postcolonial critics, namely, that the study of the Other, being a form of domination, is no longer a legitimate pursuit. This led, at least for a while, to the de-cosmopolitanisation of anthropology as a discipline. Many anthropologists returned home, or turned to an historical documentation of the colonial encounter. They feared studying the ongoing traditions and customs of real people beyond the West.

On the positive side, the move has been towards a more dialogical anthropology, in which the process of fieldwork and the interactive dimensions of research have become a necessary feature of anthropological ethnographic writing. There is far greater consciousness that the texts anthropologists produce are non-realist in the sense of being selective and politically charged. The danger here is a move towards romantic navel gazing, but at its best dialogical anthropology extends the cosmopolitan vision of anthropology by incorporating the other and the self into a single universe of discourse, shared though not necessarily (as my own fieldwork highlights) always harmonious.

Nations, Closed Cultures or Social Fields?

Recent debates on cosmopolitanism in sociology and political science have confronted the need to revise basic assumptions, and in particular the unquestioned assumption that 'society' and the 'nation-state' coincide and are one and the same. Increasingly, sociologists are seeking to challenge this unwarranted conflation[8] (see Urry 1999). Unlike sociology, anthropology has never assumed such a straightforward coincidence between 'society' and the nation-state. Instead, anthropology's unit of analysis has been small-scale worlds located in social fields – ethnic groups, tribes, cultures, villages, cults – within, or cutting across, colonial and postcolonial states. The comparative task in anthropology was thus never defined by nations, as it may have been in sociology. This is evident in a famous passage on the 'Unit of Study' in which Radcliffe Brown argued that

> It is rarely that we find a community that is absolutely isolated, having no outside contact. At the present moment of history the network of social relations spreads over the whole world... This gives rise to the difficulty which I do not think that sociologists have really faced, the difficulty of defining what is meant by the term 'a society'. They do commonly talk of societies as if they were distinguishable, discrete entities as, for example, when we are told that a society is an organism. Is the British Empire a society or collection of societies? ... If we say that our subject is the study and comparison of human societies we ought to be able to say what are the unit entities with which we are concerned. If we take any convenient locality of a suitable size, we can study the structural system as it appears in and from a region, i.e. the network of relations connecting the inhabitants amongst themselves and with people of other regions. (1952 [1940]: 193)

In a sense, anthropology has moved in the opposite direction to sociology. An important advance in social anthropology has been the recognition that the study of part societies and cultures must take cognisance of the impact of colonial or postcolonial states and regimes on local, regional and transnational relations (see R. Werbner 1996). If sociology assumes implicitly an identification between culture, society and nation, anthropologists continue to study socially or culturally distinct part-societies, but as they relate to other such groups, and articulate with and across emergent postcolonial states. Hence, as Kwame Anthony Appiah points out (1998) in his seminal article, cosmopolitanism is equally an argument *within* postcolonial states on citizenship, equal dignity, cultural rights and the rule of law, as it about globalisation.

The problem of boundaries is critical here. How do anthropologists define cultural boundaries as against social boundaries, and in what sense are boundaries blurred, situationally highlighted, permeable or violently marked? The distinction Fredrik Barth draws between social boundaries and the 'cultural stuff' they may or may not enclose (1969: 15) is key to many anthropological studies. As Barth says, boundaries persist despite a flow of personnel across them (ibid.: 9), and so, too, cultural differences can persist despite interethnic contact and interdependency (ibid.: 10). Hence beyond the project of cross-cultural comparison, anthropology may claim to be a cosmopolitan discipline because its subject matter is not closed societies but interethnic interaction across permeable, blurred or situationally marked cultural and social boundaries.

Anthropology and the Study of Transethnic Cosmopolitan Spaces

If we accept the definition of cosmopolitan spaces as a transethnic, collectively emergent 'worlds', much flows from this regarding the contribution that anthropology can make towards a cosmopolitan social science. Most fundamentally, as I have argued elsewhere (P. Werbner 1999), anthropologists are particularly expert at depicting the demotic worlds of transethnic and transnational interaction and communication, a world populated by non-elite, working-class cosmopolitans. These migrants and transnationals meet on building sites and oil rigs in the Gulf, in mines and factories in Africa or India, in plantations in California or Fiji, to create new shared cultures, and even new creolised languages. They belong to global religious fraternities and to new diasporas proliferating throughout the world today. Diasporas are not, however, intrinsically cosmopolitan (P. Werbner 2000, 2002). Their members may be focused inwardly, on the national projects of their homelands, or join exclusive global religious movements. Nevertheless, many diasporans are open to the world. They often struggle for more inclusive forms of citizenship in their places of settlement, while diasporic artists and intellectuals create new, original cosmopolitan bridging-worlds of art, music and literature. In Kantian terms, settled diasporas afford havens of hospitality and safety for travellers and refugees.

Whereas Hannerz appears to endorse an elitist definition of the cosmopolitan subject,[9] Clifford (1992, 1998) has argued for a view of 'discrepant' cosmopolitan-isms, to include servants and migrants workers as well. Nevertheless, Clifford retains the stress on the individual traveller, rather than on the open, interethnic interaction across borders or the emergence of cosmopolitan spaces beyond the West. This is an interest anthropologists share with cultural historians and comparative sociologists. In a masterly account of cosmopolitanism, Sami Zubaida describes the cosmopolitan enclaves that emerged in Egyptian cities under colonial rule and in Istanbul, in which diplomats, missionaries, Christian minorities, traders, Muslim modernists, secular intellectuals (and, one might add, Greeks and Jews) exchanged ideas and intermingled (Zubaida 1999). Sheldon Pollock describes the cosmopolitan world of Sanskrit literature and poetry that from the fifth century BC onwards stretched from today's Afghanistan to Java, Sri Lanka and Nepal.

Paralleling this, he tells us, Latin was disseminated over an equally vast space, from Britannia in the West to Mesopotamia in the East (Pollock 2000, Pollock et al. 2000). The 'Sanskrit cosmopolis' was created, according to Pollock, 'by the circulation of traders, literati, religious professionals and freelance adventurers' (Pollock 2000: 603). So too, the love of Persian and later Urdu poetry and art stretched across a vast region during the reign of the Mughal empire and persisted during British colonial rule, and even after its demise. Ashis Nandy describes the cosmopolitanism of contemporary Cochin on the Malabar coast – 'the ultimate symbol of cultural diversity and religious and ethnic tolerance' (Nandy 2002: 158 *passim*).

Such emergent worlds are necessarily culturally hybrid, boundary crossing and often iconoclastic. On the surface, they do not appear to constitute the kind of cultures normally thought to be studied by anthropologists. But this would be to misread the history of the subject as practised in Britain, in the way that postmodernist and postcolonial critics seem almost deliberately to have done. Against such critics, the need is thus: first, to clarify what social anthropology is *not*. It is not, and never has been, the study of closed, immutable, bounded and homogeneous cultural communities.[10] This is one of the most pernicious and persistent rumours directed at the discipline. Social anthropology has been perennially concerned with how certain social boundaries, whether geographically, socially or culturally defined, were cut across by other forms of sociality.

This is evident in the classic study of Trobriand Islanders by Bronislaw Malinowski, commonly regarded as the founder of modern social anthropology. As Marcel Mauss recognised so brilliantly (Mauss 1966: 19–20, 79–81), this was not, as might be assumed, an ethnography of a single island. It was the study of international commerce between islands, a cultural institution known as Kula (Malinowski 1922). So, too, Evans-Pritchard's study of the Nuer (1940, 1951), although apparently focused on a discrete ethnic group, in reality was a study of situationally shifting boundaries and nesting identities. It recognised the predatory movement of the Nuer in the Sudan, who incorporated neighbouring Dinka into their society through raiding and intermarriage, a process EP theorised as 'the python-like assimilation by the Nuer of vast numbers of Dinka' through the genealogical grafting of women on to dominant lineages (Evans-Pritchard 1951: 23; see also 1940: 227). A salient argument EP makes is that 'The limits of the tribe are therefore not the limits of social intercourse' (Evans-Pritchard 1940: 124). As a study of the dynamics of segmentary opposition and multiple shifting identities, *The Nuer* laid the grounds for later research on urban ethnicity (or tribalism as it was then called), among labour migrants on the Zambian Copperbelt by Clyde Mitchell (1956), Bill Epstein (1958), and others. They showed that ethnic identities and alliances were formed oppositionally, through fission and fusion, in the urban context, anticipating later discussions of identity.

There were other early examples of the concern for cosmopolitan spaces and blurred boundaries. Nadel studied a multi-ethnic state (1942), Fortes the blurring of boundaries of the Tallensi generated by their ritual shrines, which extended beyond any clear definition of tribe (1954, 1949; see also R. Werbner 2004: 136). From Schapera's study of the civic incorporation of strangers among Tswana (1938: 118–124), to Leach's analysis of the alternating cultural-cum-political model of Highland Burma (Leach 1954), the founding generation of British social anthropology studied cross-ethnic engagements. Although Mary Douglas, a Catholic, is famous for her analysis of the symbolic or ritual construction of boundaries, in reality she too stressed the way that boundaries were transgressed, and the peculiar qualities of symbolic figures of boundary transgression – wives, witches or Pangolins (Douglas 1966, 1970). This points to the fact that many of the arguments in anthropology were disagreements over the permeability of boundaries or the kind of conceptual frameworks needed to study multi-ethnic empires or pilgrimage flows and central places.

Some social anthropologists recognised early on the need to locate cultures within nation-states. Radcliffe-Brown, for example, and following him Gluckman, Schapera and Fortes, argued for a vision of a racially divided South Africa as a single society. The anthropologist, Gluckman argued, 'must work with communities rather than customs ... [with] a unit of life ... of common participation in the everyday political, economic and social life' (1958: 51). Such multi-ethnic, conflictual communities form a single, organised society, he proposed, rather than a social aggregation of heterogeneous cultural groups, as Malinowski would have it. Importantly, then, for Gluckman – as indeed for Fortes and Schapera – social relations, even those marked by difference, hierarchy and domination, nevertheless are constitutive of a shared 'social system': not as unified by a homogeneous set of beliefs, but as a fragmentary, contradictory and conflict-ridden social formation.

Analysing the opening of a new bridge in 1938 in modern Zululand, a harmonious event welcomed by blacks and whites alike, Gluckman highlights the *naturalness* of the ceremony for participants. The whites took it for granted that they should be drinking tea on the banks of the Black Umfolosi River just as the blacks took for granted the ceremonial cutting of a tape across the bridge, and the sacrificial beast offered them by the native commissioner. This naturalness of what Hobsbawm and Ranger have aptly called an invented tradition (1963), referred to by Bakhtin as *organic hybridity* (1981: 358), is something which anthropologists increasingly began to study in the new postcolonies.

In his analysis, Gluckman recognises that as conflicts between black and white sharpened, new configurations of existing cultures tended to surface as means of social and political mobilisation which stressed cultural difference (1958: 61), an argument that later came to be known through the work of Abner Cohen as 'political ethnicity' (Cohen 1969). Yet such social movements, like radical Islam today, even when they announce their cultural purity and sharp distinction, are necessarily hybrid culturally, since they arise from within the new social and cultural configurations of the historically transformed, organically hybridised community.

The harmony of the ceremony at the bridge was necessarily an ambivalent one, given the pervasive inequalities and separations between white and black in modern South Africa. As Homi K. Bhabha recognises, hybridity may be produced by a 'doubling up of the sign', a 'splitting' which is 'less than one and double' (Bhabha 1994: 119).[11] The same object or custom placed in a different context acquires quite new meanings while echoing old ones. Hence new cosmopolitan worlds studied by anthropologists are ones in which customs and objects displaced and de- or re-contextualised, are endowed with new meanings. British social anthropology, and particularly the Manchester School as it came to be known, has recognised this process of cultural change, movement and cosmopolitanisation.

Naive Holism and the Study of Pilgrimage and Regional Cults

The argument against anthropology as the study of closed, bounded cultural groups is one pursued by anthropologists of religion, denying the validity of certain 'closed' structural functional models. In South Asia the study of religious communalism and nationalism, of zones of interaction between different castes and religious or ethnic communities, is paralleled by studies elsewhere of regional cults and pilgrimage centres that often draw their followers from a vast region, across different ethnic communities. Such studies go against assumptions in anthropology of 'naive holism', according to which 'essential relations with a wider context get stripped away when a small group, little community or tribe is studied as an isolated whole' (R. Werbner 1977: IX; R. Werbner 1989). In my recent study of Sufi mystical Islam (P. Werbner 2003) I show that Sufi lodges and shrine complexes cannot be studied in isolation from the wider regional and transnational cult generated around the cult sacred centre, or the migratory and political contexts in which the cult operates. The further point implied by regional cult networks, crucial to cosmopolitan theory, is that the many diverse ethnic, caste or national groups converging on the sacred centre are held together by an ideology of peace and toleration.

When do culture and society coincide? 'Correspondence' theory, according to which different domains (ritual, political, economic) underwrite each other, so that ritual and belief become mere representations of political divisions or economic interests, increasingly came to be regarded with suspicion by anthropologists of religion in the 1970s (R.Werbner 1977: XVIII). Such theories draw, Werbner argued, on simplistic readings of Durkheimian or Marxist texts. In the Sufi transnational cult I studied, the symbolic order cut across political divisions and remained in tension with the postcolonial and capitalist economies of modern-day Pakistan, and even more so in post-imperial Britain. The relationship between the political centre and the sacred centre is a changing, historically contingent one, and in this sense, as in others, pilgrimage centres and regional cults are historically evolving social formations, as Victor Turner recognised (1974). They enable the movement of strangers across territorial boundaries, often over vast distances. Pilgrimage cult centres and Sufi order lodges create havens of hospitality and, as Evans-Pritchard records for Sanusi (Evans-Pritchard 1949), places of peaceful mediation between feuding groups.

The Limits of Cosmopolitanism: Migrants, Urbanites and Other Strangers

In an age of globalisation, international migration has generated the movement of people across national boundaries and with it the emergence of many new religious diasporas. As in the past, boundary-crossing Sufi orders with their traditions of hospitality, nurturing and shelter (P. Werbner 2003) continue to foster an ethos of inclusiveness and afford moral spaces for transients, such as South Asian migrants working on building sites in the Gulf or in British factories. In these contexts a wider cosmopolitan subjectivity may evolve among fellow co-workers (P. Werbner 1999).

Contemporary research on international migration has parallels with earlier studies of circulatory labour migration in Africa: in South-Central Africa, for example, African migrant workers moved to multi-ethnic colonial cities from diverse ethnic hinterlands, crossing the radical disjuncture between cultural worlds. In the Kalela dance performed on the Copperbelt, barbed, vulgar insults and ironic commentaries on tribal differences were associated with the custom of providing ritual and practical burial assistance between joking partners who died away from home (Mitchell 1956; see also Boswell 1969). Joking thus both marked and transcended tribal divisions in town, creating the grounds, perhaps, for a new cosmopolitan milieu. In East London, dominated by Xhosa and close to their tribal hinterland, divisions in the countryside were mirrored in town. Theorising networks spanning town and country, Philip Mayer (1961) distinguished between 'Red' and 'School' Xhosa-speaking labour migrants in East London, whose life-styles represented two radically opposed orientations towards urban living: open and closed, loose-knit versus encapsulated in homeboy networks, 'Christianised' versus 'traditionalist-tribal', 'progressive' versus 'conservative' (1962: 586). The division paralleled that of Xhosa in the tribal areas. The question Mayer posed was how far the 'pull of the hinterland' prevailed for Red and School in town (ibid: 580–1).

By disregarding the politics of race, one might be tempted to label School Xhosa, whether resident in town or the rural hinterland, 'cosmopolitan' – certainly by comparison to Red Xhosa, who were hostile to all things white – but this would be to simplify the cosmopolitics of apartheid South Africa which led to the Red resistance to hegemonic 'white' civilisation.

These early studies may be set against a recent Africanist anthropological tendency to define any kind of opposition to the local ('home', the 'village') as 'cosmopolitan': Zambian 'School' urbanites rejecting the countryside or frequenting multi-ethnic bars (Ferguson 1999); displaced, Malawian Pentecostals who – although continuing to value rural ties and ancestral authority – seek other worldly redemption against the all-pervasive, mundane rule of the devil, exclusively within a deterritorialised church (Englund 2004). Appiah (2006) labels such ethical yet highly exclusive global religious movements 'counter-cosmopolitan'. Invocations of cosmopolitanism as lifestyle, in one case, or as being locked in battle with a diabolised world, in the other, deflect from a more serious engagement with the new cosmopolitanism, seen as an ethical impulse conjoining particular *and* universal commitments – an active toleration for religious, cultural or ethnic diversity. At the present cosmopolitan moment in anthropology, the need is, it seems to me, to guard against an over-promiscuous tendency to label cosmopolitan anyone or anything that is no longer purely local or parochial. When it comes to urban milieus of multi-ethnic cosmopolitan *practice*, however, of living together in amity – even *without* conscious cosmopolitan conviction – the lines between cosmopolitans and locals cannot be drawn too sharply. Pentecostals in Malawi do foster widely ramifying interethnic networks in their everyday lives.

Charles Piot (1999) typifies as 'cosmopolitan' cultural exchanges between centre and periphery in Togo, among the Kabre, that highlight the fluid, highly receptive cultural lives of modern Africans, in order to rebuff a 'neo-evolutionary master narrative' (ibid.: 23) perpetuated by theorists of globalisation, including anthropologists. He thus rejects the contrast drawn by Appadurai, for example, between the fluidity of the contemporary transnational world and the supposedly 'tightly territorialized, spatially bounded, historically unselfconscious, and cult-urally homogeneous' societies anthropologists study (1999: 22, citing Appadurai 1991: 191). Rather than a scholarly departure from the past, Piot locates his study in a long tradition of anthropological engagements with African relations 'in flux' within the wider social field. Among Kabre, 'spirit trees' in the ancestral north – originating from beyond the community and demanding periodic animal sacrifices bartered with external 'bush people' – constitute fixed anchorage points in an annual cycle of ritual performances for a widely dispersed 'cosmopolitan' diaspora within Togo and beyond, whose members also bury their dead in ancestral lands.

One thing is evident: not only are anthropologists strangers in the societies they study; many anthropologists have historically had an enduring interest in strangerhood, ethnicity and boundary crossing. This is, of course, true of more recent historical anthropological studies of early cultural encounters with missionaries, colonial officials, Captain Cook or the postcolonial state, or of studies of ethnogenesis, ethnic violence and state terror.

Sufi orders, we saw, highlight the fact that in a cosmopolitanising world of increased mobility, cosmopolitanism is no longer class specific. Just as the anthropologist sojourner is frequently the recipient of open hospitality from strangers, so too working-class cosmopolitans throughout the developing world travel across continents and experience hospitality from strangers. They learn to share cosmopolitan convictions as they reach out beyond their local milieu.

Workers in developing countries also develop a cosmopolitan consciousness. In Botswana, for example, the Manual Workers Union of Botswana, the subject of my recent study, has fought fiercely for their right to a minimum working wage through strike action, nationwide protests and appeals to the High Court. These workers share a cosmopolitan sensibility, conviction and consciousness of workers' struggles elsewhere, expressed in union songs which speak of worker oppression, unity and solidarity.

Trade unions in Africa were historically extremely important civil society organisations in the colonial era, mobilising different ethnic and even national groups in demand of basic rights, in unitary opposition to colonial regimes. This was made evident in early anthropological studies of miners on the Zambian Copperbelt (Epstein 1958), and on the railways in East Africa (Grillo 1973, Parkin 1969). African nationalism arose on the back of such alliances, only to be subsumed and suppressed by newly independent African states after independence. In Botswana in the early years after independence, unions, never strong, were actively discouraged and the demand for workers' rights construed as unpatriotic, as striking at the country's development effort (Selolwane 2000: 89; see also Molokomme 1989). It thus took an act of moral courage to challenge the status quo from the lowly position of a manual unskilled worker. Union workers may be uneducated but they are rights experts and this has made them unflinching, tenacious negotiators who have gained the respect of university-educated top Batswana civil servants.

Conclusion: The New Anthropological Cosmopolitanism

In the academy today the new cosmopolitan discourse of human rights and world citizenship is said to be remote from the concerns of local citizens. Its utopian ideals are not anchored in the real politics of any country, it is claimed, or even in the bureaucratic structures of the United Nations. At its best it is merely a vision of hope.[12] At its worst, human rights discourse is seen as a legitimising discourse for imperialist invasion of other countries – Kosovo, Afghanistan, Iraq (Beck 2006).

Given the radical changes that have occurred in the developing world, and in the face of transnational migrations and so-called Islamic extremism and global terror, the present chapter has argued for the need to build upon earlier anthropological studies of the social field, and of expansive, transethnic relations within it, in order to explore vernacular and demotic as well as elite forms of cosmopolitanism arising from the contemporary engagement of the local with the global. Cosmopolitans – in trade unions, factories, building sites, mines and oil rigs, among artists, intellectuals, diasporans, Filipina international carers, labour unions or foreign correspondents – all in one way or other aspire to resolve the conjunctural dialectics of a universal ethos and particular commitments. The comparative project in anthropology, as Kuper has argued, remains 'to confront the models current in the social sciences with the experiences and models of our subjects, while insisting that this should be a two-way process (1994: 551).

It is evident that both cosmopolitanism and anthropology have become highly politicised terms, ever beleaguered by sceptics who doubt their utopian mission (see Archibugi 1998; Smith and Fine 2004). No longer able to achieve that naive cosmopolitan exhilaration of the early generation of anthropologists, the question of what a cosmopolitan anthropology might look like is not one easily answered. The magic of exotic anthropology, the experienced desire of the cosmopolitan anthropologist to study the Other as other and as self, to submerge oneself in another culture and understand it from within, is difficult to explain (given the frequent boredom and often inconvenient living conditions) and even more difficult to abandon in the face of theoretical or political critiques. I do not think that the call for 'multi-sited' anthropology, or an anthropology of the media or Internet, is the most useful way out of this impasse. Anthropology's methodological strength lies in studying 'community' and other forms of 'thick' solidarity in all their complexity. This takes time and patience; it requires intimate knowledge, trust and long-term involvement.

The new 'situated', 'rooted' cosmopolitanism recognises the strength and viability of multiple solidarities and commitments in the public sphere (Calhoun 2002; Appiah 1998). If we accept the Kantian notion of cosmopolitan right as the right to hospitality leading to greater interdependency and communication across boundaries, it becomes possible to argue that such a vision opens up scope for a cosmopolitan anthropology which builds on anthropological strengths of fieldwork in particular locales. It is obvious, however, that in studying the local today, anthropologists must take cognisance of the global, of the media, the Internet, the press, international mobility, the postcolonial state and human rights, since this is the cultural and political environment in which the subjects of anthropology live their daily lives in the twenty-first century. It is equally evident that our research depends, as ever, on the kindness and hospitality of strangers.

Notes

1. This paper was first presented to the Workshop on 'Cosmopolitan Realism: towards a cosmopolitan social science', London School of Economics, 19–20 February 2004, convened by Ulrich Beck, and later as a public lecture at the Australian National University, and at a workshop at the National University of Singapore's Asian Research Institute. It benefited greatly from comments by Joel Kahn, Roy Dilley and discussions with my husband, Dick Werbner, on the history and mission of anthropology.
2. See David Mills (2003) and Stocking (1995: 427–41) on the history of the ASA and its debates regarding the cooperation with, and the inclusion or exclusion of, American anthropologists.
3. This may well still be the most salient theoretical rebuff to the 'nativist' argument that only natives can understand and study other natives (Kuper 1994: 546–7)
4. On this issue and consequent obstacles to fieldwork or dialogue with postcolonial bureaucrats and intellectuals that anthropologists encounter in postcolonial Malaysia, see Joel Khan (2003 and 2005).
5. It needs to be stressed, perhaps, against a common misrepresentation, that Kant did not advocate a 'world government' which he thought would be despotic, but a voluntary federation of like-minded 'republics' practising human rights and democracy. For a superb discussion of Kant's argument in *Perpetual Peace* see Benhabib (2004), especially Chapter 1 (pp. 25–48).
6. See, for example, in relation to Kosovo, Beck (2002: 37) and Habermas's critique of the work of Carl Schmitt, which adopts this line (Habermas 1998: 193–201).
7. Arguably, as Britain's role in the world has diminished, the tendency has been to marginalise and shut down anthropology departments in provincial universities (Liverpool, Hull, Keele) beyond the core elite institutions. Many established red brick and new universities with large social science faculties (Leeds, Sheffield, Warwick, Leicester, Lancaster, York, Essex, Exeter) never attempted to set up anthropology departments, although most foster 'development' or 'postcolonial' studies.

8. Ulrich Beck (2006) critiques this so-called 'methodological nationalism'.
9. But see his revision of this earlier view where he talks of 'cosmopolitanism from below (Hannerz 2004).
10. For a trenchant critique see Sahlins (1999). American cultural anthropologists, in particular Kroeber and Leslie White, did however see culture as a superorganic determinant of individual behaviour but others denied such cultural closure (ibid.: 409–10).
11. On the limits and politics of cultural hybridity, see Werbner and Modood (1997).
12. Habermas disagrees with this view, arguing more optimistically that 'The contemporary world situation can be understood at best as a transitional stage between international and cosmopolitan law', but that the world has gone a long way towards instituting legal mechanisms and conventions for a world polity (1998: 183). See also Nussbaum (1994).

References

Appadurai, Arjun (1991), 'Global Ethnoscapes', in Richard Fox (ed.), *Recapturing Anthropology*, Santa Fe NM: SAR.

Appiah, Kwame Anthony (1998), 'Cosmopolitan Patriots', in P. Cheah and B. Robbins (eds), *Cosmopolitics: Feeling and Thinking beyond the Nation*, Mineapolis: University of Minnesota Press, pp. 94–114.

—— (2006), *Cosmopolitanism: Ethics in a World of Strangers*, London: Allen Lane.

Archibugi, Daniele (1998), 'Principles of Cosmopolitan Democracy', in Daniel Archibugi, David Held and Martin Köhler (eds), *Re-Imagining Political Community: Studies in Cosmopolitan Democracy*, Cambridge: Polity Press, pp. 198–220.

Asad, Talal (ed.) (1973), *Anthropology and the Colonial Encounter*, London: Ithaca Press.

Barth, Fredrik (1969), 'Introduction', in Fredrik Barth (ed.), *Ethnic Groups and Boundaries*, London: Allen and Unwin, pp. 9–38.

Bakhtin, Mikhail (1981), *The Dialogic Imagination*, trans. Caryl Emerson and Micael Holquist, Austin: University of Texas Press.

Beck, Ulrich (2006) [2004], *The Cosmopolitan Vision*, trans. Ciaran Cronin, Cambridge: Polity Press.

Becker, Howard S. (1982), *Artworlds*, Berkeley: University of California Press.

Benhabib, Seyla (2004), *The Rights of Others: Aliens, Residents and Citizens*, Cambridge: Cambridge University Press.

Bhabha, Homi K. (1994), *The Location of Culture*, London: Routledge.

Boswell, David (1969), 'Personal Crises and the Mobilisation of the Social Network', in J. Clyde Mitchell (ed.) *Social Networks in Urban Situations: Analyses of Personal Relationships in Central African Towns*, Manchester: Manchester University Press for the Institute of Social Research, Zambia, pp. 245–96.

Calhoun, Craig (2002), 'Imagining Solidarity: Cosmopolitanism, Constitutional Patriotism and the Public Sphere', *Public Culture* 14 (1): 147–71.

Clifford, James (1988), *The Predicament of Culture*, Cambridge, MASS: Harvard University Press.

—— (1992), 'Travelling Cultures', in Lawrence Grossberg, Cary Nelson and Paul A. Treichler (eds), *Cultural Studies*, London: Routledge, pp. 96–116.

—— (1998), 'Mixed Feelings', in Pheng Cheah and Bruce Robbins (eds), *Cosmopolitics: Thinking and Feeling Beyond the Nation*, Mineapolis: University of Minnesota Press, pp. 362–70.

Clifford, James and George Marcus (eds) (1986), *Writing Culture*, Berkeley: University of California Press.

Cohen, Abner (1969), *Custom and Politics in Urban Africa*, London: Routledge & Kegan Paul.

Douglas, Mary (1966), *Purity and Danger*, London: Routledge and Kegan Paul.

—— (1970), *Natural Symbols*, London: Barrie & Rockliff, Crescent Press.

Englund, Harri (2004), 'Cosmopolitanism and the Devil in Malawi', *Ethnos* 69 (3): 293–316)

Epstein, A.L. (1958), *Politics in an Urban African Community*, Manchester: Manchester University Press.

Evans-Pritchard, E.E. (1937), *Witchcraft, Oracles and Magic among the Azande*, Oxford: Clarendon.

—— (1940), *The Nuer*, Oxford: Clarendon Press.

—— (1949), *The Sanusi of Cyrennaica*, Oxford: Clarendon Press.

—— (1951), *Kinship and Marriage among the Nuer*, Oxford: Oxford University Press.

Ferguson, James (1999), *Expectations of Modernity: Myths and Meanings of Urban Life on the Zambian Copperbelt*, Berkeley: University of California Press.

Fortes, Meyer (1945), *The Dynamics of Clanship among the Tallensi*, Oxford: Oxford University Press for the International African Institute.

—— (1949), *The Web of Kinship among the Tallensi*, Oxford: Oxford University Press for the International African Institute.

Gluckman, Max (1958), (first published 1940), *Analysis of a Social Situation in Modern Zululand*, Rhodes-Livingstone Papers No. 28, Manchester: Manchester University Press for the Rhodes-Livingstone Institute.

Grillo, Ralph (1973), *African Railwaymen: Solidarity and Opposition in an East African Labour Force*, Cambridge: Cambridge University Press.

Habermas, Jürgen (1998), 'Kant's Idea of Perpetual Peace: At Two Hundred Years' Historical Remove', in Ciaran Cronin and Pablo de Greiff (eds), *The Inclusion of the Other*, Cambridge MA: MIT Press, Chapter 7.

Hannerz, Ulf (1996), *Transnational Connections*, London: Routledge.

—— (2004), 'Cosmopolitanism', in David Nugent and Joan Vincent (eds), *A Companion to the Anthropology of Politics*, Oxford: Blackwell, pp. 69–85.

Hobsbawm, Eric and Terence Ranger (eds) (1963), *The Invention of Tradition*, Cambridge: Cambridge University Press.

Jones, Jonathan (2004), 'Carving a Way to Heaven', *Guardian Weekend*, 3 January 2004, pp. 21–4.

Kant, Immanuel (1784/1970), 'Perpetual Peace: a Philosophical Sketch', in Hans Reiss (ed.), *Kant's Political Writings*, Cambridge: Cambridge University Press, pp. 93–130.

Kleingeld, Pauline and Eric Brown (2002), 'Cosmopolitanism', *Stanford Encyclopedia of Philosophy*, (website http://plato.stanford.edu/).

Kuper, Adam (1994), 'Culture, Identity and the Project of a Cosmopolitan Anthropology', *Man* (NS), 29 (3): 537–54.

Leach, Edmund (1954), *Political Systems of Highland Burma*, London: G. Bell for the LSE.

Lévi-Strauss, Claude (1985), *The View from Afar*, London: Peregrine.

Malinowski, Bronislaw (1922), *Argonauts of the Western Pacific*, London: Routledge.

Marcus, George and Michael Fischer (1986), *Anthropology as Cultural Critique*, Chicago: University of Chicago Press.

Mauss, Marcel (1966), *The Gift*, London: Cohen & West.

Mayer, Philip (1961), *Townsmen and Tribesmen*, Cape Town: Oxford University Press.

—— (1962), 'Migrancy and the Study of Africans in Town', *American Anthropologist* 64 (3): 576–92.

Mills, D. (2003), 'Professionalising or Popularising Anthropology? A Brief History of Anthropology's Scholarly Associations in the UK', *Anthropology Today* 19(5): 8–13.

Mitchell, J. Clyde (1956), *The Kalela Dance: Aspects of Social Relationships among Urban Africans in Northern Rhodesia*, Rhodes-Livingstone Papers No. 27, Manchester: Manchester University Press for the Rhodes-Livingstone Institute.

Molokomme, Athaliah (1989), 'Political rights in Botswana: Regression or Development?', in John Holm and Patrick Molutsi (eds), *Democracy in Botswana*, Athens: Ohio University Press, pp. 163–73.

Nadel, S.F. (1942), *A Black Byzantium*, Oxford: Oxford University Press for the International African Institute.

Nandy, Ashis (2002), *Time Warps*, London: Hurst.

Nussbaum, Martha (1994), 'Patriotism and Cosmopolitanism', *The Boston Review* XIX, 5 (Oct/Nov) (Internet source: www.soci.niu.edu/~phildept/kapitan/nusbaum1.html).

Parkin, David (1969), *Neighbours and Nationals in an African City Ward*, London: Routledge & Kegan Paul.

Piot, Charles (1999), *Remotely Global: Village Modernity in West Africa*, Chicago IL: University of Chicago Press.

Pollock, Sheldon (2000), 'Cosmopolitan and Vernacular History', *Public Culture* 12 (3): 591–625.

Pollock, Sheldon, Homi K. Bhabha, Carol A. Breckenridge and Dipesh Chakrabarty (2000), 'Cosmopolitanisms', *Public Culture* 12 (3): 577–89.

Radcliffe-Brown, A.R. (1940), 'On Social Structure', *Journal of the Royal Anthropological Institute* 70: 1–12.; reprinted in (1952), *Structure and Function in Primitive Society*, London: Cohen & West.

Sahlins, Marshall (1999), 'Two or Three Things that I Know about Culture', Huxley Memorial Lecture, 1998, *Journal of the Royal Anthropological Institute* (NS) 5 (3): 399–422.

Schapera, Isaac (1938), *A Handbook of Tswana Law and Custom*, London: Frank Cass.

Selolwane, Onalena D. (2000), 'Civil Society, Citizenship and Civil Rights in Botswana', in Shirin M. Rai (ed.), *International Perspectives on Gender and Democratisation*, London: Macmillan, pp. 89–99.

Smith, William and Robert Fine (2004), 'Kantian Cosmopolitanism Today: John Rawls and Jurgern Habermas on Immanuel Kant's *Foedus Pacificum*', *Kings College Law Journal* 15 (1): 5–22.

Stocking, George W. Jr. (1984), 'Radcliffe-Brown and British Social Anthropology', in George W. Stocking (ed.), *Functionalism Historicised: Essays on British Social Anthropology*, Madison: University of Wisconsin Press, pp. 131–91.

—— (1995), *After Tylor: British Social Anthropology 1888–1951*, Madison: University of Wisconsin Press.

Turner, Victor (1974), *Dramas, Fields and Metaphors*, Ithaca: Cornell University Press.

Urry, John (1999), *Sociology Beyond Societies: Mobilities for the Twenty-First Century*, London: Routledge.

Werbner, Pnina (1999), 'Global Pathways: Working-Class Cosmopolitans and the Creation of Transnational Ethnic Worlds', *Social Anthropology* 7 (1): 17–35.

—— (2000), 'Introduction: The Materiality of Diasporas – Between Aesthetic and "Real" Politics', *Diaspora* 9 (1): 5–20.

—— (2002), *Imagined Diasporas among Manchester Muslims*, Oxford: James Currey, and Santa Fe: School of American Research.

—— (2003), *Pilgrims of Love: the Anthropology of a Global Sufi Cult*, London: Hurst Publishers, and Bloomington: Indiana University Press.

Werbner, Pnina and Tariq Modood (eds) (1997), *Debating Cultural Hybridity: Multi-cultural Identities and the Politics of Anti-Racism*, London: Zed Books.

Werbner, Richard (1977), 'Introduction', in Richard Werbner (ed.), *Regional Cults*, London and New York: Academic Press.

—— (1989), *Ritual Passage, Sacred Journey: The Process and Organization of Religious Movement*, Washington DC: Smithsonian Institution Press.

—— (1996), 'Introduction: Multiple Identities, Plural Arenas', in Richard Werbner and Terence Ranger (eds), *Postcolonial Identities in Africa*, London: Zed Books, pp. 1–26.

—— (2002), 'Cosmopolitan Ethnicity, Entrepreneurship and the Nation: Minority Elites in Botswana', *Journal of Southern African Studies*, 28 (4): 731–53.

—— (2004), *Reasonable Radicals and Citizenship in Botswana*, Bloomington: Indiana University Press.

Wood, Allen W. (1998), 'Kant's Project for Perpetual Peace', in Pheng Cheah and Bruce Robbins (eds), *Cosmopolitics: Thinking and Feeling Beyond the Nation*, Mineapolis: University of Minnesota Press, pp. 59–76.

Zubaida, Sami (1999), 'Cosmopolitanism and the Middle East', in Roel Meijer (ed.), *Cosmopolitanism, Identity and Authenticity in the Middle East*, London: Curzon, pp. 15–34.

–4–

Towards a Rooted Anthropology: Malinowski, Gellner and Herderian Cosmopolitanism
Chris Hann

Introduction

Many anthropologists think of their discipline as inherently more cosmopolitan than others. After all, unlike our colleagues in departments of history or sociology, we claim to deal systematically with the full range of human societies. We also tend to take it for granted that, in the globalised world of the twenty-first century, we are more cosmopolitan than our anthropological predecessors. Our distant ancestors were infected by the prejudices of imperialism; more recently the barriers of the Cold War imposed other kinds of blinkers and restricted mobility and communication between scholars. But does the lifting of most political barriers and the digital communications revolution warrant complacent assumptions? Of course everything hinges on one's definition of cosmopolitanism. The anthropologists of Victorian Britain and Wilhelmine Germany read each other's works more assiduously than is the case today, when German scholars must publish in English to stand a chance of being read outside the German-speaking countries. At the same time the persisting vigour of national scholarly associations and journals suggests that the dominance of the English language has by no means eliminated the significance of national traditions in our discipline (see Barth et al. 2005).

Before we set about analysing the cosmopolitanism of other people in other places, it may be instructive to ask some of the same questions of our own discipline. A comprehensive answer would require a careful examination of the intertwining of intellectual and social history, and that cannot be attempted here. This paper considers the impact of two scholars from Central Europe on social anthropology in Britain and proceeds to draw out more general themes concerning the possibilities for a rooted cosmopolitanism in our discipline. Bronislaw Malinowski liked to present his functionalist theory as a modern science. Those who signed up to this paradigm could largely dispense with the intellectual history of their discipline, just as they could dispense with historical speculation about the peoples they studied, all sacrificed in favour of ethnographic excellence through fieldwork. By contrast, Ernest Gellner was always eager to pursue intellectual genealogies, and he became especially interested in the unacknowledged roots of Malinowski's functionalism. In a similar exercise of reinterpretation I shall argue that, while Gellner's central insights concerning Malinowski are convincing, his own basic categories betray a common Central European legacy. Behind their modernist universalism both Malinowski's romantic notion of culture and Gellner's radical 'modernist' exposition of the construction of nations are soaked in another variant of cosmopolitanism, which I shall term the Herderian current.

The work of Johann Gottfried Herder is nowadays little known in the English-speaking world, at any rate within anthropology. Elsewhere – in Germany, for example – he is widely regarded as a founding father, as the pioneer of cultural relativism (Streck 1997: 27). Herder's influence extended well outside the academy. His ideas had an impact on many nationalist movements in the nineteenth century, especially in Eastern and Central Europe. In the process they helped to mould national traditions of anthropology (often termed ethnology or 'national ethnography' – see Hofer 2005) that have persisted into the postsocialist present. At first glance Herderian nation-centred ethnology is the antithesis of the comparative, generalising discipline that emerged above all in countries endowed with colonial empires (see Stocking 1982). Yet in some ways Herder was every bit as much a cosmopolitan as his teacher Immanuel Kant. The Herderian current is one that we can recognise as 'rooted'. Kant's universal individual subject has an elective affinity to the discipline whose name means literally 'the study of man'. But, irrespective of the changing labels, our intellectual enterprise has always involved a tension between this universalism and the current that emphasises groupness, 'ethnology' as the study of peoples, differentiated from each other in terms of their 'cultures'. I shall argue that, certain appearances to the contrary notwithstanding, both Malinowski and Gellner were profoundly influenced by the Herderian current. Their views on cultures and nations reflect the Central European milieux in which they grew up. I have reservations concerning this brand of cosmopolitanism and draw attention briefly in the conclusion to an alternative current, one that is morally and intellectually more attractive, though it has been epistemologically unfashionable in recent decades. The main conclusion is that the challenge to establish a genuinely rooted cosmopolitan anthropology has not yet been met, either in British social anthropology or in the national ethnographies of Central and Eastern Europe.

Bronislaw Malinowski (1884–1942)

Malinowski's high standing in the history of anthropology is of course based primarily on his fieldwork in the Trobriand Islands during World War I. The quality of this ethnography has enabled its author's reputation to withstand countless attacks (e.g. Geertz 1988), not to mention the furore caused by the publication of his fieldwork diary (Malinowski 1967) and the detailed revelations of Michael Young's definitive biography (Young 2004). Malinowski is widely perceived to be not merely the founder of the modern British School (Kuper 1983) but also a giant on the international stage. Yet his intellectual background was for a long time hardly understood at all. Textbooks commonly quoted Malinowski's own recollection that he discovered anthropology in a moment of revelation in his native Cracow, where he had studied physics. In fact his dissertation at the Jagiellonian University in 1908 was a study in philosophy. The significance of Ernst Mach's positivism and of the other influences imbibed by the young Malinowski in what was then the Habsburg province of Galicia only became clear in recent decades as a result of Polish scholarship. In particular, the papers from a centennial conference in 1984 offered rich insights into Malinowski's 'Polish roots' (Ellen et al. 1988).

Ernest Gellner took a close interest in this Polish scholarship, helped to edit the conference volume, and contributed a scintillating chapter (Gellner 1988). Accepting that Malinowski's anthropological functionalism owed much to the individualist empiricism of Ernst Mach and its associated ethic of cosmopolitanism, Gellner proceeded to draw out a basic tension facing all anthropologists:

> But this internationalist, individualist, 'cosmopolitan' option, the cult of the Open Society, is perhaps less likely to constitute the whole answer for a man who knows full well, professionally, that the human condition in general is not like that – who knows ... that a greater part of mankind lives or lived in absorbing, relatively self-contained communities. In other words, can an anthropologist wholeheartedly adopt the 'cosmopolitan' model of man? He may well be cosmopolitan himself, but can he conceivably see the human condition in general in such terms? And if indeed he cannot, is he therefore condemned to embrace its best known and most favoured alternative, and indulge in the 'organic' sense of historic communities and of continuity? ... Must he choose between cosmopolitanism and Hegelianism? (1988: 168).

According to Gellner, Malinowski solved this tension by combining the two in a unique 'cocktail'. His Hegelianism expressed itself in Polish 'cultural nationalism', but since the Polish nation had been poorly treated by history, Malinowski tempered his organic romanticism with a radical rejection of history in favour of synchronic functionalism. This highly speculative interpretation is consistent with what we know of Malinowski's life. The late Habsburg era was the apogee of national movements in *Mitteleuropa* and Cracow was the conservative intellectual centre of Poland's national movement. It can be readily demonstrated that Malinowski was influenced by the creative writers as well as the scholars of the 'Young Poland' movement, that he never lost interest in the affairs of his native country during all his years in Britain, and that he was engaging himself actively on behalf of Poland when he died in New Haven in 1942.[1] At the same time he has impeccable internationalist credentials. He seems to have appreciated the Habsburg Empire as a multicultural polity and was from his childhood able to speak and read several European languages. He made no special effort to teach his daughters Polish, or to inculcate any knowledge of Polish culture and history. For their holidays the family went not to the Polish Tatras but to the Italian Alps.

The ambiguities of Malinowski's intellectual foundations can be detected in the major posthumous publications, which document his fascination with the concept of culture (1944a) and his general political creed and values (1944b). The latter were typical for a 'conservative-liberal' European intellectual of that age (Mucha 1988). By the end of his life, Malinowski had apparently transferred his loyalties from the empire of the Austrians to the empire of the British; he thought that anthropology could be put to use to improve the efficiency of colonial administration, and certainly not to subvert it.

As far as the history of anthropology is concerned, the department built up by Malinowski in the inter-war decades at the London School of Economics was highly international in both its staff and its students. But despite the fame of this seminar, there was something about this Pole that did not endear him to everyone in the British establishment (e.g. Evans-Pritchard 1981: 199). Even before his early death his theories were ignored or dismissed. Without the loyal efforts of Raymond Firth (see 1957), it is doubtful he would enjoy anything like his present stature.

Ernest Gellner, 1925–1995

When Ernest Gellner died in November 1995 he was hailed by Adam Kuper in *Anthropology Today* as 'the last of the Central Europeans'.[2] He was 'our emissary to the intellectuals, our link to the great traditions of modern European thought, our precious Voltaire'. Kuper drew attention (as had others before him) to the affinity to Malinowski; together with Karl Popper, they were 'all the progeny of Franz-Josef's Vienna, that extraordinary school of all our modernities' (Kuper 1996).

Like Malinowski, Gellner initially studied philosophy and was attracted to rigorous empiricism. Of course the differences are considerable. Gellner received his higher education in England, and in his case the most influential philosopher was not Ernst Mach but David Hume. As a Jew forced to leave his homeland as a schoolboy, his route from Prague to Britain was utterly different from Malinowski's journey from Cracow a generation earlier. Though multilingual, fieldwork in the vernacular was not one of Gellner's strengths. In his ethnographic work in Morocco and voluminous other writings he is generally more concerned with structure in a Radcliffe-Brownian sense than with the details of culture, which he tended to dismiss as mere 'wallpaper'. His strong interest in long-term historical change stood in sharp antithesis to Malinowski's synchronicism. Whereas Malinowski prioritised the 'native point of view' and often wrote in a relativist way about the differences between cultures, Gellner is usually perceived as the most explicit of the followers of Karl Popper, as indeed he is when proclaiming the West's 'cognitive superiority' (e.g. 1994).

Yet Malinowski and Gellner had much in common. Like Malinowski, Gellner was a nostalgic admirer of Franz Joseph's *Vielvölkerstaat* (the fact that the empire had ceased to exist before Gellner was born in 1925 did not prevent him from constant evocations, notably in his work on nationalism with the ideal type of 'Ruritania' (1983)). Like Malinowski, Gellner was respectful of the traditions of his adopted country, but he too was an acute observer of its quirks and absurdities. As intellectuals, both Malinowski and Gellner were trained in Western philosophy and both aimed in their anthropology to reach levels of scientific generalisation at which the details of local cultures were of no relevance. Malinowski found an ultimate basis for his functionalism in the 'biological needs' of the individual. Gellner's universalism is grounded in Popper's epistemology and his vision of the 'open society'. Our modern forms of knowledge are necessarily provisional and unstable, but the criteria of modern Western science have given us an incredibly powerful toolkit for acting upon the world. Gellner was frequently impatient with relativists who argued that such understanding was no more than one cosmology among others, and not inherently different from the worldview of a 'primitive society'. He was a thoroughgoing 'great divide' theorist, for whom the political breakthrough to 'civil society' coincided not only with the economic breakthrough from *Agraria* to *Industria* but also with the cognitive breakthrough that has produced modern science.[3]

It is hardly surprising that an emphasis upon a radical discontinuity in human history which revolves around a 'miracle' in Europe arouses suspicion among anthropologists. The stakes were raised by the fact that Gellner was more than a match for Malinowski in composing provocative hyperbole. In works such as *Conditions of Liberty* (1994) Gellner wrote of a collective 'we' in the post-Enlightenment West, fortunately acquainted with liberal individualism, the only possible basis for a free civil society, while most of the world has had to struggle against 'totalitarianism' or the 'tyranny of cousins'. Like the late Malinowski, Gellner leaves you in no doubt about his values and political sympathies.[4] It is important to note that he does not plead for a *moral* universalism. Other cultures have different systems of knowledge and different values. We can say that *our* science is much more powerful and the basis for universal knowledge; we can also state a preference to live in a society based on Popperian values; but I think both Gellner's cosmopolitan universalism and Malinowski's earlier variant stop short of claiming that these values are *better*.

Both of these cosmopolitan Central Europeans have to pay a price for their ambitions to theorise outside the constraints of culture. Like Malinowski, Gellner generated antipathy as well as admiration within his chosen intellectual community. He was eventually appointed to a prestigious position in Cambridge but for some critics his insistence on the superiority of the West was an affront, almost a contradiction of the prime job of the anthropologist, namely the appreciation of diversity. Somehow his style of combative rhetoric did not endear the Central European to many mainstream 'native anthropologists'.[5] His accomplishments as a fieldworker were modest and his reputation cannot be sustained on that basis alone in the way that Malinowski's has been. But perhaps the major key to explaining the different standing of the two figures in the history of the discipline is simply timing. Malinowski's theoretical premises and values could be overlooked and excused in the last days of Empire; the inspiration of his fieldwork was sufficient to justify his self-promotion as the founder of a school and confer the status that is confirmed with each new edition of Adam Kuper's textbook. But Gellner's defiant self-proclaimed 'Enlightenment fundamentalism' came in the aftermath of Empire, when all the old certainties had to be questioned and anything that smacked of Eurocentrism was inherently suspect; and nowhere more so than in anthropology, a discipline that in countries such as Britain was very largely a product of the Empire. In terms of intellect and charisma, our last Central European was at least an equal to our first: if Gellner has only a handful of loyal followers, few of them anthropologists, this is largely due to the embarrassment that a militant pro-Enlightenment stance is considered to create for our discipline in a postcolonial world.[6]

Complementing their empiricist universalism but little noticed by their critics, I wish to draw attention to one further intellectual similarity between Ernest Gellner and Bronislaw Malinowski: both were imbued with a romantic, excessively 'groupist' concept of culture which links them to the Herderian current.[7] This claim will surprise those who know Gellner primarily as a champion of the 'modernist' position that nations are invented through the nationalism of intellectuals. Certainly he rejected all forms of primordialism and enjoyed poking fun at populists and exposing the contradictions of the 'sleeping beauty' theories of national awakeners (e.g. 1983). His sociological argument that homogenous nation-states replace multinational empires in order to fulfil the basic preconditions for industrial modernity has been frequently attacked for its functionalism, though it continues to be debated by scholars in several disciplines (Hall 1998). My point is simply that, in constructing this theory of nationalism, Gellner does not abandon the notion of culture. The new unit may lack the rural integrity of the archetypal Carpathian kingdom, but the 'modular' citizens of Gellner's industrial society, literate and mobile thanks to their standardised high culture, participate in a comparable organic totality. The model is of course highly unrealistic and of little use in addressing the complexities of contemporary social life in countries such as Britain, where the persistence of local and regional differences and above all the multiplication of disparate cultural influences through immigration have generated diversity that is more reminiscent of what Gellner terms the Agrarian Age; but few of the anthropologists who study this diversity find it helpful to visualise it as an agglomeration of separate ('Ruritanian') cultures in which individual subjects identify and behave in accordance with the norms of one collectivity (see Eriksen 2008, Baumann 1996).[8]

Johann Gottfried Herder (1745–1802)

So far in this chapter I have discussed the reception of two trained philosophers of Central European origin who became major figures in British social anthropology. Both have been much criticised, especially for the Eurocentrism that vitiates their attempts to construct general theories. But I have also drawn attention to another similarity between them: both Malinowski and Gellner, especially in their use of the concept of culture, draw on an intellectual tradition that has its origins with Herder in the last decades of the eighteenth century, and which set out explicitly to refute universalist pretensions. Let us look a little more carefully at this neglected figure.

Herder has long been viewed as a pivotal figure in the Counter-Enlightenment, leading a reaction against the philosophers of Paris and Königsberg and pointing towards romanticism, populism, and movements of national liberation in Europe and elsewhere.[9] Of course there is room to argue about what is genuinely a counter-current and what is encompassed in the whole. Isaiah Berlin draws attention to what Herder had in common with his Christian humanist predecessors as well as contemporary Weimar cosmopolitans, and yet concludes that his works, though ridden by contradictions, constitute 'perhaps the sharpest blow ever delivered against the classical philosophy of the West' (2000: 238–9). Compared with Kant, Herder is nowadays not taken seriously as a major philosopher. He is, however, treated with the utmost seriousness by the leading historians of popular culture in Europe (Burke 1978). His pioneering role in the 'discovery of the people' paved the way for those who set out to document the life of 'other cultures' all over the world over the following two centuries. It is therefore a little odd that he receives so little attention in histories of anthropology.

Herder made a famous analogy between a 'people' (*Volk*) and a sphere, which had its own unique centre of gravity.[10] He had no *Favoritvolk* but emphasised pluralism and questioned basic Enlightenment convictions about progress (*Fortgang*). Berlin argues that Herder's notions of belonging to a group are central to his thought: he pitied those who, for whatever reason, could not partake in the elementary forms of human association (including 'superfluous cosmopolitans' who fed off the creativity of others). Language was not a mere vehicle to express thought, it was the incarnation of collective experience. Herder was obsessively attracted by origins, by the vitality of the primitive. It was in popular culture – for example, in folk songs – that one could find the 'genius of a people' (*Volksgeist*, *Volksseele*). The concept of *Kultur* remains, however, confused in his works.[11] Herder often used the term in the usual universalist sense, for example when speaking of 'der Fortschritt der Kultur'. On the other hand, in the Preface to one of his most important texts, the *Ideen zur Philosophie der Geschichte der Menschheit*, he asked '*Welches Volk der Erde ists, das nicht einige Kultur habe?*' His first English translator in 1802 rendered *Kultur* here as cultivation:

> Is there a people on earth totally uncultivated and how contracted must the scheme of Providence be, if every individual of the human species were to be formed to what *we* call cultivation, for which refined weakness would often be a more appropriate term? Nothing can be more vague, than the term itself; nothing more apt to lead us astray, than the application of it to whole nations and ages. (1966: v)

It seems we need to recognise the kind of complexity that is common enough in intellectual history. Herder's 'organic diversitarianism' (Stocking 1982) did imply the kernel of what came to be called cultural relativism, but he did not name it as such; and it was to be more than a century before the word culture was adapted from its traditional humanistic sense to serve this new purpose; indeed the adaptation has never been complete, which is why so much confusion surrounds the term in the present day.[12]

The Herderian equation of language and *Volk* had political implications from the very beginning, above all in Central Europe. Well before the birth of Malinowski in 1884 the national awakeners were hard at work. By the time of Gellner's birth in 1925 the major empires of the continent had been dismantled and another World War was not far off. From this point of view, Herder's humanist counterpoint to Enlightenment universalism turned out to be a false trail: his invitation to explore the *Kultur des Volkes* became compromised by a vision of humanity as divided into essentialist *Kulturen*. Should one therefore conclude that the Herderian emphasis on culture and nation is anti-cosmopolitan? Is the only genuine cosmopolitanism the liberal individualism of the 'Open Society' agenda?

Reconciling Anthropologies

The preceding excursus to the eighteenth century was no antiquarian exercise, since contemporary discourses of 'rooted cosmopolitanism' resound with echoes of the Herderian position. But let us stick to the history of anthropology and consider briefly how the discipline has evolved in the common Eastern European homeland of Herder, Malinowski and Gellner. Germany is the pivotal case since here one finds down to the present day not one but two intellectual communities. The *Völkerkunde* strand was at least as strong and creative as the equivalent comparative social anthropology in Britain and France until Germany lost two World Wars; *Volkskunde*, on the other hand, was the study of one's own people, very much in the spirit of Herder. In the era of nationalism the specialists of this branch, even those whose prime interests were in details of local or regional folklore, could hardly avoid becoming caught up in celebrations of the nation. *Volkskunde* lost much of its scholarly capital in Germany following the Nazi catastrophe (though in West Germany it was able to reinvent itself under names such as *Europäische Ethnologie* or *Empirische Kulturwissenschaft*). The smaller countries of Eastern and Central Europe lacked overseas empires and, even if some individual scholars worked outside their countries (notably Hungarians), the anthropology which became institutionalised was a variant of *Volkskunde*.

In the socialist era, which began after World War II, it looked at first as if a new internationalism would overturn this status quo. In some countries, notably the German Democratic Republic, efforts were made to impose a Marxist philosophy of history and to merge *Volkskunde* and *Völkerkunde*. These attempts were not very successful. Surprisingly, the discipline previously condemned as contaminated with bourgeois nationalism and rural nostalgia was increasingly tolerated and even encouraged. Socialist power holders were willing to expand subsidies for a discipline that appeared politically harmless and cemented a certain 'traditional' national identity for a future-orientated Communist Party that lacked democratic legitimacy (Hann, Sarkany and Skalník 2005).

The postsocialist era has brought new tensions between an academic establishment that is still primarily devoted to documentation of the folk culture of the nation and rival currents with quite different concerns that tend to appeal to younger scholars (Skalník 2002). One of the strongest of the new currents is Social or (more usually) Cultural Anthropology (others include Cultural Studies, Media Studies, etc.). In some countries, notably in Poland, it has proved possible since the late socialist decades to integrate new approaches and to re-label institutions accordingly (e.g. 'Department of Ethnology and Cultural Anthropology'). Elsewhere, in Hungary, for example, there has been considerable resistance to integration. As a result, where new programmes have been introduced they have been separately institutionalised. In some cases the two kinds of anthropology have become bitter rivals, with personal rifts and feuds. Those lacking a command of English tend to perceive the new currents (which some see exemplified in the vigour of the *European Association of Social Anthropologists*) as a juggernaut that threatens to put an end to their intellectual community. Some say that it reminds them of the dogmatism which threatened them from the opposite direction in the early socialist years, when 'cosmopolitan' was a term of abuse in socialist vocabulary.[13] Those in the other camp complain bitterly about sterile provincialism, the lack of funding for projects that do not conform to the established paradigm, and the blocking of positions.

To an external observer such as myself, such fragmentation of an already small discipline can only be regretted, especially in view of the real intellectual convergence that has taken place in recent decades. Many social and cultural anthropologists now work 'at home', just like the national ethnographers. Similarly, some of the latter have begun to move away from their traditional specialisation with the pre-industrial peasantry. However, despite the considerable areas of intellectual overlap the future of anthropology is in many places uncertain. The factional politics vary from one institution to the next, but behind them it is possible to identify certain issues of principle. Tamás Hofer, the distinguished Hungarian ethnographer who has sought throughout his career to build bridges between national ethnography and cultural anthropology, expresses the concern that a formal merger with the 'new' anthropology would mean the end of a distinguished Hungarian research tradition (2005). He argues that the two intellectual communities should continue to complement each other, the local scholars contributing their linguistic and historical expertise while it is left to the sociocultural anthropologists to engage with issues of comparison and sociological generalisation.

Some division of labour along these or similar lines seems reasonable enough to me, though, unlike Hofer, I would prefer to see the two communities brought together to conduct their dialogue *within* unified institutions. Contrary to some of the 'Young Turks' agitating on behalf of the new anthropology, I do not view the expertise of the 'native ethnographer' on his/her home society as inimical to the generalising comparative perspective of more cosmopolitan styles. It is hard not to feel some Herderian *Einfühlung* (empathy) with those who see the foreign variant as an unwelcome instrument of cultural homogenisation, part of the process by which English is rapidly replacing German and Russian as the prime academic *lingua franca* of the region. For example, at the Central European University in Budapest (closely allied with Open Society Foundation, also funded by philanthropist George Soros) all programmes are taught in English. At the time of writing the home variant of anthropology, including the study of folklore and the material culture of the pre-industrial peasantry, continues to flourish in the Humanities Faculty at Budapest's major university; but a new Department of Cultural Anthropology was established in 1990 in the Social Sciences Faculty, and the programmes are not well integrated. Yet it seems to me that the detailed study of the traditions of one's own country, which a Herderian will value for their own sake, can also provide a useful bedrock for scholars with wider ambitions, such as engaging systematically with the *Volkskunde* of neighbouring countries, as well as with multifarious strands of *Völkerkunde*. From this point of view the British student of social anthropology, exposed to a highly cosmopolitan curriculum that conveys selective snippets of knowledge about societies all over the world, is not necessarily better served than students in Eastern and Central Europe who acquire detailed, 'holistic' knowledge of the recent past of their own societies. For example, the study of folklore hardly exists as an established academic field in Britain, where the only way to study the pre-industrial rural population is to enrol for courses in social and economic history. If students of anthropology in Britain were required to engage more seriously with British traditions, this might help to overcome the bias which continues to dog our version of the discipline, which grew out of the study of the 'savage' and the 'primitive', and even when practised at home has tended to neglect history and to focus on minorities, on the marginal and 'exotic'.

Conclusion

The discipline of social anthropology in Britain became much more diverse and international through the expansion that began in the era of Bronislaw Malinowski. Later debates concerning universalism and relativism, or synchronicity versus history, or structure versus process, debates to which Ernest Gellner was a distinguished contributor, took place within a highly cosmopolitan intellectual community.[14] The incorporation of these Central Europeans was overwhelmingly successful, but in neither case entirely frictionless. I drew attention to similarities in their intellectual ambitions and general values, but also to their common vision of humanity as a mosaic of organic cultures. This is the less frequently noted complement to their modernist individualism. I suggested that their holism derives from their upbringing in *Mitteleuropa* in the heyday of nationalism.[15] Malinowski and Gellner mixed Herderian cultural romanticism with liberal individualism. The latter tends to dominate the more political and polemical works each published towards the end of his life; but to many contemporary anthropologists the very notions of individual and culture are suspect, and Eurocentrism undermines the larger theoretical projects of both of these scholars.

The Herderian cosmopolitanism of Gellner and Malinowski can be contrasted with another strand in social anthropology, exemplified in Malinowski's day by Alfred Reginald Radcliffe-Brown and sustained in recent decades most prominently by Adam Kuper. For these scholars the subject matter of anthropology is a social field. They are particularly critical of the concept of culture. According to Kuper (1999) the present centrality of this concept in English-language anthropology is largely the result of a post-World War II division of labour with sociology, which assigned to anthropology the prime responsibility for the 'ideational' or 'symbolic'

Chris Hann

fields. This US-led idealism built upon traditions imported from continental Europe. Whether or not Franz Boas read Herder, in the hands of Boas's student Ruth Benedict (whose *Patterns of Culture* (1934) was acknowledged by Clifford Geertz as a major influence), the concept lost its dynamism; the totalities presented by Benedict are reminiscent of Herder's spheres. Many contemporary analysts of accelerating globalisation processes, whose tool kit includes novel terms such as 'postcolonialism' and 'transnationalism', remain extraordinarily loyal to the old term 'culture'. They would not wish to be associated with Herderian populism, let alone a nationalist world view; but, as numerous critiques of liberal multiculturalism have shown, a degree of 'methodological nationalism' is hard to avoid so long as culture remains the central concept of the discipline. Social anthropology can offer an alternative: the radical comparative cosmopolitanism of Radcliffe-Brown.

Of course the first President of the Association of Social Anthropologists has been epistemologically unfashionable for more than half a century. The social anthropology that he helped to institutionalise in Britain has never been a rooted discipline comparable to national ethnography as it developed in other parts of Europe. The works of the cosmopolitans Malinowski and Gellner are being translated into their native languages, so that they can be read more widely, perhaps also by students whose prime interest is in their own country. Similarly, I think it would make for a healthy balance if more works by historians such as E.P. Thompson, Hans Medick and Peter Burke would find their way into the basic curricula of anthropology departments in Britain. A rooted cosmopolitan anthropology would be a true synthesis of *Volkskunde* and *Völkerkunde*, neither the celebration of one's own people nor a preoccupation with 'the other'.

Notes

1. Malinowski gave up his Polish passport for a British one in 1931, but he never became so British that he lost his ability to maintain a critical distance, e.g. towards the snobbery of colonial society, including that of the family into which he married (Young 2004).
2. If Malinowski and Gellner are the first and last of British anthropology's Central Europeans, how many do we find in-between? Apart from Siegfried Nadel perhaps only Franz Steiner really qualifies: Prague, like Malinowski's Cracow, was still living off Habsburg credit long after the Empire's formal demise in 1918 (Adler and Fardon 1999). The later contributions of Ladislav Holy and Milan Stuchlik belonged clearly to another era. Overall, the influence

from Central Europe has been modest in comparison, say, to the influence from South Africa.

3. Gellner did not deny that the mechanisms through which this knowledge is produced have specific cultural dimensions. But I don't think he would have been very excited by the work that has been carried out in 'science studies' in recent years, since for him this has no bearing on his fundamental insistence on the 'effective knowledge' of the modern West. In view of Gellner's lifelong anti-idealist polemics, there is a distinct irony in the weight he sometimes appears to attach to a revolution in cognition (McNeill 1996).

4. Although Gellner was a frequent critic of Clifford Geertz, I do not see much difference in practice to the values to which Geertz owns up more obliquely in some of his later writings (2000).

5. Gellner served for a few years as the President of Royal Anthropological Institute; but it is hard to imagine him being elected as Chair of the Association of Social Anthropologists.

6. This analysis is based in part on personal observations at the Department of Social Anthropology in Cambridge, where I was a junior colleague of Gellner for much of the 1980s. Temperamentally, he sometimes revelled in his minority position. Though he supervised many students, both in London and later in Cambridge, there is no Gellnerian school.

7. I do not know if either scholar ever read the works of Herder (as we saw in the quotation above, Gellner preferred to term this option 'Hegelian') but in the *Mitteleuropa* in which they lived there was simply no escaping the spirit of populism and nationalism.

8. One reason why Gellner perceived the contemporary world in such groupist terms may have something to do with his own Jewish identity, strongly felt at least in some periods of his life (Davis 1991).

9. In this discussion I rely heavily on the sympathetic commentary of Isaiah Berlin (2000 [1965]). though the level of his scholarship is hardly comparable to the recent study by John Zammito (2002).

10. *Jede Nation hat ihren Mittelpunkt der Glückseligkeit in sich wie jede Kugel ihren Schwerpunkt'* (Herder 1774, V, 509).

11. Herder appears not to use *Kultur* in the plural. Nations (*Nationen*) and peoples (*Völker*) were his usual categories, and the only sense in which he pluralises *Kultur* is in distinguishing the *Kultur des Volkes* from the *Kultur der Gelehrten*.

12. For comprehensive discussion, see Bunzl 1996 and Gingrich et al. 2005.

13. For further discussion of the socialist semantics of the term in Russia, see Humphrey 2004.

14. Much more might be ventured here about how the community of the Association of Social Anthropologists has been shaped over the years by

changing patterns of international recruitment. My impression is that the academic job market is more open in Britain than it is elsewhere in Europe; the decisive factor is the English language rather than any greater propensity to cosmopolitanism on the part of our politicians and educational managers.

15. It would be an interesting exercise in the history of anthropology to link these two giants of the British tradition to others, especially in North America, where George Stocking and others have long drawn attention to the significance of the German connection (Boas, Kroeber, Lowie, etc.). Karl Polanyi's formative years were spent in Budapest and Vienna. The contributions of Géza Róheim, Mircea Eliade and many more were decisively shaped by their socialisation and training in these parts of Europe. In comparison with the non-émigrés who dominated in the discipline of national ethnography, all of these scholars were cosmopolitans; but I am not claiming that all anthropological emigrants from Central Europe took with them similar Herderian influences.

References

Adler, Jeremy and Richard Fardon (1999) 'An Oriental in the West: the Life of Franz Baermann Steiner', in F.B. Steiner, *Selected Writings*, Volume 1, New York: Berghahn, pp. 16–100.

Barth, F., Andre Gingrich, Robert Parkin and Sydel Silverman (2005), *One Discipline, Four Ways*, Chicago: University of Chicago Press.

Baumann, Gerd (1996), *Contesting Culture: Discourses of Identity in Multi-Ethnic London*, Cambridge: Cambridge University Press.

Benedict, Ruth (1989 [1934]), *Patterns of Culture*, Boston: Houghton Mifflin.

Berlin, Isaiah (2000), *Three Critics of the Enlightenment; Vico, Hamann, Herder*, Princeton, NJ: Princeton University Press.

Bunzl, Matti (1996) 'Franz Boas and the Humboldtian Tradition: from *Volksgeist* and *Nationalcharakter* to an Anthropological Concept of Culture', in George W. Stocking Jr. (ed.), *Volksgeist as Method and Ethic: Essays on Boasian Ethnography and the German Anthropological Tradition*, Madison: University of Wisconsin Press, pp. 17–78.

Burke, Peter (1978), *Popular Culture in Early Modern Europe*, London: Pelican.

Davis, John (1991), 'An Interview with Ernest Gellner by John Davis,' *Current Anthropology* 32 (1): 63–71.

Ellen, Roy, Ernest Gellner, Grażyna Kubica and Janusz Mucha (eds) (1988), *Malinowski Between Two Worlds: The Polish Roots of an Anthropological Tradition*, Cambridge: Cambridge University Press.

Eriksen, Thomas Hylland (2008) 'Ernest Gellner and the Multicultural Mess', in Mark Haugaard and Sinisa Malesevic (eds), *Ernest Gellner and Contemporary Social Thought*, Cambridge: Cambridge University Press, pp. 168–86.

Evans-Pritchard, E.E. (1981), *A History of Anthropological Thought*, London: Faber & Faber.

Firth, Raymond (ed.) (1957), *Man and Culture: An Evaluation of the Work of Bronislaw Malinowski*, London: Routledge & Paul.

Geertz, Clifford (1988), *Works and Lives; The Anthropologist as Author*, Cambridge: Polity Press.

—— (2000), *Available Light; Anthropological Reflections on Philosophical Topics*, Princeton NJ.: Princeton University Press.

Gellner, Ernest (1983), *Nations and Nationalism*, Oxford: Blackwell.

—— (1988), 'Zeno of Cracow' or 'Revolution at Nemi' or 'The Polish revenge: a Drama in Three Acts', in Roy Ellen, Ernest Gellner, Grażyna Kubica and Janusz Mucha (eds), *Malinowski Between Two Worlds: the Polish Roots of an Anthropological Tradition*, Cambridge: Cambridge University Press, pp. 164–94.

—— (1994), *Conditions of Liberty: Civil Society and its Rivals*, London: Hamish Hamilton.

Gingrich, Andre (2005), 'The German-Speaking Countries', in Fredrik Barth, Andre Gingrich, Robert Parkin and Sydel Silverman (eds), *One Discipline, Four Ways*, Chicago: University of Chicago Press, pp. 61–153.

Hall, John A. (ed.) (1998), *The State of the Nation: Ernest Gellner and the Theory of Nationalism*, Cambridge: Cambridge University Press.

Hann, Chris, Mihály Sárkány and Peter Skalník (eds) (2005), *Studying Peoples in the People's Democracies. Socialist Era Anthropology in East-Central Europe*, Münster: Lit Verlag.

Herder, J.G. (1774), *Auch eine Philosophie der Geschichte zur Bildung der Menschheit*, Riga: Hartnoch.

—— (1966 [1784]), *Outlines of a Philosophy of the History of Man*, New York: Bergman.

Hofer, Tamas (2005), 'Anthropologists and Native Ethnographers in Central European Villages: Comparative Notes on the Professional Personality of Two Disciplines', in Chris Hann, Mihály Sárkány and Peter Skalník (eds), *Studying People in the People's Democracies. Socialist Era Anthropology in East-Central Europe*, Münster: Lit. Verlag, pp. 343–61.

Humphrey, Caroline (2004), 'Cosmopolitanism and *Kosmopolitizm* in the Political Life of Soviet citizens', *Focaal* 44, Utrecht: Stichting Focaal and Berghahn Books, pp. 138–52.

Kuper, Adam (1983) *Anthropology and Anthropologists: The Modern British School*, London: Routledge & Kegan Paul (revised edition).

—— (1996), 'Obituary of Ernest Gellner', *Anthropology Today* 12 (1): 19–20.

—— (1999), *Culture: The Anthropologist's Account*, Cambridge, Mass.: Harvard University Press.

Malinowski, Bronislaw (1944a), *A Scientific Theory of Culture and Other Essays*, Durham, NC: University of North Carolina Press.
—— (1944b), *Freedom and Civilization*, New York: Roy.
—— (1967), *A Diary in the Strict Sense of the Term*, New York: Harcourt, Brace & World.
McNeill, William H. (1996), 'A Swan Song for British Liberalism?', in John A. Hall and Ian Jarvie (eds), *The Social Philosophy of Ernest Gellner*, Amsterdam: Rodopi, pp. 565–72.
Mucha, Janusz (1988), 'Malinowski and the Problems of Contemporary Civilisation', in R. Ellen et al. (eds), *Malinowski between Two Worlds: the Polish Roots of an Anthropological Tradition*, Cambridge: Cambridge University Press, pp. 164–94.
Skalník, Peter (ed.) (2002), *A Post-Communist Millennium: The Struggles for Sociocultural Anthropology in Central and Eastern Europe*, Prague: Set Out.
Stocking, George (1982), 'Afterword: A View from the Center', *Ethnos* 47 (1–2): 172–86.
Streck, B. (1997), *Fröhliche Wissenschaft Ethnologie; eine Führung*, Frankfurt: Edition Trickster, Peter Hammer.
Young, Michael W. (2004), *Malinowski; Odyssey of an Anthropologist, 1884–1920*, New Haven: Yale University Press.
Zammito, John H. (2002), *Kant, Herder and the Birth of Anthropology*, Chicago: University of Chicago Press.

Section II
Feminist and Non-Violent
Cosmopolitan Movements

Gender, Rights and Cosmopolitanisms
Maila Stivens

The recent political developments in Malaysia have added the impetus and urgency to strengthen women's participation in the cultural, economic and political life of the nation. We deplore the manipulation of ethnicity and religion, as well as the use of fear and oppressive forces to divide us. We want to contribute towards the building of a just, democratic and peaceful society for ourselves and future generations.

Women's Agenda for Change, Malaysia (1999)[1]

The virtually insignificant presence of gender issues in the now voluminous literature on cosmopolitanism is remarkable. Yet over the same period, feminisms have engaged both theoretically and practically with many of the besetting difficulties within the cosmopolitanism debates: important gender-based movements around the globe have worked painfully through accusations of universalism, ethnocentricity, neo-imperialism and worse, towards ideas of transversal politics and versions of what can be seen as grounded cosmopolitanism. This chapter argues that a gendered reading of the recent cosmopolitan debates points us to significant sites for exploring questions of cosmopolitanism in its many meanings. In the chapter I discuss one particular case, that of the Malaysia women's movement.

Habits of neglectfulness

Efforts to theorise the relationship of gender to cosmopolitanism confront ongoing androcentrisms within social theory and the inevitable awkwardnesses exposed by attempts to engender readings of emerging debates. This was also the case, for example, with the theorising of the key concepts, 'modernity', 'post modernity' and 'globalisation', which feminist theorists have seen as inherently excluding gender concerns and neglecting feminist debates (Felski 1995; Marshall 1994; see Stivens 1998a). Analysing 'gender' as an increasingly fractured and contested term, with multiple claims made on it, is a task for another paper (see Stivens 2007b), except to say that it is still often conflated with 'woman' (Cornwall 2001). The familiar problems of gender blindness within recent cosmopolitan debates, however, are evidence of habits of neglectfulness that reflect continuing problems in the relationship between social theory and issues of gender.[2]

As yet only a very small body of work has addressed directly the question of gender and cosmopolitanism or the gendering of cosmopolitanism. Women and gender seem to be almost wholly absent from much of the theorising about the linked futures of nationalisms and cosmopolitanisms: a Google search of the phrases 'gender and cosmopolitanism' and 'gendering of cosmopolitanism' produced no hits for work addressing the relationship between the two; similarly 'gendered cosmopolitanism' and 'women and cosmopolitanism' yielded only a handful, including an interesting paper 'Women and the New Cosmopolitanism', by Josna Rege (2003). While many hits discussed both, none specifically addressed these conjunctions. A search of journal databases produced similar results. The Google count is not infallible, however: Mica Nava (2002, 2003, 2006) has important work in progress. As she notes, 'the specificity of *gendered* relations to elsewhere and otherness, whether racist or anti-racist' has attracted little attention (2006: 42).

There are some exceptions to the neglect of gender in the core cosmopolitan literature: Ulrich Beck has noticed the complex negotiations around domestic violence at the Vienna human rights conference in 1993 (2004); Sheldon Pollock et al. (2000) have pointed us to significant attempts to 'think the cosmopolitan' by looking to feminism, or better, feminisms. Thus:

> Many of the key terms central to these debates – "universal," "theoretical," "abstract," "conceptual" – have been characterized as implicitly masculine because of their properties of mastery, distance from experience, indifference to specifics, and concern for absolutes in human life. These are the terms of a disembodied, free-floating, or generalizing scientific or humanistic thought. To focus, therefore, on these three historical practices is to ignore another pressure and inspiration to think the cosmopolitan, namely, feminism. Feminism has learned to wrestle with problems and attendant possibilities while struggling to keep the situated rather than the universal subject in the foreground.

> Thus, for cosmopolitanism, feminism may serve a role similar to but different from the other contested "isms" of the late twentieth century – nationalism, multiculturalism, and globalism – whose critiques are grounded in other economies and ideologies of difference and similarity. U.S. mainstream feminisms have noted that the "our" of our times is a noninclusive our that consists of able-bodied, white, heterosexual men. (Pollock et al. 2000: 583)

This point looks very much like an afterthought, however: gender dimensions of cosmopolitanism are not discussed elsewhere in the work.

The overall relative neglect of gender may be due in part to the neglect of popular and vernacular cosmopolitanisms in the prevailing concern with the privileged and mobile individual cosmopolitan: Peter van der Veer (2004: 167) observes that in gender terms the cosmopolitan is obviously [conceived of as] a man; an individual who has the ability to live anywhere and the capacity to tolerate and understand the barbarism of others'. This echoes the emblematic, problematic figure of modernity, the equally male flâneur, equally the sole bearer of agency (Marshall 1994). Werbner makes the important point that the study of women activists has been 'a glaring blind spot' in the new cosmopolitan literature (2004). Catherine Eschle (2001), too, underlines the surprising lack of interest in social movements in the new cosmopolitanism literature. But the neglect of gender issues may also be connected to a long-term disdain in political thought for what is deemed the 'private', 'domestic' or intimate, still often assumed to be 'women's business' within a universal domestic domain. Women's movements have of course been concerned centrally with democratisation within the so-called domestic sphere. Perhaps, ultimately, many theorists in their ongoing neglect of gender as ever feared their own internal other, the 'feminine'.[3]

The significance of the absence of gender concerns from 'mainstream (male-stream) theorising around cosmopolitanism becomes apparent when we consider a series of highly influential feminist arguments about intersectionality, the mutually constitutive nature of gender, race and class. Writers like Nira Yuval-Davis have argued convincingly since the 1980s that the making of nation, culture/s, ethnicities, classes and new religions can only be understood fully when they are seen as gendered phenomena, constituted within gendered relations (Anthias and Yuval-Davis 1984, Yuval-Davis 1997, Lister 2003). As Joel Kahn has suggested, some writers argue that the cosmopolitan imperative must be grounded in culturally neutral terrains, 'beyond culture as Gupta and Ferguson put it' (cited in Kahn, 2006: 14). 'Anything to do with the universal, the transnational, the hybrid, the cosmopolitan or "complexity" presumes the possibility of deculturalised or culturally neutral spaces which one may enter after having left one's particular cultural coat at the door as it were.' One presumably has to leave one's gendered coat at the door as well.

Yet the painful debates within recent women's movements about the proper path to gender justice and rights[4] offer many lessons for the theoretical, political and moral projects of cosmopolitanisms. Yuval-Davis points out that the first-wave feminist movement was internationalist from its inception: 'its cosmopolitan approach was expressed in Virginia Woolf's famous declaration "As a woman I have no country"' (2004: 10). Against that, many feminist writers have emphasised how the struggle for women's equality and liberation was frequently formulated by women's groups as part of their people's national and anti-colonial struggles (ibid.). The most painful of these debates swirled around the hurt and upset that many 'third-world'/Southern feminists felt at the continuing exclusionary epistemologies and practices of first-world feminists: of particular concern was the neocolonial thrust of pronouncements about genital cutting, foot binding, *sati*, and so on. Answers were sought for ways to construct a new feminist politics that acknowledged its late modern (second modern) – possibly post-postmodern – situatedness in a world in a flux of unfixed identities: these included such concepts as strategic essentialisms/sisterhoods, unity within difference and finally transversal politics. Perhaps as a result of these battles, feminist scholarship is now wary of the perceived universalisms and utopianisms of cosmopolitanisms in their many guises.

It could be argued, however, that a voluminous literature on transnational feminisms is *de facto* dealing with cosmopolitanism(s), but mostly evading the term. Why has this feminist scholarship not embraced the 'c' word? Aihwa Ong suggests populations in former colonies have been understandably sceptical of cosmopolitan discourses invoked by the civilising mission of imperialism (2006:18). Eschle, too, is somewhat dismissive of the possibilities of feminist cosmopolitanism, which like some other critics she associates with the problems of a universalising exclusionary liberal cosmopolitanism upholding certain universal values (2001: 156). She prefers Nira Yuval-Davis's *transversal politics* (Yuval-Davis 1997). Transversal politics, enthusiastically embraced in some feminist circles, is based on the idea of dialogue and debate that take into account the different positioning of women (1997: 125). 'Concretely this means that all feminist (and other democratic) politics should be viewed as a form of coalition politics in which the differences among women are recognized and given a voice' (1997: 126). In Yuval-Davis's formulation this also implies that women will approach disagreement and conflict with a cosmopolitan openness to an interlocutor's viewpoint, 'shifting' and 'rooting', in order to try to achieve a move towards mutually acceptable agendas *without effacing one's own positioned identity*. What is important more than the name, Yuval-Davis emphasises, 'is the realisation that transversal politics is not only a dialogue in which two or more partners are negotiating a common political position, but it is a process in which all the participants are mutually reconstructing themselves and the others engaged with them in it' (2006 [2004]: 278).[5]

Gendering Cosmopolitan Spaces

There are many other arguments to be made for gendering accounts of cosmopolitanism, and in turn for a feminist embrace of the concept. Nava suggests that the emotions and imaginaries associated with cosmopolitanism as a structure of *feeling* have largely been neglected by social and cultural theorists (2006: 42):

she contends that affective cultures are deeply implicated in political resistance and transformation (2006: 51). In a piece looking at trans-ethnic relationships, she argues for a viscerally experienced, domestically located and gendered cosmopolitanism in relation to the imagined and geopolitical spaces of contemporary metropolitan England. She proposes that women have figured more strongly than men in the history of twentieth-century cosmopolitanism in Britain, and that they have identified with Others more strongly (2006: 48–49; see also Sichone, Chapter 15). As she points out, we need to 'sharpen and clarify some of the neglected theoretical possibilities of the concept and to highlight absences in current debates' (2006: 46).

One significant area that can underline these possibilities is the role of 'family' and kinship in the making of transnational spaces. Anthropology has often been more interested in the ways in which 'familism' can be socially exclusionary by constructing borders of class, race, ethnicity, and so on. But we might also highlight how much 'family' is part of and creates globalisation and can construct cosmopolitan spaces in several senses of the term: for example, according to the World Bank, migrants officially sent home more than US$167 billion to their families in developing countries in 2005 – a figure more than twice the level of international aid (World Bank 2005). Pnina Werbner, writing about Pakistani cosmopolitans in Manchester, suggests that labour migration forges global pathways, routes along which Islamic and familial transnational worlds are constituted (Werbner 1999a). Such work increasingly involves global women, as part of the panoply of practices like cross-border labour circuits (Sassen 2003: 264) which constitute globalisation. These circuits are deeply imbricated with some of globalisation's major constitutive dynamics: the formation of global markets, the intensifying of transnational and translocal networks, and the development of communication technologies that easily escape conventional surveillance – alternative circuits for survival (ibid.). Thus, there has been growing scholarly attention to the relationships that the rising tide of migrant and transnational 'nannies' has with their employers, their charges and their own distant children.[6] Such work as Barbara Ehrenreich's and Arlie Hochschild's book *Global Woman* (2003) has focused on the importance of mothering on a global scale, including the social conditions of mothering and the emotional negotiations involved in these relationships – what Parreñas (2001a, 2001b) calls 'diverted [absentee] mothering'. The scale of this new internationalisation of mothering is clearly unprecedented (Ehrenreich and Hochschild 2003; see also Stivens 2007a). Arlie Hochschild suggests that migration for her interviewees in California constructs new subjectivities – love for their charges that partly develops on American shores, informed by an American ideology of mother-child bonding and fostered by intense loneliness and longing for the migrants' own children (2003: 24). Ehrenreich and Hochschild are especially interested in the growing number of female-headed transnational families originating in the Philippines, in which the mother works abroad, while some or all of her dependants reside at home. The authors estimate that some 30 per cent of children in the Philippines (eight million children) have a parent who works abroad, the majority mothers.[7] For absentee Filipino mothers their transnational worlds become concrete in the large public gatherings of Filipino domestic workers, desperate for some fun on their rare days off, in Central in Hong Kong or at the Lucky Plaza shopping centre on Orchard Road, Singapore. In the last few years, for example, the latter shopping centre has filled up with businesses servicing these migrant workers – forwarding agents, dressmakers and Filipino restaurants. These gatherings can be seen to form highly significant spaces, literally embodying a deterritorialised identity and space.

The mothering practices of global 'nannies' suggest some interesting ways in which the purportedly intimate and domestic can be seen to configure cosmopolitan spaces and practices.[8] Pollock et al. ask, 'if cosmopolitanism seeks to take the large view, how can we think the intimate under its sign without restricting intimacy to the domestic sphere?' (2000: 584). In their view 'any *cosmofeminism* would have to create a critically engaged space that is not just a screen for globalisation or an antidote to nationalism but is rather a focus on projects of the intimate sphere conceived as a part of the cosmopolitan' (ibid.) (Interestingly, there are few takers for the term 'cosmofeminism' in the literature). They suggest that such a critical perspective would also open up a new understanding of the domestic, which would no longer be confined spatially or socially to the private sphere (2000: 584). This conceptualisation of the intimate/domestic, however, echoes the problematic ideas that society is universally divided into fixed, reified 'public' and 'private' domains, and evades the long history of feminist critique of these imaginaries. These critiques have included proposals for a political restructuring of these domains, a posing of multiple links between shifting realms, an emphasis on the permeability of the divide, rejections of such a dichotomy, and, finally, a suggestion that the divide is fracturing, albeit in inconsistent and contradictory ways (Fraser 1997: 115; Stivens 2000a).

Without being too essentialist, one might well look to revisit and revise the earlier feminist literature on maternal practice in looking for a neo-Kantian seeking after peace, justice and equity. Pnina Werbner among other has pointed to the virtues of caring, compassion and responsibility for the vulnerable which have often been the product of specifically women's campaigns (Werbner 1999b). Martha Nussbaum's cosmopolitan, the person whose primary allegiance is to the community (1994), could find a powerful echo here in the long-term feminist interest in maternal thinking (Ruddick 1989) in spite of all the well-documented problems with maternalism as a basis for political action.

Rethinking/Reframing Rights

The end of the twentieth century saw many social movements around the world moving to articulate their central claims in the language of rights, especially that of human rights. Those naming their struggle a human rights struggle have included advocates of the rights of women, the lesser-abled, LGBTQ groups (lesbian, gay, bisexual, transgender and queer), the ageing, and indigenous peoples, as well as those working for ecological and land rights. These rights claims are clear signs of what many see as new universalising trends in global politics, including a new humanitarianism, which many interpret in part at least as a response to the traumas experiences by the 'global community' in response to the Yugoslav and Rwanda tragedies.

One feminist attempt to deal with the postmodern and postcolonial decon-structions of universalising feminisms was a reassertion (and perhaps reinvention) of women's rights as human rights. Feminists worldwide moved strongly to lay claim to, expand and reconfigure the idea of human rights, even though legal humanism has clearly been a 'discourse of exclusion, not just of foreign barbarians but also of women and people of colour' (Douzinas 2003: 164). The slogan 'women's rights are human rights' became a central claim of the global women's movement from the 1990s on; feminist theorists argued for an explicit inclusion of women and gender into human rights tenets; and United Nations forums became central sites of a new global feminist 'counter public', providing unprecedented avenues for feminist initiatives and action (Stivens 2000a). One important result of this expansion of the human rights project has been a global recasting of core second-wave feminist concerns as 'human rights' claims, with an insistence that the 'private' is an important site for human rights claims which had hitherto only considered 'public' claims (ibid.).

Elsewhere, following Nancy Fraser, I have seen this project as both drawing on and reshaping a global feminist public in an avowedly neouniversalist mode (Fraser 1997; Stivens 2000a). But I also saw a number of difficulties with this cosmofeminism, which was not named as such: what are the consequences of the development of this human rights project and new global space? What happens to both the feminist and human rights projects when feminists adopt the concept of 'human rights' as the core claim of a global feminist politics in which identity politics had been so prominent (Stivens 2000a)? Will we see a collapsing of the two projects – subsuming women's gendered, interests-based politics within a reclaimed utopian 'human'?

It is clear, first, that the strategic use of UN forums, especially the women's and the Human Rights conferences, as critical global arenas by feminists, has been spectacularly successful in some senses: it has provided an unprecedented promotion of women's rights, interests and activism over the last twenty years, spurred on by the Vienna Conference on human rights (1993) and specific issues like the systematic sexual assaults of the war in the former Yugoslavia. Amnesty International and Human Rights Watch have also made important interventions, dating from the late eighties, with very active Women's Rights projects. I am not suggesting that the engagement with the UN and globally-operating NGOs has not also been highly problematic: it has seen the subsumption of local concerns to hegemonic 'global' discourses, especially to the power of agendas driven by global NGOs. Nonetheless, in my view, these international political mobilisations may still usefully be termed an international counter-public, a cosmopolitan space inseparable from globalisation/globalism, in spite of the continuing geopolitical tensions within feminist/womanist/women's movements and in spite of the highly problematic character of the UN.

As I argue elsewhere, many of the women involved in such struggles in the 'South' reject northern poststructuralist and some postcolonial feminist depictions of activists' rights claims as 'Western-derived' and of little relevance in the South (Stivens 2000a, 2003); indeed some see such critiques as mirroring the cynical arguments made by their own authoritarian governments. Instead, they make overt demands in terms of a common, shared humanity that has many roots in global discourses and practices, and in a long history of global ideas about rights, justice and democracy.[9] This history includes the legacy of Christianising missions – for all their close links to imperialism – anticolonial nationalisms and liberation struggles, and engagements with contemporary liberal modernity. Some women human rights activists are ambivalent about explicitly 'feminist' struggles, associating feminism with 'Western' women's politics. But many make considerable strategic use of the multiple and complex links they have to the global feminist counter-public. These links are very variable, ranging from fragile links between small local NGOs and the UN in some small Pacific states to the complex and multilayered links of the large-scale Indian women's movement (ibid.). A point to be emphasised here, however, is that women's struggles are not simply drawing on these long-circulating ideas – women are engaged in a process of actively redefining and reimagining ideas like democracy and rights on a global scale (see Stivens 2000a, 2003).

Malaysian Women's Movements

Let me now turn to explore some of the dimensions of these issues in relation to the recent women's movement in Malaysia. Malaysia has seen extraordinary 'development' over the last forty years, now ranking as a middle-income country. Massive urbanisation, the development of large new middle classes and large-scale female entry in to 'modern' occupations and education have dramatically reshaped women's lives in particular.[10] The New Economic Policy was instituted in the 1970s, aiming to improve the situation of Malays, but arguably leading to the rule of a technocratic elite. According to its futurist child, the Vision 2020 policy, Malaysia is to be a fully developed country by the year 2020. This modernist project imbued with developmentalist ideology somewhat contradictorily embeds much state-level rhetoric about the exceptionalism of Asian civilisation and 'Asian Values'. The latter discourse has expounded an explicit and unrelenting critique of the West. Ideas of re-invention are critical to the disparate versions of the desirable Malaysian modern, with both state and religion invoked. State, religious and consumerist rhetoric alike exhorts the citizenry to re-invent themselves as modern Malaysians and new Asians, invoking a further modern imaginary, the New Asia/Truly Asia. It is significant that the long-term Tourism Malaysia campaign commodifying and packaging Malaysia for foreign consumption ('Malaysia Truly Asia') consistently features four glamorous women representatives from the four essentialised ethnic/'race' groups commonly identified within a society that some have described as hyper-ethnicised (Martinez 2003). This campaign locates women as the symbolic keepers of culture and of the harmonious interweaving of the Asian continent's greatest civilisations within Malaysia. A further Islamic modern imaginary operates powerfully for Muslims.

The last few decades have seen a thoroughgoing Islamicisation of Malaysia, arising from developments in Islam internationally and the growth of Islamic organisations, especially *dakwah* (missionary) groups locally. This Islamicisation was also championed by the state in its quest for modernity. The state established a well-endowed Islamic think tank, the Malaysian Institute for Islamic Under-standing (IKIM), designed to shape an Islamic work ethic (see Nagata 1994). Other initiatives have included the development of Islamic banking and Islamic industrialisation. There have also been many campaigns against forms of enter-tainment considered un-Islamic, including 'traditional' Malay song and dance forms, and controversial attempts in the states of Kelantan and Terengganu to introduce Islamic criminal law (*hudud*). The previous prime minister, Mahathir Mohamad, however, and the present one, Abdullah Badawi, have both been keen to present Malaysia in a post- 11 September 2001 world as the very model of a modern, 'moderate' Muslim nation.

As part of research projects on new Malay middle classes and Malaysian modernity with Joel Kahn,[11] I carried out intensive interviews with forty house-holds in Penang and Kuala Lumpur. Over a quarter were overt supporters of versions of revivalism, a figure which echoes national figures for the new middle classes as a whole at the time. I have suggested elsewhere that my middle-class informants' narratives present what can be seen as evidence for a postmodern-isation of Muslim identity and of Islamic practices within the shifting complexes of meaning surrounding the idea of an Islamic modernity in Malaysia (Stivens 2006). It is commonly argued that radical Islam derives its support from those who feel socially dislocated, but my informants fit a pattern of middle-class embrace of such 'fundamentalisms' globally. These informants have been offered, taken up, and created a range of positionings within the recent Islamisation of the country, from adherence to revivalism, to reformist 'liberal' Islam, to somewhat more secular modernism, and even to repudiation of religion (the latter being a highly problematic position, possibly attracting apostasy charges (Stivens 2006)). Modernity and religion were mutually constituted within many narratives: a number saw being a proper Muslim as the only way to be(come) modern in a way that removed them from a difficult positioning as 'Western', a particular issue for women.

These dramatic economic and political changes have reshaped the spaces within which Malaysian women can act politically as gendered agents. A wider push for reform has produced rights claims made on the state and on sections of 'civil society' for a complex array of women's rights. The *Reformasi* (reform) movement which arose in the late 1990s, however, has stalled badly. Women's claims have faced especially complex terrains, which have included: ethnonationalist pressures around a revivified Islam among Malays, that have defined the spaces available to women for such contestation; a complex politics of meaning around the many imaginaries of the modern; extensive support for ideas about an alternative 'Asian way' to becoming modern; and the tangled and often tense relationships among a range of women's NGOs themselves, in which discourses of 'ethnic' belonging and divisions have been central. There have been clear divisions between those conceiving of rights in more universalist terms, mostly left-leaning, 'progressive' non-Malay organisations, and those embracing more culturally particularist aims (Stivens 2003). An important area of activism has been the long-term, concerted campaigns seeking trans-ethnic coalitions among women over a number of years in the 1990s: one prominent example is the successful campaign for new laws relating to domestic and sexual violence (see Lai 2003; Martinez 2003).

In 1999 a number of Malaysian women's groups, in an explicitly proactive move, built on an earlier (1990) Women's Manifesto to draft a detailed eleven-point document, the Women's Agenda for Change (WAC). The coalition of women's groups was drawn from all the major ethnic groups and their respective organisations, including Jamaah Islah Malaysia (Wanita JIM), a Muslim women's organisation, Sisters In Islam, a reformist women's group working for women's rights within Islam (SIS), which I shall look at below, [the] All Women's Action Society (AWAM), Persatuan Sahabat Wanita Selangor (PSWS, a support group for women workers), Malaysian Trade Union Congress (Women [*sic*] Section), the Women's Development Collective (WDC, a 'progressive' women's group) and the Selangor Chinese Assembly Hall (Women [*sic*] Section). The eleven sections in the Women's Agenda for Change (WAC) looked at the relationships between women and: development, participatory democracy, religion and culture, violence against women, land, health services, the law, work, Aids, environment, and sexuality.

The declared aims of the women's groups were to:

1. Draw attention to specific problems, issues and needs of women which should be recognised and addressed;
2. Raise awareness of women and men on the position of women in Malaysia;
3. Strengthen the political participation and voices of women in Malaysia so as to promote and achieve gender equality and to work for a just and democratic society; and strengthen a network of women's organisations and NGOs to work towards the advancement of the status of women in Malaysia.

The epigraph at the beginning of this chapter highlights the way the WAC document deplores the manipulation of ethnicity and religion and the use of fear and oppressive forces to divide women. 'We want to contribute towards the building of a just, democratic and peaceful society for ourselves and future generations'.

The women sent the document to 192 members of parliament, asking them to endorse it and raise its issues as part of their election platforms. But the response was poor (Martinez 2003; Derichs 2005). Although Malaysia's political parties have a female membership of around 50 per cent, only seven members out of the 192 replied. Seeking an alternative strategy, the women planned an initiative to increase women's representation in parliament, the Women's Candidacy Initiative (WCI), launched in September 1999, which garnered a number of votes.[12]

These rights claims can be seen as evidence for a growing willingness by a range of women's NGOs to make local versions of more 'universalist/universalising' rights claims (see Stivens 2003). The term 'rights' within women's activism in Malaysia has been elusive, highly contested and deployed in a series of shifting meanings by a range of political actors (Stivens 2000a, 2003). But, as the WAC organisation website shows, some of these actors have explicitly rejected the contentions of local leaders that human rights is a 'Western' concept. Their initiative instead resonates with liberal universalist discourses on human rights and democracy (cf. Martinez 2000, 2003). While Malaysia has recently seen a considerable rise in ethnic tensions, which is distressing to the many cosmopolitan-minded NGOs, nonetheless such moves towards '[human] rights' can also be understood as clearly reinventing ideas of rights, joining both local and more global turns to mediated, grounded or rooted neo-universalisms (Stivens 2000a, 2003).

Sisters in Islam

Some of these dialogues can be illustrated by looking at the tactics and experiences of one prominent constituent group of the WAC coalition, Sisters in Islam (SIS). A small group of professional tertiary-educated women, including anthropologist Norani Othman, SIS was formed in 1988. It has had a large impact nationally, and within feminist circles globally, receiving many overseas invitations to speak and holding a very successful workshop at the Beijing Women's Conference in 1995. The group has very self-consciously positioned itself as part of an internationalist movement working for a social justice agenda within Islam.[13] SIS 'believes in an Islam that upholds the principles of equality, justice, freedom and dignity.' Their stated mission is 'to promote the rights of Muslim women ... based on the principles of equality, justice and freedom enjoined by the Qur'an as made evident during our study of the holy text' (http://www.sistersinislam.org.my/). Their key objectives are:

• To promote and develop a framework of women's rights in Islam, which takes into consideration women's experiences and realities;
• To eliminate injustice and discrimination against women by changing practices and values that regard women as inferior to men;
• To create public awareness, and reform laws and policies, on issues of equality, justice, freedom, dignity and democracy in Islam (see the SIS website http://www.sistersinislam.org.my/).

The group has operated very strategically: they have prepared submissions to pressure government (see these listed on its website), organised important conferences on Shari'a law, *hudud* (Islamic criminal law) and Islam, Reproductive Health and Women's Rights and made other interventions, especially with conservative religious forces, all designed to contribute to a 'more informed public debate on topical issues of concern'. The regular study sessions they run are an important site for many interested liberals – mostly women and including many non-Muslims – to talk about burning topical issues. It is significant that their key concentration on Islamic family law engages with matters concerning the 'family' which are both specific to Muslim women but also link to non-Muslim concerns about the domestic sphere. In Malaya under the colonial regime, family law for Muslims became the main site for the operation of Islamic law.

SIS's main strategy has been to engage Malaysian society in a highly reflexive and participatory process of 'cultural' mediation or dialogue by constructing women as the subject of more communitarian, culturally particularist claims to rights.[14] They contrast this to the 'secular' approach of arguing for rights on the basis of universal claims to human rights (Othman 1999). Scholar-activist members like Norani Othman have provided sharply conceptualised programmes which involve finding sources for women's rights and internationally recognised human rights in the local Muslim 'culture' and religious teachings, while also questioning the meanings and implications of dominant cultural norms within an explicit attachment to ideas of women's rights as human rights.

It is important to note that Malaysian Muslim women were rarely given public speaking positions as religious 'experts' in the past. SIS members have energetic-ally sought time and space as public intellectuals to debate important religious issues in media fora like television panel discussion shows. Ong argues that they have sought to widen that space for debates about Islamic truths by an educated Muslim public (2006: 43). We can argue for what one might term an Islamic, cosmopolitan reimagining of rights as inherent in the Sisters' project, negotiated within tense, delicate, and constantly shifting engagements with both a repressive 'soft-authoritarian' state and religious authorities (Stivens 2003).

It is significant that Malaysian women activists have come together attempting to transcend 'ethnic' divisions, especially in relation to key issues like domestic violence against women: they have mobilised 'local' versions of overtly modern ideas of rights, democracy and gender equality within campaigns to advance feminist/womanist identity politics, including within Islamic practices; these ideas have their origins in the specifically situated, rooted histories and politics of local forms of modernity. In spite of the misgivings shared by many NGOs about the language of 'women's [human] rights' (Stivens 2003), the scrolling banner on the SIS website reads 'Visit Rights at Home Website: An Approach to an Internalization of Human Rights in Family Relations in Islamic Communities.' It is especially significant, perhaps, that such initiatives have come from Muslim-identified groups reaching out to other groups. Not only SIS, but some more 'conservative' Islamic women's organisations opposed to the government have also attached themselves to ideas of democracy and justice (Mohamad 2003). Such seeking after rights is clearly to be understood as part of a long, rich history of dialogue and negotiation by Malaysian women's organisations with local nationalist, reformist and radical discourses and global discourses on (human) rights, equality, justice and democracy.

The specificities of local rights discourses and claims illustrate some of the slippages between apparently universalistic, ethical notions and their long-term historical reworkings in local contexts (see discussion in Stivens 2000a). SIS's highly reflexive strategy of making mediated claims for rights underlines the argument that it is possible to transcend some of the polarities of the debates about universalism versus particularism and cultural relativism within global feminist politics by looking at how claims to rights are embedded – 'rooted' or 'grounded' – in situated, specific local contexts and struggles (cf. Stivens 2000a).

At the same time, SIS face everyday pressures in their advocacy that are considerably more complex than dualistic accounts of 'conservatives' versus 'liberal' religious polarities might suggest. It is clear that the group has been useful to – and explicitly drawn upon by – the government at some points in its conflicts with PAS (*Parti Islam SeMalaysia*), the Islamist party, as a voice of 'moderate' Islam. Until the 2004 elections PAS had made headway in the north-eastern states of Malaysia. (It is also the case that PAS had an uneasy relationship for some time within the opposition Reformasi alliance.) But SIS has also been fielding accusations voiced during the ruling party UMNO (United Malays National Organisation)'s general assembly in November 2006 that SIS is 'against Islam'. The ways in which the Sisters have constructed women as the subject of more communitarian, culturally particularist claims to rights may have been well received – indeed co-opted – prior to this by both elements within the authoritarian, anti-Western government and by some sections of the larger Malaysian public. But one can also question the level of popular support for SIS. Ong suggests that SIS should not be dismissed or marginalised for accommodating Islamic ethics and paternalistic nationalism in forging gendered citizenship (2006: 51). The members of SIS and of other women's organisations were cynical about the appeals to women made explicitly in the last election campaign in 2004. But these appeals also pointed to the state apparatus mobilising gender relations as a key site for national politics (see Mohamad 2003), which will further constrain the spaces available for feminist politics (cf. Stivens 2003, Mohamad 2003). By the time of the 2004 election, for example, it is reported that a Barisan Nasional (BN, the ruling government coalition) advertisement 'screamed' ... 'A Yes to BN is A Yes to Women's Rights' (Hassan 2004). Attracting women's votes had clearly moved onto novel ground in Malaysia.

The SIS project illustrates the problems Malaysian women's groups have had in constructing spaces within which effectively to lay claims. The WAC and WCI contributed a strongly gendered dimension to the Reformasi democratisation process. This further complexified the dialogue between gendered rights and democracy. Some see gains, including the appointment of a new minister of women's affairs (she is now the Minister of Women and Family Development, after a change of ministry name). The government and conservative religious forces, however, can be seen as defining the 'public' very much within clearly delimited boundaries, which are closely tied to the problems for the state apparatus in managing opposition ideologies, activities and identities. Given all this and a surge in ethnic conflicts in 2006, many women activists are quite pessimistic about the possibilities for Malay women to contest women's place from within these circumscribed discursive and political spaces. Nonetheless, the participatory processes of 'cultural' mediation may on occasion be highly effective in relation to the wider public in the organisation's refusal of the opposition between 'universalism' and a relativist concept of 'culture'.

The middle-class character of such NGOs, and their close links to global feminist circuits, agendas and funding are key factors. Malaysian women's movement struggles have been increasingly linked to the 'global feminist counter public' proposed above (Stivens 2000a). Members of many NGOs have sizeable engagements with cosmopolitan global networks, operating on a global stage. Local Malaysian commentaries on the women's movement in the country, however, tend to be quite parochial, concentrating on internal processes and politics, not least the 'ethnic' divisions that so dominate Malaysian political practices and spaces. This is understandable, but overlooks the considerable international prominence of SIS, for example. There is widespread enthusiasm for the SIS project within global feminist and some Muslim reform circles. Moreover, its presence on the Internet, an increasingly critical site for such politics-making, both nationally and internationally, is also crucial: all the pamphlets and documents it produces are available online. This global presence – cosmopolitan in several senses of the term – is significant for understanding the nature of its ideas, practices and constituencies, and of emerging forms of Islamic feminism in general.

How might we characterise the cosmopolitan subjectivity of the Malaysian women's movement members discussed? Arguably, they can aptly be termed rooted, grounded cosmopolitans in several senses. They invoke universal notions of equality and human rights in seeking gender justice, but in the process also actively reconfigure such ideas of rights. The earlier campaigners for domestic violence laws (see Amirthalingam 2003) and the Women's Agenda for Change in particular have sought transethnic alliances within national political activism, proactively seeking dialogue across a hyperethnicised divide. In so doing, they follow a common pattern in contemporary feminist and womanist practices: of strategic alliances rather than a unified struggle around a universally shared interest or identity (Fraser and Nicholson 1990 [1981]: 35). Many members, of course, are also mostly cosmopolitanism in the elite sense of the word, frequent international travellers, and conversant with the esoterica of new global middle classes.

The nature of the Islamic national and transnational worlds in which Sisters in Islam operates is of particular interest. I have suggested that SIS imagine, draw on, and in the process further develop, a highly reflexive Islamic cosmopolitanism. It is clear that they have successfully created multilayered and complex, highly gendered cosmopolitan spaces with robust links to global feminist and womanist cosmopolitan spaces. They articulate a global discourse of women's rights that at the same time is grounded in a clear understanding of the need to deal with the situated specificities of local 'culture'. As suggested, these global spaces may usefully be termed an international counter-public, a cosmopolitan space insepar-able from globalisation or globalism. It is especially significant that Muslim womanists – their preferred term – (personal communication, Norani Othman) are part of a transnational world of Islamic feminism; their location in Southeast Asia puts them at the crossroads of multiple historically important transnational flows.

This raises a further key question: some of these spaces traverse those within which operate groupings that Olivier Roy (2004) terms neofundamentalists and radical neofundamentalists:[15] both seek 'a pure Islamic countermodernity' or what Juan Cole calls an alternative [Islamic] modernity (2003: 771). Anthony Appiah (2006) wants to nominate the radical neofundamentalists as counter-cosmopolitan. In so doing it is arguable that he is echoing the dominant geopolitical representa-tions of a dualistic clash of civilisations between the supposedly particularistic 'tradition' of the 'Islamic' world and the supposedly pure universalism of the 'Western' world (Kahn 2006; Roy 2004). Joel Kahn repudiates the Appiah view, arguing for understanding these fundamentalists as cosmopolitans. While the neofundamentalists' search for universal justice for the *ummah* (the worldwide 'community' of Muslims that today is itself very much a product of globalisation) perhaps marks it off from the Sisters' search for gender justice within the *ummah* and beyond, its cosmopolitanism is nonetheless an issue.[16]

Concluding Points

I have been asking why the cosmopolitanism literature has seemed so uninter-ested in questions of gender, and in turn why some feminist scholarship has been wary about appropriating the c-word. I have suggested that gendered readings have much to offer the recent cosmopolitan debates: they point us to significant sites for exploring questions of cosmopolitanism in its many meanings (Nava: 2006:46), and offer many lessons for the theoretical, political and moral projects of cosmopolitanisms. I have asked in particular why the women's movements of the last few decades have so little presence in the malestream cosmopolitanism literature, suggesting both habits of neglectfulness and theoretical awkwardnesses as factors, and exploring one case, the Malaysian women's movement. I also proposed that we might think further about the ways in which the historically contingent intimate and domestic can configure cosmopolitan spaces and practices.

Appiah hopes that the concept of cosmopolitanism can be rescued (2006: xx): he wants to make it harder to divide the world between the West and the rest, locals and moderns, 'us' and 'them' (2006: xxi). In this chapter, I have been concerned with how the gendering of these debates can contribute to this 'rescue'.

The concept 'cosmopolitanism' has multiple politicised, contested, elusive, even fanciful meanings, and has attracted many critiques, some of them from feminists, as noted, including accusations of universalism, essentialism, ethnocentricity and imperialism. Nonetheless there is an argument to be made for placing gender at the heart of notions of rooted or grounded cosmopolitanism in order to promote Appiah's project. Nava insists with Rege (2003) that cosmopolitanism must always be understood as a historically contingent, geographically specific formation (2006: 43). I have been arguing here that feminist perspectives offer this project many possible insights from their theoretical and practical engagements with the issues that so concern the cosmopolitanism debates: exploring the grounded, rooted, gendered relations and imaginaries within the workings of cosmopolitanisms might well play a fruitful part in developing such understandings.

Notes

1. See Women's Agenda for Change, Malaysia website (http://wa4change.tripod. com/index.htm), for gender, public and private and rights claims within the Malaysian women's movement.
2. See Vertovec and Cohen (2002) and the *British Journal of Sociology* special issue on cosmopolitanism (March 2006). Beck and Sznaider mention gender just once (2006: 20).
3. I am grateful to Maree Pardy for this point.
4. See Mohanty et al. (1991) Mohanty (2003) for discussions of these debates.
5. See, however, Yuval-Davis's (2006) reflection on this, including issues with human rights parallel to those raised in Stivens (2000a).
6. See, for example, Adams and Dickey (2000), Chin (1998), Constable (1997), Ehrenreich and Hochschild (2003), Parreñas (2001a, 2001b), and Yeoh and Huang (1999).
7. It is estimated that between 35 and 54 per cent of the Philippines population is sustained by remittances (Parreñas 2001a, 2001b).
8. See Stivens (2007a) for a discussion of the internationalisation and post-modernisation of mothering in Asia.
9. See Hilsdon, Mackie, Macintyre and Stivens (2000).
10. See Stivens (1998b, 2000b).
11. Australian Research Council funding is gratefully acknowledged for the projects: *Work and Family in the New Malay Middle Classes* (1990–1993), *Public and Private: Gender and Southeast Asian Modernities* (1995–1996), and *Inventing the 'Asian Family': Gender, Globalisation and Cultural*

Contest in Southeast Asia (2000–2002). I am also extremely grateful to Goh Beng Lan, Jomo Sundaram, Joel Kahn, Azizah Kassim, Clive Kessler, Norani Othman, and Ikmal Muhd Said for much help. Particular thanks for research assistance to Hah Foong Lian and Zainab Wahidin, Lucy Healey, Linda Pang, Nur Amali Ibrahim, Zarinah Ali, Lester Chua, Ro Yule, Nicki Tarulevicz, Elizabeth Nelson and Satia Zen. Many thanks too to the Asia Research Institute, National University of Singapore, and its Director Professor Anthony Reid, who hosted a visiting fellowship in 2004.

12. See http://www.candidate.freeservers.com/object.html, for WCI history and activities; and Martinez (2003).
13. See Wadud-Muhsin (1992) for an account of this movement.
14. See Aihwa Ong's approving account (1996).
15. Roy sees a division within neofundamentalism between the mainstream and radicals – the latter advocating jihad and violence as an individual act (2004: 254).
16. It is interesting that 'Islamic cosmopolitanism' has a large scholarly presence.

References

Adams, Kathleen M. and Sara Dickey (eds) (2000), *Home and Hegemony: Domestic Service and Identity Politics in South and Southeast Asia*, Ann Arbor: University of Michigan Press.

Amirthalingam, Kumaralingam (2003), 'A Feminist Critique of Domestic Violence Laws in Singapore and Malaysia', Asia Research Institute, National University of Singapore, Working papers no 6, July, http://www.ari.nus.edu.sg/docs/wps/wps03_006.pdf (accessed 13 March 2006).

Anthias, Floya and Nira Yuval-Davis (1984), 'Contextualizing Feminism: Ethnic, Gender and Class Divisions', *Feminist Review* 15: 62–75.

Appiah, Kwame Anthony (1997), 'Cosmopolitan Patriots', *Critical Inquiry* 23 (3): 617–39.

—— (2006), *Cosmopolitanism: Ethics in a World of Strangers*. NY, London: W.W. Norton.

Beck, Ulrich (2004), 'The Truth of Others: A Cosmopolitan Approach', *Common Knowledge*, 10 (3): 430–39.

Beck, Ulrich and Natan Sznaider (2006), 'Unpacking Cosmopolitanism for the Social Sciences: a Research Agenda', Special Issue on Cosmopolitanism, *British Journal of Sociology* 57 (1): 1–23.

Chin, Christine B.N. (1998), *In Service and Servitude: Foreign Female Domestic Workers and the Malaysian Modernity Project*, New York/Chichester: Columbia University Press.

Cole, Juan R.I. (2003), 'The Taliban, Women, and the Hegelian Private Sphere', *Social Research, Part III: Individual, Family, Community, and State* 70 (3): 771–808.

Constable, Nicole (1997), *Maid to Order in Hong Kong: Stories of Filipina Workers*, Ithaca, NY: Cornell University Press.

Cornwall, Andrea (2001), 'Making a Difference? Gender and Participatory Development', IDS Discussion Papers 378, Institute of Development Studies, http://www.ids.ac.uk/ids/bookshop/dp/dp378.pdf (accessed 1 May 2005).

Derichs, Claudia (2005), 'Strategy, Action, Transition: Women as Agents of Change', Project Discussion Paper No. 14, Universität Duisburg-Essen und Universität Erlangen-Nürnberg.

Douzinas, Costas (2003), 'Humanity, Military Humanism and the New Moral Order', *Economy and Society* 32 (2): 159–83.

Ehrenreich, Barbara and Arlie Russell Hochschild (2003), 'Introduction', in Barbara Ehrenreich and Arlie Russell Hochschild (eds), *Global Woman: Nannies, Maids, and Sex Workers in the New Economy*, New York: Metropolitan Books, pp. 1–14.

Eschle, Catherine (2001), *Global Democracy, Social Movements, and Feminism*, Boulder, CO: Westview.

Felski, Rita (1995), *The Gender of Modernity*, Cambridge, Mass.: Harvard University Press.

Fraser, Nancy (1997), *Justice Interruptus: Critical Reflections on the 'Post-socialist' Condition*, London: Routledge.

Fraser, Nancy and Linda J. Nicholson (1990 [1988]), 'Social Criticism Without Philosophy: An Encounter Between Feminism and Postmodemism', in Linda J. Nicholson (ed.) *Feminism/Postmodernism*, London: Routledge, pp. 19–38, (reprinted from *Theory, Culture and Society* 5, 1988: 373–94).

Hassan, Saliha (2004), 'Women in the 2004 Malaysian General Election', see http://www.google.com.au/search?q=cache:pH0NyPjy5uoJ:phuakl.tripod. com/pssm/womeninelection2004.doc+%22saliha+hassan%22+%2B+women &hl=en (accessed 31 May 2004).

Hilsdon, Anne-Marie, Martha Macintyre, Vera Mackie and Maila Stivens (eds), *Human Rights and Gender Politics: Asia Pacific Perspectives*, London: Routledge, pp. 1–36.

Kahn, Joel S. (2006), 'Other Cosmopolitans: Islam versus Culture in the Malay Worlds', paper prepared for ASA Diamond Jubilee Conference 2006 – 'Cosmopolitanism and Anthropology', University of Keele, 10–13 April.

Lai, Suat Yan (2003), 'The Women's Movement in Peninsular Malaysia', in Meredith Weiss and Saliha Hassan (eds), *Social Movements in Malaysia: From Moral Communities to NGOs*, London: Routledge, pp. 46–74.

Lister, Ruth (2003), *Citizenship: Feminist Perspectives*, 2nd edn, Basingstoke: Palgrave.

Marshall, Barbara L. (1994), *Engendering Modernity: Feminism, Social Theory and Social Change*, Cambridge: Polity Press.

Martinez, Patricia (2000), 'From Margin to Center: Theorizing Women's Political Participation from Activism on the Margins to Political Power at the Center', see http://www.philanthropy.org/GN/KEN/gntext/politicalrights_women_power_patricia.htm (accessed 7 February 2002).

—— (2001), 'The Islamic State or the State of Islam in Malaysia', *Contemporary Southeast Asia* 23 (3): 474–503.

—— (2003), 'Complex Configurations: The Women's Agenda for Change and the Women's Candidacy Initiative', in Meredith Weiss and Saliha Hassan (eds), *Social Movements in Malaysia : From Moral Communities to NGOs*, London: Routledge Curzon, pp. 75–96.

Mohamad, Maznah (2003), 'Shifting Interests and Identities: The Politics of Gender, Ethnicity and Democratisation in Malaysia', in Maxine Molyneux and Shahra Razavi (eds), *Gender Justice, Development, and Rights*, Oxford: Oxford University Press, pp. 347–83.

Mohanty, Chandra T. (2003), '"Under Western Eyes" Revisited: Feminist Solidarity Through Anticapitalist Struggles', *Signs* 28 (2): 499–535.

Mohanty, Chandra T, Anne Russo and Lourdes Torres (eds) (1991), *Third World Women and the Politics of Feminism*, Bloomington IN: Indiana University Press.

Nagata, Judith. A. (1994), 'How to Be Islamic Without Being an Islamic State: Contested Models of Development in Malaysia', in Akbar Ahmed and Hastings Donnan (eds), *Islam, Globalization and Postmodernity*, London/New York, pp. 63–87.

Nava, Mica (2002), 'Cosmopolitan Modernity: Everyday Imaginaries and the Register of Difference', *Theory Culture & Society* 19 (1–2): 81–99.

—— (2003), 'Visceral Cosmopolitanism: The Specificity of Race and Miscegenation in UK', *Politics and Culture* 3, see http://aspen.conncoll.edu/politicsandculture/page.cfm?key=255.

—— (2006), 'Domestic Cosmopolitanism and Structures of Feeling: The Specificity of London', in Nira Yuval-Davis, Kalpana Kannabiran and Ulrike Vieten (eds), *The Situated Politics of Belonging*, London: Sage, pp. 42–53.

Nussbaum, Martha (1994), 'Patriotism and Cosmopolitanism', *Boston Review* 19 (5): 3–9.

Ong, A. (1996), 'Strategic Sisterhood or Sisters in Solidarity?: Questions of Communitarianism and Citizenship in Asia', *Global Legal Studies Journal* 4 (1), (http://www.indiana.edu/glsj/vol4/no1/ongpgp.html, accessed 11 August 1999).

—— (2006), *Neoliberalism as Exception: Mutations in Citizenship and Sovereignty*, Durham NC: Duke University Press.

Othman, Norani (1999), 'Grounding Human Rights Arguments in Non-western Culture: Shari'a and the Citizenship Rights of Women in a Modern Islamic State', in J.R. Bauer and D.B. Bell (eds), *The East Asian Challenge for Human Rights*, Cambridge: Cambridge University Press, pp. 169–92.

Parreñas, Rhacel S. (2001a), 'Mothering from a Distance: Emotions, Gender, and Intergenerational Relations in Filipino Transnational Families', *Feminist Studies*, 27: 361–90.

—— (2001b), *Servants of Globalization: Women, Migration, and Domestic Work*, Stanford: Stanford University Press.

Pollock, Sheldon, Homi K. Bhabha, Carol A. Breckenridge and Dipesh Chakrabarty (2000) 'Cosmopolitanisms', Introduction to Special Issue on 'Cosmopolitanism', *Public Culture* 12 (3): 577–89.

Rege, Josna (2003), 'Women and the New Cosmopolitanism', Curricular Crossings: Women's Studies and Area Studies, Five College Women's Studies Research Center, http://womencrossing.org/rege.html (accessed 24 April 2004).

Roy, Olivier (2004), *Globalized Islam: The Search for a New Ummah*, New York: Columbia University Press.

Ruddick, Sarah (1989), *Maternal Thinking: Towards a Politics of Peace*, London: Women's Press.

Sassen, Saskia (2003), 'Global Cities and Survival Circuits', in Barbara Ehrenreich and Arlie R. Hochschild (eds), *Global Woman: Nannies, Maids, and Sex Workers in the New Economy*, New York: Metropolitan Books, pp. 254–74.

Stivens, Maila (1998a), 'Sex, Gender and the Making of the Malay Middle Class', in Krishna Sen and Maila Stivens (eds), *Gender and Power in Affluent Asia*, London: Routledge, pp. 86–126.

—— (1998b), 'Introduction: Theoretical Perspectives on Sex and Power in Affluent Asia' in Krishna Sen and Maila Stivens (eds), *Gender and Power in Affluent Asia*, London: Routledge, pp. 1–34.

—— (2000a), 'Introduction: Gender Politics and the Reimagining of Human Rights in the Asia Pacific', in Anne-Marie Hilsdon, Martha Macintyre, Vera Mackie and Maila Stivens (eds), *Human Rights and Gender Politics: Asia Pacific Perspectives*, London: Routledge, pp. 1–36.

—— (2000b), 'Becoming Modern in Malaysia: Women at the End of the Twentieth Century', in Louise Edwards and Mina Roces (eds), *Women in Asia: Tradition, Modernity and Globalisation*, Michigan: University of Michigan Press, pp. 16–38.

—— (2003), '(Re)-Framing Women's Rights Claims in Malaysia', in Virginia Hooker and Noraini Othman (eds), *Malaysia: Islam, Society and Politics, Essays in Honour of Clive Kessler*, Singapore: Institute of Southeast Asian Studies, pp. 126–46.

—— (2006), '"Family Values" and Islamic Revival: Gender, Rights and State Moral Projects in Malaysia', *Women's Studies International Forum*, Special Double Issue on 'Human Rights, Gender and Islam', 29 (4): 354–67.

—— (2007a), 'Postmodern Motherhoods and Cultural Contest in Malaysia and Singapore', in Theresa W. Devasahayam and Brenda S.A. Yeoh (eds), *Working and Mothering in Asia: Images, Ideologies and Identities*, Singapore: Singapore University Press, pp. 29–50.

—— (2007b), 'Gendering Asia', in Helle Rydstrøm, Cecilia Milwertz and Wil Burghoorn (eds), *Gendering Asia*, Washington: Washington University Press.

Veer, Peter van der (2004), 'Cosmopolitan Options', in Jonathan Friedman and Shalini Randeria (eds), *Worlds on the Move: Globalization, Migration and Cultural Security*, London: I.B. Tauris, in association with the Toda Institute for Global Peace and Policy Research, pp. 167–78.

Vertovec, Steven and Robin Cohen (eds), (2002), *Conceiving Cosmopolitanism: Theory, Context, and Practice*, Oxford/New York: Oxford University Press.

Wadud-Muhsin, Amina (1992), *Qur'an and Woman*, Kuala Lumpur: Penerbit Ajar Bakti.

Werbner, Pnina, (1999a), 'Global Pathways: Working Class Cosmopolitans and the Creation of Transnational Ethnic Worlds' *Social Anthropology* 7 (1): 17–35.

—— (1999b), 'Political Motherhood and the Feminisation of Citizenship: Women's Activisms and the Transformation of the Public Sphere', in Nira Yuval-Davis and Pnina Werbner (eds), *Women, Citizenship and Difference*, London: Zed Books, pp. 221–45.

—— (2004), 'Cosmopolitans, Anthropologists and Labour Migrants: Deconstructing Transnational Cultural Promiscuity', Proceedings of the Asia Research Institute Workshop on Identities, Nations and Cosmopolitan Practice: Interrogating the Work of Pnina and Richard Werbner, sponsored by the Asia Research Institute at the National University of Singapore, 29 April, see http://www.ari.nus.edu.sg/docs/Monograph.pdf (accessed 24 April 2006).

Women's Agenda for Change (1999), see http://wa4change.tripod.com/index.htm (accessed 24 April 2004).

World Bank (2005), 'Global Outlook and the Developing Countries', in *GEP 2005*, New York: World Bank, pp. 1–25.

Yeoh, Brenda S.A. and Shirlena Huang (1999), 'Singapore Women and Foreign Domestic Workers: Negotiating Domestic Work and Motherhood', in Janet Momsen (ed.), *Gender, Migration, and Domestic Service*, New York: Routledge, pp. 277–300.

Yuval-Davis, Nira (1997), *Gender and Nation*, London: Sage.

—— (2006 [2004]), 'Human/Women's Rights and Feminist Transversal Politics', in Myra Marx Ferree and Aili M. Tripp (eds), *Global Feminism: Transnational Women's Activism, Organizing, and Human Rights*, New York: New York University Press, pp. 275–312 (originally given as Lecture 2 in the Bristol Lecture Series on the Politics of Belonging, June 2004, pp. 275–295).

–6–

Islamic Cosmopolitics, Human Rights and Anti-Violence Strategies in Indonesia
Kathryn Robinson

Introduction

Indonesia, the nation with the world's largest Islamic population, has been undergoing a process of continuous conversion since the thirteenth century. Like most of the Muslim world, Indonesian Muslims have engaged with the global Islamic renewal following the Iranian revolution. Since the authoritarian, centralising ruler Suharto was forced to resign in 1998, Indonesia designates itself as in a period of Reform (*Reformasi*) where competing visions for the form of the state and its fundamental values are in contestation. Political Islam, with philosophical (and sometimes organisational and financial) links to the Middle East – for example, the ideas of the Muslim Brotherhood and its offshoots – and a movement for gender equity, are important fractions in this emergent political flux.

The influence of reform traditions arising in the Middle East is not something new in Indonesia: Islamic modernism developed through the embrace of the ideas of Muhamad Abduh in the late nineteenth and early twentieth century.[1] Like earlier waves of Islam, the influences were expressed in a variety of organisational forms and through local debates and contestations. By the third decade of the twentieth century, Indonesian Islam had a political face, firmly harnessed to the anti-colonial and increasingly nationalist movement, and both the 'traditionalist' and 'modernist' strands of Indonesian Islam gave rise to political parties which competed in the free elections of the 1950s, in the new republic (Feith 1962).

Islamism is popularly associated with quintessentially communitarian politics, valorising the collective identity of the *ummah* over non-believers. However, for significant sectors of the contemporary Indonesian Islamic community, Islam is associated with cosmopolitan values, here understood as a commitment to 'the human' as 'a complex singularity over and above proximal categorisations and identifications of nation, ethnicity, class, religion, gender, locale and so on' (Rapport 2006: 23), a commitment to 'planetary conviviality' (Mignolo 2000:721) which in Indonesia is expressed in a commitment to 'pluralism'.[2] In contemporary

Indonesian politics, there is a significant Muslim voice that asserts that Islam provides an authentic path to democracy, equity and social justice, arising out of humanistic ideals that express Qur'anic values; an alternative path to Western post-Enlightenment political ideologies.[3] In this chapter, I examine emergent positions in Islamic feminism in Indonesia, which draw inspiration from a global Islamic movement for gender equity associated with the names of scholars such as Fatima Mernissi, Riffat Hassan, Asghar Ali Engineer and Amina Wadud. This contemporary form of Islamic practice utilises hermeneutic readings of Islamic texts that support the idea of Islam as a basis for gender equity.[4]

In Indonesia, the Islamic pro-democracy and gender equity positions claim political space alongside a secular nationalist ideology associated with the founding president of the republic, Sukarno, that claims the ideals of democracy, social justice and humanitarianism as autochthonous Indonesian values, rather than ascribing them a singular history as post-Enlightenment, post-French revolutionary ideas, and rejects the neofundamentalist (and neoconservative) proposition of a basic conflict between Islam and the West as two opposing civilisations (*peradaban*). There is a growing group of Indonesian Islamic scholars (men and women) trained in Arabic and the formal skills of Qur'anic exegesis who claim their legitimacy to arrive at original interpretations of the Qur'an and Sunnah; that is, they challenge the literal textual interpretations associated with neofundamentalist groups (which they describe as '*Islam keras*' or 'stern/hard Islam'), and the presumed centrality assumed by the Arabic-speaking Middle East in the Islamic world. They use the language of Western textual critique – terms like deconstruction and reconstruction – to describe their interpretive practices, although these encompass the body of interpretive practices specific to Islam, as I show below. Islamic feminism, an important strand within this movement, 'makes the teaching of Islam the foundation for examining the position and role of women' (Munir 1999: 5).

Whereas, from the point of view of the Middle East, Southeast Asia is regarded as marginal to Islamic orthodoxy (Martinez 2005: 137), there is a school of indigenous Indonesian Islamic intellectuals who promote '*Islam Pribumi*' or indigenous/vernacular Islam as a legitimate variant (Rahman et al. 2003), and contrast it with 'Middle Eastern' and 'Westernised' Islam (pers. comm., Ciciek Farha 2006). *Islam pribumi* is committed to social equity (including gender equity), human rights, tolerance and pluralism, and these values are regarded as having Islamic and indigenous roots. These thinkers (for example, former president Abdurrachman Wahid (1999–2001)) position themselves in opposition to a global Islamism and a 'generic transnational Islamic identity' (Bubalo and Fealy 2005: viii) which originates in the Middle East.

Islam pribumi is particularly associated with the so-called 'traditionalist' Islam of the country's largest Islamic organisation, the Nahdlatul Ulama (henceforth NU).[5]

They have been termed 'traditional' because they endorse the accommodation of Islam to local cultural practices, (and Sufi influences) and reject the modernist/ fundamentalist endeavour to 'purify' Indonesian Islam. Claiming a voice that (bowdlerising Mignolo) is a 'cosmopolitanism from the margins', they argue for a uniquely Indonesian variant of Islam, which is nonetheless true to the essential spirit of the Qur'an, arising from the specifically Indonesian embrace of the universal values contained in Islam. While to an outsider their practices may appear as accommodation to Western liberalism, so that their neofundamentalist critics accuse them of corruption by the poison of Western thought, the political doctrine of *Islam pribumi* appears to have an organic connection to the political ideology of Indonesia's radical nationalist founding president, Sukarno, encapsulated in the idea of the Panca Sila or Five Principles that are formally accepted as the ideological basis of the Indonesian state. The Sila are usually glossed in English as Monotheism, Humanitarianism, Democracy, Social Justice and National Unity. Sukarno asserted these as autochthonous values of the people of the Indonesian archipelago, which he 'discovered'.

The emergent Islamic feminism locates support for gender equity in the general proposition that Islam stands for social justice and equity, and for a tolerant and pluralistic society. Leading figures in the Islamic movement for gender equity, apart from former president Abdurachman Wahid (popularly known as Gus Dur), include his wife, Siti Nuriyah, who heads an organisation concerned with gender analysis of the *kitab kuning*, or classical texts studied in Islamic schools (*pesantren*) associated with NU;[6] NU activist and scholar Lily Munir; Ciciek Farha, who heads the civic rights organisation Rahima; Lies Marcoes-Natsir, who among other things prepares a weekly gender section for the principle Jakarta metropolitan daily, *Kompas*; Khofifah Indar Parawansa, who heads the NU women's organisation Muslimat, (also a former Minister for Women's Empowerment); the social activist Wardah Hafidz; and Siti Musdah Mulia, the Islamic scholar who heads the department of Religious Affairs' 'gender mainstreaming' team. Lily Munir and Musdah Mulia in particular have developed textual interpretations to support their claims for gender equity.

There are also important male scholars engaged in analysis and reinterpretation, like Faqihudin Abdul Kodir, Nasaruddin Umar, Masdar F. Mas'udi and Syafiq Hasyim (see below). The other major Islamic organisation, the 'modernist' Muhammadiyah also has its champions of women's rights: for example, the woman feminist scholar, Sri Ruhaini Dzuhayatin, who was appointed as the head of the Muhammadiyah Marjlis Tarjih (Assembly for Decisions on Islamic Law in Muhammadiyah) in 1995. But activists and scholars associated with the 'traditionalist' group, NU, have been a stronger force in the gender equity movement.[7]

Islamic and Gender Politics in the Suharto Era

Under the authoritarian regime of Suharto, Islam was eclipsed as a political force. After an initial alliance in which the military utilised Islamic youth in the mass slaughter of communists, their main opposition, the Suharto regime moved to domesticate Islam, its principal potential political rival, through banning Muslim parties, rolling them into one of two loyal opposition parties (the other representing secular nationalism) and in the early 1980s, enacting a law obliging all political organisations to accept the state ideology, *panca sila*, as their ideological basis. NU chose to withdraw from politics, re-emphasising its role as a religious and social organisation. The mass women's organisations of NU (Fatayat and Muslimat) also withdrew into a role more focused on social service, as they were fearful of the consequences of political engagement in the political climate of the New Order.

NU was important in a social justice movement which engaged in public discussion about issues of equity and human rights, but also in social activism, for example through NU *pesantren* (religious schools) and associated NGOs. Abdurrachman Wahid, as a leading NU figure, was an important critic of the authoritarian New Order, using Islam, but also in interfaith alliances to promote a social justice agenda and critique the worst excesses of the regime.

In regard to gender issues, the New Order engaged in a similar homogenising movement, and independent women's organisations were rolled into two principal state-sponsored organisations (under the Minister of Home Affairs, rather than Women's Affairs) that organised women as 'citizen mothers' in the service of a state familism that provided ideological rationale for the authoritarian regime (Robinson 1994).

Nonetheless, Indonesia was characterised by a growing secular women's movement throughout the Suharto period, a movement of middle-class women who found 'democratic space' in the apparently paradoxical engagement of the Suharto regime with the global movement for women's rights through the UN-sponsored agenda. Indonesia was one of the first nations in the region to establish a women's machinery – a Ministry of Women's Affairs, in 1975 (after the first UN Conference on Women in that year), and has participated in all of the International Conferences on women and ICPD in Cairo. CEDAW (the Convention on the Elimination of all Forms of Discrimination Against Women) was one of a small number of international instruments ratified by the government. Under the influence of the UN agenda, official policy as well as NGOs took up ideas of 'gender equity', 'gender analysis' and 'gender mainstreaming'. The New Order government endorsed the long-standing demand of women's organisations (see below) with the passage of a Marriage Law in 1974, which set minimum marriageable ages, outlawed forced marriage and placed bureaucratic restrictions on men's right to polygamous unions. (This move was probably principally motivated by a modernising commitment to population control) (Robinson 2006).

Women's organisations in the 1980s focused on issues such as the rights of women workers, especially overseas labour migrants, and legal aid for women in cases such as polygamy, divorce and domestic violence. By 1990 there was also growing protest at the use of violence against women as a state tactic in crushing dissidence. The dominant voice in these debates was secular feminism, drawing on the international agendas and seeking legitimacy through them (Robinson 1998). Islamic women's organisations remained in the background, focusing on religious and social issues (Marcoes 2002).

The Suharto government responded fearfully to the international waves of the Iranian revolution, and banned literature from that source. There has always been interest in events in the Middle East among Indonesian Muslims who had – since easier passage to Mecca opened up in the late nineteenth century – engaged as 'players' in the international world of Islam. By the 1980s, some of the public symbols of the Iranian revolution were appearing in Indonesia, for example young women wearing the fitted headscarf (*jilbab*), replacing the loose headscarf (*kerudung*) that had been worn by Indonesian women since the 1920s (introduced by the modernist organisation, Muhammadiyah). In the meantime, there was an Islamic revival happening on Indonesia's campuses, especially in West Java (the so-called *dakwah*, or call to Islam) and these young urban students were interested in reading Islamic literature, much of it originating in the Middle East. One important genre of the works were primers for the proper conduct of Muslim women, in their spiritual role and their worldly duties as wives and mothers.[8] Under this 'neofundamentalist' influence some organisations were adopting a conservative position on women's rights, which included winding back freedoms that women in the archipelago had long enjoyed. The Islamic resurgence incorporated a dimension that was engaging with the global discourse of women's rights, however, and real interest was developing in the possibility of discovering an Islamic argument for women's freedom, that would avoid the secularist foundation of international Human Rights discourse.

Islamic Feminism: its Reception in Indonesia

Indonesian Islamic supporters of gender equity have engaged with Middle Eastern and South Asian feminist thinkers such as Rifat Hasan, Fatimah Mernissi and Asghar Ali Engineer, whose ideas were first introduced to Indonesia in the early 1990s. In 1991, a translation of an article by Riffat Hassan was published in

Ulumul Qur'an, a leading journal in what Hefner has termed the move for civil Islam (2000). The journal subsequently published a special gender issue with both Indonesian and 'foreign' authors in 1995.

According to Ciciek Farha, the director of Rahima, one of the principal Islamic women's rights NGOs in Indonesia, among the first translations of Mernissi and Hassan were those published by the NGO LSPPA (involved in education for women and children). Situated in the central Javanese town of Yogyakarta, its members were part of the Indonesian women's movement that had been influenced by the international secular feminist agenda associated with the UN World Conferences on Women, and it also identifies its historical roots back to the engagement with European feminist ideas of the late nineteenth-century Javanese culture hero, RA Kartini (1883–1904) (see Coté 1992). However, as Muslims, women in these secular organisations became interested in new ideas originating from critical Muslim thinkers in other parts of the world. Whereas in the late nineteenth century, Islamic ideas were transported globally by lengthy sea travel, and few Indonesians were literate, by the late twentieth century the cultural flow of ideas were through more intense travel connections, including international labour migration (Robinson 2000) as well as the Haj, and through the flow of ideas via the Internet and translated books. Higher levels of literacy in both Roman and Arabic scripts have democratised exposure to global conversations.

The LSPPA discussion groups were attended by young women from the nearby State Islamic Institute (IAIN). Literate in Islamic texts, they sought Islamic answers to feminist questions. Having read the 1991 translation of Riffat Hassan, they sought out her work which they saw as providing an insight into feminist textual critique. A visit by Hassan further excited their interest. In addition, Ciciek Farha, who was part of this group, had been introduced to the writing of Fatima Mernissi through a resource centre run by the prominent secular feminist group, Kalyanamitra. The LSPPA group laboured to translate hers and Hassan's works from English into Indonesian, and published an Indonesian edition of collected works by both writers, *Setara di Hadapan Allah* (*Equal before Allah*) (1996). A translation of Mernissi's *Women in Islam* (*Wanita Dalam Islam*) was published in 1994 by Pustaka, Bandung. Engineer's translated work *Hak-Hak Perempunan Dalam Islam* (*Women's Rights under Islam*), was published in 1994. Prominent in publishing this work was the Bandung publisher Misan, who also published a translation of *The Tao of Islam* in 1996, which is a less orthodox exploration of gender relations based on an analysis of Islamic texts. The ideas of Islamic feminist writers began to circulate as they were taken up in discussion groups among students and activists in Jakarta, Bandung and Yogyakarta (Viviani 2001: 4). A number of Indonesian feminist Islamic thinkers began publishing their own contributions to the debate, notably Lies Marcoes-Natsir and Wardah Hafidz. In Marcoes-Natsir's 1993 co-edited book, *Wanita Islam dalam Kajian Tekstual dan Kontekstual (Muslim Women in Textual and Contextual Study)* many of the contributing authors cited Mernissi and Hassan.

Throughout the period of the Suharto government, there had been an expansion in formal Islamic education, especially through the tertiary-level State Islamic Institutes. This has produced a rich crop of home-grown Islamic intellectuals skilled in reading and interpreting the Islamic texts, with important inputs from Indonesian scholars who studied abroad at institutions like Al Azhar in Egypt, but also Islamic intellectuals who have studied for higher degrees at secular institutions in the West, as well as in Indonesia. By contrast, many of the groups opposing their ideas, with literalist textual interpretations, come from a middle-class, technically educated group – indeed the *dakwah* movement has been particularly strong in the campuses of technical faculties like Bandung Institute of Technology (ITB) or the Agricultural University in Bogor (IPB).[9]

The 1996 compilation *Membincang Feminisme (Debating Feminism)* engaged the debates around Islamic textualism and gender relations. Interestingly, in the light of the assumption that the Middle East, in particular Saudi Arabia, is the source of new Islamic ideas, this efflorescence of Islamic feminist writing in Indonesian translation shows, *par excellence*, how Indonesia draws on a range of global intellectual currents. Most of the works supporting feminist contextual analysis mentioned above were not translated from Arabic but from English, French or German. *Membincang Feminisme* also provided a voice for scholars arguing against the feminist position – for example, Ratna Megawangi whose argument, presented as an Islamic position, nonetheless draws heavily on US Christian anti-feminist positions.[10] Women's advocacy groups such as Rahima established links with Sisters in Islam in Malaysia (see Stivens, this volume).

A unique feature of this Islamic movement for women's rights in Indonesia is the significant influence of male scholars who have been subjected to criticism and even threats for their stance. Two major books that emerged from the debates of the 1990s were Nasaruddin Umar's *Argumen Kesetaraan Jender: Perspectif Al-Qur'an* (1999) and Syafiq Hasyim's *Hal-Hal yang Tidak Dipikirkan tentang Isu-isu Keperempuanan dalam Islam* (2002). Both cite Mernissi and Hassan, with Umar using an illustration from their book *Women in Islam* on the cover. The Monday section (*Swara*) of the major Jakarta daily *Kompas* edited by Lies Marcoes-Natsir,[11] is a venue for (male and female) Indonesian Islamic intellectuals to engage in debates about gender equity and Islam, as are the websites of organisations like Jaringan Islam Liberal (liberal Islam network) and Rahima. A popular figure in these public venues is the Ulama Faquihuddin Abdul Kodir, whose textual interpretation of Islam's 'pro-woman' position was published by Rahima in 2006 (*Bergerak Menuju Keadilan: Pembelaan Nabi terhadap Perempuan* – 'Moving Towards Justice: the Prophet's support for women').The Bandung publisher Misan prides itself on its contribution to this debate. Many of the intellectuals involved are active within major Islamic organisations, especially Nahdlatul Ulama and also Muhammadiyah. Indonesian Islamic intellectuals are bringing the ideas of a cosmopolitan Islamic discourse to a wider Indonesian audience through translation, but they are also developing the ideas they have taken up and embedding them in Indonesian Islam.

The fundamental idea in Islamic feminist writing is that discriminative practices arise from gender-biased interpretations of the Qur'an and Hadith (the latter refers to reports of the words and actions of the Prophet). It proposes a reconstruction of Islamic values, weeding out the patriarchal traditions that have taken root in Islamic thought and practice that are in contradiction with the true egalitarian spirit of Islamic values (Viviani 2001).

Proponents of gender equity argue for a contextual (socio-historical) rather than a textual (literalist) approach to interpretation.[12] Almost all of the verses that refer to gender in the Qur'an and Hadith can be understood in the light of the historical context at the time of revelation (*asbab al-nuzul*). Local differences are inherent in the transmission of Islam, and these local particularities can assume the basis of doctrine. For example, the story in the Hadith by Bukhari concerning the creation of Eve from Adam's rib shows the influence of Judeo-Christian ideas. Authors like Wadud, Mernissi and Hassan contend that there is no verse in the Qur'an which argues that men and women were created differently. Mernissi, for example, uses semantic analysis to weigh up the historical context (*asbab al-nuzul*) in the interpretation of the verses of the Qur'an and Hadith. In order to deconstruct the textual basis of Islam, it is necessary to understand its metaphorical dimensions and to test the Hadith for reliability and credibility (*sanad shahih*, the rules by which scholars judge the verity of the chain of transmission). Other considerations used by these advocates of gender equity in order to challenge what are regarded as misogynist interpretations are the *jalur periwayat* (chain of transmission), the substance of the report (*matan*) and its history (*asab al wurud*). These interpretive traditional tools are used to analyse Qur'anic texts to 'reveal' the basis for gender equity. Proponents of this view argue that one objective of the Qur'an is to transform social reality gradually and in stages (*bi al-tadri*), including in gender relations: that is, that the idea of gradual social change is fundamental to the Qur'an.

The flood of new Islamic feminist literature exemplifies the cosmopolitan character of Islamic social and political thought as a counterpoint and complement to Western thinking in a manner remarkably similar to the development of Indonesian nationalism in the early twentieth century. The principles of gender equity discovered through hermeneutical readings of texts are similar to the principles put forward by proponents of Islam as a basis for democracy, or for a distinctive Islamic form of human rights. For these scholars, feminism (like democracy and human rights) is not exclusive to Western cosmopolitan ideals.

New Interpretive Practices and Women's Activism Against Violence

There has been continuity in the concerns of the Indonesian women's movement since the early twentieth century. Women's rights in marriage and the family, and the role of the state in protecting those rights have been enduring concerns, especially early or forced marriage, divorce rights and polygamy. These central issues were raised in the first women's congress in 1928, which brought together representatives of secular nationalist, Muslim and Christian groups. In subsequent congresses, the issue of family law was divisive, especially in regard to polygamy. Islamic women felt constrained to publicly support the practice, although individual leaders from these organisations commented on their private opposition at the time (see Wieringa 2002).

Anti-violence developed as a strong theme of the Indonesian women's movement through the 1980s; for example, the Islamic group Rifka Anissa established a women's refuge in Yogyakarta to support victims of violence, and women's groups became increasingly vocal critics of military and paramilitary violence against women in areas of conflict like West Papua and East Timor. Activists drew parallels with the rape of women in Bosnia, decrying the use of women as 'instruments of war'. Several hundred women, mostly of Chinese descent were brutally raped during the riots which forced President Suharto to resign in 1998. Women claimed similarities between the experiences of these women and those in other conflict areas, invoking a widely held belief that these women too were used as 'instruments of war', as a part of a state strategy to scapegoat the Chinese minority for the economic collapse (the so-called Krismon – monetary crisis or Kristal – total crisis). Public outrage at the rapes (which the government initially tried to deny) led to mass public demonstrations and a significant shift in public discourse in which violence against women became widely accepted as a major political issue. Women began regularly demonstrating on the issue and the government established a Commission on Women's Human Rights (KOMNAS Perempuan) to address the issue.[13]

Return to Democracy: Feminist Islam Contested

Increasingly, in the post-Suharto period, the concerns originating in secular feminist organisations have been expressed in a new register that engages an imaginative space defined by Islam. Opposition to gendered violence, in particular within the family, is a dominant theme in current women's activism, and draws its force not only from secular global instruments like CEDAW, but also by appealing to a cosmopolitan form of Islam, which emphasises women's individual human rights over men's prerogative as household heads.

Reformasi (the Indonesian term for the movement towards greater democratisation that toppled Suharto) opened the doors for the re-emergence of some old arguments that women perhaps felt had been settled or at least tamed. The new climate of political freedom has allowed a greater public voice to neofundamentalist groups that had formed in the '80s and '90s in the climate of growing opposition to Suharto and frustration at the marginalisation of Islam from politics. These groups take the form of new political parties as well as socio-religious organisations. Many had developed with financial and other support from Saudi Arabia, and these close ties concern some Indonesians, who are uneasy at the 'Arabisation' of Indonesian Islam (Bubalo and Fealy 2005:76). With this new politicisation of Islam, issues that seemed to have been resolved in pluralist Indonesian society have resurfaced. New political challenges to supporters of gender equity and women's rights have arisen from groups championing literalist interpretations of Islamic family law, including men's rights to polygamous marriage. Of concern to women, there have been demands for the repeal of the 1975 Marriage Law, for example, on the grounds that it interferes in the private world of the family which is properly regulated by religion. In the following discussion, I will take up three major issues in which Islamic feminists have taken political action, and have been countered by conservative Muslims: the issues of polygamy, marriage law reform, and the outlawing of domestic violence.

Polygamy

The New Order had kept polygamy behind closed doors: under the Marriage Law, men had to meet conditions to the satisfaction of religious courts, and obtain permission from their first wives to legally take a second wife. Civil servants faced extra restrictions,[14] contributing to the negative image of polygamy. Post-Suharto, polygamy has been accorded renewed public legitimacy, through the very public polygamy of Megawati Sukarnoputri's vice president, Hamzah Has (2001–4), and the promotion of Polygamy Awards in 2003 by a well-known restaurateur (Robinson 2006). Both of these public displays drew the wrath of women – from both secular and Islamic organisations – who became more vociferous in demanding radical changes in the Marriage Law, including the outlawing of polygamy on the grounds that it violated Indonesia's obligations as a signatory to CEDAW. Prior to this, the most strongly voiced objection to the 1975 marriage law, articulated by groups like LBH-APIK (Legal Aid Institute for Women's Human Rights), related to the formal institutionalisation of gender inequality through the Law's definition of men as household heads and women as managers of the household. In contrast to the conflict between secular and Islamic women's organisations in the 1940s and 1950s on the polygamy issue, many Islamic feminists have now arrived at anti-polygamy positions supported by textual analysis. That is, there has been convergence between political demands arising from a secular women's rights agenda and the developing Islamic feminist discourse. The support for polygamy in the Qur'an rests on a single verse in Surah An Nisa which is concerned with the plight of orphans. An anti-polygamy stance put by NU activist and scholar Lily Munir (2005: 201) is representative:

> The core issue of polygamy in current Muslim societies is that it has been taken as a general attitude of Islam, ignoring the social justice reasons for the revelation of the verse. Polygamy, which was common in pre-Islamic society, apparently has a new meaning in Islam. Islam intended to change it from a male right to female privilege in limited circumstances beneficial to women and children, not in circumstances detrimental to women. If it is acceptable to women, polygamy may be a way to protect them and give them sexual access to men in a time when women outnumber men. However, the Qur'an itself does not refer to the sexual nature or needs of women or men in dealing with polygamy: it refers only to the need to ensure social justice for orphaned girls in a time when unprotected women were open to all kinds of abuse. Even so, polygamy is not the Qur'an's ideal.

Marriage Law Reform

Pro-gender equity Muslim intellectuals are challenging the polygamy and divorce provisions of the 1975 law and its further iteration through the 1989 Compilation of Islamic law (Kompilasi Hukum Islam). The Kompilasi has been praised for its legitimation of *fiqh* of a uniquely Indonesian character, enshrining as positive law many rights women have under custom (*adat*) (e.g. common property rights; see, for example, Lev 1996) and the rights afforded Indonesian women by the provisional divorce or *ta'lik* (Robinson 2006). In particular, women's rights advocates criticise discriminatory clauses of the marriage law relating to age at marriage, the stipulation of male household heads, the requirement for a *wali* (guardian) to be male, differential divorce rights and the continued legal support for polygamy (argued, as mentioned, to be in breach of Indonesia's obligations as a signatory to CEDAW). The women critics also want to revisit unequal inheritance laws.

In late 2004, the government signalled its intention to upgrade the status of the Kompilasi Hukum from Presidential Instruction to Law.[15] Women's rights advocates saw this as an opportunity to argue that the sections of the Kompilasi dealing with family law should be further revised to reflect principles of democracy and gender equity and contemporary Indonesian social practice. The Gender Mainstreaming Team in the Department of Religious Affairs, led by Siti Musdah Mulia and supported by the Commission on Women's Human Rights (KOMNAS Perempuan), undertook to devise a 'counter legal draft'.

The key figure in this counter legal draft, Siti Musdah Mulia, is an Islamic scholar who is a lecturer at the Islamic University Syarif Hidayatullah in Jakarta and Head of the Research Bureau (Litbang) in the Department of Religious Affairs (which is in practice the government department for the regulation of Islam). She is an erudite textual scholar with a command of Arabic and the Qur'an and Sunnah. She is confident, articulate and a clear thinker. Siti Musdah Mulia studied under Nurcholish Majid, who in turn was a student of Fazlur Rahman at the University of Chicago, noted for his distinction between 'eternal and historically specific Qur'anic verses' (Bowen 2003: 149n.2). Musdah Mulia confidently utilises the language of Western textual analysis and employs classical techniques for 'deconstruction', including philology, historical approaches to the Hadith and comparisons between different Qur'anic texts, to discern underlying eternal values. The fundamental Islamic values she 'reconstructs' are social justice, including gender equity, respect for individual rights and humanitarianism. She has been active in analysing Indonesian law, especially family law, and arguing on the basis of her analysis of basic Islamic values for improvement in the law to benefit women. Like Lily Munir, she is a strong advocate of the view that polygamy is tolerated but not condoned by Islam, and has published a closely argued textual critique entitled *Islam Menggugat Poligami* ('Islam Reproaches Polygamy'). Musdah Mulia confidently finds her way around Islamic texts and through her writing stakes her claim as an *alim*, an interpreter of the texts, an originator of *fiqh*. In this, she is part of the wider Islamic women's movement claim to recognition of female *ulama*. The Counter Legal Draft has taken form under the rubric of Gender Mainstreaming, a concept and process directly arising from the international women's rights agenda of the UN. The content, however, draws its inspiration from contemporary practices of Qur'anic exegesis.

Musdah Mulia (2005) has been at the forefront of new feminist textual interpretations, through careful deconstruction of the relevant passages in the Qur'an and Hadiths. Her reasoning questions the legitimacy from an Islamic point of view of the exercise of unequal power within the household, enshrined in the 1975 Marriage Law. A key concept for 'deconstruction' is that of *qawwam*, usually translated in Indonesian as *pemimpin*, or 'boss'. According to Musdah Mulia this has rather the sense of protector of the family and household (2004: 142), a different kind of relationship and responsibility. Her most innovative interpretation relates to her application of the ideas of the fundamental Islamic belief in *tauhid*, or the unity of God, from which she deduces that a commitment to gender equity is a fundamental value in Islam. She argues that the doctrine of *tauhid* renders illegitimate unequal social relations such as master–slave, men dominating women: in such unequal relations, the dominant partner positions themselves as a God to the dominated. The idea that 'the absolute sovereignty of God makes any human hierarchy impossible' (Esposito and Voll 1996: 25) has been utilised as an argument for democracy being an Islamic value, even the overthrow of dictators in parts of the Muslim world. In Indonesia, this argument was developed by Nurcholish Majid, a teacher of Musdah Mulia at IAIN Jakarta.

The counter-legal draft did not garner the same level of support as the law on domestic violence, however, and has been withdrawn.

Feminism and Anti-violence

Anti-violence has been a strong theme of the Indonesian women's movement and since the fall of Suharto it has become one of the major organising tropes. On four different days – International Women's Day, the UN day of opposition to violence against women and Indonesia's national days celebrating women (Mother's Day and Kartini Day) – women take to the streets and invade government offices to demand action by both the state and civil society to curb violence against women.

The Indonesian term glossed as violence, *kekerasan*, is used to mean a range of practices involving the abuse of male (or state) power and prerogatives against women, from physical abuse to polygamy. Opposition to gendered violence within the family is a dominant theme in current women's activism, and draws its force not only from secular global instruments like CEDAW, but also by appeal to cosmopolitan values argued to be inherent in Islam. Women's organisations began organising to draft a bill outlawing domestic violence in the New Order period, and their actions gained momentum in the Reform period. The bill was enacted by parliament in 2004, after extensive lobbying of political parties and religious and secular groups. By the time it came before parliament it had widespread support and was passed, including controversial clauses on marital rape. There has been some public opposition from voices within Islam who wish to interpret particular Qur'anic verses as legitimating the rights of men to slap (but not beat) their wives, and who also argue on a textual basis that women must always be ready to 'serve' their husbands. Neofundamentalist groups like Hizb ut-Tahrir oppose the extension of state regulation of family relations. They argue that Islam condemns bad acts (like hitting a spouse) and hence there is no need for special state law on domestic violence. Some Islamic groups argued that the activities within a household enjoy a special privileged position and cannot be shared with outsiders (like counsellors or refuge workers, or the courts). For Islamic feminists like Lily Munir, the exercise of certain male prerogatives, such as in marital rape, are instances of 'patriarchy' which are at odds with fundamental values of Islam that do not support male privilege.

The 'Counter-cosmopolitan' Backlash

Gender equity is a terrain for the dispute over competing visions of Islam in Indonesia. There have been some voices arguing against the feminist gender equity position (e.g. Ratna Megawangi) which, though argued with Islamic rhetoric, are based on arguments derived from secular Western anti-feminism. However, the growing significance of Islamic feminism's claims for gender equity based on Islamic interpretation have attracted an Islamic opposition as well – that is, an Islamic opposition that tries to set the terms for the debate in styles of interpretation. The most strident of these critiques come from neofundamentalist groups who feel that Islamic values are under threat from the Westernisation of society and culture and the opening up of the Indonesian economy and mass media to the capitalist world under Suharto's New Order.

An interview with Ridha Salamah published in December 2005 on a neofund-amentalist website, WIBeramuslim, clearly sets out the terms of this attack. She is an Islamic scholar, the highest-ranking woman in Hizb ut-Tahrir (HT) and a member of the Commission for Research and Development of the Majelis Ulama Islam (MUI), the government-sponsored body charged with making fatwah. As part of the struggle over Islam in contemporary Indonesia, Salafi groups like HT have been seeking membership of politically important bodies like the MUI (although they eschew involvement in parliamentary politics).

In a 'counter-cosmopolitan' attack (Appiah 2006), Salamah presents a vision of a malevolent globalisation, with capitalism as the dominant power, and sees the cosmopolitan vision of international governance through common instruments of law as a sinister plot to retain the inequalities of the existing world order.

> This is a western view point (*wacana*) – the nations that are dominated (*terjajah*) (in the global system) are obliged to follow what is targeted for them by the dominating powers who want one global order under their hegemonic control. So whatever becomes a global issue (*isu*) must be ratified, adopted by the dominated countries. Muslim women embracing feminism are 'lured into a trap' (*terjebak*).
>
> ...the problems they raise are not addressed by the solution they propose. Their solution is only that women should have an equal bargaining position with men. But what is the connection between this goal and addressing the problems of poverty, backwardness, injustice, violence and so forth?

According to Ridha Salamah, the issue of gender (*isu*, implying, is not true) is the *alat paling ampuh* (most powerful tool) to ruin Muslim women, and destroy future generations.

The position put forward reflects the anti-cosmopolitan stance of global fundamentalist thinking. Values such as gender equity are interpreted as part of a plot for global domination by the West in a postcolonial world. Islam as a civilisation has a differing and legitimate set of values to regulate relations between men and women, and women's social responsibilities. So-called Islamic feminists have been duped into an agenda which blinds them to the correct analysis of the causes of social evil such as domestic violence, which is not a consequence of patriarchal social structures and unmitigated male authority, but results from the very Western influence from which they draw their intellectual and political inspiration. In Salamah's view, the declining status of women is due to global Western domination, and to secularism.

> The pressure on life from the effects of secularism-liberalism and capitalism, has the effect of making women's role as mothers very difficult (*berat*). They think about the quality of their children's education while at the same time thinking about whether the money for buying food is adequate. The gender perspective is not the solution to the problem of the declining social status of women. We must look to a solution that addresses the roots of the problem – not a solution that only addresses the symptoms. For example, in order that women seem not to be held in contempt, disdain, they are given the title 'professor', or to improve their bargaining position they are allowed to be leaders in congregational prayer (*imam sholat*) for men. These acts only address the symptoms, not the root causes.

Salamah does not deny that women face oppression (*ketertindasan*) but she sees this as a consequence of secularism, a kind of *ekses* (something that has gone too far) from the application of a set of principles that is devoid (*steril*) of God's principles (*aturan Allah*).

> The gender equity outlook will increase problems. In the countries where the gender movement originates, the problems have already emerged, created difficulties for family life in the West. This is triggered by the *isu* of gender equity: women want to be freed from the regulations of Islam with the consequence that they don't want the responsibility of serving their husbands. They also feel despised (*terhina*) if they undertake domestic tasks because they consider that they are not counted as part of the national economy as they don't generate income. This is what makes women abandon their domestic tasks, which are given by God and should be carried out in a harmonious fashion. In the end the household is ruined, a generation destroyed. And this is very effective destruction. This is the danger. This is a global conspiracy which makes the dominated / oppressed (*jajahan*) countries remain backward, through the destruction of a generation.

She is critical of educated Muslims, the graduates of State Islamic Institutes (IAIN), who are the proponents of Islamic democracy and Islamic Human Rights, which are in fact products of Western liberalism and do not arise on the basis of

Islamic practice (*aquidah Islam*). They have 'abandoned their muslimness' in their approach to the nation's problems. She signals that '*genderisme*' is being considered, along with '*secularisme*', '*pluralisme*' and '*liberalisme*' (identified as a complex through the acronym '*sipilis*') as the subject of a fatwa by the MUI.

This is a strong statement from a member of the Muslim elite which sees cosmopolitan values as part of a Western conspiracy to destroy family relations that are the basis of a 'true' Islamic society. The use of international instruments of global governance and the manner in which they spread secularist and liberal values are targeted as foundational elements of this conspiracy.

Popular Engagement with Gender Equity and Anti-violence

Of course, I have been discussing highly intellectual debates, predicated on a familiarity with the Qur'an and Sunnah; a confidence with *fiqh*. But what is happening outside the elite and urban spheres, the intellectual and political circles of these debates? In discussions in early 2006 with women activists involved in supporting victims of domestic violence (in the South Sulawesi capital Makassar), the women (from the local branch of the women's legal aid support group LBH APIK and a local women's refuge) commented that outside of the city, the domestic violence law was not well known. In rural communities, in cases of domestic violence, women were more likely to seek the advice of religious leaders than women's groups, and were commonly told to accept their chastisement as a trial from God.

Feminist ideas generally are frequently dismissed as 'Western'. In one area (Mangkutana in North Luwu) where the Makassar-based activists tried to promote awareness of the new law to the local Muslim population, the latter were unwilling to accept its terms; they saw it as 'Christian' because it was seen as coming from the West. In the view of these activists who are all Muslim, by contrast, Christian women were in fact worse off than Muslim women because of the lack of tolerance for divorce. Despite this, however, the activists saw the anti-domestic violence law and its associated debate as important in changing attitudes: at both national capital level and in the province, LBH APIK had experienced a rise in the number of women reporting domestic violence. Police procedures for handling rape and other criminal violence against women were dramatically improved by innovations during Abdurrachman Wahid's presidency under the woman he appointed as Minister for Women's Empowerment, Khofifah Indar Parawansa, the NU woman politician who heads one of the NU women's organisations (Muslimat) as well as sitting in the national parliament (Indar Parawansa 2002). She initiated special procedures to handle the cases of victims of violence, including dedicated rooms in police stations ideally under the authority of women police officers.

These procedures have been embraced in the procedures outlined in the Domestic Violence Act. The activist women in Makassar say that this had made palpable changes in the way police handle victims, and the activists work closely with a senior police officer. According to the women anti-violence activists in Southeast Sulawesi organisations, however, in the current era of decentralised government (regional autonomy), it is necessary to have local regulations (*perda*) as well as national law to ensure it is acted on by state authorities, and this is one of their areas of activism. They complained that the judges were unfamiliar with the new legislation, as the state had not provided awareness training, and tended to prosecute ceases under the criminal code, which has lesser penalties for domestic violence (interview in Kendari with Kapal Perempuan). It is difficult to raise awareness of the new laws, especially in rural communities, and both state and religious authorities remain part of the problem of obtaining justice for women.

Women activists associated with NU have evolved an imaginative strategy for spreading their message that gender equity (indeed, democratic and pluralistic values) is a fundamental Islamic value, and that domestic violence is not tolerated by Islam. Having experienced opposition in their attempt to win the support of *kiai* (religious scholars) through use of the 'Western' concept of gender analysis (see Bowen 2003), they have drawn on the NU tradition of adapting local cultural practices to spread Islamic values through the tradition of *Salawat Kesetaraan*. *Salawat* is joyous singing in praise of the Prophet Muhammad that is performed in different ways throughout the archipelago, in areas where Islam is practised. In its 'acculturated' form it blends with local musical traditions. It is a common form of worship in NU circles. The group Rahima have developed the *Salawat Kesetaraan* or Equality Salawat, drawing on Qur'anic verses to sing songs of praise stressing the values of social equality and mutual respect. They also call it *Salawat Keadilan* (Justice Salawat) or simply *Salawat Jender*. The *Salawat Kesetaraan* rituals are becoming accepted, for example in the Islamic schools (*pesantren*), which are the heartland of NU and are presided over by NU-affiliated *kiai*. Significantly, the mass NU women's organisation, Fatayat NU, with four million members all over the country, is now promoting the practice. The joyful singing of the messages in the Qur'an which, they argue, demonstrates the fundamental commitment of Islam to gender equity and to decent behaviour of men towards women, is well received by many (even conservative) *kiai*, and is a way of promoting a gender-equity interpretation in a manner that elicits wide acceptance outside elite circles. It mimics extremely popular pop cultural television shows like Indonesian Idol and Akademi Fantasi Indonesia by staging public competitions where men and women join in the performance of *Salawat Jender*. The performance of *salawat*, through which people affirm – in their dress, rhythms, instruments, singing and lyrics – their identity as Muslims, simultaneously embraces cosmopolitan values of respect for individual rights, social justice and humanitarianism. Through the performance, participants enact their identity as Muslims, while simultaneously claiming universal values. These are 'alternative cosmopolitans' rather than the 'counter-cosmopolitans' identified by Appiah (2006)

Conclusion

What threat does Islamism pose to gender equity in Indonesia? The current efflorescence of the *jilbab* (tight veil) – in proliferating styles – as a marker of Islamic identity, of piety, even as a fashion statement (in the words of the elegantly veiled women scholar Musdah Mulia), is seized on by many observers as a symbol of a current drive to delimit women's access to the public sphere and to roll back gains women have made – for example, new challenges to the restrictions on the male prerogative of polygamy from the 1974 Marriage Law (Robinson 2006) and the imposition of gender-specific curfews in the name of Sharia law. However, the veiled women chanting *Salawat Kesetaraan* indicate the complex significations of the *jilbab*: in contemporary Indonesia it is as likely to signify the performance of Islamic identity by a woman who sees that identity as embracing a fundamental commitment to gender equity, as it is to signify an Islamic identity which denies women equal rights with men.

'In a globalised world, the flow of Islamic ideas into Indonesia is less and less a function of specifically Middle Eastern influences than a broader, global process of intellectual exchange and adaptation' (Bubalo and Fealy 2005: ix). Part of this global engagement is with critical Islamic thought defending social justice, humanitarianism and pluralism. Muslim feminists also seek inspiration from Western political and scholarly traditions, and in Indonesia, they form alliances with secular feminists to achieve goals such as the passage of the law on domestic violence. While they have developed a programme of action motivated by a specifically Islamic and Indonesian understanding of gender relations, they are also 'hailed' by the analysis and political programmes of international feminism and secular feminism in their own country. They have negotiated with the Indonesian state and secular and Islamic organisations in a dialogue highly conscious of the concerns and positions of their interlocutors, as well as of their own commitments. This transversal dialogue (Yuval Davis 2006) has led, in the Indonesian instance, to shared cosmopolitan values across what may appear to be incommensurable 'ideologies'.

In creating a local consensus, Indonesian Islamic scholars do not all position themselves in textual exegesis as passive recipients of textual interpretations and authoritative positions from the Arab-speaking Middle East. There are many who confidently engage in the process of textual analysis, claiming their own legitimacy and authority. Many of these scholars and activists are pushing the boundaries of Islam with their feminist Islamic practice, while at the same time they are successfully pursuing strategies to take their activism outside the realms of elite politics and bring a 'counter-globalisation' based on Islamic precepts to non-elite Indonesians, which simultaneously challenges Western cultural domination and the 'counter-cosmopolitanism' (Appiah 2006) of global fundamentalist Islam.

Notes

1. The main Wahabist modernist organisation that developed in the early twentieth century is Muhammadiyah, now Indonesia's second largest Muslim organisation. Its founder, K.H. Ahmad Dahlan was influenced by the ideas of purification of the faith from Muhammad ibn'Abd al-Wahab (1703–1787) as developed by the Egyptian scholars Al-Afghani (1839–1897) and Muhammad Abduh (1849–1905), including taking up the latter scholar's endorsement of the use of *ijtihad* (the exercise of judgment, interpretation in reading the Qur'an and Hadiths).
2. The idea of 'civilisational pluralism' is an important concept in the liberal strand of contemporary global Islam which is challenging the influence of neofundamentalism – see, for example, Tibi (2003: 254) ; 'let us … talk about a new world order based on justice and democratic peace in which cultural and civilisational pluralism and mutual respect determine how people of different religions live in peace with one another'.
3. Some Islamic intellectuals assert the importance of Islamic influence in Hellenic political thought (see Tibi 2003).
4. Wadud argues, for example, that the Qur'an intended to erase all notions of women as subhuman, and that Islam brought changes that challenged the patriarchal character of seventh-century Arabia in matters such as rights to inheritance, independent property rights and divorce rights, and in forbidding violence against women (see www.newint.org/issue345/legacy.htm).
5. This appellation was popularised through Geertz's (1960) analysis of *The Religion of Java*, contrasted with the 'modernist' approach of Masyumi and Muhammadiyah. The 'traditional/modern' dichotomy was embraced by political scientists as a way to understand political – especially electoral — behaviour in the 1950s and beyond. Indonesia's current complex social and political contestations are not easily encompassed by this dichotomy.
6. Gus Dur and Siti Nuriyah are also leading figures in the interfaith movement.
7. However, in Muhammadiyah's initial period of formation, the founder Haji Dahlan was very progressive on women's issues, founding a special women's section in 1917 which had spiritual, social and educational aims.

8. Meuleman [1993] analyses a number of these texts circulating in the early 1990s.
9. Suzanne Brenner speculates on the attraction of the 'purification' movement for young women students, many of whom were of the first generation of their families to attend university: 'Besides giving them a sense of belonging to a community of people with shared experiences and values, the Islamic organisations also offered them codes of behaviour, morality, and often dress that may have alleviated their sense of confusion or discomfort at being on their own in the city for the first time' (Brenner 2005: 99).
10. Her 1999 book *Membiarkan Berbeda*? ('Let There be Difference?') was also published by Misan. She has a PhD in International Food and Nutrition Policy from Tufts University, Massachusetts, USA.
11. Lies Marcoes-Natsir is also employed by *Kompas* and a 'gender ombudsman' to ensure that the newspaper's reporting is not gender-biased.
12. The Islamic feminists discussed here seem to be in the 'spirit of the Qur'an'-type mould of Fazlur Rahman (Saeed 2006: 6).
13. The first street demonstration in the period leading up to Suharto's resignation was the so-called 'demo susu', or milk demo, when a group called Suara Ibu Peduli (Voice of Concerned Mothers) protested at the difficulties for women in feeding their families under the conditions of the Krismon. They took over a major intersection in Jakarta, stopping traffic and offering flowers to motorists. They were consciously emulating the strategy of Argentinian housewives who used 'mother power' to protest against the disappearance of their children. The symbolic gesture of handing out flowers has been taken up by the movement against gender violence in their now regular protests in Indonesia.
14. Civil servants were required to obtain the permission of their superior officer, in addition to the permission of the first wife, as required by the 1975 Marriage Law.
15. Whereas under the Suharto regime, a Presidential Instruction was a stronger legal instrument than a law passed by Parliament, the constitutional changes post-Suharto limited executive power and increased the power of Parliament, rendering presidential Instructions weak legal instruments.

References

Appiah, Kwame Anthony (2006), *Cosmopolitanism: Ethics in a World of Strangers*, New York: W.W. Norton.
Bowen, J. (2003), *Islam, Law and Equality in Indonesia*, Cambridge: Cambridge University Press.

Brenner, Suzanne (2005), 'Islam and Gender Politics in Late New Order Indonesia', in Andrew C. Willford and Kenneth M. George (eds), *Spirited Politics: Religion and Public Life in Contemporary Southeast Asia*, Ithaca: Cornell Southeast Asia Program Publications, pp. 93–118.

Bubalo, Anthony and Greg Fealy (2005), *Joining the Caravan? The Middle East, Islamism and Indonesia*, Alexandria NSW: Longueville Media for the Lowy Institute of International Policy.

Budianta, Melani (2002), 'Plural Identities: Indonesian Women's Redefinition of Democracy in the Post-Reformasi Era', *Review of Indonesian and Malaysian Affairs (RIMA)* 36 (1): 35–50.

Coté, Joost (1992), *Letters from Kartini. An Indonesian Feminist 1900–1904*, Clayton Vic./Melbourne: Monash Asia Institute in association with Hyland House.

Engineer, Asghar Ali (1994), *Hak-hak Perempuan dalam Islam* ('Women's Rights under Islam'), Yogyakarta: Yayasan Bentang Budaya.

Esposito, John L. and John O. Voll (1996), *Islam and Democracy*, Oxford: Oxford University Press.

Fakih, Mansour, Ratna Megawangi, Syu'bah Asa, et al. (1996), *Membincang Feminisme: Diskursus Gender Perspektif Islam* ('Debating Feminism: Gender Discourse in Islamic Perspective'), Surabaya: Risalah Gusti.

Feith, Herbert (1962), *Decline of Constitutional Democracy in Indonesia*, Ithaca: Cornell University Press.

Geertz, Cliford (1960), *Religion of Java*, New York: Free Press.

Hassan, Riffat (1994), 'Women's Interpretation of Islam', in Hans Thijssen and Judith Saffe (eds), *Women and Islam in Muslim Societies*, The Hague: Netherlands Institute of International Relations, pp. 113–21.

Hassan, Riffat and Fatima Mernissi (1991), *Setara di Hadapan Allah* ('Equal before Allah'), Yogyakarta: LSPPA Yayasan Prakarsa.

Hasyim, Syafiq (2002), *Hal-Hal yang Tidak Dipikirkan: Tentang Isu-isu Keperempuanan dalam Islam* ('Matters not Considered: On Women's Issues in Islam'), Bandung: Misan.

Hefner, Robert (2000), *Civil Islam: Muslims and Democratisation in Indonesia*, Princeton: Princeton University Press.

Indar Parawansa, Khofifah (2002), 'Institution Building: an Effort to Improve Indonesian Women's Role and Status.' in Kathryn Robinson and Sharon Bessell (eds), *Women in Indonesia: Gender, Equity and Development*, Singapore: ISEAS, pp. 68–77.

Kodir, Faqihudin Abdul (2006), *Bergerak Menuju Keadilan: Pembelaan Nabi terhadap Perempuan*, Jakarta: Rahima

Lev, Daniel S. (1996), 'On the Other Hand?', in Laurie J. Sears (ed.), *Fantasising the Feminine in Indonesia*, Durham: Duke University Press, pp. 191–203.

Marcoes, Lies (2002) 'Local Level Islamic organisations', in Kathryn Robinson and Sharon Bessell (eds), *Women in Indonesia: Gender, Equity and Development* Singapore: ISEAS, pp. 187–97.

Marcoes-Natsir, Lies and Johan Hendrik Meuleman (1993), *Wanita Islam dalam Kajian Tekstual dan Kontekstual* ('Muslim Women in Textual and Contextual Study'), Jakarta: INIS (Indonesia-Netherlands Cooperation in Islamic Studies).

Martinez, Patricia A. (2005), 'Is it always Islam versus Civil Society?', in K.S. Nathan and Mohammad Hashim Kamali (eds), *Islam in Southeast Asia. Political, Social and Strategic Challenges for the 21st Century*, Singapore: ISEAS, pp. 35–161

Megawangi, Ratna (1999), *Membiarkan Berbeda?*, Bandung: Mizan.

Mernissi, Fatima (1994), *Wanita dalam Islam* ('Women in Islam'), Bandung: Pustaka.

Mignolo, Walter D. (2000), 'The Many Faces of Cosmo-Polis: Border Thinking and Critical Cosmopolitanism', *Public Culture* 12 (3): 721–48.

Mulia, S.M. (2005) *Muslimah Reformis: Perempuan Pembaru Keagamaan*, Bandung: Mizan.

Munir, Lily Zakiyah (ed.) (1999), *Memposisikan Kodrat: Perempuan dan Perubahan dalam Perspektif Islam*, Bandung: Mizan.

—— (2002), '"He is your garment and you are his...": Religious Precepts, Interpretations and Power Relations in Marital Sexuality Among Javanese Muslims', *Sojourn: Journal of Social Issues in Southeast Asia* 17(2): 191–220.

—— (2005), 'Islam and Gender: Reading Equality and Patriarchy', in K.S. Nathan and Mohammad Hashim Kamali (eds), *Islam in Southeast Asia: Political, Social and Strategic Challenges for the 21st Century*, Singapore: ISEAS, pp. 191–205.

Noerdin, Edriana (2002), 'Women and Regional Autonomy', in Kathryn Robinson and Sharon Bessell (eds), *Women in Indonesia: Gender Equity and Development*, Singapore: ISEAS, pp. 179–86.

Rapport, Nigel (2006), 'Anthropology as Cosmopolitan Study', *Anthropology Today* 22 (1): 22–3.

Robbins, Bruce (1998), 'Introduction Part 1: Actually Existing Cosmopolitanism', in Pheng Cheah and Bruce Robbins (eds), *Cosmopolitics: Thinking and Feeling Beyond the Nation*, Minneapolis: University of Minnesota Press, pp. 1–20.

Robinson, Kathryn (1994), 'Indonesian National Identity and the Citizen Mother', *Communal/Plural* 3: 65–82.

—— (1998), 'Indonesian Women's Rights, International Feminism and Democratic Change', *Communal/Plural* 6: 205–223.

—— (2000), 'Gender, Islam and Nationality: Indonesian Domestic Servants in the Middle East', in Kathleen M. Adams and Sara Dickey (eds), *Home and*

Hegemony: Domestic Service and Identity in South and Southeast Asia, Ann Arbor: Michigan University Press, pp. 249–82.
—— (2004), 'Islam, Gender and Politics in Indonesia', in *Islamic Perspectives on the New Millennium*, Virginia Hooker and Amin Saikal (eds), Singapore: ISEAS, pp. 183–98.
—— (2006), 'Muslim Women's Political Struggle for Law Reform in Contemporary Indonesia', in Carolyn Evans and Amanda Whiting (eds), *Mixed Blessings: Women, Laws and Religion*, Leiden: Brill, pp. 183–210.
Saeed, Abdullah (2006), *Interpreting the Qur'an. Towards a Contemporary Approach*, London/New York: Routledge.
Subhan, Zaitunah (2002), *Rekonstruksi Pemahaman Jender Dalam Islam: Agenda Sosio-kultural dan Politik Peran Perempuan* ('Reconstructing the Understanding of Gender in Islam: The Socio-Cultural and Political Role of Women'), Jakarta: el-Kahfi.
Tibi, Bassam (2003), 'Dialogue Among Civilisations: In Search of a Just and Pluralistic World Order', in Chaider S. Bamualim, Dick van der Meij and Karlina Helmanita (eds), *Islam and the West: Dialogue of Civilisations in Search of a Peaceful Global Order*, Jakarta: Pusat Bahasa dan Budaya IAIN Syarif Hidayatullah and Konrad-Adenauer-Stiftung.
Umar, Nasaruddin (1999), *Argumen Kesetaraan Jender: Perspectif Al-Qur'an* ('Arguments About Gender Equality: The Perspective of Al-Qur'an'), Jakarta: Paramadina.
Viviani, Nefisra (2001), '*Sketsa gerakan perempuan Islam Indonesia: Mengukir Sejarah baru*' ('A Sketch of the Islam Women's Movement in Indonesia: Carving Out a New History'), *Swara Rahima* Edisi 1, http://www.rahima.or.id/SR/01–01/Fokus.htm (accessed 15 November 2005).
Wieringa, Saskia (2002), *Sexual Politics in Indonesia*, Basingstoke: Macmillan.
Yuval Davis, Nira (1994), 'Women, Ethnicity and Empowerment', *Feminism and Psychology* 4 (1): 179–97.
—— (2006), 'Human/Women's Rights and Feminist Transversal Politics', in Myra Marx Ferree and Aili Mari Tripp (eds), *Global Feminisms: Transnational Women's Organizing, Activism, and Human Rights*, New York: NYU Press: 275–95.

'A new consciousness must come': Affectivity and Movement in Tamil Dalit Women's Activist Engagement with Cosmopolitan Modernity

Kalpana Ram

To Stella, who may have lost her speech, but not her voice.
I am the daughter of a fisherman, and I am married to a rice trader who is now in Saudi Arabia, working on an oil rig in the ocean. We were a poor family. I have studied up to the SSLC, but more important, I now have *arivu* [consciousness, awareness, knowledge in the widest sense] which dispels fears. I talk freely about periods and menopause since my training and I am now asked to attend births. The girls I teach are initially embarrassed but there is great curiosity afterwards. You should see the difference between me and my *akka* [elder sister]. When I began to have overbleeding in my periods, I went to the doctor, and looked at the scan with her. (Interview with health guide Jansi in fishing village, Kanyakumari, 1991)

Those exposed to our [health] talks stand out in any crowd. *They talk differently to the others*. There is great progress [*munnetram*]. (Interview with Amber, a trained midwife, from agrarian village, employed by a leading non-government organisation in Kanyakumari, 1991)

The voices of women such as Jansi and Amber are heard here as extracts from interviews I conducted in the early 1990s, part of a wider project on the changing nature of puberty and maternity among rural Tamil women from labouring classes, both fishing communities (Ram 1991) and agricultural castes in Chengalpattu District. But the dimensions of activism I explore in this paper will not do justice to the wide variety of class and caste formations I found in the course of this research. The term 'Dalit', used in the title of this chapter, is itself shaped by activist discourses rather than the local particularities I uncovered as a researcher. The term Dalit seeks to displace older, more stigmatising and patronising forms of nomenclature (such as 'untouchables', 'Scheduled Castes', 'Harijans') with a militant reference to oppression. Yet this particular experience of caste oppression does not sit very easily with the sociology of fishing communities in Kanyakumari, where caste is more a dimension of community identity – along with belonging to the sea and Catholicism – than a relationship of direct subordination to upper castes (Ram 1991). By contrast, the accounts given by activist women in the agricultural Hindu castes of Chengalpattu discussed below, draw directly from personal, often bitter, experiences of caste-based ideologies of exclusion and pollution in relations with upper castes.

In the activities and aspirations of activists such as Jansi and Amber, however, these specificities of power and place all but disappear. Even the ordinary lived experience of place – strikingly affirmed and elaborated as central to the constitution of social identity by Tamil discourses of the *ūr* or one's 'native place' (Daniel 1984) – emerges quite transformed. One's *ūr* now becomes nothing more than a site of oppressive traditions to be superseded through engaging in a wide range of transformative practices. Both Jansi and Amber worked for the Kottar Social Service Society (hereafter KSSS), managed by Belgian Catholic missionaries. During the 1980s and 1990s it ran health clinics in which babies were weighed, pregnant women monitored and medicines dispensed. The organisers gave health talks to pregnant women and mothers about a balanced diet, and advised women to have their first babies in hospitals. None of these activities, in themselves, quite capture the larger significance of what this and similar non-government organisations hope to accomplish. In south India, non-government organisations (hereafter NGOs) often use the English word 'awareness' to describe the missing dimension they hope to inculcate in villagers. The direction and character that such 'awareness' should take are equally anticipated. 'Awareness' involves adopting an essentially modern attitude, one capable of drawing a strong distinction between the self and society, in which society inevitably figures as the source of wrong, irrational or backward beliefs. Of all the categories of women I interviewed about their experiences of life transitions around puberty and maternity (Ram 1998b), it was this group of women whose representations came to the interview, as it were, already sharply thematised by the tropes of conversion and enlightenment:

I now have *aṟivu* [knowledge, awareness] which dispels my previous fears.

Amma [mother] would keep a *katti* [iron knife] in the ashes of the stove to keep the spirits from hearing the cry of the baby. When my baby was small, I was told not to go in front of women who had lost babies before birth – if I did chance on one, I was told I should give them my baby to hold for a little while. There are many *mūṭa nampikkai* [backward, foolish, irrational beliefs] around. But 75 per cent change their minds after we answer their questions.

Such distinctions flow into and help constitute these women's construction of their own identity through a sharp opposition between past and present selves. In retrospect, the old self is viewed as hedged about with fears and false beliefs, and the new self is one that may be characterised equally by the English word 'awareness' and by the Tamil word '*aṟivu*'.

On their own, giving talks on health and weighing babies could not have achieved this anticipated transformation of subjectivity. For all the language of consciousness adopted by the NGOs, it was clear that the degree to which they could shape identity and discourse depended a great deal on the temporality and durability of engagement by the women in a varied range of practices. For instance, women who, in addition to hearing talks and attending the clinics, were also organised into '*Matar Sankams*' (Tamil, or Sangham in Sanskrit) or Mothers' Organisations, tended to meet with some regularity. The women who spoke 'most differently to the others,' to use Amber's phrase, were those who had themselves received prolonged training with the NGO to act as health guides back in the villages. One of the organisers explained the training programme in Kanyakumari to me:

> Every year we train sixteen to twenty girls. If they are to be health workers, they are given six months' training, with some refresher training offered in subsequent years. If they are to be health guides, we offer them a basic training in minor ailments. Girls who are chosen for this training are chosen from those who have already been working in villages as volunteers for us for between one to four years. We began in 1971 and at its peak, we had health centres in one hundred and twenty seven villages in the district, with Colachel as the main centre. Each centre has one health guide and two health workers. In addition we run the *Matar Sankam* [mothers' groups]. (Interview 1992)

Again, the training in itself would have been insufficient to secure the change of consciousness recounted by the women. After their training, however, health guides were expected to move around between different villages, running the mothers' groups, conducting health talks, and occasionally organising village women for various forms of direct action. Mothers' groups mobilised over specific issues, such as villages' lack of water supply or proper distribution of government food rations. This was particularly the case in the 1980s after communal disturbances between Hindus and Christians in the coastal areas, and again after the recent tsunami.

Maria was a woman in her early thirties in the coastal village of Pallam. She had been involved in the *Matar Sankam* for the last nine years. In her account she moves *without pause* from her training in hygiene, to mobilising village women for direct protest action against the district level Collectorate, police and the parish priest:

> I joined to learn about *cuttam* [cleanliness, hygiene], about nutrition and care of babies and children. It has been useful – we know now about how to take care of diarrhoea in infants at home, about vaccinations, about the varieties of vegetable types, and about

not discarding the water we cook vegetables in. We learn about quarantining food and clothing during infectious diseases such as measles and chicken pox, about not using the same washing water for others, about hygiene for eye infections. We have also taken up issues concerning women – three years ago, we had a campaign opposing alcoholism among men, and now there is no longer alcohol sold in the area. We have become bolder with the police. Two years ago we went to the priest and to the collectorate to change the salt water we were being supplied with, to good water. Before that we had to travel for a kilometre for a tap, or even two if that one was broken.

Another organiser makes the same effortless transition in her discourse:

> There is great awareness about immunisation and hygiene, and treatment for diarrhoea. Where before no liquid was given, now they give the sugar and salt solution. For *vaicūri* [small pox], they seek hospital treatment. At the last Mothers' Meetings the women suggested writing to the Block Development Officer over the lack of electricity and water pumps in the village; finally they went there themselves and broke their water pots outside the office.

From the perspective of activists, then, bringing modern reforms to the village and taking direct action against administrative authorities such as church and state, are not two distinct operations but one. Nor is it possible to draw a boundary around the *type* of activity that might be fostered by such forms of engagement. Being organised into "Mothers' Groups" did not limit activity to the domain of "women's business". As with many other 'mothers' organisations' around the world such as the Mothers of Plaza de Mayo in Chile and other parts of Latin America, the very experience of organising to meet women's needs and experiences in a collective fashion was capable of generating its own political momentum and public awareness. Indeed, it was a lengthy article about fisherwomen's protests in the Indian feminist media published in Mumbai that drew me to the coastal villages of Kanyakumari in the first place, as a young feminist ethnographer back in the early 1980s. On closer inspection the women's protests, which were over the mechanisation of their work of weaving of fishing nets, emerged out of an innocuous activity – the collective weaving groups organised by an activist Catholic nun in the convent at Kanyakumari. Let me give a couple of further examples from among my close circle of acquaintances.

My research assistant during the early eighties was Seraphim, a supremely confident young woman, who had studied up to high school level, and was one of the many bright, educated yet unemployed young women with whom I found ready companionship. On subsequent trips I found her variously engaged in a diverse set of collective organisational activities – organising the older women fish vendors into a credit union, actively involved in a district-wide protest campaign over a rape case. In January 2006 I returned to take part in the memorial services one year after the tsunami – over 200 had died in Seraphim's village alone, over a hundred of them children. There were photographs of the dead everywhere, on walls and house exteriors. As I caught up with stories of the disaster, I heard from Seraphim that her activist impulse had erupted even in the midst of her own grief and chaos. Barely had she ascertained that her loved ones were alive after an agonising search among the dead bodies, than she began organising a massive collectively run kitchen erected in makeshift shelters in order to feed vast numbers of men, women and children. As aid organisations came pouring into the coastal villages, she helped mediate between villagers and aid. She even managed to locate and utilise the statistical economic data we had collected together many years earlier, as a baseline for working out the neediest families.

These 'movements' between forms of action, between different geo-political spaces, are not unproblematic for women activists, particularly insofar as they involve real physical travel out of the village and into the district, state and nation space. Another activist health care organiser and close friend of mine, Stella, who has recently suffered a stroke (and to whom this chapter is dedicated), was experiencing in the 1980s, a strong tension between the life she was expected to lead as a young widowed mother of two children and her life as a social work organiser, moving constantly around the district, having meetings in her home which included hosting local male activists, one of whom became a close personal friend of hers. I lived with the family at the time and felt daily the pressures placed on her and the two young children by the unpleasant moral scrutiny of the village gossip and innuendo. In an attempt to alleviate the tension, she moved out of the village and into the district's main town of Nagercoil and leapt at the chance when I helped find work for her in the late eighties with another activist organisation through an academic activist friend of mine, in the district of Chengalpattu, close to the metropolis of Chennai. She never looked back, eventually founding an NGO of her own, with the title of Rural Education and Animation Centre. The two children have absorbed their mother's experiences. Her daughter trained to help mentally ill children among the poor, and herself is now struggling to combine that training and aspiration with her role as wife and mother of two young children. Her son learned skills in alternative technology to help the poor build low-cost housing, and is now the charismatic leader of an international organisation based in the east coast township of Pondicherry, promoting a holistic, environmentally conscious spiritual philosophy that attracts Europeans as residents in the Ashram. In her capacity as activist organiser Stella travelled across India to Delhi for an All-India women's movement conference. Again, it was a trip that generated its own tensions. She told me wry, deprecatory stories about being 'frozen' out in Delhi, as a southerner unfamiliar with cold winters, but also blocked by the manoeuvrings of a prominent local Tamil feminist who interposed herself as a broker between the Tamil rural activists and the other delegates.

Organised activism brings with it, for these women, a fluid crossing of boundaries between village, district and nation-state. At the same time, this fluidity itself generates tensions that illuminate the underlying sexual construction of female embodiment. Language itself alerts us to this feature. 'Movement' and 'ability to work with others', both valued aspects of politicised identity, become transmogrified into the heavily loaded sexualised language of 'looseness' and 'availability' when applied to women. Nevertheless, women are not imprisoned by these meanings – the new experiences they have as activists also engender in them new capacities.

The experiences I describe are not to be sequestered within a 'present' that can be understood in isolation from the past. Shaping today's NGOs in India there lies a history of women's mobilisation that has flowed like a river through Indian modernity. That river has been fed by various streams. Kumar (1993) describes two such streams in her illustrated 'History of Doing' for the period 1800–1990. One stream includes movements such as the communist-led food campaigns of the 1940s, and the anti-alcohol and anti-price rise movements of the 1970s, which 'focused on issues which are regarded mainly as "women's concerns", because they were ancillary to the role of a housewife: water for the home, fuel for heating and cooking, food, money for food' (1993: 3). This history is to be discerned in the very readiness with which NGOs choose particular issues over which to mobilise, such as opposition to male alcoholism. Even the bodily gestures described by the coastal women, such as breaking water pots in front of the local administrative office, are themselves also part of a history of political performance: theatrical gestures that connect one struggle to another.

A second strand of mobilisation is identified by Kumar in movements dominated by men but involving large numbers of women as activists. These include the nationalist movement, but also the peasant movements known as the Tebhaga movement in Bengal and the Telengana movement in south India. Male leadership of these movements did not preclude the capacity of such movements to tackle problems related to male dominance, such as alcoholism, wife-beating and male control over familial resources. In Kumar's final characterisation, both streams mingle insofar as they exercise very similar *effects* on the women themselves. In both cases, Kumar states, 'women learnt to confront capital and the state, to work together in groups or organisations, and to feel united as women' (Kumar 1993: 3).

Cosmopolitanism, but of what kind?

I would suggest therefore that what is released by organised mobilisation is not to be defined by the specific concerns that generated it in the first place, but rather by a set of *skills*, bodily orientations and a fundamental stock of politicised gestures that can be used, in a labile fashion, in varying contexts.[1] Such an approach to understanding women's activism, based on the acquisition of skills and orientation rather than on specific issues, is particularly apposite to the literature on cosmopolitanism. While the debates often do refer to specific content of consciousness – such as an awareness of rights – what more typically emerges as 'cosmopolitan' is an *orientation*, not specific *tenets*. Held, for example, describes cosmopolitanism as an 'ability to stand outside a singular location (the location of one's birth, land, upbringing, conversion) and to mediate traditions' (Held 2002: 58). As an orientation, this would describe all the diverse situations and activities I have mentioned thus far. Indeed, I began this chapter with a reference to ideologies that *demand* that their adherents step outside the 'location of their birth', regardless of whether the activist continues to live in the village, like Seraphim, or has moved out, like Stella.

However, there is something about the very resoluteness, the absolute quality of the language used by activists that ought to suggest to us immediately that we are dealing with a very specific kind of cosmopolitanism here. Their discourse does not simply allow them, in a gentle fashion, to 'mediate traditions'. It requires of them to shun and abjure all that comes under the label of tradition, mobilising themselves and others to achieve a particular kind of 'awareness' in order to transcend and leave behind these zones of backwardness. This is not the kind of unselfconscious movement between the local and the global that Kwame Appiah celebrates in his father, in an influential article that has been described as 'perhaps the closest thing to a classic text yet generated by the new cosmopolitanism' (Hollinger 2002). For his father, according to Appiah, there was simply no contradiction between acknowledgement of one's roots and belonging as a world citizen (Appiah 1998). The activist discourse taken up by rural Tamil women is in sharp contrast both to this kind of unselfconscious acknowledgement of two planes of belonging, and to the versions of 'cultural cosmopolitanism' that celebrate a hybridity associated with diaspora and globalisation.[2] Instead, we are dealing here with something much more sharply and consciously articulated as a political philosophy. The requirements for re-making subjectivity are far more absolute than the requirements for an urban and urbane appreciation of difference. *Both* kinds may entail a transformation of identity and a broadening of horizons, but there the resemblance ends. The genealogy of these activists lies in social movements whose leadership has been informed by political ideologies that include socialism and feminism – ideologies which, far from being noted for their appreciative stance towards difference, have been notoriously vulnerable to the charge of *suppressing* differences. And unlike the humanist vision of a rights-based universalism that flows from valuing a shared essence inhering in all human beings, the politics I refer to has fostered an attitude resolutely partisan, aligned with a particular oppressed group ('the proletariat', 'women').

Yet, there is an undoubted universalism at work here. This is so in two senses. First, the category of 'the oppressed' is not limited to one location, but, by its very defining characteristics, is understood to suggest certain features of existential plight shared with similarly situated groups around the world. The very determinants of this plight are by nature *global*. Capital, by its nature, will flee the more organised sectors of the working class and find fresh sources of unorganised labour to exploit. And the global flows of capital in turn provoke, for an adequate response, a resistance that cuts across nation-states. Such a logic gives us the rationale for the *internationalism* of nineteenth- and twentieth-century socialist, anarchist and communist movements. 'Second wave' feminism made its political entry in the 1970s on a similar basis, anticipating a universal 'sisterhood' of women based on overwhelming similarities in male domination the world over.

Second, these movements have been universalist in the sense that they have held out the promise that if their struggle comes to fruition, they will bring about a new world order that is more truly universal than the 'sham' universalism of the bourgeois order they have overthrown. The liberation of the oppressed group has been linked, in this utopian vision, with the overthrow of class society and of patriarchy itself, bringing freedom for the majority rather than the minority.

This kind of *partisan* universalism is not only very different from the cosmopolitan politics of tolerance and diversity; it has been particularly vulnerable to the charge of positively *suppressing* difference. The story of second-wave feminism can be told as a triumphal resurgence of earlier activism, but it could equally be told as the story of a narrative that has generated continual challenges to its own claims of a universal sisterhood. The claim to a universality of female oppression almost immediately produced challenges from groups of women who could not see their history and location – whether of 'class, race, sexuality, ethnicity, nationality, First World/Third World' (Sinha, Guy and Woollacott 1999: 1) – being reflected in the dominant narrative.

These challenges have in turn made a powerful contribution to the reappraisal of the meanings of modernity and emancipation that has occurred over the last thirty years. I have taken part in these challenges, and have no desire to rehearse them here. My concern is rather with appraising a shift of discourses that appears to have left these rural activist women stranded in a backwater, their sentiments and language outmoded, their talk of progress and emancipation rendered anachronistic, and their version of cosmopolitanism out of step with the current debates on cosmopolitanism, which flow out of a different concern – a concern with difference and identity politics rather than with internationalism, social class and the promise of emancipation.

Reappraisals of Critiques of Modernity and Cosmopolitanism

Kumar's representation of women learning to 'confront capital and the state' is itself a register for a more widespread phenomenon, the depth of intellectual engagement in India with a broad left socialist tradition. The language she uses springs from a faith in modernity's emancipatory horizons, a tangible sense of the potential it held out as a liberator from the burdens of caste, class and gender oppression. In sharp contrast, prevailing tendencies in postmodern and postcolonial scholarship have urged us to exercise a close and hard scrutiny of progress and emancipation in order to view these discourses themselves as modalities in the workings of power. At its sharpest, the critique takes as its target the universalist aspirations and tenets of an Enlightenment modernity, denouncing them as so many presumptions, as sham universalisms. The debates on cosmopolitanism are in many ways simply an extension of these debates on the nature of modernity itself. The parallels are readily apparent. Is cosmopolitanism really a mask for the privileged existence of a white European minority of 'high flying cosmocrats'?

There is more than one way of responding to these critiques. The collection entitled *Feminism and Internationalism* (Sinha, Guy and Woollacott 1999) seeks to sustain the critique of a 'false universalism' while explicitly rejecting 'national or cultural feminisms'. The volume seeks to highlight cross-cultural alliances that are adequate to the challenge posed by the global dimensions of a 'world wide social formation fashioned by imperialism and colonialism' (ibid.: 2). We note continuities here with the logic of earlier socialist internationalisms. In India, for the most part, intellectuals have had a similar response, incorporating recent critiques into a deepening and strengthening of a local emancipatory politics rather than choosing between the two. It is predominantly in this spirit that social reform movements in India have been reappraised, in order to bring to light their class and patriarchal limitations. The history of gender and modern social reform is being rewritten as the history of a new Indian middle class, formed in the interaction between colonialism and nationalism (Sangari and Vaid 1989; Mani 1998, 1998; Uberoi 1996). Modernity is no longer unproblematically equated with female emancipation, but is increasingly understood in terms of a class relationship. Commenting on the All India Women's Congress of the 1920s and 1930s, Whitehead captures the flavour of such an analysis:

> Since the elevated nutritional, hygienic and educational standards were difficult to achieve by the majority of working-class or peasant women, they became a mark of differentiation within India itself. The 'new woman's' access to education and hygienic knowledge symbolically defined the new boundaries of the 'respectable community' within India itself. The metaphor of the mother's body as nation generated continuing

symbolic distinctions between urban middle-class and lower-status women within India, and between coloniser and colonised without, as the motherhood symbol was continually re-negotiated during this period. (Whitehead 1996: 206)

The productive insights of such an approach have entered into and shaped my own work on maternity and midwifery in rural Tamil Nadu. I have tried to illuminate the price that is paid by the poor for the privilege of coming to be regarded as educated modern subjects. The price to pay is an admission of inadequacy, the shame of the inferiority of their existing knowledge (Ram 1998a, 2001).

This injunction to re-examine the emancipatory discourses of modernity has been a source of much illumination and insight. But there has been blindness as well. In some cases, modernity is represented in action as little more than a series of exclusions, exercised in the name of progress and emancipation. Chatterjee, for instance, closes his chapter in the influential collection *Recasting Women* (1989) with the sweeping conclusion that the Indian middle class affected a *social closure* through the use of emancipatory ideals:

Ideas of freedom, equality and cultural refinement went hand in hand with a set of dichotomies which systematically excluded from the new life of the nation the vast masses of people whom the dominant elite would represent and lead, but who could never be culturally integrated with their leaders. (Chatterjee 1989: 251)

His critique represents the poor as only ever experiencing modernity as oppressive and external, as remaining forever locked outside the citadel of modernity. Yet Chatterjee is manifestly wrong on at least one count. If such understandings were originally meant to exclude the poor, they have certainly not been successful in doing so. While the style of characterisation seems to side sympathetically with the poor it does not impel one to explore or even anticipate the effects of such understandings once they begin to circulate within the ranks of the poor themselves. Yet there is by now a rich and long history of social interventions designed to bring about a change of subjectivity among the labouring classes. The forerunners of today's NGOs are to be found not only in peasant and left social movements, but in the women's organisations led by the middle class and founded in the context of the nationalist movement. *Mahila samitis* (women's associations), village and municipal women's groups were set up in Bengal in 1913 in the aftermath of the Swadeshi movement, and later formalised into umbrella organisations such as the Saroj Nalini Dutt Memorial Association (Engels 1996).

We now have empirical studies that show how the micro-interventions of conscious modernisers are related, often across social classes, with the macro-politics of colonialism and the nation. But on the *consequences* of this lengthy history of interventions, aimed precisely at reshaping the subjectivities of poor women, there is a resounding silence in the literature. The detailed ethnographic and historical work that it takes to write such subaltern experiences becomes readily subsumed, even within 'subaltern studies', under the rubric of examining dominant discourses. Conclusions such as Chatterjee's, that modernity has effected a series of exclusions as far as minorities are concerned, are destined to remain foregone conclusions in the absence of independent enquiry into the lives of minorities. By contrast, the voices of the poor women I spoke to have a distinct ring about them. Disowning or ignorant of the view that they have been excluded by modernity, or even rendered inferior by modernity, they take up a stance as active *claimants* of modernity.

I wish to examine this staking of claims in closer detail. I met Victoria as an NGO worker in Stella's new organisation, the Rural Education and Animation Centre, in the 1990s. Her narrative affords us a glimpse of how a familiar, seemingly outmoded, discourse can nevertheless be renewed and given fresh significance by a Dalit woman who integrates it into the specificities of her own life.

The Narrative of Self-Transformation: Victoria, a Dalit Non-Government Organisation Worker

My family are Roman Catholic, and we owned a little land. In my village the dominant caste is Reddiar. Before I was born, my family must have worked on their land. We had to have give way to them, not to have worn slippers in front of them, nor walked on the same path as them. Over the last thirty years or so, all that has changed. Maybe five out of every hundred still keep to the same habits and practices [*palakkam*]. In Porur, we have our own water supplies, pumpsets, handpump and new well. So we don't have to rely on the upper castes any more. We also know now that we are numerically dominant, and that frightens them a little.

Intermarriage between castes is still frowned upon. A Reddiar girl eloped with one of our (Dalit) boys, a Hindu, but the girl was brought back. In another village, an unmarried Mudaliar boy has been courting one of our SC [Scheduled Caste] girls, and the community is trying to make her marry one of the same-jati boys. But in this case, the boy might succeed.

My mother's family had some educated and important members. My mother's father was a *Tehsildar* [district administrator] and there was a school headmaster in the family. Her brother works in the railways. My mother was determined to educate her children, even though she was married at fifteen with little education. One of my brothers has finished teachers' training, another has finished 10th class at school, and I have studied up to 10th class, done a typewriting course in English and Tamil, and completed seven years of social work with the Madras Social Service. We would get food supplies from the US of soy bean oil, wheat and fish powder, which we distributed among villages. We weighed infants monthly. I did house visits and ran a twenty-day class for mothers, one hour daily. I taught them about hygiene, about infectious diseases, about the importance of weighing children, about eye infections, and about how to manage pregnancy.

In the *Matar Sankam*, which were held at night, we spoke about *penkal nilaimai* [the situation and dilemmas of girls and women], we read literature, made charts. We would encourage them to make small savings with their own credit society, get them a bank book. We held a Mother's Day one year after opening, showed a film on women's situation, organised the women into performing a play, a *kummi* [rural women's dance in Tamil Nadu].

But my upbringing was actually quite sheltered. My elder siblings got married and moved away, and my family brought me up very protected in case I went on to a bad path, or boys developed relations with me. When I was first sent to Bosco School in Madras for a better education, I was very afraid. I had to stay in a school hostel, and thought that I was to be locked up somewhere. I stuck it out for one year, very afraid of all the people. I even ran away. My father and brothers would visit me, and I could go home on weekends. Gradually I got used to everyone and eventually became so fond of my friends I didn't even wish to go home with my brothers. Eventually, they would just bring me delicacies on feast days.

I was no sooner back from school in my village of Porur, than a sister in the convent called me to do social work. My parents worked for the convent. They carried water, watered their plants, my mother washed their dishes, my father put up fences for them, did agricultural work. The Sisters had always been kind, putting aside any extra food for us. They trusted us with money lying around the place. The Mother Superior also liked us, and would say to us kids 'Your mother got you all educated'. My father sometimes got fed up with the number of children, and was doubtful about getting us educated, but my mother never gave up, because her father was educated. So the Sister from the convent called me and gave me training in how to speak and dress, simply, so you can communicate with the poor. They gave me a cycle to move around on. I was only fifteen, so the sisters had to convince the village women that I could take responsibility, despite my youth. I was afraid of the big *kūttam* [crowds] and refused to go a couple of times. The Sisters told me about their own dedication, the efforts they had to make. They taught us morality – not to laugh and mix too freely with men; they said that when we go to work we must conduct ourselves *olunka* [decently] so we could be good for marriage. They would read out from newspapers and stories for us. I saw others attending meetings, and thought, I should like to be like them. So I began to go around on my bike, taking doubles sometimes. I got insults from others. If I carried an umbrella, the villagers would say: 'Oh, look at her go with a *kuṭai* [umbrella], just like some big teacher.' I would ignore them, or retort: 'So what, have *you* paid for my umbrella?!'

[I ask about her marriage.]

I got married when I was 21 to my *atai*'s son [father's sister's son]. I had never met him before marriage. He works as a salesman for the cooperative society, selling rice and kerosene in the town of Tirumedi. I have got a man such as I prayed for. He is not abusive, does not drink or beat me, like so many women I counsel. We use the rhythm method of contraception advocated by the Sisters – so I watch my discharges, and know my fertile period. I was afraid of men when I first got married. I told my husband quite early that I did not want to be harassed [for sex] when my body is not feeling right, like during my periods. My husband agreed. Now sometimes he says he is tired and not wanting [sex], sometimes I say it. He says, you and I are both not strong, it is not good for us to have too much.

[I ask her about how she manages with her little girl while doing social work with other mothers.]

Doing this work has been difficult since I had the baby. My little girl Sharmi is two years old. I had to leave her with my husband for a ten-day training period. My mother-in-law also moved in for the time. He would come home to play with her. Later I learned he had actually stayed at home for five of those days, afraid that I would scold him for not taking care of her properly. I gave him a lot of instructions before I left. I explained to him that infections could come if she was not cleaned properly and fresh clothes changed after having a pee. But since then I have not left her at home alone – she just comes with me everywhere unless I have a night meeting.

I have changed since my mother's ideas. She brought me up not to be able to speak in front of four people, not to be able to move around. I plan to give my daughter confidence and will tell her everything she needs to know about her body and how to live her life.

Affect, Agency and Activism

Focusing on activist versions of modernity among poor women can help restore missing dimensions. Even the most powerful critiques of modernity and cosmopolitanism sometimes leave us unable to understand how so exclusionary a set of discourses could succeed in galvanising poor Dalit women. I will argue that certain missing elements have been overlooked. They perpetuate an inadequate account of the *affective* power of modernity and cosmopolitanism. In particular, we lack an adequate phenomenology of the modern activist version of cosmopolitanism. Integrally linked with this missing element, I will argue, are limitations with the conceptual tools currently available. These tools do not enable use to describe the heightened sense of agency described by activist women.

As I only have room to consider here a limited range of models, I have restricted myself to Foucault, the single most important theorist to prompt a reappraisal of what were considered 'progressive' aspects of modernity (see Merry 2006 for a recent instance of this legacy). His version of agency, properly applied, is subtle and sophisticated. Indeed, his famous insistence that we study power, not as a purely punitive exercise, but as a capacity to exercise productive effects, *relies* on an understanding of agency within power. The modern institutions of reform he investigates work not so much by outright punishment but by a process of continual monitoring, assessment, and refinement of measuring techniques. Their effectiveness depends on subjects taking hold of the discourse and fashioning themselves as active agents of the discourse. Our neoliberal universities are a classic instance of this, relying on academics fashioning themselves through both external and self-assessment forms of reporting. But so, too, are forms of agency found in Tamil rural villages. As I have described elsewhere (Ram 1998b), ordinary young women in coastal villages had developed a complex relationship to the codes of sexualised morality, creating themselves as responsible adult female subjects in and through these codes of conduct.

Foucault's later corpus of work explains the genealogy of the 'modern individual [who] could experience himself as a subject of a "sexuality"' (Foucault 1985: 5–6). Here he studies subject formation and the exercise of agency in a gentler context. Far from the institutional disciplines of prisons and asylums, his concern now is with philosophical texts, manuals of advice meant to help individuals attain their own inherent potential as rational human beings. He seems willing to allow a more substantial agency to the individual. The Greek and Roman formulations and practices discussed by Foucault do not resemble later Christian 'juridifications' that regulate sexuality within marriage and procreation. What is proposed by Plutarch, for instance, is 'not a regulation that would draw a division between permitted and forbidden acts. It is instead a mode of being, a style of relations' (Foucault 1986: 184). Commenting on the shift in his own work, Foucault (1988) describes a distinction between forms of power 'which determine the conduct of individuals and submit them to certain ends or domination' and those forms 'which permit individuals to effect by their own means or with the help of others a certain number of operations on their own bodies and souls, thoughts, conduct and way of being, so as to transform themselves in order to attain a certain state of happiness, purity, wisdom, perfection, or immortality' (1988: 18).

Certain elements of this later work – in particular, his description of projects that entail 'the affect of change, of rupture with self, past and world' (Foucault 1988: 43), resonate strongly with the voices of the women in this chapter. But there are essential continuities of approach between his earlier and later work which make his conception of agency less than adequate for a phenomenology of activism. As his defenders are among the first to point out, 'The task of studying subjectivity did indeed require a different approach, but [Foucault's own] previous researches acted more as background material than as mistakes to be corrected' (Ransom 1997: 56). Foucault himself describes the material he is seeking to explore in *The Care of the Self* in the following terms:

> The domain I will be analyzing is made up of texts written for the purpose of offering rules, opinions, and advice on how to behave as one should: "practical" texts, which

are themselves the object of a "practice" in that they were designed to be read, learned, reflected upon, and tested out, and they were intended to constitute the eventual framework of everyday conduct. These texts thus serve as functional devices that would enable individuals to question their own conduct, to watch over and give shape to it, and to shape themselves as ethical subjects; in short, their function was "etho-poetic", to transpose a word found in Plutarch. (Foucault 1986: 13)

The concern that links the earlier and the later work could be described as the investigation of an authoritative framework that becomes the basis for the sub-jectivity of an agent. The same preoccupation guides Foucault to the feature of Christianity that best fits such a description – the confessional. Foucault again shows his gift for breaking with the 'repressive hypothesis' of power: far from simply exercising punitive power, the confession is immensely productive in making desire into a discourse, in prompting the 'nearly infinite task of telling – telling oneself and another, as often as possible, everything that … had some affinity with sex' (Foucault 1976: 20). This is indeed a formulation that has enabled us to breathe a little more freely than is permitted by the tight embrace of the binary dichotomy we have inherited, that of determinism and pure freedom. We have been given a powerful formulation that works for a very particular version of agency, one that entails a productive relationship between didactic, authoritative discourses and subjectivity.

The heat generated by the debate over whether there is agency in Foucault's oeuvre has obscured a question just as important: is his version of agency adequate for describing all situations? Where, for instance, would a Foucauldian subject, shaped by confessionals, locate the emotional reserves a woman such as Victoria draws on, reserves that enable her to endure the taunts she must encounter for moving out of the circumscribed arena allotted to a Dalit woman? The Christian genealogy is certainly not irrelevant to activism among south Indian Dalits, but the Christianity that has bearing in Victoria's case is not the Christianity of the confessional incitement to talk. It is, rather, that *missionary* Christianity which galvanises subjects to *act* and to move out into the world in order to engage with transforming others. The voice of Victoria, which tells us of braving insults for moving around with bicycle and umbrella 'like some big teacher', finds an almost uncanny echo in the voice of a nineteenth-century low caste 'Bible Woman' in Nagercoil, Kanyakumari District, narrating her 'visits' to a Muslim village:

For six months we walked past the mosques round the streets without getting permission to go to a single house to teach the women, not one of whom could read Tamil. The men were at times angry with us for continuing to come, but at length one day a man took us to his house to teach his wife and then some others began to learn. This made some of the people very angry and they would not allow us to carry an umbrella or a bag and sometimes snatched away our books and tore them. They often threatened to kill

us saying that anyone who did so would gain heaven. (Records of the London Mission
Society, 1897, cited in Haggis 1999)

These 'Bible women', recruited and trained by the British Protestant missions in
the nineteenth century from the poor and lower castes such as the Nadars (Haggis
1998), are very much the prototypes of village trainees such as Victoria, Jansi or
Amala. Trained by missionaries in Travancore as intermediaries who could enter
the citadel of the upper-caste 'zenana ladies', Bible women had, in the course of
their activity, to make a striking departure from the gender norms of their communities. As women from a low status caste, they had to face hostility for presuming
to teach anything to upper castes. Even the details we hear from Victoria about the
resentment of villagers at a young girl using an umbrella, recur in the nineteenth-
century narratives. Long a prerogative of those who need not work bare-headed
under the hot sun, the use of the umbrella by a low-caste woman draws on a long
history of the semiotics of contestation (cf. Guha 1983). These moves by lower
castes could well fit Foucault's description of micro-moments of resistance. What
moves them into another sphere of action is their *organised* nature. Missions, like
today's NGOs, which have their source in India in the history of the 'voluntary
sector', consciously aim at producing social change through collective forms of
action. It is not at all a matter of infinitesimal moments of resistance, too fine
grained to last, let alone to prevail.

Foucault's formulation is well able to illuminate some aspects of the mission
experience but would plunge others into darkness. Armed with his formulation,
we can certainly trace the way in which Victoria fashions herself by employing an
available discourse which seeks to instil in her the discipline of dressing simply,
of conducting herself decently, so that she will be 'good for marriage'. We can
see how this discipline may better equip her for reforming 'the poor', from whose
ranks she has been plucked for training. But how are we to explain why the
reformist activities in which women like her may engage flow over so readily into
collective forms of action aimed at the state?

We are *systematically* missing some element of emancipatory discourses when
we stick too close to the Foucauldian formulation. In what follows, I will seek
to identify the missing element in terms of the phenomenology underlying two
very different *emotional* frameworks. In the first, which characterises Foucault's
version of agency, subjects *split themselves*. They become both the subject and
the object of discipline. As he explains in the introduction to *The Use of Pleasure*,
Foucault wishes to

analyze the practices by which individuals were led to focus their attention on themselves, to decipher, recognize, and acknowledge themselves as subjects of desire,
bringing into play between themselves and themselves a certain relationship that allows

them to discover, in desire, the truth of their being, be it natural or fallen. (Foucault 1985: 5)

Not only is the primary emphasis here on the subject's relationship to the self, a feature which has led some commentators to detect an element of solipsism at work (e.g. Werbner 2005), but the emotional tone of this relationship is slow, calculated and deliberate. The reigning verbs are 'to decipher, to recognise, to acknowledge and to act on that recognition'. This project bespeaks a certain privileged use of time, which is singularly inapposite for rural poor women.

Activism, by contrast, moves by *contagion* and releases energy precisely because it allows agents a reprieve, however temporarily, from a relationship to the world that is modelled on the relationship of subject to object. The outward-directedness of the activist project can actually *obliterate* the self/other distinction. There is an absorption in others which is not a matter of locating empathy within oneself, but of recognising essential aspects of one's own history in the history of others similarly situated. The feminist activist self *rushes ahead of itself* to find itself already there, present in the plight of the girl child married off before maturity, or in that of the bride burned for dowry – to name just two of the issues that have mobilised activists in the Indian women's movement. In the light of my earlier remarks on the problem of blindness to internal differences, I hope not to be misunderstood as romanticising such an endeavour. However, cosmopolitanism may take more than one form. It need not consist only in an appreciation of the difference between self and other. It may, as in the forms of universalism under discussion here, consist rather in a rush of identificatory emotion from self to other, where the self is enlarged by the perception of sameness and shared predicaments, generating the sense of solidarity and collective energy to act and bring change to the world.

I have used the word 'emotion' thus far to describe the qualities of activism Elsewhere I have used Heidegger's concept of *sorge* or care to explore the emotional features of feminist projects (Ram 2006). But the specifically *bodily* energy of such projects is particularly well captured by the term 'affect' as developed by Deleuze and Guattari (1987). For the activist project is precisely a mobile flow of energies and intensities that are outward directed, and social in orientation. It is a flow between bodies, augmenting the body's capacity to act. Unlike the considered deliberations in the Foucauldian version of agency, affect conveys the sense of collective excitement, the *contagious* movement of energy that allows us to be affected by others and to affect others (1987: 278). For it is this collective effervescence of organised action which allows an individual woman – to again quote Held's definition of cosmopolitanism – to 'stand outside a singular location (the location of one's birth, land, upbringing, conversion).' For Dalit women such as Victoria, the strength to stand apart comes not simply from her identification with other women, or from her place within an organisation, but from her sense of the collective energy generated in Dalit communities by a history that includes the 'Self Respect' fought for by an earlier anti-Brahmin social movement in Tamil Nadu, the importance of sheer numerical dominance in an electoral democracy, and a sense of greater autonomy. Caste has not disappeared – it is fiercely policed at the level of inter-caste marriages – but the Dalit communities know that they have the upper castes 'a little frightened'.

The somewhat hypostatised English term used by non-government organisations in Tamil Nadu now takes on a fresh meaning. NGOs train local women to become, in turn, 'animators' of others. Activist projects, with their orientation to movement and intervention in the world, seek to tap into this affective flow between bodies, to energise and, quite literally, to 'animate' others. Affect has also been described as disruptive, working *against* our habituated forms of perception 'through the force of altered, juxtaposed or disordered sensations' (Paterson 2006: 5). This feature is an integral characteristic of activists who do not, characteristically, accept the social world as a 'given'. Instead they seek to heighten 'awareness' and *arivu* or knowingness about that which hitherto been taken for granted.

Conclusion

Debates over cosmopolitanism have renewed interest in the relationship between universalisms, translocal flows, and the necessarily emplaced aspects of human identity. Scholars who seek to go beyond the legacies of the Enlightenment re-conceptualise cosmopolitanism as 'entailing multiple, uneven and non-exclusive affiliations' (Caglar 2002: 180). I have tried to explore the ways in which one strand of Enlightenment modernity, which I have typified as a *partisan* universalism on the part of the working classes and of women, continues to 'animate' the poor and the marginalised in countries like India. This form of universalism does not reflect the high value recently placed on difference, and on local identities. Quite the opposite. Impatient with differences and local boundaries, it calls on its adherents to move out of the circumscribed spaces allotted to them as women, as Dalits, and as rural poor, and to challenge the power structures of caste, the state, and the church. Its antecedents lie in the missionary structure of conversion and action, rather than in a contemplative confessional Christianity. While it may not concern itself with issues of cultural pluralism and "Otherness", this partisan, action-oriented universalism has in fact enabled those who have been cast(e) in the very role of "Other", to challenge that circumscribed location. For such women, the question of 'recognising' and 'prizing' difference is not the urgent one.

I have emphasized the new forms of mobility that embody this challenge – the fluid movement between concerns of very different kinds, and the physical mobility between village, district and nation. But equally, this mobility is present in the very structure of affective involvement which propels the self out into the world, transcending its original location and finding itself in an expanded sphere of agency and identifications that have the capacity to dissolve the boundaries between the local and the global.

Notes

1. This thesis is amply substantiated by the literature surveying women's mobilisations around the world. See for example, Basu (1999).
2. See Featherstone 2002 for an overview.

References

Appiah, Anthony Kwame (1998), 'Cosmopolitan Patriots', in Pheng Cheah and Bruce Robbins (eds), *Cosmopolitics: Thinking and Feeling Beyond the Nation*, Minneapolis: University of Minnesota Press, pp. 91–114.

Basu, Amrita (ed.) (1999), *The Challenge of Local Feminisms, Women's Movements in Global Perspectives*, New Delhi: Kali For Women.

Caglar, Ayse (2002), 'Media Corporatism and Cosmopolitanism', in Steven Vertovec and Robin Cohen (eds), *Conceiving Cosmopolitanism, Theory, Context and Practice*, Oxford: Oxford University Press, pp. 180–90.

Chatterjee, Partha (1989), 'The Nationalist Resolution of the Women's Question', in Kumkum Sangari and Sudesh Vaid (eds), *Recasting Women, Essays in Colonial History*, New Delhi: Kali for Women, pp. 233–53.

Daniel, Valentine (1984), *Fluid Signs, Being a Person the Tamil Way*, Berkeley: University of California Press.

Deleuze, Gilles and Felix Guattari (1987), *A Thousand Plateaus, Capitalism and Schizophrenia*, Minneapolis: University of Minnesota.

Engels, Dagmar (1996), *Beyond Purdah? Women in Bengal 1890–1939*, Delhi: Oxford University Press.

Featherstone, M. (2002) *Theory, Culture and Society*, Special Issues on Cosmopolitanism, 19 (1–2).

Foucault, Michel (1976), *The History of Sexuality, Volume One: An Introduction*, Harmondsworth: Penguin Books.

—— (1985), *The Use of Pleasure, The History of Sexuality, Volume 2*, Harmondsworth: Penguin Books.

—— (1986), *The Care of the Self, The History of Sexuality, Volume 3*, Harmondsworth: Penguin Books.

—— (1988),'Technologies of the Self', in Luther H. Martin, H. Gutman and P. H Hutton (eds), *Technologies of the Self: A Seminar with Foucault*, London: Tavistock Publications.

Guha, Ranajit (1983), *Elementary Aspects of Peasant Insurgency in Colonial India*, Delhi: Oxford University Press.

Haggis, Jane (1998), '"Good Wives and Mothers" or "Dedicated Workers"? Contradictions of Domesticity in the "Mission of Sisterhood",' in Kalpana Ram and Margaret Jolly (eds), *Maternities and Modernities:, Colonial and Postcolonial Experiences in Asia and the Pacific*, Cambridge: Cambridge University Press, pp. 81–113.

Held, David (2002), 'Culture and Political Community: National, Global and Cosmopolitan', in S. Vertovec and R. Cohen (eds.), *Conceiving Cosmopolitanism. Theory, Context and Practice*, Oxford: Oxford University Press, pp. 48–58.

Hollinger, David (2002), 'Not Universalists, Not Pluralists: The New Cosmopolitans Find Their Own Way', in Steven Vertovec and Robin Cohen (eds), *Conceiving Cosmopolitanism, Theory, Context and Practice*, Oxford: Oxford University Press, pp. 227–39.

Kumar, Radha (1993), *The History of Doing: An Illustrated Account of Movements for Women's Rights and Feminism in India, 1800–1990*, New Delhi: Kali for Women.

Mani, Lata (1998), *Contentious Traditions: The Debate on Sati in Colonial India*, Berkeley: University of California Press.

Merry, Sally Engel (2006), *Human Rights and Gender Violence, Translating International Law into Local Justice*, Chicago: University of Chicago Press.

Paterson, Mark W.D. (2006), 'Affecting Touch: Towards a "Felt" Phenomenology of Therapeutic Touch', paper given at 'Senses, Postcolonialism and Globalisation,' Research Cluster of Centre for Research on Social Inclusion, Macquarie University.

Ram, Kalpana (1991), *Mukkuvar Women: Gender, Hegemony and Capitalist Transformations in a South Indian Fishing Community*, St Leonards: Allen and Unwin (also published 1992 by Kali for Women, New Delhi.)

—— (1998a), 'Maternity and the Story of Enlightenment in the Colonies: Tamil Coastal Women, South India' in Kalpana Ram and Margaret Jolly (eds), *Maternities and Modernities: Colonial and Post Colonial Experiences in Asia and the Pacific*, Cambridge: Cambridge University Press, pp 114–43.

—— (1998b), 'Uneven Modernities and Ambivalent Sexualities: Women's Construction of Puberty in Coastal Kanyakumari, Tamilnadu' in Mary E. John and

Janaki Nair (eds), *A Question of Silence? The Sexual Economies of Modern India*, New Delhi: Kali for Women, pp. 269–303.

—— (2001), 'Modernity and the Midwife', in Linda H. Connor and Geoffrey Samuel (eds), *Healing Powers and Modernity, Traditional Medicine, Shamanism and Science in Asian Societies*, Westport: Bergin and Garvey, pp. 64–84.

—— (2006), 'Temporality and Sorge in the Ethical Fashioning of the Feminist Self,' in Elizabeth McMahon and Brigitta Olubas (eds), *Feminist Temporalities*, Perth: University of Western Australia Press, pp. 191–220.

Ransom, J. (1997), *Foucault's Discipline: the Politics of Subjectivity*, Durham/London: Duke University Press.

Sangari, Kumkum and Sudesh Vaid (eds) (1989), *Recasting Women: Essays in Colonial History*, New Delhi: Kali for Women.

Sinha, Mrinalini, Donna J. Guy and Angela Woollacott (eds) (1999), *Feminisms and Internationalisms*, Oxford: Blackwell Publications.

Uberoi, Patricia (ed.) (1996), *Social Reform, Sexuality and the State*, New Delhi: Sage.

Werbner, Pnina (2005), 'Dialogical Subjectivities For Hard Times: Expanding Political and Ethical Imaginaries of Elite and Subaltern Southern African and South Asian Women', keynote address, Conference on 'Self and Subject: African and Asian Perspectives,' September, Ferguson Centre, Edinburgh.

Whitehead, Judy (1996), 'Modernising the Motherhood Archetype: Public Health Models and the Child Marriage Restraint Act of 1929,' in Patricia Uberoi (ed.), *Social Reform, Sexuality and the State*, New Delhi: Sage Publications.

Section III
Rooted Cosmopolitanism,
Public Cosmopolitans

–8–

A Native Palestinian Anthropologist in Palestinian-Israeli Cosmopolitanism
Aref Abu-Rabia

Background

This chapter will dwell on the meaning of being a native anthropologist in Palestine-Israel in the twenty-first century. It will also explore the roles of the native anthropologist in conflicted Palestinian-Israeli society. Complex questions will be discussed – such as whether cosmopolitanism can really exist in such types of societies and whether anthropologists have a role in facilitating or maintaining cosmopolitanism – and the issues raised will be illustrated by case studies from fieldwork in Israeli and Palestinian societies.

I will begin by describing my background, in order to present my position and, more importantly, to be very explicit to you concerning myself. I was born into the Abu-Rabia tribe, a Bedouin tribe in the Negev Desert. My tribe migrated to Palestine in the seventeenth century as descendants from Bili clans in the area of the Hejaz in the Arabian Peninsula (Abu-Rabia 2001: 130–31; Al-Aref 1934; Bailey 1985: 20–49, 1989: 9–21). I have, to date, never visited the Arabian Peninsula. Nonetheless, I am a Bedouin man whose spiritual and ethical universe and worldview is based on the Arabic language and civilisation, and the Islamic religion.

I grew up as part of a semi-nomadic family, and until the age of twenty I lived in a tent with my parents, brothers and sisters. My family raised livestock and camels and pure breed horses. When I was a young boy I studied three to four hours a day with a tribal teacher along with half a dozen other boys. When I was eight, my father sent me to follow my three brothers at a tribal primary school run by the Israeli Ministry of Education, situated seven kilometres from our encampment. I shared a donkey with my brothers and it was very hot in the summer and cold in winter. We were all sons of the leaders and notables of our tribe (Abu-Rabia 2001). I did not like school very much, but one day, the teacher gave me his bicycle to ride and this made me feel happy. That was the first time in my life I saw a bicycle. When I completed primary school my father sent me with my eldest brothers to the high school in Nazareth. It was one day's travel by bus. There, we rented a house to live in. That was the first time I studied with Arabs who came from towns and villages (*fellahin*). It was very difficult for me to adapt and speak in fellahin or the city dialects of my classmates. Living outside my tribe was certainly a signature event in my life. Once a term (of four months) we returned home for the holidays to visit our family. The whole tribe waited and welcomed us when we arrived in the car of my uncle – the Sheikh of the tribe. That was the best feeling one can imagine. However, the last day of the holiday was very sad. We were rooted in our culture, but we were obliged for the sake of our tribe to be educated, and there was no compromise.

After four years I completed high school and was appointed as a teacher in my tribal school. I decided to go on to the university and completed a BA in Pedagogy, and a Master's degree in Public Health at Israeli universities. I was later granted a scholarship from the British Council for one year to go to University College London to study Anthropology and Health Education for two years. (The second year was at my own expense, assisted by other charities and friends, and I never ceased to complain about the unwillingness of the British Council to support me for one more year, given that Great Britain ruled mandated Palestine as an imperialist power for thirty years.)

Financial problems brought me back to Israel, to study for my PhD in anthropology at Tel-Aviv University under the supervision of Professor Emanuel Marx. I continued to work as a teacher and later on as a superintendent of Bedouin Education. For me, studying anthropology was my first priority while for my parents and community it was the last one. Above all, my job has been as a mediator, a go-between among my people, the Bedouin, and the Israeli authorities. The mediator has a unique function among the Bedouin (Marx 1981: 119–26). The Bedouin have seen in me one of them and I stand on their side and identify with them. Since I held a higher university degree and served as a senior official in the Education Ministry, some of my people considered me as a 'friend' (the euphemism for a collaborator, a very insulting title in Arab society) of the Israeli authorities. The more I helped them to solve crucial problems (appointing more than a thousand teachers (male and female) during ten years), the more they considered me a 'friend of the Israeli authorities'. On the other hand, the Israeli authorities regarded me as 'their' official and asked me to carry out the Israeli law and to be loyal to the state. When I hesitated, disagreed or finally opposed some of the authorities' policies, they considered me an Arab, Palestinian, Muslim – in short, a person not loyal to the ethos of the state of Israel. It was very difficult for me, and sometimes impossible, to convince the Israeli authorities that reforms can only be done slowly, and by persuasion, in order to narrow and close the gaps between the state and its minorities.

The Palestinians and Israel have been in a struggle over land since long before the establishment of the state of Israel in 1948. It should be noted that the conflict between the Bedouin and Israel over the land has an ethnic dimension, as Israel considers the Bedouin a separate segment of the (repressed) Palestinians inside Israel (Marx and Meir 2005: 43). Israel views itself as the only democratic state in the Middle East, representing Western modern culture and enlightenment, and sees the Bedouin as the most backward of all Middle Eastern communities. Israel views its Bedouin citizens as Arabs, Palestinians and Muslims rather than full citizens. Despite the fact that some of the Bedouin have served in the Israeli army since 1948, and many have been killed in the line of duty, these citizens are not yet integrated into Israeli society. Many of their villages are awaiting basic infrastructure. More than 50 per cent of them are waiting to be supplied with running water and electricity.

It is worth mentioning that during the last several years, the Israel Lands Authority has leased large parcels of confiscated Bedouin lands to Jewish settlers in 'individual farms' in order to prevent what the Israeli officials call the 'encroachment of the Bedouin on State Lands'. In these farms the new settlers raise goats and cows. Needless to say, these 'individual farms' are immediately supplied with running water and electricity, financial supports and governmental grants.

Case Study

My nuclear family and I had planned to visit Jordan and we put our baggage in our car and drove to the Eilat-Aqaba border between Israel and Jordan. At the Israeli checkpoint we were checked very carefully. The security officers examined our car, the car documents, baggage and passports and asked us a series of questions: 'What is the purpose of your visit to Jordan? What is your job title? Where do you work, etc.?' I told them that I am a lecturer in the university, showing them my university identity card. Then they gave us some instructions about security awareness, etc. We paid the travel taxes on the Israeli side. To be honest, the Israeli officials treated us with respect, although they maintained the strict security procedure. They wished us all the best in Jordan, and said to me: 'We [the Israelis] trust that you [the Bedouin] will represent us in a good manner in Jordan.' I answered: 'Of course, of course.'

Then we moved to the Jordanian checkpoint. There, we were welcomed in English, and I answered in Arabic. The Jordanian official asked me where we were from, and I answered from Israel. Then I added that we are Palestinians inside Israel. (The term '*Arab al-48*' is coined by the Arab countries in order to make clear and perhaps draw a line between the Palestinians who live on the West Bank, the Gaza Strip and Arab countries, and the Palestinian citizens of Israel who remained inside Israel after its establishment in 1948). He began checking our documents and passports. Then he turned to our baggage and ordered me in a very officious way: 'Open the suitcases, please. What do you have in them? Who packed them?' These were more or less the same questions that were asked on the Israeli side. While I was opening the suitcases, an officer approached us and welcomed us, asking me where I was coming from. I gave him the same answers. Then he added one more question: 'Where are you living exactly?' I told him that I live near Beer-Sheva, in the Abu-Rabia Tribe. The next question, asked with half a smile, was: 'Are you a relative of Sheikh Hammad Abu-Rabia?' My answer: 'Yes, yes, he was my uncle.' It is worth noting that Sheikh Hammad Khalil Abu-Rabia was my cousin, but I never referred to him this way, but rather by the title of Uncle as a show of respect for him in that position. Sheikh Hammad was the sheikh of the Abu-Rabia tribe since 1948; he was elected by the Bedouin in Israel as a member of the Knesset (the Israeli Parliament), from 1973 to 1977 and 1979 to 1981, until he was murdered by a Druze in 1981. During his term, he became the leader of the Bedouin throughout the country, and helped many Palestinians, solving their problems with the Israel authorities – mainly the military administration in Gaza and the West Bank. After his murder, sheikhs and leaders of the Bedouin and urban Arabs from all over the Middle East came to console our family, notably the sheikhs of Jordan and the representative of King Hussein (Abu-Khusa 1994: 124–5; Abu-Rabia 2001: 130–1).

The officer shook my hand warmly and asked me to follow him to his office, ordering the official to stop checking our suitcase; as I followed him to his office, he said, 'I have sworn that the luggage of Abu-Rabia will not be checked in the Jordanian land'. There, while drinking Bedouin coffee, he told me that he is a Bedouin, and his tribe has excellent relations with my uncle and the Abu-Rabia tribe. His sheikh knew our sheikh personally. Finally, he invited me and my family to be his guests. I thanked him very much and apologised that as I had duties and only limited time, my next visit would be better for me. When I approached my car I found my family was being served cold drinks by the Jordanian officials. My children felt very happy about the warm welcome. We thanked the officials and left to make our way to Aqaba, directed by a Jordanian police jeep to guide us until we arrived at the Crystal Hotel. I should mention that at the border they removed our car number plates and replaced them with Jordanian ones (this was for security reasons in accord with the Israeli–Jordanian peace treaty). In the hotel reception they welcomed us and asked for our passports, 'Are you Israelis, please?' I answered in Arabic, 'We are from Israel, but we are Palestinians – *Arab al-48.*' The official answered, 'Yes, yes I know that.' Then he said, 'Welcome to the Palestinians in Jordan.' The next day, on our way to Petra, we met some Bedouin and talked to them for some time before arriving at our hotel in the centre of Amman. At the reception they asked me the same questions and I gave the same answers. The receptionist told me that he was originally from Jerusalem. I kept talking to him in the Palestinian dialect of the Galilee. In Amman, Jarash and Irbid I kept talking with people in that same dialect.

One evening, near the reception of the hotel in Amman, I met a group of Arab teachers on an organised trip coming from Israel talking mixed languages – namely, Arabic, Hebrew and English. One of the teachers approached me asking me if I am Aref. I told him, yes. He shook my hand and welcomed me. He told me that I appointed him as a teacher in the Bedouin schools in the Negev when I was the superintendent there. He and other teachers invited me for a coffee and we chatted for a long time. One of the teachers said that he was happy to meet me there in Jordan: 'Where the Bedouin find each other in any place, they greet each other as brothers (*alakhow*) even when not acquainted; we feel sympathy and commitment for each other – like the Jews *kol yisrael arevim ze la ze* – which means 'all Jews are responsible for each other'– We are brave and maybe one day we will control all the Middle East... We [the Bedouin] need to be like them [the Jews] and to have their smart mind and their money. What do you think, Aref?' I said, without any hesitation: 'We need to be highly educated like them and to have all the petrol money of the Middle East, and then we can join the Jews or the Jews can join us to control the world.' The group burst out laughing. We did not notice that the Palestinian receptionist stood nearby and overheard us. He looked at us seriously and said: 'Really I don't care if you control the world or not, but please make your friends – the Israelis – leave my Palestine. Who said that you are Palestinians?' And he left in complete silence. I went back to my bedroom, thinking about that.

After some days we came back from Jordan to Israel through the Sheikh Hussein checkpoint. We were checked by the Jordanian officials, with the same routine process. They removed the Jordanian car number plates and brought back the Israeli car number plates as we moved to the Israeli side. There we underwent more or less the same routine, in addition also checking my car with a special monitor device to detect any sabotage material. The official ordered my wife to get out of the car, and asked her to take off her eye glasses, comparing the passport photograph to the real colour of her eyes. Then the official asked my eldest son (8 years old), Amir, to get out of the car. Amir refused and told the official that he has the right to stay in his father's car and to be checked there, saying that in Hebrew. I tried to intervene but the official refused and called a patrol policeman to come. They asked Amir, 'Where did you learn such stupid rights?' Amir answered: 'In a Beer-Sheva Jewish Kindergarten, my teacher Golda had taught us the rights of children in Israel.' Surprisingly, the police and the official burst out in laughing and told Amir: 'You are a clever boy but you have Israeli *chutzpah*,' and left us. After that we were checked by the Customs and Excise section. After this unpleasant procedure we found ourselves free of this border ordeal. The temperature was above 41 degrees. After three and half hours we arrived in our tribe. They were waiting for us, more than happy to receive us, and were astonished as to why we had taken such a long time (one week) away from the tribe.

Discussion

The word 'cosmopolitan', is derived from the Greek, meaning 'citizen of the world', and has been used to describe a wide variety of important views on moral and socio-political philosophy. The core idea is that all human beings, regardless of their political affiliation, do belong to a single community (see *Stanford Encyclopedia of Philosophy* 2002).

According to Hage (1998: 200–2), the term cosmopolitan has been used to describe individuals that are well travelled and can immerse themselves comfortably in various cultural settings. Hage portrays the 'cosmopolites' ironically as elites who are 'white' 'class figures' that are 'open to all forms of otherness' and consume 'high quality' commodities and cultures, including 'ethnic' cultures. In his view, the language of tolerance of such white multicultural cosmopolites obscures an underlying racism. For Calhoun too (2002: 86–109) cosmopolites who have citizenships beyond affiliations with local places or nation-states, are most often elites. Waldron (1992: 751–93), like Hage, argues that it is all very well to be a cosmopolitan if you are a white American academic, or, if you are not a member of the white privileged elite, 'play their tune'.

This critical view of cosmopolitanism is countered by Hiebert (2002: 212), who argues that cosmopolitanism is a way of living based on openness to all forms of otherness and associated with appreciation and interaction with people from other cultural backgrounds. Unlike critics of cosmopolitanism, he uses this term not in the sense of a disconnected elite, but in the sense of the capacity to interact across cultural lines. Whereas most scholars have white Europeans in mind, Hiebert acknowledges the possibility that others too can also be cosmopolitan.

Arab-Muslim empires established cultural and scientific centres that in their golden age comprised aspects that could be called cosmopolitanism. For example, the Abbasid court in its golden age in the eight and ninth centuries (Hitti 1952: 311–12; Ullmann 1978: 7–40), and in the Western end of the Islamic empire period (Andalus-Islamic Spain) in the eight to the fifteenth centuries (Al-Najjar 1994: 159–229; Johnstone 1998: xxxi–xxxii) are examples of cosmopolitan centres. In such cosmopolitan milieus, Muslims, Jews and Christians participated in translating and inventing arts, literature, medicine, philosophy, music, poetry, and other sciences, of different cultures and civilisations from Greece, Persia, Arabia, as well as from Europe. In the late nineteenth and early twentieth centuries, Cairo, together with Alexandria, was one of the cosmopolitan centres. For example, the dialogue between Muslims and Christians in Cairo revealed the centrality of

Cairo as a cosmopolitan city with intellectual resources, a developed publishing industry, and open political discourse reflecting the existence of a vibrant civil society at the start of the twentieth century (Ayalon 1995: 51–62; Gershoni 1999: 44–54). It is worth mentioning that Cairo and Alexandria are called by Zubaida (2002: 32–41) the golden age of Middle Eastern cosmopolitanism, which occurred in the political context of European imperial dominance.

I believe that caution should be exercised in drawing conclusions about cosmopolitanism on the basis of conditions in one particular Western country such as Australia or the USA. Even when considering a single country, caution should be exercised in drawing analogies from one period to another. The processes of socialisation, modernisation, and integration are related to those of cultural adaptation. It behoves one to remember that Arab-Muslim civilisation, spanning as it has almost two millennia, cannot be discarded, abandoned or superseded in a single, albeit modern, century.

A person has many layers of identification which may be private or revealed to the public. If nomadic Bedouin have perhaps always been cosmopolitan in some sense, the founding of the state of Israel and the ambitions of my tribe created the conditions which compelled me to be and act like a cosmopolitan. Being an anthropologist and an academic impelled me further into cultural worlds far beyond the place of my birth.

Due to the fact that the native anthropologist belongs to multiple worlds, both professionally and personally, he becomes bi- or multicultural (Narayan 1993: 673–682). Indeed, according to Bauman (1996) one often settles with a combination of overlapping identities and lives on the strength of this combination. But in contexts of global inequality arising from a post-national distribution of labour and wealth and the globalisation of the job market (Elkins 1995), rich countries export their low-skill jobs to poor countries while reserving the high-skilled jobs for themselves. Hence, whereas globalisation blurs identities and boundaries, it also erects new ones (Beck 2002: 81).

Boundaries of countries in the Middle East are barriers that two World Wars and local conflicts have established. In the Middle East it is quite usual for borders to shift, become fluid or hold varying meanings for different peoples and identities. Boundaries include the symbolic and social dimensions associated with the border divisions that appear on maps, or other dividing lines that cannot be found on any map at all. According to Migdal (2004: 5–6) 'One may think of people acting according to a set of laws on one side of a state boundary, and others acting on the basis of a different code on the other side of the boundary.' Rules, customs that are clear on one side of the border, could be understood differently on the other side for sociocultural, political, security, or even racial, reasons. What is permitted on one side could be forbidden on the other side.

Carrying my many identities or mixed identities (and sometimes frustration identities), I crossed the borders between Israel and Jordan through the Palestinian West Bank. In crossing these recently created borders, one of my identities was minimised, the other ignored, the third was more profound, but in other situations that identity was ignored. Each one was used at the checkpoints, hotels, etc., according to the situation. As a traveller, I felt that I needed all of them, so I kept them in one 'mind box' applying each one according to the situation in Jordan and Israel, as well as with Palestinians.

It should be noted that the attitude of Israel towards the Palestinian citizens in its midst was determined according to one central goal, to supervise them (Asmar 1975; Lustick 1980), to control them and to render them manageable and transparent to state power (Kemp 2004: 80), using the state's security needs as a pretext for suppressing them. The policy of limiting access to national membership based on racial distinctions has become the norm in Israel, rather than the promotion of the greater inclusion of all her citizens, as happened in the USA in the nineteenth century (Basson 2004: 176). Held (1995: 233) argues that some bureaucracies fail to comprehend that people have come to enjoy multiple citizenships and political membership in diverse political communities and have become citizens of both their immediate political communities and of the wider regional and global communities, thereby becoming more cosmopolitan.

Theories of globalisation and multiculturalism imply a process which assumes that dominant and minority cultures will become integrated both within nation-states and globally. But this openness can be seen by individuals living exclusively within the domain of what they perceive to be their homogeneous cultural community as a dangerous threat. Furthermore, as argued by Hiebert (2002), the more people interact between dominant and minority cultures and become more multicultural, the more they become cosmopolitan. Therefore, cosmopolitanism has been depicted as complimentary to globalisation and the movement of people around the world, particularly in major cities like Paris, London and New York.

Yet these cosmopolitan cities in the twenty-first century are, in fact, closed to most people from Asia and Africa, who can only enter as illegal migrants, and are constructed as a threat to the integrity of the nation. Ironically, as the European Union expands, with fewer border checkpoints between member countries, new barriers are being erected to prevent Asians and Africans from migrating into the Union and participating in its 'cosmopolitan theatrical play.' Not having free access to the West, they can only dream about the 'white cosmopolitan' cities, beyond the 'dark and racist' checkpoints. It doesn't matter if you are a black worker or a tenured professor, you are conceived of as a dark/coloured skin, so you can't be belong to the twenty-first century 'white' European Union. In simple words, please don't be a threat or a danger to our Union.

So, too, the exclusionary practices of successive Israeli governments, and the regional conflict, have turned former cosmopolitans into eternal strangers. Indeed, this may be the fate of all true cosmopolitans. Yet we remain steadfastly rooted in our land.

The Palestinian citizens in Israel have the feeling that 'when we are in Israel we miss the Palestinian people, but when we are in the Palestinian territories or Arab countries they consider us as Israelis or Israeli friends; then we miss Israel.' It hurts me personally that most of the time we feel that we should apologise for staying to live in steadfastness (*samidun*) in Israel, or what is called the 'captured Palestine' by Arab countries. The term *samidun* means steadfastness in the face of the Zionists, and is used to describe Palestinians citizens in Israel (Bardenstein1999: 148–70; Khalidi 1997: 177–209; Pettet 2000: 195–6; Sayigh 2000: 464–94; Schulz 2003: 105–7). Our predicament in Israel cannot be understood by any Arab citizen, but only by ourselves. The healing process must be initiated, motivated and carried out by ourselves in Israel, for good and for bad. Time heals all wounds and, I hope, political situations.

Palestinian intellectuals in Israel must wear spotless white gloves. If favouring their relatives in the Palestinian authority, living under occupation, they must at the same time show that they are not supporting terrorists. As a result, they cannot help feeling that there is something wrong with them – perhaps they have collaborated with the Israeli authorities, or betrayed their Palestinian people! That bad feeling reminds me of the Jews after World War II who survived the Holocaust, when they were faced with such questions. How could they have survived when six million Jews were killed by the brutal Nazis (see Segev 1991: 99–170; Yablonka 1999: 9–78)? Sometimes, understanding tragic situations threatens to cripple judgement, because to understand is almost to justify; but I am not intending to justify anyone but myself. Needless to say, there is no comparison (at least, for me) between the misery caused by the Israeli Authorities/State of Israel and Nazi cruelty.

The attitude of the Bedouin and the Israeli authorities towards me caused me to feel like a stranger. My academic profession and position as a senior government official, and later as an academic, made me more and more a stranger. Simmel (1950a) suggested in a most interesting way that in the modern cosmopolitan world every individual becomes a stranger (Simmel 1950b). This idea reappears in the work of many native and non-native sociologists and anthropologists, such as Bauman (1995), Coser (1977), Lipman (1997), Lofland (1973), Marx (2005), Nakhleh (1979), Narayan (1993) and Ohnuki-Tierney (1984).

The role of Palestinian-Israeli intellectuals and political leaders in the face of the daily suffering, killings and dispossession of their fellow Palestinians is painful and risky. Those who speak out in public are often vilified or ridiculed.

Behind the scenes, reforms can sometimes be achieved by persuasion, such as when I helped expand Bedouin education during the time I was employed as a civil servant. As an academic anthropologist, teaching in a department of Middle East studies, I used my position to present my students and colleagues with a more balanced picture of the Middle East conflict and Palestinian society, to humanise its members and make their case.

There have been distinguished Arab-Palestinian activists who have been recognised by a wider public in Israel, and beyond it, in the Arab world. Emile Habibi, a founder and member of the Communist Party in Israel, was awarded the Israel prize. He was, in many senses, a truly rooted cosmopolitan who never abandoned his native city of Haifa but continued throughout his life to speak out against injustice, while accepting his citizenship in the State of Israel. Israel has never had an Israeli-Palestinian minister (until January 2007), and has never included left-wing Arab parties in its coalitions. Arab members of the Knesset who speak out there – for example, against the war in Lebanon – are regarded as traitors by the majority and sometimes even condemned by left-wing Israeli parties.

Within the university and anthropological community in Israel there are some who document the Palestinian minority's predicament, and this is true of some members of the Jewish and Jewish-Palestinian peace movement. Not all are 'false' cosmopolites. In this respect, I do not feel that I am alone. But we rooted cosmopolitans are weak politically and marginalised socially.

Despite all this, I am not a stranger. I live in my own land and want its long-term welfare, the welfare of my people, Israel, Palestine and the whole Middle East. In this sense, perhaps, I am a 'rooted' cosmopolitan, or cosmopolitan patriot (see Appiah 1998: 91–114).

Instead of this feeling of estrangement, I would argue that segments of the Palestinian citizens in Israel may be equally, if not more, cosmopolitan than the elites in business, religious movements, politics, media, arts and academia. I am not as naive as to think that it is easy to achieve that sense of cosmopolitanism in Israel, since the Palestinians at all times have to feel the suspicions and 'stranger-hood' inflicted upon them by the Israeli authorities and the majority society, which imposes itself tangibly on their senses.

Nevertheless, despite this, I would like to say and express my feeling clearly and frankly: I am not a stranger like Simmel, nor the 'stranger of Simmel' but I am the stranger of Aref in my Bedouin community, in my academia in Israel, among the Palestinians, as well as among the Arabs. Because I also feel that I am a part of most of these communities with my own kind of cosmopolitanism, I think that I am one among a handful of the Israeli and Palestinian cosmopolitans. I hope they think the same of me; but if they don't think so, I forgive them! And I hope they forgive me because some of them love me more even than I do myself. This loving feeling gives me the optimism to survive, endure and feel cosmopolitan.

References

Abu-Khusa, Ahmad (1994), *Mausw'at Qabayil Beer al-Saba' wa-'Ashairiha al-Raiysiah*, Amman: Sherket al-Sharq al-Awsat le-Teba'a, pp. 124–5.

Abu-Rabia, Aref (2001), *A Bedouin Century: Education and Development Among the Negev Tribes in the 20th Century*, Oxford: Berghahn Books.

Al-Aref, Aref (1934), *Tarikh Beer al-Saba' wa-Qabai'liha*, Jerusalem: n.p.

Al-Najjar, Amer (1994), 'al-Ttibb fi al-Andalus,' in *Fi Tarikh al-Ttib fi al-Dawlah al-Islamyya*, ('History of Medicine in the Islamic Empire'), Al-Qahira: Dar al-Ma'aref, pp. 159–229.

Appiah, K. Anthony (1998), 'Cosmopolitan Patriot', in *Cosmopolitics*, Pheng Cheah and Bruce Robbins (eds), Minneapolis: University of Michigan Press, pp. 91–114.

Asmar, Fouzi El- (1975), *To be an Arab in Israel*, London: Frances Pinter.

Ayalon, Ami (1995), *The Press in the Arab Middle East*, Oxford: Oxford University Press.

Bailey, Clinton (1985), 'Dating the Arrival of the Bedouin Tribes in Sinai and the Negev', *Journal of the Economic and Social History of the Orient* 28 (1): 20–49.

—— (1989), 'The Janabib Tribe in the Negev: Facts and Folkloric Traditions', *Notes on the Bedouin* 20: 9–21.

Bardenstein, Carol (1999), 'Trees and Forests Reconsidered: Palestinian and Israeli Acts of Memory', in Mieke Bal, Jonathan Crewe and Leo Spitzer (eds), *Acts of Memory: Cultural Recall in the Present*, Dartmouth: University Press of New England, pp. 148–70.

Basson, Lauren (2004), 'Challenging Boundaries and Belongings: Mixed Blood, Allotment at the Turn of the Twentieth century', in Joel Migdal (ed.), *Boundaries and Belonging: States and Societies in the Struggle to Shape Identities and Practices*, Cambridge: Cambridge University Press, pp. 151–76.

Bauman, Gerd (1996), *Contesting Culture: Discourses of Identity in Multi-Ethnic London*, Cambridge: Cambridge University Press.

Bauman, Zygmunt (1995), *Life in Fragments: Essays in Postmodern Morality*. Oxford: Blackwell.

Beck, Ulrich (2002), 'The Cosmopolitan Perspective: Sociological in the Second Age of Modernity', in Steven Vertovec and Robin Cohen (eds), *Conceiving Cosmopoloitanism: Theory, Context, and Practice*, Oxford: Oxford University Press, pp. 61–85.

Calhoun, Craig (2002), 'The Class Consciousness of Frequent Travelers: Towards a Critique of Actually Existing Cosmopolitanism', in Steven Vertovec and Robin Cohen (eds), *Conceiving Cosmopoloitanism: Theory, Context, and Practice*, Oxford: Oxford University Press, pp. 86–109.

Coser, Lewis (1977), 'George Simmel', in *Masters of Sociological Thoughts: Ideas in Historical and Social Context*, 2nd edn, New York: Harcourt Brace Jovanovich, pp. 177–215.

Elkins, David (1995), *Beyond Sovereignty: Territorial and Political Economy in the Twenty-first Century*, Toronto: University of Toronto Press.

Gershoni, Israel (1999), *Light in Shadow: Egypt and Fascism 1922–1937*, Tel Aviv: Am Oved.

Hage, Ghassan (1998), *White Nation: Fantasies of White Supremacy in a Multicultural Society*, Sydney: Pluto Press.

Held, David (1995), *Democracy and the Global Order: From the Modern State to Cosmopolitan Governance*, Cambridge: Polity Press.

Hiebert, Daniel (2002), 'Cosmopolitanism at the Local Level: The Development of Transnational Neighbourhoods', in Steven Vertovec and Robin Cohen (eds), *Conceiving Cosmopolitanism: Theory, Context, and Practice*, Oxford: Oxford University Press, pp. 209–23.

Hitti, Philip (1952), *History of the Arabs, From the Earliest Times to the Present*, London: Macmillan.

Johnstone, Penelope (1998), 'Introduction', in *Ibn Qayyim al-Jawziyya: Medicine of the Prophet*, trans. Penelope Johnstone, Cambridge: Islamic Texts Society, pp. xxxi–xxxii

Kemp, Adriana (2004), 'Dangerous Populations: State Territoriality the Constitution of National Minorities', in Joel Migdal (ed.), *Boundaries and Belonging: States and Societies in the Struggle to Shape Identities and Practices*, Cambridge: Cambridge University Press, pp. 73–98.

Khalidi, Rashid (1997), *Palestinian Identity: The Construction of Modern National Consciousness*, New York: Columbia University Press, 177–209.

Lipman, Jonathan N. (1997), *Familiar Strangers: A History of Muslims in Northwest China*, Seattle: University of Washington Press.

Lofland, Lyn (1973), *A World of Strangers: Order and Action in Urban Public Space*, New York: Basic Books.

Lustick, Ian (1980), *Arabs in the Jewish State: Israel's Control of a National Minority*, Austin: University of Texas Press.

Marx, Emanuel (1981), 'The Anthropologist as Mediator', in John G. Galaty, Dan Aronson, Philip C. Salzman and Amy Chouinard (eds), *The Future of Pastoral Peoples*, Ottawa: International Development Research Centre, pp. 119–26.

—— (2005), 'The Bedouin's Lifeline: Roving Traders In South Sinai', in Majid Al-Haj, Michael Saltman and Zvi Sobel (eds), *Social Critique and Commitment: Essays in Honor of Henry Rosenfeld*, Lanham ML: University Press of America, pp. 193–206.

Marx, Emanuel and Avinoam Meir (2005), 'Land Towns and Planning: The Negev Bedouin and the State of Israel', *Geography Research Forum* 25: 43–61.

Migdal, Joel (2004), 'Mental Maps and Virtual Checkpoints: Struggles to Construct and Maintain State and Social Boundaries', in Joel Migdal (ed.), *Boundaries and Belonging: States and Societies in the Struggle to Shape Identities and Practices*, Cambridge: Cambridge University Press, pp. 3–23.

Nakhleh, Khalil (1979), 'On Being a Native Anthropologist', in *The Politics of Anthropology: From Colonialism and Sexism toward a View from Below*, Gerrit Huizer and Bruce Mannheim (eds), The Hague: Mouton.

Narayan, Kirin (1993), 'How Native is a "Native" Anthropologist?', *American Anthropologist* 95 (3): 671–85.

Ohnuki-Tierney, Emiko (1984), 'Critical Commentary', *American Anthropologist* 11 (3): 584–6.

Pettet, Julie (2000), 'Refugees, Resistance and Identity,', in *Globalizations and Social Movements: Culture, Power, and the Transnational Public Sphere*, John A Guidry, Michael D Kennedy, Mayer N Zald (eds). University of Michigan Press, 195–6.

Sayigh, Yezid (2000), *Armed Struggle and the Search for State: The Palestinian National Movement 1949–1993*, Oxford: Oxford University Press, 464–94.

Schulz, Helena Lindholm with Julian Hammer (2003), *The Palestinian Diaspora: Formations of Identity and Politics of Homeland*, London: Routledge.

Segev, Tom (1991), *The Seventh Million, the Israelis and the Holocaust*, Jerusalem: Keter Publishing House/Domino Press (in Hebrew).

Simmel, Georg (1950a), 'The Stranger', in Kurt H. Wolff (ed.), *The Sociology of Georg Simmel*, trans. Kurt H. Wolff, New York: Free Press of Glencoe, pp. 402–8.

—— (1950b), 'The Metropolis and Mental Life', in Kurt H. Wolff (ed.) *The Sociology of Georg Simmel*, trans. Kurt H. Wolff, New York: Free Press of Glencoe, pp. 409–24.

Stanford Encyclopaedia of Philosophy (2002), Edward Zalta (principal ed.), Stanford, CA: Center for Study of Languages and Information.

Ullmann, Manfred (1978), *Islamic Surveys: Islamic Medicine*, Edinburgh: Edinburgh University Press.

Waldron, Jeremy (1992), 'Minority Cultures and the Cosmopolitan Alternative', *University of Michigan Journal of Law Reform* 25 (3): 751–93.

Wolff , Kurt H. (trans./ed.) (1950), *The Sociology of Georg Simmel*, New York: Free Press of Glencoe.

Yablonka, Hanna (1999), *Survivors of the Holocaust: Israel after the War*, Basingstoke: Macmillan.

Zubaida, Sami (2002), 'Middle Eastern Experiences of Cosmopolitanism', in Vertovec and Cohen (eds), *Conceiving Cosmopolitanism: Theory, Context and Practice*, Oxford: Oxford University Press, pp. 32–41.

9

Responding to Rooted Cosmopolitanism: Patriots, Ethnics and the Public Good in Botswana

Richard Werbner

Introduction

Kwame Anthony Appiah ends his brilliantly insightful essays on postcolonial Africa and culture with his moving story of his father's funeral in Kumasi (Appiah 1992: 181–92). It is, *surprisingly*, a story of conflict, of putting the ties that bind to severe and very public test, to the point of damage, perhaps beyond repair. Appiah's father, Joe, was a rooted cosmopolitan and a man of high social rank, who apparently saw no conflict between his multiple, somewhat overlapping loyalties – to his matriclan, which he headed, to his church, to the Asanti people whose king was his brother-in-law, to Ghana, which he served as opposition leader and later government minister – and his final message of *noblesse oblige* to his family was, 'Remember that you are citizens of the world' (Appiah 2005: 213). Cosmopolitan patriotism is the phrase which the son Kwame uses for his father Joe's exemplary practice. Joe Appiah had, also, the maverick's capacity for being his own master; he was admired, his son Kwame recalls, for being fiercely tenacious in a matter of right but resolute, no less, in pursuit of the good reconciliation. Widely regarded as a founding father of his country, he led fearlessly, first, in the anti-colonial struggle, then, even in prison at the risk of his own life, in resistance to postcolonial tyranny under President Nkrumah. Later, in a gesture of personal reconciliation and national homage to his former good friend and comrade-in-arms, he brought Nkrumah's body home from exile.

What was surprising, even to those close to Joe Appiah, and remarkable for a *rooted* cosmopolitan is that the one who chose to make the test of conflict inevitable was Joe Appiah himself. He did so by adding a codicil to his will, virtually on his deathbed, against the matrilineal tradition of Asante and with his son's help. The unorthodox codicil removed control of his funeral from his matriclan and gave it to his church and his immediate family, and thus pitted both against his matriclan and even the Asante king, tested his son's determination under great moral pressure, and eventually embroiled Ghana's head of state, who made an explicit rebuke during the funeral, calling the king's dignity, his respect for his stool, into question at his own capital. Kwame Appiah himself wonders and does not know how much his father 'would have foreseen, whether he knew his funeral would provide the occasion for conflict between monarch and head of state, between Asante and Ghana' (1992: 192). Perhaps the answer reflects as much proud confidence – in a maverick tradition, the son following in the father's footsteps – as it does the chosen self-development of the individual. Kwame Appiah, a distinguished philosopher of Western liberalism, often leaves us thoughtful with Asante proverbial wisdom, and it may be that in his English mother's remarkable collection of Asante proverbs, there is one that suggests that it is a wise father who knows his own son.

Rooted Public Cosmopolitans: From Ghana to Botswana

Following Kwame Appiah's example – and I return later to Appiah's insights into cosmopolitan patriotism – I want to approach the life of another rooted cosmopolitan, Richard Ngwabe Mannathoko (Figure 9.1), and his funeral's

Figure 9.1 Richard Mannathoko. Courtesy of Rosinah Mannathoko

postcolonial significance.[1] My approach is through biography and ethnography for a first-hand account of stories and responses, including my own, at his funeral in Botswana.

Richard Ngwabe Mannathoko died aged 79, and was buried early in December 2005 in his home city, Francistown. Mannathoko, like Joe Appiah, exemplifies the rooted public cosmopolitan who was something of a maverick. Such cosmopolitans are rooted, because they are proud and assertive of their ethnic or other origins and home identities, while recognising the cultural good of being engaged with a variety of others; and public, because they deliberately bring cosmopolitanism to bear in their engagement with the state and in their creative impact on the public sphere. They are also mavericks, being hard to pen in and given to striking out on their own, ahead of any popular herd, sometimes following them, sometimes not. Popularity as such is not their great driver. Their public cosmopolitanism is about justice, no less than about culture and the self.

In my present biographical and ethnographic account, I take a stage further the argument I put about cosmopolitan ethnicity in *Reasonable Radicals and Citizenship in Botswana* (2004a). There, I suggest cosmopolitan ethnicity has a characteristic tension, because it is

> urban yet rural, at once inward- and outward-looking, it builds interethnic alliances from intra-ethnic ones, and it constructs difference while transcending it. Being a cosmopolitan does not mean turning one's back on the countryside, abandoning rural allies, or rejecting ethnic bonds. (2004a: 63, italics in my original)

I am not about to argue that Appiah's approach to 'cosmopolitan patriotism' is wrong, the better to defend my own term of art, 'cosmopolitan ethnicity'. On the contrary, I agree with Appiah's conclusion:

> you can be cosmopolitan – celebrating the variety of human cultures; rooted – loyal to one local society (or a few) that you count as home; liberal – convinced of the value of the individual; and patriotic – celebrating the institutions of the state (or states) within which you live. (1998 [1997]: 106)

Against this background of agreement, I do see a significant difference in approach, signalled by the two terms. As Appiah himself takes care to explain, his approach was intended to be – and indeed was – a turning point in the 1990s debate about multiculturalism in American democracy. Having chosen to become a naturalised citizen of the United States, Appiah contributes deliberately as a patriotic advocate of cosmopolitanism. A liberal in politics and philosophy, he continues to write forcefully in defence of the freedom of choice, the autonomy of the individual and the right of self-invention or the right one has to rework and recombine, to play up or play down, for oneself, the many identities one derives from society (Appiah 2005, 2006; see especially his *tour de force* on John Stuart Mill and the ethics of individuality, 2005: 1–35). Belonging counts – the tribe is not a hateful throwback – and we cannot be moral beings without owing and meeting special obligations. Appiah is pragmatic, explicitly aware of the need for working compromise, but he has a deep concern, suspicious of the tyranny of the community, of the group's claim to command the 'authentic' script for a life way. On his agenda for a currently relevant philosophy of liberalism is, as a priority, autonomy and with that, self-development. Being a gifted philosopher, Appiah integrates; he presents the theoretical consistency and satisfying harmony between the ideas he holds, following his father's example, as liberal, patriot and cosmopolitan. His long-term intellectual project has its agenda for reconciling troublesome, possibly contradictory, priorities in the theory of liberalism.

Ideas all of one piece: that, in my view, is tempting and yet analytically blinding, because it minimises their actual tension, in practice, which people find problematic in public life, which often becomes a passionate concern, and which drives forward one predicament after another.

Cosmopolitanism appears impoverished, when it is made out to be all of one piece, actual and not ever 'about-to-be', and when it seems to lack any creative tension between disparate, unstable, possibly contradictory elements. Worse still, contrary to Appiah's holistic optimism, that impoverishment may open the way to the very subversion of cosmopolitanism against which Appiah pitches his argument. We must keep in mind the demonising of cosmopolitanism in the twentieth century under totalitarian regimes. For Stalin's regime, 'rootless cosmopolitan' was a hateful euphemism legitimising the persecution on unpatriotic grounds of prominent Jewish intellectuals and professionals. Perhaps for any cosmopolitan, but certainly for the public cosmopolitan, the cosmopolitan who engages actively with the state and contributes to the public sphere, this question of how to be patriotic and cosmopolitan at the same time is sensitive and pressing.. Never a merely academic question, it is inescapable for the scholarly understanding of the changeable force that public cosmopolitanism has in civic culture and civil life in postcolonial Africa, no less than post-imperial Europe.

Richard Mannathoko: Family, Ethnic Group, Inner Circle

I consider such changeable force ethnographically in my study of Kalanga elites, including very prominently Richard Mannathoko himself (see Figure 2, captioned, 'The author with Richard Mannathoko, wearing VIP rosettes, at the installation of a village headman in the North East District,' Werbner 2004a: 66). A cosmopolitan in more than the familiar sense of being worldly and widely travelled, Mannathoko came from a long stigmatised though now powerful ethnic minority, the Kalanga, and was a leading member of the first postcolonial generation to be senior civil servants in the highest decision-making echelon. He was also a founding and leading member of the civil servants' association (the precursor of a union), an NGO head, ambassador and multinational director, real estate investor, lawyer and large-scale farmer.

Mannathoko's cosmopolitanism continues to be known and effectively carried forward by the women closest to him, his wife, the former mayor of Botswana's capital now a leading philanthropist, and his daughters. One daughter was, at the time of his funeral, Regional Director of a UNICEF programme for Eastern and Southern Africa; a second, the Assistant Director General of the World Health Organisation in Geneva (she is now in Washington DC, a Vice-President for Development in the World Bank); and a third daughter, a senior economist formerly with USAID, now also with the World Bank. These women are in the forefront of Botswana's new generation of international public servants, a significantly growing number. True to a public cosmopolitan ethic, they take upon themselves a more inclusive responsibility for bettering the quality of life, not merely for people in their own country but reaching well beyond that to a wider, shared world. Elegant women in black, they came, living proof of the realisation of their father's public cosmopolitan vision, from across the world to mourn at his funeral.

Richard Mannathoko himself belonged to an inner circle, mainly Kalanga and drawn from the first postcolonial generation of top echelon civil servants who built up Botswana's interlocking big-business directorates. The establishment of Botswana's postcolonial technocrat-directorate complex is, in good measure, their accomplishment, though not exclusively theirs, of course (Werbner 2004a). Members of this inner circle have also been influential in making public cosmopolitanism meaningful in Botswana by both constructing difference and transcending it. In assertion of minority rights and ethnic dignity, they founded cultural associations, for example, the Society for the Promotion and Advancement of the Ikalanga Language (SPIL). But they also took leading roles in the growth of public forums and other racially and ethnically integrated institutions concerned with good governance or critical of current public policy (Werbner 2004a: 187). Not that they ignored the hot arenas of party politics – and Mannathoko himself was identified with a faction, at least in the media – but it was in these forums and institutions, above all, that Mannathoko and other public cosmopolitans sought, recognised, and sustained allies in the realisation of their cosmopolitan potential. Their attention to their changing problem of alliance contributed significantly to the remarkable growth of voluntary associations as NGOs in Botswana, admittedly, in Botswana as elsewhere across Africa, a growth at its peak much driven by foreign donor funding. Where to create alliances was the open question from one postcolonial moment to another, a question, of course, relative to the life course and repositioning of the public cosmopolitans themselves. In Mannathoko's case, the move in responsive alliance was from one extreme of founding leadership to another, from his service in the 1960s as Secretary General of the Botswana Civil Servants' Association to his establishment of the umbrella council, the Botswana Confederation of Commerce, Industry and Manpower (BOCCIM), which for a decade under his presidency, in the nineties, brought together state officials and business executives and had a major impact on public policy (on BOCCIM, see Maundeni 2004: 77). Mannathoko's contribution as a bridge-builder was acknowledged by BOCCIM's Representative, speaking before me at the funeral.

Hope and Three Aspects of Public Cosmopolitanism

From the very start, I want to anticipate likely criticism: that here I merely celebrate, perhaps glorify, public accomplishment. After all, as Mannathoko's funeral programme registers, I speak as Family Friend. But, even to do that, faithfully, I must still pursue the cosmopolitan interest in hope beyond accomplishment. For important as accomplishment is, it pales before the importance of three aspects of public cosmopolitanism which Mannathoko's life exemplified in the large: first, the restless quest for the further horizon; second, the imperative of moral recentring; and third, the construction and transcending of difference.

As for the first aspect – the restless quest for the further horizon – in public cosmopolitanism, such as Mannathoko's, that exceeds mere curiosity. Nor is the horizon quest primarily about the stranger's entry into Ali Baba's cave: seeking consumption, or the desire to taste the unfamiliar and sample the strange, or even the aesthetic pleasure in wonder and revelation, given the delights of alien things and unexpected experiences. Sometimes explosive, sometimes merely volatile or not quite tamed and wholly domesticated, the horizon quest of the public cosmopolitan makes for a somewhat risky, even uncertain reach in public life, rather than solely the safe grasp in accomplishment. In saying that, I do not intend to yield too much to Britain's trusted 'Man on the Spot', or any empire's Old Guard, and their feel for 'the safe pair of hands' (not those of a maverick like Mannathoko, my account shows). But perhaps most important in public cosmopolitanism is daring. In public cosmopolitanism, frontiers represent not limits but temptations, open zones calling to be crossed, all the more so because the ways to do so are not yet routine or even hardly tried.

Second, the imperative of moral recentring: my cue comes from the debate on patriotism and cosmopolitanism in *The Boston Review* (Nussbaum 1994). In it, Martha Nussbaum rehearses the cosmopolitanism of Stoic philosophers in imperial Rome. Aware of great human diversity, Stoics reflected upon the origins and development of consciousness in living beings according to their peculiarity. Stoics' ethics embraced the whole of mankind (Zeller 1957 [1931]).²

For their recognisably diverse world, the Stoics' sociologic was concentric from the self in the innermost circle, to the extended family, to neighbours, other city-dwellers, fellow countrymen, and so on. Outermost, and all encompassing, was the largest circle, that of humanity as a whole.

Taken as static, the concentric idea might appear an ancestral ghost, haunting the Diamond Jubilee Conference of the Association of Social Anthropologists. For the idea calls up the celebrated, but otherwise untitled, Diagram 1 of British Social Anthropology (Fortes and Evans-Pritchard 1940: 277). Changeless still, of course, Diagram 1 shows the view of social distance from the hut outwards through the outer circles of Nuerland, Dinkaland and Other Foreign Countries to the outermost circle of The Government Operating From Various Centres. Looking backward, and with tongue in cheek, we might be cynical, not stoical, and dismiss our venerable Diagram 1 as if it were merely imperial, for it does locate the British at the outer limits, rather than our encompassing humanity as a whole.

But my point is that for the Stoics, the sociologic had to be dynamic to be civic and truly moral. Stoics demanded active, deliberate change of a certain kind in the light of moral reason and perceived virtue. As the second century Stoic philosopher Hierocles put it, the essential task is to 'draw the circles in somehow toward the centre' (Nussbaum 1994: 3–6). The far has to be brought morally near, but without obliterating the many circles of difference; that is the dynamic aspect of cosmopolitanism which I call the imperative of moral recentring.

Perhaps the most influential response to Nussbaum's essay is Kwame Appiah's 'Cosmopolitan Patriots' (1998 [1997]), which David Hollinger rightly labels 'perhaps the closest thing to a classic text yet generated by the new cosmopolitanism' (Hollinger 2002: 230). Before commenting on what the new cosmopolitanism is as an intellectual movement, it is worth positioning its 'classic text'. This appre-ciation might appear to be something of an aside, but in fact, it takes us forward in our main argument about cosmopolitanism and postcolonial Africa. For the classic text is written by one of Africa's foremost diasporic intellectuals, it is a product of a diasporic imagination, it is very much in the mainstream of postcolonial studies, and it makes the vanguard of the new cosmopolitanism distinctively postcolonial and diasporic (on Africa, the diasporic and the postcolonial, see Werbner 1996; Werbner and Ranger 1996: 7). Perhaps most importantly, and largely neglected in debate about the movement, it makes the new cosmopolitanism intellectually indebted to theoretical reflection on cultural and political struggles in Africa.³ Carrying forward that reflection is our present aim.

By the new cosmopolitanism, Hollinger identifies a cross-disciplinary move-ment of intellectuals, mainly liberals, who since the mid-1990s seek a mid-way between extreme doctrinal positions. Of these, one is overcommitted, Hollinger argues, to universalism and its appeal to identification with humanity as a whole, to moral obligation without borders and the same treatment for all – Nussbaum's approach, for Hollinger, is the leading example, although he gives short shrift to her concern for the cosmopolitan dynamic of recentring which works with and through circles of difference. At the other extreme, again emerging within liberal philosophy, is a communitarian form of pluralism which disregards multiple, overlapping identities, 'is likely to ascribe to each individual a primary identity within a single community of descent ... [and is] more concerned to protect and preserve the cultures of groups that are already well established' (Hollinger 2002: 231). For Hollinger, the leading exponent of such pluralism is the Canadian philosopher Will Kymlicka (on Kymlicka's ideas, see also Werbner 2004a: 34, 2004b: 261, 267), although, especially for postcolonial Africa, it is in my view Charles Taylor who has contributed even more to what I call 'the new dialogue with post-liberalism' (Werbner 2004b: 261–73) in work on the politics of recognition, multiculturalism, and citizenship. Appiah's argument, striking a liberal middle way, between the universalist and the pluralist, illuminates a third aspect of public cosmopolitanism, the construction, reconstruction and transcending of difference. This is the aspect that I, too, focus upon in my conceptualisation of 'cosmopolitan ethnicity' (Werbner 2002b; 2004a).[4]

Cosmopolitanism as Socially Viable: Inclusion and Alliance

The liberal stress in Appiah's approach is on the individual, and what that does not lead him to do is to ask, in any depth, what makes cosmopolitanism *socially viable*.[5] It is because I have to explore that, specifically in a postcolonial context of debate about the rights of collectivities, pluralism and tribalism, that I find it useful to start from a circle of inclusion: it is that circle which attracts an emerging set of significant insiders who, as collectivities and individuals, make the dialogue of cosmopolitanism meaningful and viable. It is a contended circle, and its membership amounts to a controversial cosmopolitan Who's Who. The problem is: How are allies sought, mutually recognised, and sustained in the realisation of the cosmopolitan potential? And how, on a great civic occasion such as the funeral of a public cosmopolitan, is that potential seen and documented as more or less realised?

Civic Culture: Biography and Documentary Practice

Hundreds of mourners, people from all walks of life, including many of the great and the good in the country, came to Richard Mannathoko's funeral. This very public event was hosted, in between a requiem mass and the other solemn last rites, with a generous excess of feasting on much loved local foods from juicy, fresh-killed goat meat to thick porridge and rich stews, with abundant greens and other tasty relishes. Grand and lavish as Mannathoko's funeral was, it was nevertheless a moment common and true to the civic culture, now widely shared throughout much of Botswana, in remote villages no less than in the towns and cities (for a very illuminating account of funerals, civil discourse and the public space of sentiment in Botswana, see Durham and Klaits 2002).

This civic culture fosters very careful regard for social biography. The individuation of the subject matters a great deal. Not individualism or the cult of the heroic individual, I stress, but that individuation which strains to do justice to the problem of the member as a special and vital part of a greater whole. Careful individuation calls, at death and faithful to life, for a highly ceremonious relating of the subject to significant others. First, it is through their recognised presence and solemn procession in last rites, normally wearing their respectful best; second, through illuminating biography in oratory and, third, through the reading of personal, written messages, along with the display of their floral wreaths.

Funerals proceed, accordingly, with an announced, meticulously detailed programme. It is often printed to list the schedule of times and places, the main participants, their immediate roles and usually their relationships to the deceased. The deceased's personal profile, briefly given on the programme, usually with a characteristic photograph, is always rehearsed in the round. From their distinct perspectives, significant others trace the special moments of a life course, individual and highly specific, through to the fine particulars of death. The details matter; an honest, or at least credible, account is expected; the life, at death, must be put on the public record as a meaningful chain of events for a known and now memorable character. No one, not even a young woman or teenage boy, dies without a bare trace and without some public oratory of personal dignity. There is a cherishing in memory of the life that was, including quirks, jokes, and moments comic enough to make everyone laugh, unchecked by the solemn presence of the casket and its corpse, before whose exposed face, composed in death, mourners bend their heads in reflection – that is the carefully observed and respected truth of this civic culture in Botswana.

Civic Culture: The Predicament of Public Cosmopolitanism

Endemic in all this is a predicament of civic culture which can be highly problematic for the public cosmopolitan in particular. In Botswana people value highly the smooth surface of social life, indeed, civility itself. Yet the documentary practice in funerals puts that value at risk, making it precarious and vulnerable to tensions, even open quarrels and the exposure of personal grievances. Even beyond that, the predicament takes on a special sensitivity when the occasion responds to the life of a public cosmopolitan well known to be a controversial maverick, never branded someone else's own or fully domesticated.

It hardly needs saying that such a maverick is not likely merely to serve social life's smooth surface, even when his time comes to rest in peace. But what does need saying for the public cosmopolitan, more generally, goes to the horizon above the surface. The force of public cosmopolitanism is uncontained and uncontainable, for it comes from looking beyond, seeing a horizon as open, perhaps barely glimpsed yet with potential somehow to be realised in the public sphere. If restless in life, and given to seeking beyond the horizon, the public cosmopolitan makes an uneasy subject for the documentary practice of funerals to command.

The Partial Measure of the Public Man: Funeral Programmes

So too in Mannathoko's funeral: a partial measure of the public man was made visible in each of two programmes, one for the requiem mass on 9 December at St James's parish church, ending with the 'Profile of a Gifted Son of Botswana', and the other programme, for 10 December, the day of his burial.

This second programme, folio size with computer-generated personal graphics on each of its twelve pages, is a remarkable representation of public distinction in an exemplary life. The first page reprints the *Profile* on the requiem programme. Next appears the Mannathoko *Family Tree*, with the couple's 1962 photograph from Leeds and law student days above a diagram spread across the whole page. It is as if to remind all, including the social anthropologist, that genealogy lives on; it is not passé.

The third and fourth pages are devoted to the *Funeral Programme: Order of Service*. Listed, among others, and in English and Kalanga, but not Tswana, are the two Masters of Ceremonies, the three Traffic Masters, the 32 Pall Bearers (turn-takers along the way from house to grave), the ten Speakers at the Hall (each identified by relationship, i.e. in-law, BOCCIM Representative, BP Representative), the thirteen Readers of Messages, the Wreath Bearers and the several Speakers, including Members of Parliament, at the Graveside. The whole list registers the richness of personal and public association over a lifetime. Considerable as the list is, nearly 70 participants in all, it conveys but a bare hint of the funeral's substantial logistics in mobilising so many kin, friends and the general public, very quickly, from across the country and beyond.

Pages 5 to 8 portray Mannathoko's *Professional Life*, illustrated by his photographs with the country's first president, with his colleagues at the Ministry of

Local Government, with fellow trainees for the foreign service in 1966, with fellow ambassadors at the OAU in Addis, 1968, as High Commissioner with the Zambian vice-president in 1967, and with other Barclays Bank of Botswana Board Members. The narrative of *Family Life* on page 10 follows him from birth to marriage, to his own and his wife Rosinah's early education and practice as teachers both in Botswana and the then Southern Rhodesia, to the birth and upbringing of the surviving four of his six children and eight grandchildren, to his retirement and active advisory role as senior uncle to the current Chief Masunga, sometime Head of Botswana's House of Chiefs. (Among all his public distinctions, Mannathoko much prized his claim to chiefly descent. 'I am always a Headman, wherever I go,' he would boast to me, with a characteristic chuckle.) The accompanying illustrations are brim-full of family, children and grandchildren, and their glowing smiles, around Mannathoko and his wife. 'Dick', the physical giant, the champion athlete, football and tennis player, emerges in the account and photos for Social Life on page 11; all this is above the final section for the proudest of his lifelong passions, for breeding and accumulating cattle. He was President of the Nata Farmers Association at the time of his death, and this section's illustration, 'Breeding at the Farm', shows stock from his highly valuable prize herd, some from his remarkable accomplishment in cross-breeding Brahman, Charolais and Simmertals. Finally comes his full-page portrait, with the caption *Rest in Peace*, and in Kalanga, *Ezelani Nge Dothodzo Ntombo*.

If not *Cosmopolitan*, Worldly Cosmopolitan?

If not a candidate for the slick magazine cover of *Cosmopolitan*, Mannathoko could easily have passed for the most familiar appearance of the worldly cosmopolitan. Widely travelled as an ambassador on behalf of his country, he had shaken the hands of the sheikhs of this world, taken their oil and his seat on the international board of BP, the first ever for an African, yielded hugely increased corporate profit, and drunk copiously from the best of the British Empire's legacy in Scotch and from the rest of the world's good red wines. A trained lawyer, who helped write his country's constitution, he had the advocate's skill in making the best of a case, of getting sharply to the rights and principles in conflict. It was a skill he brought to bear in the civil service, diplomacy, corporate enterprise, in the designing and leading of NGOs and on presidential commissions, but not in legal practice as such. Of the worldly cosmopolitan's competence in languages, he again had a broad grasp, being fluent in at least three African languages and two European. He made close and strong friendships across national, racial and ethnic differences. As a host, he had the rare gift for putting his guest at welcome ease. A charming *bon vivant*, he apparently never felt himself a stranger however strange the place he was in – or at least, his stream of jokes and spontaneous banter made people laugh, whether they were San herders on his huge farm or 1960s, 'with it' Oxford dons (when I saw him at Oxford on his diplomatic training).

That said, I must add a significant qualification to the word 'never'. There came a time of retirement, when he felt he had enough of life in the capital, Gaborone, a city of which he was not very fond, and he and his southern-born wife moved their home back north to Francistown, the city near the chiefdom of his birth. It was to be, as he told me, 'near my roots'.

Rooted Public Cosmopolitanism: Biography and Ethnography

The story of Mannathoko's Professional Life in the larger programme represents him as 'a free thinker', 'never constrained by tradition, rules or conformist approaches.' He was regarded as a charismatic, strong leader already as a head boy at St Joseph's College. At the time, the Protectorate's leading southern boarding school, St Joseph's became a major crucible for postcolonial elite formation, its powerful old-boy and old-girl network including at least one vice-president of Botswana and numerous other politicians, very senior civil servants and big entrepreneurs in the country's interlocking directorates. Mannathoko wrote and spoke fearlessly, even recklessly at a high moment of deference to alien rule. Among other things, ahead of revisionist postcolonial historians, he dismissed the founding myth of the Protectorate: that Queen Victoria gave her protection as grace and favour to Tswana chiefs petitioning her with missionaries in the Christian civilising mission.

The point is that his debunking was not taken lightly by the authorities as mere schoolboy posturing. At heavy personal cost, he gained a lifelong reputation for daring to stand his ground against the powers that be. 'His scholarship at college was withdrawn when he insisted that British Colonial Rule had been imposed on the country,' the programme reports, 'when what our Botswana Chiefs had sought was an alliance. This led to him being perceived as a threat and troublemaker, and he was forced to teach in Southern Rhodesia rather than Bechuanaland.' The programme goes on to tell of his 'sentencing a white man to imprisonment while he was a [Protectorate] District Officer, because it was the right thing to do: an act which was considered unthinkable at the time.' In explaining this daring to think the unthinkable and act upon it, the programme does not use the word cosmopolitan, but it represents his motivation in cosmopolitan terms, in terms of moral principles, rights and universals of humanity, beyond race or nation, 'He respected all men and believed in equality before the law.'

This representation catches the nub of the legend that surrounded Mannathoko in his lifetime, for being anti-imperialist and anti-racist. When, before

Independence neared in 1966, he studied to become one of the country's first handful of university graduates, he was the only one whose radical politics ruled him out of the Protectorate government's largesse for overseas courses. Nor did his legend and tactically sharp tongue endear him to the Old Guard of senior former Protectorate officials who at first dominated the President's Office and most of the ministries, in the very early years of the postcolony (on the opposition between the Old Guard and the Young Turks, see Werbner 2004a: 174–6). He was watched with more than suspicion. As a radical activist, he was a founding member of the Bechuanaland African Civil Service Association and later Secretary-General of the Botswana Civil Servants Association. He helped draft and present the Protectorate Association's thoroughgoing critique of the colonial government's discrimination in favour of expatriates at the expense of locals (see *Report on Localisation and Training* (1966) cited in Werbner 2004a: 161). This is still regarded as an opening salvo in a continuing controversy over localisation.

The Old Guard consensus was that Mannathoko was a dangerous tribalist; that his talk of rights, justice, principle was no more than a cover for self-interest; that he was always on the make to look after his own Kalanga people, above all. In the cocktail parties of the small world of the capital in those days, his wife told me, one or another senior expatriate official would come up to him and say, whatever the merits of the case, 'I see you got another job for one of your people.' Or, 'Not yours this time, eh!' If not deliberate divide and rule, after the celebrated caricature of Perfidius Albion's imperial policy, it was nevertheless more than a casual response to the expanding horizons of local elites, to their rooted cosmopolitanism in the making. There was a late imperial mind-set, with a long self-congratulatory wisdom of its own, that reserved the moral high ground for the Old Guard themselves. They left, among the likes of Mannathoko, little or no room for what the British call 'a safe pair of hands'.

It is worth saying that the vicissitudes of his career never made Mannathoko bitter against the British, or for that matter, bitter at all. After all, human beings would get up to their antics, and that for him was a source of endless jokes and shared humour. Of course, as an American, I am myself perhaps a poor judge of the British, although I am told by a Fellow of the British Academy, 'You have become truly English.' But, characteristically, in 1964, when Mannathoko and I first sat drinking together in a Francistown bar, then usually segregated by race, on an informal basis, he warned me that being seen with him would cause me trouble with some people and then laughed heartily. Or, rather, we both laughed heartily.

Not surprisingly, the programme passes silently over a consequence for Mannathoko of being such a maverick: conspiracy theories, defamation and rumour, even about plotting a coup d'etat with other top Kalanga civil servants. 'Guns under the Bed' ran the headline in a 1969 pre-election issue of the *Bulawayo Chronicle*, then the main source of gossip and news in the absence of any local newspaper in Botswana. The story had leading Kalanga, including Mannathoko and a future cabinet minister, plotting for a take-over and arming themselves at night, in the capital. At the time, however, they were actually President Khama's guests for Easter in his Serowe home. The President traced the rumour to expatriate police officers in the CID and sacked them. But the rumour never quite died; it has become one of those 'truths', often whispered in the capital, about the 'hidden agenda' of Kalanga elites as a minority about to take over from the majority (see Werbner 2004a: 71–4). A Tswana cabinet minister told me frankly, but only on the basis of anonymity, that in his view Mannathoko, who was regarded as a potential head of the civil service, never attained his potential in the civil service, nor became a minister, in part because the accusation of being a tribalist plotter gave him a reputation that stuck.

Family Friend: Richard Werbner

I took up some of these issues in my own speech at the funeral, which follows. Speaking first in Kalanga, I made the customary opening address to the funeral, announced I would speak in English, and then took the liberty of asking the interpreter to rest. Otherwise, he offered a clean but hurried translation in Tswana between each Kalanga or English speaker's sentence or two. And rest he did, after translating my request into Tswana. I felt I had to concentrate, myself, and be aided in that by a close, moved hearing from my fellow mourners. If a liberty, then perhaps a wise one, or so the interpreter himself conveyed later, when he somewhat jokingly told me, after the speeches, that he would have been bound to edit some of my remarks.

> *The passing of a great man leaves lasting inspiration for generation after generation. Some great men get riches for themselves, their families, even their country. Other great men give public service of the highest value. Still other great men build the institutions and the organizations upon which daily life depends. But the true mark of the great man is always powerful vision. To see beyond, to open out the horizon of hope, of trust and of promise, to dare to be ahead of the times, all that marks out the great man.*
>
> *Richard Ngwabe Mannathoko was such a great man. Here we can only begin to tell of his remarkable life. He did not have to wait for us to eulogise him in endless stories and in his fund of jokes. He was already a legend living in our midst. But I have a confession to make to put the record straight. We carried on our conversation over more than forty years, from the time when he was a young law student and I, a novice anthropologist. During that time, I sometimes referred to him and his ideas in my published work; the references are a dozen in my latest book. What I want to confess is – and I know he forgave me for*

this – I ought to have made dozens and dozens more acknowledgements to his contributions. He was such a good talker, so cogent, so sharp and persuasive in his analysis of the issues, that I often came away thinking I had got the point by myself even before he had driven it home.

This confession takes me to the heart of the matter, which in this country cannot be distant from diamonds and the public good. Every Motswana now knows the answer to the question: Who owns Botswana's diamonds? The people of Botswana, of course. Obvious and to be taken for granted? Perhaps! But the fact is, for it to be effectively true took, and still does take, much deliberate effort by this country's leading decision-makers. Here Richard was in the vanguard. Early on, he saw that the many tribes of the Bechuanaland Protectorate had to give way to the one nation-state in the Republic of Botswana, when it came to mineral rights. To realise his republican vision, he set about as Principal Secretary to the Prime Minister and as Permanent Secretary of the Ministry of Lands and Local Government, campaigning very successfully to get the chiefs on board. No longer, as a result, did tribes claim mineral rights. Of course, I am not saying that Richard was single-handed in the founding of this basis for a stable, viable Republic. Obviously, Sir Seretse Khama took the lead. But I am saying that Richard's republican contribution was outstanding.

Richard had a well-deserved reputation for being bold, outspoken, fearless and ready to speak truth to power. I will say more about that, shortly. But first I want you to have in mind his virtue as a gentle giant, the diplomatic virtue which made his republican contribution possible. In this, Richard brought to bear his skill as a consummate negotiator; he did so much to convince chiefs, men proud of their dignity and honour, that they would be respected all the more by agreeing to put the national interest first, before the tribal.

Many of you may immediately wonder whether Richard the republican was also Richard the tribalist. For you will well recall Richard's much publicised blast at the height of the recent Balopi Commission. Then he called the late Ngwato regent Tshekedi Khama 'a terrorist'. It was for Tshekedi's part during the 1940s in unleashing violent regiments leading to the imprisonment and exile of the prominent Kalanga chief Nswazi and his subjects. Many were Richard's relatives. As a youth, he visited them doing hard labour in prison. The injustice rankled with Richard. It made him determined to fight for what he saw as oppression of the many by the few. The immediate lesson he drew was about wrongs against Kalanga, his own people, and it led him to be a proud founding member of the first Kalanga student cultural association. But he also looked beyond that immediate lesson to the wider moral horizon in his vision of public respect and dignity for all minorities on an equal basis with the majority. Richard was a strong advocate of the universal rights of the citizen, every citizen without discrimination.

Richard Werbner

Let me quote from one of those places in my most recent book where I did acknowledge his ideas. This quotation, explaining the remarkable importance of Kalanga as lawyers, is actually about a perception Richard had from his own experience:

Mannathoko notices that facing stigma and inequality often makes minorities great supporters of universal rights. Minorities turn to law as a profession, he suggests, because the experience of discrimination by a majority gives them a passion for justice, and even more the determination to know how to get it. (2004a: 108)

A passion for justice, yes, Richard was moved by that. While serving on a highly sensitive Presidential Commission of Enquiry, he felt he had to expose a trail of scandal and corruption no matter where or to whom it led. If this made him unforgiving enemies, well, so be it and, indeed, so it was. He had taken an oath as a Commissioner and could not go back on that, he told me.

Richard was a passionate, determined man who enjoyed being a politically controversial figure. A good number of leading civil servants felt he had the potential to be the head of the civil service or, at least, a minister. In his prime, some talked of a glass ceiling against Kalanga, especially to keep them from certain sensitive areas of public security. I had the gall to ask Richard why that potential of his was never fully realised. He was philosophical about it. With a twinkle in his eye and a characteristic grin, he told me he was by nature better suited to being a general. As I have said, he was ahead of his time – nowadays in Botswana, a Kalanga can be Minister of State in the President's Office and not merely Attorney General or Chief Justice, and like anyone else, a general, too, can hold high office, perhaps the highest.

If something of a general, Richard was at his very best in crisis, when, so to speak, the war was on. Take the oil crisis, for example. In the 1970s when sanctions were hitting apartheid South Africa, and thus the refineries for Botswana's oil, the cabinet and permanent secretaries, including Richard, suddenly faced the emergency of oil supplies running out almost immediately. So critical and outspoken was Richard on the folly of those responsible, I am told, that by general consensus, he was given the brief to get the oil somehow, somewhere, and very quickly. But where?

You will appreciate that at that time to give the answer, Botswana had no central intelligence agency of its own. Or rather, the agency was so undercover in a library that only Richard knew that the one who could come to the rescue was the librarian, the beautiful woman he loved from his youth at their boarding school, his wife Rosinah. Rosinah did the library research; she identified the oil sources, and off Richard went on his successful, if hair-raising, hunt, eventually finding an old friend from his student days who turned out to be a most highly placed Saudi, eager to help a poor country like Botswana.

The rest of the story is familiar history to many of you who will recall often seeing Richard's face in the Botswana Telephone Directory ad for BP. Having reached his peak in the civil service and as a top diplomat and ambassador, Richard became, of course, the first African to be a member of the international board of BP. Not that this was his only achievement in the world of corporate capital and wise investment. It is enough to say here that he managed often to beat the manager of Barclays at his own game, tennis.

My last memory of Richard brings to mind the biblical verse from Exodus (13: 21) about the Israelites on their trek in the Wilderness. What the Israelites followed by the day was a pillar of cloud sent by God. So too did my wife and I follow a great pillar of dust, just a few months ago, when enjoying the freedom to speed at the wheel of his old yet still fast-moving van, Richard led us like an angel to his Nata farm, to his promised land. I savour still the liver he roasted so skilfully, on an open fire outside, from the goat he slaughtered in our honour. And very nearby, I recall too, was the sound of the prize bull, eager to be on the job, a bellow which was always music to Richard's ears. Richard's farm was a Spartan place, without luxuries, and with hardly any creature comforts from the city. It spoke of a highly productive man, caring for his capital investment in his herd, but who rather disdained the world of consumer goods; a brave old man who was determined, above all, to die as he lived, rooted and still nourished by the countryside.

Finally, in Richard Mannathoko's honour, I recited the praises of his clan, which are partly in Pedi and partly in Kalanga:

Bo Mannathoko, Zwitetembo zwenyu zwiapo zwinodha mo ludzi gwa ba Pedi. Ndoti Ntombo, Mperi, Bamagwasa, Bamagadagadang majwana, matlhari aana magwasa. Bantswi la tswiritswiri. Bari tjindigwi kiya. Hakilagwi nyama mbisi, kiya ndambala. Bari Mannathoko tiya. Baka sebona atama, atsena semokopela. Moswazi o tlhabile pologolo. Boelela motlhaba tlou, osekare maabane ke tlhabile. Nswazvi gogola kwano, shango haina bathu.

Ezelani nde dothodzo, Ntombo.

Public Cosmopolitanism, Patriotic Divide: The Senior Statesman's Speech

The next to speak was the most honoured mourner, Sir Ketumile Masire, Botswana's second president. For our understanding of Mannathoko's public cosmopolitanism, we need to appreciate a remarkable divide, both in sensibility and in cultural politics, because that divide set Mannathoko and Masire apart. Patriotism united them, of course, but patriotism also divided them. If apparently a paradox, it is important, because it is revealing for patriotism and public cosmopolitanism more generally, and because it reaches the respect for constitutional order, which citizens of a republic, like Botswana or the United States for that matter, must owe (on the general issues, see Appiah 1998: 101). I want to unpack the paradox and then say more about the divide in sensibility and cultural politics.

At the heart of the matter is the debate about difference and variety. This debate we know, in Botswana as elsewhere, is about that many splendid chameleon, multiculturalism (for an insightful analysis on Botswana, see Solway 2002; and also, Werbner 2002a, 2002b, 2004a; Nyamnjoh 2006). As Appiah, above all, has made us recognise, one can be a patriot of some sort without valuing difference and variety highly, but not a cosmopolitan patriot (Appiah 1998 [1997]). I have to rehearse the point for the multiculturalism debate, even at the risk of labouring over the now perhaps all too familiar. The point is this: public cosmopolitans, finding discrimination in their country's laws or constitution, have to press for legal reform and constitutional change because they are patriots who respect constitutional order and because they are also cosmopolitans who value difference. Not being cosmopolitans, opponents of such change can still take their stance as patriots. On both sides of the divide lies actual or claimed motivation by patriotism.

In Botswana, and for Mannathoko and Masire in particular, the opposition between the sides came to a head at the height of the recent Presidential Commission on tribal and other discrimination in Botswana's constitution. Earlier, in nationalist speeches about the danger of 'letting The Tiger loose', the spectre of ethnic violence on the horizon, Sir Ketumile, while president, repeatedly gave dire warnings. In 2000, during a Presidential Commission hearing at the capital, in a moment which I, too, felt to be electric, the former president raised the full weight of his reputation as a founding father and one of the authors of the Constitution, and he brought that weight to bear forcefully in defence of the *status quo*. He spoke very movingly of his fears for the danger to unity and public order, if minority cultural and language politics went unchecked (see Werbner 2004a: 44). Against that view, Mannathoko, himself also responsible for the drafting of the Constitution, fought for change; the time had come to end tribal clauses. Speaking before the Commission in his home city but capturing much publicity in the national media, Mannathoko made his battle cry heard before the Commission, by calling the late Ngwato regent Tshekedi Khama 'a terrorist', as I recalled at his funeral. The two national leaders thus stood, with outspoken passion, on opposite sides of what is still a great and sensitive debate about minorities and multiculturalism in Botswana.

That said, I turn to illuminate more of the contrast in sensibility as it relates to cultural politics and cosmopolitanism. Of the two men, only Mannathoko spoke the other's home language, Masire being renowned in his prime as one of the most gifted popular orators in Setswana, the national language, the official one being English. Where Mannathoko was a pluralist[6] – the cosmopolitan who celebrated the variety of culture and the patriot who insisted on public recognition and support for his language along with others – Masire was more the unitarian, the one-nation advocate of homogeneity. Masire's government carried forward an assimilationist policy, a policy that virtually reserved the public cultural space for a perceived majority, the Tswana, including Masire himself. In Botswana's first postcolonial period, building one state was building one nation – the Tswana nation (on the One Nation Consensus and its fate from the first to the second postcolonial period, see Werbner 2004a: 38–9, 79–83; Masire 2006: 144).

In the funeral, former President Masire came to praise Mannathoko, and not merely to bury him along with the still simmering factional disputes of the ruling party, the BDP. Mannathoko had been a founding BDP member, one of the most prominent, and of unwavering party loyalty. Being myself something of a relic of fieldwork BDBP – Before Diamonds in the Bechuanaland Protectorate – I was nevertheless bemused to hear the octogenarian Sir Ketumile apologise in his eulogy for not being an anthropologist. Unlike the anthropologist who spoke immediately before him, this surviving father of his country could not recite Mannathoko's clan praises in Mannathoko's own languages – Kalanga and Pedi. He also joked about the way two of the speakers before him (Colleague and Friend, Gobe Matenge and Family Friend, Richard Werbner) appeared to have got together to talk up Kalanga issues, which left other things for him. Significantly, even if no one had addressed Mannathoko's sense of outrage at Tswana cultural dominance over Kalanga, that would still have been documented at the funeral, because the programme records, 'Throughout his adult life he [Mannathoko] promoted the use and development of the Ikalanga language, because he considered it a *crime* to let part of Botswana's rich, diverse culture and tradition die' (my italics). Later gossip with well-informed others, off the record, confirmed my feeling that the former president was defusing a politically charged moment very deftly, for his concern might well have been that he had come to be regarded, even by some Kalanga once close to him, as being too suspicious of minorities like Kalanga, and perhaps an enemy or at least somewhat hostile to their advancement (on perceived discrimination in his Office of the President and the Leno Affair, see Werbner 2004a: 74, 79–80).

Sir Ketumile rose gracefully to the occasion, at the funeral. His eulogy, given spontaneously with much personal affection, was a seamless fusion of languages. It resounded with a richness of Tswana drawn from the common poetry of the people. But it was a richness commanded in the service of Development-speak, that official rhetoric without which no great civic occasion in Botswana can proceed.

In the government's own newspaper, the *Daily News*, Sir Ketumile was later quoted as saying,

> Richard Mannathoko was a man whose development ideology was rooted in his confidence in the ability of Batswana. Mannathoko was driven by an urgent desire to see Botswana recognised as a valuable global player because of the capacity of its citizens. He used every window of opportunity to enable the full realisation of Batswanas' potential. (December 2005)

In fact, this is a quotation from the last paragraph of the Profile of a Gifted Son of Botswana, on both funeral programmes. Sir Ketumile spoke without notes, and did not say that. I was too overcome by my own participation, sitting among the other speakers, and too long preoccupied later, to make even mental notes of my own. Nevertheless, I believe the Botswana Daily News rightly reported what Sir Ketumile should have said and what, at least in sentiment and sensibility, he actually did express.

'Botswana is recognised as a valuable global player, because of the potential of its citizens,' the vision is unmistakably patriotic. And the former President's presence in itself spoke in honour of Mannathoko's patriotism; after all, they came together in the state-building vanguard, creating Botswana as a new nation-state. But how plain was or is it, for all the words 'valuable *global* player' (my italics), that equally this public vision is cosmopolitan?

The Quest for the Horizon: The Promise in the People

That it is an optimistic vision no one at the funeral could have doubted of course. After all, well known in the background, the unspoken stereotype, against which Mannathoko himself fought tenaciously, was this: the country, as the Bechuanaland Protectorate, was held to be a remote, relatively unimportant outpost of Empire. It was, overwhelmingly, more a backward, custodial burden – in a word, a desert – than anything else in imperial eyes, which for long saw rather little potential in most of the people themselves – tribesmen at home with cattle, when not mine workers. 'The British were poor,' remarked Mannathoko, 'when it came to investing in our human capital.'

But the cosmopolitan optimism may have seemed less bold in this present, second postcolonial era than it was in the first, when Mannathoko, as a young diplomat at the OAU and elsewhere, began his quest for wider recognition for Botswana and its citizens. For, now, more to the foreground rings the acclaim for 'Botswana, the Cinderella of Africa', 'An African Miracle', even in the face of the AIDS pandemic, rising unemployment and dire poverty for far too many Batswana. Admittedly, the acclaim for accomplishment pleased Mannathoko, given his rightful patriotic pride in his own national contributions. But the stress, in the programme as in the sometimes explosive assertions of Mannathoko's will to change, is on his trust in human potential. Not diamonds, not more yet to be discovered natural resources for international exploitation, but here it is the world-reaching promise in the people themselves that opens the horizon, as befits a distinctively public cosmopolitan vision.

Who could have expected, at the end of the Bechuanaland Protectorate, that one man's wife would become the mayor of Botswana's booming capital and that three of their daughters would be 'global players' in our *cosmopoliticum*, in the United Nations and international agencies? But this, as I record earlier, came to be true for Mannathoko and his wife and daughters.

These daughters were the last to speak in the hall. They gave me an immediate sense of *déjà vu*, responding to their fun in the memory of their father's own playful humour. I saw them once again as the mischievous children they were, when I first knew their father as a young law student, and he was given to teasing their interest in the wonders of English.

H I P P O P O T A M U S, they chanted gleefully for the assembled mourners, spells hippopotamus. 'The rhinoceros', the programme records him reading them from wildlife books 'is found in Africa comma but comma is not as common as the elephant full stop!'

Afterthought

It is striking in African postcolonies, such as Botswana and Ghana, how dramatically revealing a rooted public cosmopolitan's funeral becomes. There are several reasons for this. Most importantly, for our purposes, we are made aware of the cultivated appeals for moral passion – tolerance, patience, reconciliation, compassion – and yet, also, the changing tensions which characterise rooted cosmopolitanism. The second reason is historic: we see how people respond to rooted cosmopolitanism, when a great civic occasion remarkably carries forward a perceived transition from one postcolonial moment to the next. In Joe Appiah's case for Ghana, it is after the time of the founding tyrant; but in his case, as in Richard Ngwabe Mannathoko's for Botswana, it is forward to Africa's emerging second liberation struggle, this time an emancipatory moment perceived, hopefully, to promise good governance and deliberative democracy and, hopefully also, development. A third reason is that the occasion, like so many postcolonial funerals in Africa, calls for richly significant biography; not a monologue, but a number of characteristic stories in a dialogue as various as the speakers themselves. For public cosmopolitanism, such occasions give us what Victor Turner called, 'a limited area of transparency on the otherwise opaque surface of regular, uneventful social life' (Turner 1957: 93).

Here some might say I should stick to the surer ground around my late friend Richard Mannathoko, and only address the immediate postcolonial horizon I study in the safety of informed biography and ethnography. Admittedly, much remains to be said about that, spelling out the distinctively postcolonial significance of the creative force a maverick has as a rooted public cosmopolitan. But the more I reflect on that, the more I am convinced that by its very unsettling nature, such force leads to reflection at the most open horizons of the patriotic, the imperial, and the cosmopolitan; that is, for us, too, about powerfully uncertain issues of our changing world order.

If compelling over centuries of world history, the imperial question looked curiously dated, even antiquarian, when the twentieth century gave a moment's notice: The End of Empire. But now we wonder anew about empire: is it about us again, though in a fresh guise? The world's dominant and, currently, its only global power, my native USA, denies officially that it wants its own American empire. The old self-proclaiming empires reached for sovereignty and subjects to the possible limits of territorial expansion. America as an empire in denial actively avoids that; it is not a return of the Romans, the Turks or the British. But it does adhere to the proposition that all men, being created equal, are entitled to be treated, for the sake of democracy, of world peace and security, to a pre-emptive strike, when their country, or rather its atrocious regime, deserves it. And in applying this proposition arrogantly and not subject to the judgement of the United Nations or any other major body of world opinion, America has already turned out to be the judge and executioner in its own devastating case against atrocity. The darkness on the horizon threatens to be vast, and it may now be in vain to try to learn lessons to go beyond that darkness. But if cosmopolitanism has any deeper value for us, it must be in opening out the urge to think the unthinkable, about in Lévi-Strauss's phrase for totemism, 'humanity without frontiers'. Our focus in this chapter has, of course, been more specific, but perhaps for that very reason, it has meant a more critical understanding of the political struggles and culturally creative tensions in and around cosmopolitanism. We have seen how through such struggles and tensions, rooted public cosmopolitanism continues to be socially viable in postcolonial Africa.

Notes

1. For an illuminating analysis of an elite postcolonial funeral in Namibia, see Fumanti (2007).

2. See also Zeller's argument that their 'metaphysics and ethics have left ineffable traces in modern times in the philosophy of Spinoza, Leibniz, Kant and Fichte' (1957 [1931]: 293).
3. See Note 5 for Appiah's view of the problematic relation between the postcolonial continent and its diaspora.
4. See also my view of 'permeable ethnicity', which continues in overlapping, multiple loyalties from precolonial to postcolonial times in contexts of migration, mixing and interchange between variable ethnic groups (Werbner 2004a: 68–69)).
5. I am aware that Appiah does comment insightfully on alliance as a problematic, when he interrogates Pan-Africanism in the light of his view of the relativity of identities. But he does not theorise the problematic as a central interest in his own intellectual project. He remarks, 'in constructing alliances across states – and especially in the Third World – A Pan-African identity, which allows African-Americans, Afro-Caribbeans, and Afro-Latins to ally with continental Africans, drawing on the cultural resources of the black Atlantic world, may serve useful purposes' (1992: 180). He goes on, however, to stipulate the right terms – terms of independence between the diaspora and the continent – for such alliance, 'If there is ... hope, too, for the Pan-Africanism of an African Diaspora once it, too, is released from bondage to racial ideologies (alongside the many bases of alliance available to Africa's peoples in their political and cultural struggles), it is crucial that we recognise the independence, once "Negro" nationalism is gone, of the Pan-Africanism of the diaspora and the Pan-Africanism of the continent' (ibid.).
6. I differ from Hollinger in my usage of cultural pluralist in order to convey an ongoing shift in postcolonial politics, rather than in the liberal or post-liberal theory of intellectuals. My usage here builds on the one in my study of postcolonial elites where I write of 'political pluralism' and mean 'the expansion of diverse pressure groups – professional, civic, and cultural – as organised lobbies for public yet distinctive and differentiated interests' (2004a: 200). My usage also allows for permeable ethnicity, and for a pluralist to have multiple, shifting and overlapping loyalties, rather than the over-determined ethnic ties and culturalism which Hollinger attributes to the pluralist position.

References

Appiah, Kwame (1992), *In My Father's House*, Oxford: Oxford University Press.

—— (1998), 'Cosmopolitan Patriots', in Pheng Cheah and Bruce Robbins (eds), *Cosmopolitics*, Minneapolis: University of Minnesota Press, pp. 91–114.

—— (2005), *The Ethics of Identity*, Princeton: Princeton University Press.

—— (2006), *Cosmopolitanism: Ethics in a World of Strangers*, London: Allen Lane.

Durham, Deborah and Frederick Klaits (2002), 'Funerals and the Public Space of Sentiment in Botswana', *Journal of Southern African Studies* 28 (4): 777–98.

Fortes, Meyer and E.E. Evans-Pritchard (eds) (1940), *African Poltical Systems*, Oxford: Oxford University Press/Press for the International African Institute.

Fumanti, Mattia (2007), 'Burying E.S.: Educated Elites, Subjectivity and Distinction in Rundu, Namibia', *Journal of Southern African Studies* 33 (3): 469–83.

Hollinger, David (2002), 'Not Universalists, Not Pluralists: The New Cosmopolitans find their own Way', in Steven Vertovec and Robin Cohen (eds), *Conceiving Cosmopolitanism*, Oxford: Oxford University Press, pp. 227–39.

Masire, Quett (2006), *Very Brave or Very Foolish? Memories of an African Democrat*, Gaborone: Macmillan.

Maundeni, Zibani (2004), *Civil Society, Politics and the State in Botswana*, Gaborone: Medi Publishing.

Nussbausm, Martha (1994), 'Patriotism and Cosmopolitanism', *Boston Review* 19 (5): 3–6.

Nyamnjoh, Francis (2006), *Insiders and Outsiders*, London: Zed Books.

Solway, Jacqueline (2002), 'Navigating the "Neutral" State: "Minority" Rights in Botswana', *Journal of Southern African Studies* 28 (4): 711–30.

Turner, Victor (1957), *Schism and Continuity in an African Society*, Manchester: Manchester University Press.

Werbner, Richard (1996), 'Multiple Identities, Plural Arenas', in Richard Werbner and Terence Ranger (eds), *Postcolonial Identities in Africa*, London: Zed Books, pp. 1–25.

—— (2002a), 'Challenging Minorities, Difference and Tribal Citizenship in Botswana', *Journal of Southern African Studies* 28 (4): 671–84.

—— (2002b), 'Cosmopolitan Ethnicity, Entrepreneurship and the Nation: Minority Elites in Botswana', *Journal of Southern African Studies* 28 (4): 731–54.

—— (2004a), *Reasonable Radicals and Citizenship in Botswana*, Bloomington and Indianapolis: Indiana University Press.

—— (2004b), 'Epilogue: The New Dialogue with Post-Liberalism,' in Harri Englund and Francis Nyamnjoh (eds), *Rights and the Politics of Recognition in Africa*, London: Zed Books, pp. 261–74.

Werbner, Richard and Terence Ranger (eds) (1996), *Postcolonial Identities in Africa*, London: Zed Books.

Zeller, Eduard (1957) [1931], *Outlines of the History of Greek Philosophy*, New York: Meridian Books.

10

Paradoxes of the Cosmopolitan in Melanesia[1]
Eric Hirsch

Is it an oxymoron to speak of Melanesian cosmopolitanism? The region is often portrayed in the popular media as inhabited by isolated 'last unknown' peoples. At the same time, as is also well known, it is a region with over 700 different languages, famous for its cultural and social diversity. It is this intensity of difference – one that often belies a sense of cultural and social 'isolation' – which significantly informs Melanesian cosmopolitanism. The emphasis on difference co-exists with its opposite, the surmounting of difference, in order to create the grounds for new forms of distinctiveness. This recurrent process, as exemplified in exchange relations, person and place-name transformations, among others, is the basis of what I refer to here as a 'grassroots' kind of Melanesian cosmopolitanism. It is perhaps akin to what Kahn (2003: 409) refers to as 'popular cosmopolitans', where he suggests that in modern Malaysia and the surrounding archipelago '[a] certain cosmopolitanism governs the practices of localized individuals and institutions, everyday interactions between individuals and groups, popular cultural activities, forms of economic relations and institutions of village government.' However, a further distinctive feature of Melanesian cosmopolitanism is its cosmology: the widespread view across the region that each collectivity occupies the centre of the world. The capacity to draw in otherness, often from great distances, is evidence of this centrality and the power associated with it. In Melanesia there is a different kind of commerce evident, compared to that typical, for instance, of large-scale mercantile, urban societies of the Mediterranean, fertile crescent or South-East Asia. It is a commerce of symbolic transactions between relatively small cultural collectivities and one that engenders a cosmopolitan world of exchange. The 'conversation' in Melanesia (Appiah 2006) is not so much verbal but nevertheless highly symbolic and communicative.

The question, however, is: how is this distinctive form of Melanesian cosmo-politanism being sustained in the face of the unequal relations produced by Westernisation and predatory economic globalisation? James Clifford has noted that cosmopolitanism '[a]llows us to hold on to the idea that whereas something like economic and political equality are crucial political goals, something like cultural similarity is not' (Clifford 1998: 365). In considering the impact of globalisation on indigenous peoples he argues that, 'the goal is not complete separation from the global systems that descended on indigenous peoples during the past few centuries. The struggle is rather for a real degree of control over areas such as land and culture, *more power in managing the ongoing interaction'* (Clifford 1998: 366, emphasis added).

In this chapter I consider two ways in which Melanesians assert power in managing interactions with others. In the first part I consider examples of symbolic exchange from my own fieldwork and that of others before considering, in the second part of the chapter, the impact of foreign mining and the expansion of Western-style education on communities in the hinterland. The first assertion of power, as indicated above, is in the context of Melanesians viewing themselves at the centre of the world and open to diverse outside influences. The second is where Melanesians view the world as influencing their cultures and where cultures should be potentially closed to diverse outside influences. The first is a sort of grassroots cosmopolitanism; the second a literate and metropolitan cosmopolitanism. Together, I suggest, they highlight the paradoxes of the cosmopolitan in postcolonial Melanesia that I seek to elucidate in what follows. I do so with reference to land and the wealth deriving from land-based resources and with reference to culture: to the control over what are considered distinct, separate cultures.

Cosmological Centrality

It would be incorrect to see Melanesian peoples as incapable of living side by side with outsiders – such as non-Melanesians. In fact, people like the Fuyuge whom I studied, and who have now been affected by mining, have a significant history of living with outsiders, of facilitating outsiders' entry to their lands and social lives: missionaries, colonialists, capitalists. It is their capacity to incorporate and live side by side with outsiders that suggests a form of cosmopolitanism. But in the Melanesian cases, at least, it is also predicated on distinct cosmological visions. These visions are ones where people imagine themselves as occupying the centre of the world – and either implicitly or explicitly understand themselves as 'centre people'. In being at the centre, their world is potentially fully open and as fully capable of appropriation as the world system that impinges upon it: '[w]ithin this world, transformation rather than reproduction (which is viewed negatively, as an undesirable restoration of the *status quo ante*) is the norm' (Biersack 1991: 231–2). Among many Melanesian peoples it could be said that 'if their boundaries were boundaries of containment, the white man [for instance] would have come as an exogenous agent. But their boundaries are the sites of expansion and incorporation and any agent who "comes" succumbs to the logic of the processes organized at these sites'.

A classic instance of this capacity for incorporation are the first contact situations described and re-described for the New Guinea Highlands (Strathern 1992). The

Australians that first contacted the inhabitants of New Guinea imagined the natives would be awed by the scale of their flight technology that followed them into the mountainous terrain and by the steel tools and other modern things they brought with them. But to the locals these were mere curiosities. It was not the distinctions or differences between the highlanders and the Australians that was to have the most important impact, but the collapse of that distinction (ibid.: 245). At first the highlanders thought the white men were people-eating spirits and many ran away in fear, but others were curious and stayed. The Australians needed pigs from the locals to feed their numerous carriers, but the men would not part with them in exchange for the things the white men brought. However, when one of the Australians noticed the gold-lip pearl shells worn by the people, he arranged that some be brought back on the next plane. Subsequently, when the case holding the shells was opened the highlanders realised the Australians were men like themselves: they were 'confronted with an image of themselves' (ibid.: 250) and it was this disclosure that made relationships possible (ibid.: 249). '[T]hey were recognizable as humans because [they disclosed] the capacity to transact' (ibid.: 251). In this regard it was also evidence of themselves, the highlanders, and their world as the centre: things that come from distant places provide 'evidence of people's local capacities to draw them in' and the Australians presented the highlanders with evidence of their own – highlander – power (ibid.: 251). If we return to Clifford's words, at this moment the highlanders were capable of powerfully managing the ongoing interaction: a set of relations that would subsequently alter, but not the conventions or expectations about relationships.

The dynamics of 'first contact' reveal the rules of cosmopolitan engagement in Melanesia: it was only when highlands men recognised things that came from distant places that they apprehended evidence of their own capacities. The outsiders presented these men with testimony of their own power. This attention to outside influences as the source of power and political authority is one that has been documented for numerous Melanesian societies. The Mountain Arapesh, for instance, were dubbed by Mead as an 'importing culture' (Mead 1938) and she documented an elaborate system of exchange and trade with coastal peoples that included not only material products (e.g. tobacco and shell valuables) but also 'immaterial' goods, such as dance complexes. Similarly, male cults in the New Guinea highlands are transacted between local groups in enchained performances that parallel the enchained ceremonial exchanges of Moka or Tee (Modjeska 1991, cited by Harrison 1993).

Harrison (1993, 2000) suggests that these forms of 'commerce' are an intrinsic feature of Melanesian regional relations and that the interest in such outside influences is that they are perceived as renowned – prestigious – and hence as the basis of power and political-ritual authority. This commerce circulates across different cultures or sub-cultures, where 'cultures are perhaps inherently relational and oppositional, generating themselves in processes of mutual differentiation' (Harrison 1993: 148). The more general point that Harrison derives from these cultural divisions is that 'Melanesian societies often seem ... to create this distinctiveness or differences in order to mediate and bridge it.' He then argues that,

> in these processes of mutual differentiation, in the deliberate mutual heightening of each other's 'otherness', there [is] the creation of a particular kind of value. The identities of others, in the form of the rituals they possess, [are] valuable to acquire just as they [are] valuable to acquire in the material form of gifts such as shell valuables. (Harrison 1993: 149)

As Harrison (2000: 667) indicates, cultural forms introduced by Europeans were often dealt with in comparable ways. He provides examples of missionary churches locally incorporated as powerful outside influences (see Neumann 1992a and Otto 1991). It should be noted that this openness to external sources of power and the internal transformations these entail was not due to an inborn Melanesian 'cultural instability' as argued by some (Brunton 1989; Whitehouse 2000). Instead, it derives from the fact that such forms are 'produced or acquired in the first place to move along lines of communication between groups' (Harrison 1993: 147). Rituals and shell valuables are analogous in this regard, not only because of their transactability, but because of their potency as performances. These entities are not conceptualised as 'traditions' with intrinsic qualities central to a group's identity, to be handed down to each generation (ibid.: 147). Rather, they are all versions of persons and are thus implicated in the persons from whom they derive. As such, people are concerned with the entities' effects, with their capacity to yield power and wealth. These effects can only be known when they are performed, seen and witnessed, that is, when they are perceived as 'images' – at once evoking past actions and foreshadowing future ones (Strathern 1990; Wagner 1986).[2] The makers of such images are concerned to appear effective and innovatory and it is this interest which leads, in turn, to the 'openness' of (potentially) renowned outside influences. Men and women speak of following in the way of the ancestors, but their way of doing so will be informed by a desire to appear powerful, to 'knock the conventional off balance' (Wagner 1975). From this perspective, each performance has the capacity to be a unique instance of the connections between past, present and future (cf. Neumann 1992b). Such a historicity[3] is different from one that views 'traditions' and the integrity of the past as a prime value in itself. In this latter historicity[4] the relation between past and present is inherently separate, as much as the relation between cultures (cf. Fasolt 2004).[5]

Among the Kaluli people, studied by Feld (1996) and Schieffelin (1976), the *gisalo* ceremony was once the most prominent spectacle for men to assert their power. In the not too distant past, this was accomplished by invited guests dancing and singing in the hosts' longhouse, performances that evoked, in turn, weeping and violent responses on the part of the hosts. The songs, also known as *gisalo*, are what contribute to an effective ceremony (Schieffelin 1976: 178). The songs performed early in the evening, when the dancers first arrive in the longhouse, often do not contain references to the lands or place names of the hosts. As the ceremony develops the songs gradually contain references to localities closer to those of the hosts. Finally, 'they cross over into the hosts' lands themselves, and the weeping and violence begin in earnest' (ibid.: 184). Here again is an instance of distinctiveness created in order for it to be bridged and obviated.

As Feld (1996: 127) notes, men no longer stage *gisalo* and have not done so in the Bosavi area since 1984. *Gisalo* songs are now performed largely by women, not in competitive ceremonial displays, but more as modes of personal expression. Feld has made sound recordings of these and other Kaluli song genres, most notably with a woman named Ulahi. His earlier recordings were produced as an LP, but more recently he asked her to sing some of the songs again for the 'Voices of the Rainforest' CD he was making. Feld and Ulahi made the recordings but immediately afterwards Ulahi performed a second song, in a Kaluli genre different from *gisalo*. The lyrics of the song ask for the names of what Ulahi refers to as 'my American and Australian men and women' (Feld 1996: 129). Ulahi then switches to a full speaking voice: 'Well ... I won't see your place but you see mine, I don't know your names ... you people in faraway lands, listening to me ... "Many people will hear your Bosavi songs", you say like that to me before, but ... singing by myself, I'm thinking, what are your names? ... I don't really know the land names, just America, Australia, so I'm sadly singing like that so that they can hear it' (ibid.: 129). Ulahi's lament refers back to a conversation she and Feld had before recording her songs again. He told her that a large number of new people would now hear her singing. Ulahi was not able to comprehend the scale of the recording venture, but she knew the *gisalo* depended on the audience and performer knowing and recognising each others' place names. How, in short, can the audiences of her song in America or Australia appreciate it if *she* does not know *their* place names? This form of reciprocal recognition – of sustaining difference in order to mediate it – is reproduced in these new, international circumstances of *gisalo* performance (see Hirsch 2002).

Among the Udabe Valley-residing Fuyuge with whom I lived, place names are periodically changed for foreign-derived ones. This occurs in different but related circumstances. In some cases men who have worked or visited other areas transform the names of their land or that of their villages with the names of distant places. So, for example, in the Udabe Valley are found villages with names deriving from Port Moresby and the surrounding coastal region, such as Bautam or Elevala. Land names are also changed in similar fashion, with names such as Taurama. A comparable change may occur following the visit of persons or collectivities from distant places, often in coercive ritual situations. For instance, a section of the territorial area I resided in (called Visi) was known as Yago. The name derives from

Fuyuge-speakers living in the distant Chirima Valley. Men and women from this valley performed as dancers in a *gab* ritual staged in Visi several decades ago. When the Visi hosts killed pigs in exchange for Yago's dancing performance, the dancers expressed their pleasure and said the hosts killed pigs just as themselves – the hosts were as Yago. Since that time, this section of Visi refers to itself by this 'foreign' name. More recently and during my first fieldwork, I extensively studied a *gab* ritual in Visi, whose village name was Uyams. When I first came to reside in this village – as I lived elsewhere in Visi – a small rite was staged whereby the name of the village was 'washed away' and the name of my 'home' village of Chicago replaced it. The village is now known by this name.

Analogous sorts of transformations occur with respect to the names of persons throughout Melanesia. Among the Maisin of Collingwood Bay, for instance, the aftermath of World War II led to a new set of names being adopted as a result of peoples' positive perception of US servicemen stationed in the area. As John Barker (personal communication) observes, one man in a nearby village was named America by his father. Anthropologists working in other regions of Melanesia have recorded similar adoptions, such as Bruce Lee or Johnny Cash. Each of these instances are locally perceived as evidence of peoples' capacities to draw in distant names, mediate their differences and thus demonstrate themselves as powerfully effective.

Cultural Loss: Strangers in their own Home

This cosmopolitan world of exchange and power, of cultural openness and fluidity, has for some decades now been challenged by imported ideas about authenticity, historical continuity and culture closure. This 'classical historicism' has been connected to the writings of Herder (Burns and Rayment-Pickard 2000: 59–61). Whereas Kant writes of the possibility of a universal cosmopolitan existence, where 'the matrix within which all the original capacities of the human race may develop' (Kant 1991 [1784], cited in Burns and Rayment-Pickard 2000: 56), Herder highlights a 'respect for human difference at both national and individual level' (Burns and Rayment-Pickard 2000: 60). Herder was Kant's contemporary, but the former writes:

> No other person has the right to constrain me to feel as he does, nor the power to impart to me his mode of perception. No other person can, in short, transform my existence and identity into his. (Herder 1969: 308, cited in Burns and Rayment-Pickard 2000: 60)

The reason I invoke Herder's legacy here is that it implicitly informs an article from *The National*, one of Papua New Guinea's English language national daily newspapers. The article in question was drawn to my attention during 2002.[6] It was pointed out to me by my friend and fieldwork associate Alphonse Hega.

He is a Fuyuge whom I have known since the mid-1980s. The media piece he suggested I consult is by one of the most 'cosmopolitan' Papua New Guineans, the current Governor General, Sir Paulias Matane. Until shortly after he became Governor General, Matane wrote a weekly column in *The National* called 'The Time Traveller'. The title of the particular column that Alphonse had in mind was 'Destruction of Papua New Guinea Culture'. Why, through our letter correspondences, did Alphonse suggest I consult this piece whose views he said he shared?

During fieldwork in 1999 Alphonse had expressed to me views about what he called his culture and how it was important to keep out influences – such as dances or place names – that originated from other cultures. I had addressed the issues he raised with me in an article I later wrote and sent him to see if he felt that I represented his views accurately (Hirsch 2001). In his response he said that I did and highlighted Matane's column as one whose views he greatly shared.

This specific column of Matane's derived from a symposium the author had participated in at the University of Sydney (during July 2002). The symposium was to reflect on the cultural decolonisation of Papua New Guinea (PNG) before and after political independence. The symposium included a very cosmopolitan group with speakers from PNG, Australia, and other countries. The title of Matane's symposium talk was 'The Rape and Destruction of PNG Cultures and Traditions by Foreign Influences'. In the adapted version, in his column, he focused on how colonial foreign influences altered the way Papua New Guineans viewed themselves, took up foreign languages and ideas and lost traditional ways. As he notes, and this is the point Alphonse emphasised to me in his letter about the column: 'Today, some do not ... even know their cultures and traditions. They have become strangers in their own homes'.

Matane is writing not only from a specific cosmopolitan perspective – literate and metropolitan – but as a powerful and influential member of the PNG elite. This elite took shape in the years prior to national Independence in 1975. Writing during the period of self-government, and three years before Independence, the Australian historian Hank Nelson (1972: 60) emphasises some of the challenges facing a new national elite:

> The need is for a sensitive regard for the past while not claiming that it is the culture of the people of Niugini [Papua New Guinea] now. The first generation of Niuginian students are reading prose, poetry and plays by Niuginians. They need to see the art forms used by the old men to demonstrate their skills and their aspirations while at the same time they themselves move confidently among newer forms. There is a richness for the student from the Papuan Gulf who can see the carved *hohao* boards and read Vincent Eri's novel, *The Crocodile*, which describes the lives of the people who abandoned the tradition of the carvers.

At around this same time Matane published his first volumes of autobiography (1972) and travel writing (1971), writings that would have reached the generation of students referred to by Nelson. In fact, some of these very students were writing their own prose at this moment. *Three Short Novels from Papua New Guinea* was published in 1976, but the pieces were clearly written several years previously. In his introduction to the collection, written in 1974, Greicus (1976: viii–ix) summarises the connections between the three authors:

> The first two short novels [by Benjamin Umba and August Kituai] are pre-occupied with transitions which though recent are evocative of a past New Guinea experience, shaped largely by the pressures of European colonization. In that way they prepare the reader for an understanding of Jim Baital's futuristic novel of New Guinea and independence ... Baital's character is at once more sophisticated and more European than the heroes of Umba and Kituai. And that sophistication, representative of a new generation of Papua New Guineans guiding the country towards self-government and independence, is the crucial element in the story. For Baital, like Umba and Kituai, is preoccupied with the anguish of an individual poised between incompatible cultures. But the problem in Baital's story has been generalized from the individual and from the clan to the country itself.

If we return to Matane's more recent newspaper article, these same themes are present: the writer refers explicitly to the effects of mission influences or Western-style education, and their general impacts on PNG cultures. Alphonse in his discussions with me was referring to his own culture and the effect of other PNG cultures and/or Western influences upon his culture. The fact that Alphonse reads *The National* (when he can obtain it, which is often not easy in his village) and columns such as Matane's, indicates that he has more explicitly cosmopolitan views than most of his fellow villagers. His perceptions are informed by different horizons, shaped by his education (agricultural college graduate) and political interests (local councillor, magistrate and parliamentary candidate). Alphonse, like Matane, is aware and concerned with the existence of distinct cultures, cultures whose integrity, they both argue, exists by sustaining their boundaries with other cultures. More specifically, Alphonse is aware that in contemporary PNG, discourses and images of culture circulate widely in media forms such as *The National* newspaper. In this context, cultures or 'legacies' – to adopt Harrison's notion – are prestigious *in themselves* and need to be sustained as such. But not all cultures become visible and circulate, let alone in an effective and positive manner. Alphonse is concerned to get his culture portrayed and to have it portrayed in a way that shows it to be effective.

This is a new kind of 'commerce of cultures' as compared to the one described by Harrison (1993). In this new kind of commerce, Alphonse's culture – and he, by implication – become renowned and distinguished. To do so, a culture must appear like a recognizable culture – it must be distinct from other competing examples. This is what is displayed in much media advertising, where Papua New Guineans are portrayed – often in 'traditional' dress – and which are perceived by other Papua New Guineans to exemplify unique cultures whether this is actually the case or not (see Errington and Gewertz 1996: 116). Although this appears to be a version of the production of difference described above, what is different is that these distinctions are not created in order to be explicitly mediated.

The radical change has come in the way that, in such a competitive, globalised world, an emphasis on avoiding intercultural transformations – maintaining cultural integrity – is highly valued by such PNG elite cosmopolitans. This is in contrast to the instances I described earlier in the chapter where explicit conversions are specifically valued, whether within cultures or between them; whether adopting Western disco to a PNG style of dance or taking place names from different areas and emplacing them in ones own place (see Hirsch 2004).

In his column Matane highlights these outside influences as a form of cultural loss:

We learned foreign poems like Baa, Baa Black Sheep, The Three Bears Goldilocks, London Bridge is falling, etc. We were being removed from our animals, tales, and cultural and traditional ways of living. As the years went by, foreign music, books and even food invaded our homes. We became materialistic in our thoughts, words and deeds. The next generations followed suit.

He is reacting to Western colonial and postcolonial culture that sought (and seeks) to render Melanesians apparently more 'cosmopolitan' and 'civilised', but at the expense, as he perceives it, of *destroying* PNG cultures – hence a universalising, effacing counter-cosmopolitanism. Alphonse concurs with his analysis, especially as this applies to his own Fuyuge culture and the outside influences he is critical of – PNG style disco being the latest form. At the same time, though, Alphonse knows that the Western-derived cosmopolitan culture that Matane condemns, but also centrally participates in, is the very culture that he also must engage with if he is to render his culture visible. This visibility is engendered through, among other means, commercially sponsored photo competitions, such as that sponsored by Coca-Cola.[7] And this is among the numerous competing versions that circulate in PNG, as displayed in biscuit and Coca-Cola advertisments.[8]

The influences from other PNG cultures or of Western-dominated universalist or commercialised culture is one Alphonse seeks to avoid. But this is contrary to how most of his fellow villagers perceive the world and how they understand what it is to be effective and powerful in the world. Like them, Alphonse is seeking to attain more power in the ongoing interaction with outside influences. Men like Matane and Alphonse are engaging in a 'commerce of cultures', attempting to appear powerful and effective in ways not so different from their village compatriots. However, the key difference between these agents hinges on the conceptions of culture and the cosmopolitan they each sustain. The paradox is that the more that people like the Fuyuge assert their own form of cosmopolitanism – as 'centre people' – to render themselves visible and powerful, the more this seems to subvert the kind of defensive cultural cosmopolitanism advocated in parallel ways by Alphonse and Matane. However, the more such men draw on this explicit literate and metropolitan literacy to render themselves or their cultures visible, the more they seem to contribute to the very predicament – of potentially infiltrating PNG cultures with outside influences – that they seek to transcend.

Unequal Transactions: Mining Companies and Predatory Globalisation

At the end of August 2005 another (brief) article appeared in *The National* (30 August 2005).[9] The article is titled 'Landowners torch TGM facilities', TGM being the acronym for Tolukuma Gold Mine. It is reported in the article that village landowners acted this way because of unhappiness about the royalty payments they had been receiving. The TGM had repeatedly tried to fly members of the mobile police unit to the mine site but had been prevented by heavy fogs. The article went on to further report how '[l]ast month, disgruntled landowners shut down the hydro plant at the Auga River to disrupt work at the mine site. They were unhappy over compensation they got from the use of their river in operating the plant. The villagers living along that river tampered with the power lines that supplied electricity to the mine to express their disappointment over compensation payment for the use of the river.'

The people directly affected by the Tolukuma Gold Mine are Fuyuge speakers residing in the Auga Valley. Their villages lie in the Wharton Ranges of the Papuan highlands about 100 km north-west of Port Moresby, the national capital.[10] There are no vehicular roads from the coast into Fuyuge lands and all transportation into and out of the mine is conducted by giant helicopters. The mine started operations there during 1995. It is currently operated by the South Africa-based mining company DRD Gold, and is one of its most profitable mines. At present, exploration is being conducted at sites neighbouring the mine, with possible expansion in the future.

To repeat the point made by Clifford: peoples such as the Fuyuge require more power in managing the ongoing interaction. But what does this mean in the example I have briefly given above – especially the idea of the 'ongoing interaction'? What sort of interaction is taking place? A cursory reading of the incidents at TGM provided by the newspaper article suggests that they are nothing more than destruction motivated by frustration. Although to some extent true, further contextualization is needed to make better sense of this brief media example and the sources of the frustration involved.

Agreements made with the PNG authorities, and with representatives of the Fuyuge, endow mining operators with control over the way the future transpires and, specifically, the way people of PNG are organised on the land – the need to form themselves into named, bounded units. It is to these units alone that money as royalties or compensation proceeds. This way of organising themselves in connection to the land is contrary to conventional relations between people and land among Melanesians (see Filer 1990: 11–12). In such a situation it is not possible for local people to perform conversions or transformations with the mine – and thus their peoples' sense of effectiveness is curtailed. Instead, the boundaries imposed by the mining concern and the way it controls the timing and direction of monetary transactions prevents the possibilities of any conversions, that is, of reciprocal exchanges of diverse forms (see Jacka 2005: 647).

This manner of bounding persons with respect to the land brings to mind the way the idea of culture has come to be understood and critiqued. Responding to globalisation theory in their much cited paper, 'Beyond culture', Gupta and Ferguson (1992) suggest that the association of peoples and cultures with defined territorial space or land was no longer possible. As they put it: 'An anthropology whose objects are no longer conceived as automatically and naturally anchored in space will need to pay particular attention to the way spaces and places are made, imagined, contested and enforced' (ibid.: 17–18). The situation in PNG seems, however, to reverse the historical trajectory identified by Gupta and Ferguson. In PNG, culture was not in the past contained within a bounded territory. It was the global penetration of Western ideas about ownership that imposed such a relationship between people, territory and culture.

The mining companies have compelled people to anchor themselves in clearly demarcated spaces or land and this is contrary to the way most PNG people constitute themselves with the land and other persons. The PNG actions against the mine, described above, amount to a kind of critique which reverses that articulated by Gupta and Ferguson. As we have seen, however, some elite and literate Papua New Guineans have developed an alternative critical view about boundaries and especially the association of boundaries and culture.

In general, mining projects in PNG are localised not by the people themselves but by the national government through the delineation of project development licence areas. These areas correspond to the graticular units of fixed dimension on official maps and it is with reference to these maps that the mining sites are drawn. The delineated area includes the immediate sites of the project and often other adjacent sites as well. After the mining project area has been delineated, then, as a matter of course, all persons specified as owning land are considered project landowners. As a result of these land demarcations, any site of major resource development is likely to become the focus of competition by persons who can claim some proprietary interest in it (Weiner 2004: 5). The mineral resources below the surface of the land are the property of the state. To gain access to these resources, though, requires the removal of local 'landowners' and the payment of royalties to them in compensation. Other forms of compensation are also paid to people affected by the mining operations due to loss of crops, houses, trees, etc.

There is now a growing literature from PNG to do with issues of compensation, landownership, and what has been labelled 'entification': 'the process of the making of "entities", or things from what have been either implicit or contingent categories' (Ernst 2004: 126). This latter process is, for example, where persons come to designate themselves as landowning 'clans'. However, notions such as landownership and even clans are not, in many cases, relevant local categories. This is why analysts have proposed the notion of entification, to capture the emergence of explicit entities that come to be formed due to the influence of resource development projects and their procedures of operations. It is to such entities, as in the case of named landowning clans, that resource rent payments then flow.

The timing of these payments are dictated by the mining concern and associated government departments. This is generally worked out at one time and the disbursements are controlled over time. And yet the effects on the people, their land and environment continue and intensify. This includes the pollution of local rivers from toxic mine tailings and chemical spills and the compromising of subsistence activities due to the loss of cultivatable land (see *The National*, 16 March 2007, 'A mining genocide'). So although the compensation agreement appears to take into account these long-term effects, what it does not take into account is the day-to-day, ongoing relationship with the mine – the ongoing interaction – and the local expectation that a relation entails a recurrent, reciprocal flow. Thus the mining operations are perceived locally to appropriate continuously from the villagers' land. Although the compensation agreement has built in this 'time-factor', what is actually experienced is an ongoing relationship that is not being properly acknowledged. In the relations between a mine such as Tolukuma and that of the local people there is a difference in the way the temporality of relations is appreciated and whether these relations are understood as being conducted appropriately by the agents involved. This is not to say that the mining operators do not have ongoing relations with the local Fuyuge people. This takes the form of Community Relations Officers, Community Projects and Community Relations exercises, such as the company-produced *Tolukuma Times*, a newsletter that appears periodically. However, this only involves a relatively small proportion of the people affected by the operations, and often the same people are already benefiting from royalty and compensation payments. A not dissimilar example to that at Tolukuma is reported for the Pogera mine in the New Guinea Highlands (Jacka 2005). The Pogera mine is located in the Porgera Valley and on land of the Ipili people. The Ipili people are connected in a ritual network with Huli people to the south and Enga people to the north. '[T]he ritual network was linked together by a giant python ... and the various ritual sites were places where the snake's body rose to the surface of the ground' (Jacka 2005: 646). From the current Huli perspective, the gold at Pogera is from this snake, while from the Pogera perspective it derives from a spirit snake located solely on their lands. As the anthropologist who worked among them explains:

> [T]he power for the Pogera mine is generated from [a gas project] located among the Huli, and in 2002, the Huli shut down the Pogera mine for several months by destroying 14 electrical pylons that transmit electricity to the mine... Their rationale for destroying the pylons was that they were not receiving enough proceeds from the mine, even though they had long-term ritual and social links with the Ipili. As several Huli men expressed to me in 2000, the Huli were at the center of the ritual network because the head of the snake was in their area. It was their ritual activities – their pigs and vegetable products – which kept the snake alive so that its skin, urine and faeces could become the valuable resources of gold, gas, and oil. (Jacka 2005: 648)

As indicated above, the Ipili view the origins of the gold as deriving from spiritual powers on their land alone. But what the Huli men were telling the anthropologist is that the conversion of the snake's skin, urine and faeces into valuable entities was enabled by their capacity to keep the snake alive. It was their transformation of pigs and vegetables at the mouth of the python that facilitated the conversions resulting in gas, oil and gold. It was these ritual alterations that further transformed the Ipili landowners into wealthy persons. And yet, there was insufficient wealth flowing in the Huli direction. Huli efforts, they perceived, really enabled the gas, gold and oil, but an analogous and substitutable form for their efforts – money – was not coming back sufficiently. By destroying the pylons and shutting down the operations the Huli sought to effect on others (stopping the flow of valuable commodities) what was being caused to them (insufficient flow of money). The anticipations of the Huli in terms of the conversions they had effected were not being returned appropriately in terms of the timing or the amounts.

It would be wrong, then, to see these actions as simple opposition to the mine (although there are those in the areas mentioned that have this view). Rather, what is being opposed is a convention of relationship that is not proceeding according to expectation. It could be said that the mine is operating with one view of relationships, premised on the bounded entities of land and landowning individuals, and how such individuals conduct their relations over time. The villagers, by contrast, have a different view of relationships and a different view of how such relations are conducted over time. The problem here, as above, is the ongoing interaction and how this should be managed.

Conclusion

Melanesians have, it seems, a long-standing interest in highlighting cultural differences in order to obviate these differences for the purposes of political-ritual power. The value ascribed to this 'otherness' also derives from Melanesian cosmology, where people view themselves at the centre of the world. The capacity to draw in difference, often from great distances, and incorporate it, is both evidence of powerful effectiveness and cosmological centrality. At the same time there are literate and metropolitan Melanesians who adopt a different kind of cosmopolitanism. From their perspective cultural differences are to be positively valued and the integrity of such differences should not be transgressed. This is a defensive, cultural cosmopolitanism: outside influences are to be avoided – such as the case with the effects of Western colonialism – and communication and exchange between cultures sustained by maintaining boundaries.

In effect, the introduction of large-scale resource extraction throughout Melanesia over the last two decades, such as mining and forestry, has meant that ideas of discrete bounded entities – not dissimilar from ideas of bounded cultures – have become locally imposed and adopted. The deployment by resource extraction operators of notions such a 'landowning clans', in order to determine ownership rights and thus the payment of royalties, is contrary to conventional Melanesian relations with the land as much as with persons and 'cultures'.

As Clifford (1998: 365) has noted more generally, peoples such as the Melanesians described in this chapter, struggle to achieve more power in managing the ongoing interactions with respect to their cultures and lands. What I have sought to highlight here is that Melanesian ideas about interaction, as much as about culture, land, or power rests on distinctive notions of difference and how difference is meant – or not meant – to be obviated in order for it to be sustained. There are paradoxes in the way Melanesians view the cosmopolitan – what I have referred to as grassroots and metropolitan – in the sense that each either implicitly or explicitly undermines the project of the other. The more power each seeks to achieve in managing the interactions they value, the more these interactions become, it seems, difficult to deal with. This is a paradox that cannot, I think, be resolved. However, by knowing its forms and limits it can perhaps be better understood and the paradox itself better managed.

Notes

1. This chapter draws on different periods of fieldwork (from the mid-1980s), most recently supported by the Cambridge and Brunel Universities joint research project, 'Property, transactions and creations: new economic relations in the Pacific', funded by the UK Economic and Social Research Council (grant no. R000237838). I am most grateful to Alphonse Hega, Kol Usi, and my other recent hosts in Yuvenise. I am also very grateful to Narmala Halstead and Daniele Moretti for their comments on a draft of the chapter and to Pnina Werbner for her very effective editing in shaping the chapter's final form.

2. As Strathern (1990: 34) notes, following Wagner (1986): 'An image ... condenses or collapses context into itself in the sense that all points of reference are obviated or displaced by its single form.'

3. Carr (1995: 586, original emphasis) provides a concise but lucid sense of historicity: 'Persons are not merely *in* history; their past, including their social past, figures in their conception of themselves and their future possibilities. Some awareness of the past is thus constitutive of the self prior to being formed into a cognitive discipline.'

4. An outgrowth of 'classical historicism' (see Burns and Rayment-Pickard 2000: 57–71, and see below).

5. As Neumann (1992b: 6) has observed: 'Whether in order to derive the present from the past, or whether because historians empathised with the past from a victor's point of view (as nineteenth-century historicists have done so convincingly), the dominant approaches in Western historiography over the past 150 years have, however unintentionally, provided an explanation of the present by means of unravelling of the past. Many, if not most, have opted for a representation of the past as some kind of linear progressive change.'

6. Published on 26 September 2002.

7. He has a limited range of possible ways in which he can display his 'culture': he can only make use of what is at his disposal.

8. One of Alphonse's entries to the 1998 national Coca-Cola calendar competition was selected and used in the nationally distributed calendar (see Hirsch 2004 for these images).

9. Thanks to Stuart Kirsch for drawing this article to my attention.

10. I have conducted research in the neighbouring Udabe Valley since the mid-1980s.

References

Appiah, Kwame A. (2006), *The Ethics of Identity*, Princeton: Princeton University Press.

Biersack, Aletta (1991), 'Prisoners of Time: Millenarian Praxis in a Melanesian Valley', in Aletta Biersack (ed.), *Clio in Oceania: Towards a Historical Anthropology*, Washington DC: Smithsonian Institution Press, pp. 231–95.

Brunton, Ron (1989), *The Abandoned Narcotic: Kava and Cultural Instability in Melanesia*, Cambridge: Cambridge University Press.

Burns, Robert and Hugh Rayment-Pickard (eds), (2000), *Philosophies of History: From Enlightenment to Postmodernity*, Oxford: Blackwell Publishers.

Carr, David (1995), 'Philosophy of history', in Robert Audi (ed.), *The Cambridge Dictionary of Philosophy*, Cambridge: Cambridge University Press, pp. 584–6.

Clifford, James (1998), 'Mixed feelings', in Pheng Cheah and Bruce Robbins (eds), *Cosmopolitics: Thinking and Feeling Beyond the Nation*, Minneapolis MN: University of Minnesota Press, pp. 362–70.

Ernst, Tom (2004), 'Land, Stories and Resources: Some Impacts of Large-Scale Resource Exploitation on Onabasulu Lifeworlds', in Alan Rumsey and James Weiner (eds), *Mining and Indigenous Lifeworlds in Australia and Papua New Guinea*, Wantage: Sean Kingston Publishing, pp. 125–44.

Errington, Frederick and Deborah Gewertz (1996), 'The Individuation of Tradition in a Papua New Guinea Modernity', *American Anthropologist* 98 (1): 114–26.

Fasolt, Constantin (2004), *The Limits of History*, Chicago: University of Chicago Press.

Feld, Steven (1996), 'Waterfalls of Song: An Acoustemology of Place Resounding in Bosavi, Papua New Guinea', in S. Feld and K. Basso (eds), *Senses of Place*, Santa Fe: School of America Research Press, pp. 91–136.

Filer, Colin (1990), 'The Bougainville Rebellion, the Mining Industry and the Process of Social Disintegration in Papua New Guinea', *Canberra Anthropology* 13 (1): 1–33.

Greicus, Mike (ed.), (1976), *Three Short Novels from Papua New Guinea: Benjamin Umba, August Kituai, Jim Baital*, Auckland: Longman Paul.

Gupta, Akhil and James Ferguson (1992), 'Beyond "Culture": Space, Identity, and the Politics of Difference', *Cultural Anthropology* 7 (1): 6–23.

Harrison, Simon (1993), 'The Commerce of Cultures in Melanesia', *Man* 28 (1): 139–58.

—— (2000), 'From Prestige Goods to Legacies: Property and the Objectification of Culture in Melanesia', *Comparative Studies in Society and History* 42 (3): 662–679.

Herder, Johann (1969), *J,G, Herder on Social and Political Culture*, edited by F. M. Barnard. Cambridge: Cambridge University Press.

Hirsch, Eric (2001), 'New Boundaries of Influence in Highland Papua: "Culture", Mining and Ritual Conversions', *Oceania* 71 (4): 298–312.

—— (2002), 'Malinowski's Intellectual Property', *Anthropology Today* 18 (2): 1–2.

—— (2004), 'Techniques of Vision: Photography, Disco and Renderings of Present Perceptions in Highland Papua', *Journal of the Royal Anthropological Institute* 10 (1): 19–40.

Jacka, Jerry (2005), 'Emplacement and Millennial Expectations in an Era of Development and Globalization: Heaven and the Appeal of Christianity for the Ipili', *American Anthropologist* 107 (4): 643–53.

Kahn, Joel (2003), 'Anthropology as Cosmopolitan Practice?' *Anthropological Theory* 3 (4): 403–15.

Kant, Immanuel (1991 [1784]), *Immanuel Kant: Political Writings*, H. Reiss (ed.) and H. Nisbet (trans.), Cambridge: Cambridge University Press, 2nd edn.

Matane, Paulius (1971), *A New Guinean Travels through Africa*, Port Moresby: Department of Education.

—— (1972), *My Childhood in New Guinea*, Oxford: Oxford University Press.

Mead, Margaret (1938), *The Mountain Arapesh: An Importing Culture*, New York: American Museum of Natural History.

Nelson, Hank (1972), *Papua New Guinea: Black Unity or Black Chaos?* Harmondsworth: Penguin Books.

Neumann, Klaus (1992a), *Not the Way It Really Was: Constructing the Tolai Past*, Honolulu: University of Hawaii Press.

—— (1992b), 'Finding an Appropriate Beginning for a History of the Tolai Colonial Past: Or, Starting From Trash', *Canberra Anthropology* 15 (1): 1992: 1–19.

Otto, Ton (1991), *The Politics of Tradition in Baluan: Social Change and the Construction of the Past in a Manus Society*, Nijmegen: Centre for Pacific Studies.

Schieffelin, Edward (1976), *The Sorrow of the Lonely and the Burning of the Dancers*, New York: St Martin's Press.

Strathern, Marilyn (1990), 'Artefacts of History: Events and the Interpretation of Images', in J. Siikala (ed.), *Culture and History in the Pacific*, Helsinki: Suomen Antropologien Seura, Finnish Anthropological Society, Transactions No. 27, pp. 25–44.

—— (1992), 'The Decomposition of an Event', *Cultural Anthropology* 7 (2): 244–54.

Wagner, Roy (1975), *The Invention of Culture*, Chicago: University of Chicago Press.

—— (1986), *Symbols that Stand for Themselves*, Chicago: University of Chicago Press.

Weiner, James (2004), 'Introduction: Depositings', in: Alan Rumsey and James Weiner (eds), *Mining and Indigenous Lifeworlds in Australia and Papua New Guinea*, Wantage: Sean Kingston Publishing, pp. 1–11.

Whitehouse, Harvey (2000), *Icons and Arguments:Divergent Modes of Religiosity*, Oxford: Oxford University Press.

–11–

Cosmopolitics, Neoliberalism, and the State: The Indigenous Rights Movement in Africa[1]
Dorothy L. Hodgson

Indigenous rights, which derive from international human rights legislation, are premised on cosmopolitan values of equality, shared rights and responsibilities as citizens, and the recognition and respect of cultural diversity (cf. Appiah 1997, 2005; Breckenridge et al. 2002; Cheah and Robbins 1998). Indigenous activists from across the globe have been extraordinarily successful at having their economic, political and cultural rights recognised and affirmed by the United Nations, transnational advocacy groups and donors. But some, especially African activists, have been far less successful at leveraging the international recognition of indigenous rights in their national struggles for recognition, resources and rights. Tensions between indigenous activists and their governments have intensified as African states have been radically transformed by neoliberal political, economic and social policies, further undermining the precarious livelihoods of historically marginalised citizens.

In this chapter, I argue that cosmopolitics, of which indigenous activism is one form, must therefore take seriously the mediating role of the state and the pressures of neoliberalism in shaping political positionings[2] and possibilities for civil society to engage with transnational advocacy networks and movements. The chapter uses an ethnohistorical case study of Maasai activists in Tanzania to explore the centrality of the state to both indigenous rights and neoliberalism, and the consequent challenges to their political struggles. It traces and explains three phases of the relationship between Maasai and the Tanzanian state: 1) a deeply modernist, paternalist postcolonial state that treated Maasai as 'subjects' rather than 'citizens', and left little space for Maasai political engagement; 2) the emergence and embrace of indigenous rights and transnational advocacy by Maasai activists in the 1990s; and 3) a recent shift by Maasai activists from discourses of indigeneity to discourses of livelihoods, from international to national advocacy, and from calling themselves non-governmental organisations (NGOs) to civil society organisations (CSOs). These shifting political positionings within international and national debates inform, challenge, and complicate ongoing theoretical and political debates about the struggles of transnational social movements, the contours of cosmopolitics and the enduring political salience of the state.[3]

The first period of the relationship between Maasai and the Tanzanian nation-state, from the early 1960s to the late 1980s, corresponds to independence and President Nyerere's forceful efforts to build a Tanzanian nation premised on the socialist principles of *ujamaa* ('familyhood'). After decades of ambivalent relationships with British colonial administrators – who veered between deeply protectionist policies designed to control, contain and conserve Maasai 'culture' (most notably in the formation of the Maasai Reserve and lack of investment in education), to fierce demands for rapid change and progress (as in the Maasai Development Project of the 1950s),[4] Maasai were disparaged by the African elites who took power as vestiges of 'savage' Africa to be either left behind or forced to change in the interests of modern progress. As a result, government officials alienated and redistributed the most fertile areas of Maasai territory to more economically 'productive' people and enterprises, launched a multi-million dollar project to rapidly increase the 'productivity' of Maasai livestock, promoted Maasai as icons of 'traditional' 'primitive' Africa in order to expand the increasingly lucrative tourist industry, and conducted national campaigns such as 'Operation Dress-up' to force Maasai men to wear trousers in towns and forbid the application of ochre on Maasai bodies (Hodgson 2001; see also Schneider 2006).

Since civil society organisations were virtually non-existent in Tanzania at this time, there were few avenues available for Maasai to protest state actions and to demand change. The one political party, Chama Cha Mapinduzi (CCM), controlled the political system, stifled political critique, and regulated meetings, organisations and collective action through a strict system of permits, permissions and laws. On occasion, elder Maasai men made public speeches to protest specific actions, and Maasai women launched collective strikes against certain Maasai and non-Maasai leaders. But a lack of education and political integration prohibited most Maasai from any meaningful political participation beyond the village level. My interviews in the mid-1980s and early 1990s revealed that few Maasai considered themselves as 'citizens' of Tanzania; rather, they thought of themselves as 'subjects' of unjust rule by postcolonial elites.

By the mid-1990s, following the retirement of President Nyerere, the introduction of multiple political parties and the imposition of neoliberal economic policies in the shape of structural adjustment, much had changed in Tanzania (Shivji 2006). Democratisation in its efforts to 'strengthen' civil society created the space for grassroots pastoralist organising (Neumann 1995; Igoe 2000, 2003, 2004). Economic liberalisation encouraged the privatisation of key industries, state disinvestments from social services such as education and health, and investment by international capital. One result was to intensify economic inequalities and political discontent among already marginalised peoples. For pastoralists and hunter-gatherers, one of the most alarming effects of liberalisation was the tremendous acceleration of illegal and quasi-legal incursions on to their lands and its alienation for large-scale commercial farms, mining, game parks, wildlife reserves, and other revenue-generating endeavors by the state, elites and international capital (Hodgson 2001; Hodgson and Schroeder 2002; Lane 1996; Madsen 2000; Brockington 2002). These neoliberal 'reforms' were deeply contradictory for pastoralists, simultaneously opening the political space for their mobilisation through the formation of NGOs and shrinking the economic space on which their livelihoods depended by further alienating their lands (Hodgson 2002b).[5]

In the context of these changes, several Maasai leaders found the possibilities of linking their struggles with those of the transnational indigenous rights movement through the formation of pastoralist organisations compelling (cf. Cameron 2004; Igoe 2000, 2004, 2006). A key figure behind this positioning was a Maasai intellectual and activist named Moringe ole Parkipuny. He was born in Nayobi, on the edge of the Rift Wall, and sent to school when his grandfather was forced by colonial officers to 'contribute' one son for schooling. Although his grandfather urged him to purposefully fail the exam to qualify for middle school, Parkipuny refused: 'I already had a sense of how Maasai were being treated. I decided I must go on.'[6] He completed secondary school and then received his BA and MA in Development Studies from the University of Dar es Salaam. His MA thesis was a critique of the huge, 10-year, $20 million dollar USAID Masai Range Project that was taking place at the time. In 1977, he was hired by the Tanzanian government to work for the Masai Range project. But USAID balked, given his harsh critiques of the project in both his thesis and published editorials. As a compromise, they sent him on a study tour of the US to visit 'proper ranches':

I travelled to Washington DC, Oregon, California, Arizona and more to visit extension schools, ranches, and so forth. But I became fed up, it was too monotonous. So at the airport one day, I met a Navaho from Windrock. We talked some and he invited me to visit. I said 'let's go!' So I stayed with them for two weeks, and then with the Hopi for two weeks. It was my first introduction to the indigenous world. I was struck by the similarities of our problems. I looked at Windrock, the poor state of the roads and reservations, it was just like the cattle trails in Maasailand. But this was *in the United States*!

Seeking a political space to advocate for justice, Parkipuny ran for and was elected to Parliament in 1980. As he explained, 'at the time, it was the only door open under the one party system to voice outcry. There were no civil society organisations at the time. You had to work through the party.' He fought tirelessly, especially against the rising tide of illegal land alienation by the government, speaking in Parliament, filing court case after court case against the government, pleading with political leaders, and rallying Maasai. As his reputation as a formidable intellectual and political leader of Maasai grew, so did the number of his enemies inside and outside of Parliament. 'They all kept their distance from me. And when I would go to Parliament and voice problems, nothing would happen, there was no action.' By 1989, he decided to 'get out of this place' – and through the support of friends and a progressive advocacy network in the US, 'I travelled to Europe, the US, as far as Berkeley!' He met with Native Americans in New Mexico and Canada, and then travelled to Geneva – where he was the first African to address the United Nations Working Group on Indigenous Populations. His eloquent speech described the historical marginalisation of pastoralists and hunter-gatherers in Tanzania under first, colonialism, and then nationalism, and the structural similarities between the status of pastoralists and hunter-gatherers in East Africa with 'the plight of indigenous peoples throughout the world' (Parkipuny 1989).

Shortly after his trip to Geneva, Parkipuny and seven other Maasai men founded one of the first Maasai NGOs, called KIPOC, which means 'we shall recover' in Maa. Although KIPOC's formal constitution (KIPOC 1990) made no mention anywhere of the term 'indigenous', the word appeared 38 times in the initial 22-page project document written to publicise KIPOC's programme and funding needs to international donors (KIPOC 1991). The project document was full of the language and logic of the sanctity of the 'cultural identity' of 'indigenous' peoples, and their 'basic human rights' to choose the form, content and pace of changes in their lives. According to KIPOC, the Maasai struggle was 'part of the global struggle of indigenous peoples to restore respect to their rights, cultural identity and to the land of their birth' (KIPOC 1991:7).[7]

Since the formation of KIPOC, over a hundred non-governmental organisations (NGOs) have emerged in predominantly Maasai areas in northern Tanzania. Initially, most were organised around diverse claims of a common 'indigenous' identity based on ethnicity (such as 'being Maasai'), mode of production (being a pastoralist or hunter-gatherer) or a long history of political and economic disenfranchisement by first the colonial and now the postcolonial nation-state. Moreover, these Maasai activists and NGOs tried, with mixed success, to link with each other and with other groups on the continent to form a series of national, regional and continent-wide networks to pressure African states to recognise the presence and rights of indigenous peoples within their borders, to support and coordinate the activities of African NGOs within the UN process, and to promote the United Nations Declaration on the Rights of Indigenous Peoples (United Nations 2007; see Hodgson 2002a more generally).[8]

By reframing their long-standing demands and grievances against the Tanzanian state in the language of indigenous rights, Maasai NGOs like KIPOC turned the cultural politics of their treatment by the colonial and postcolonial states on its head. Rather than continue to challenge enduring stereotypes of Maasai as culturally (and even, at times, racially) distinct, inferior, backward and primitive, these NGOs appropriated and reconfigured these fixed, ahistorical images in order to appeal to global indigenous rights advocates and initiatives. As KIPOC (1991) argued in one of their project documents, the dominant 'national culture' conceives the 'modern Tanzanian' to be a Kiswahili speaker and either an active farmer or of 'peasant origin'. In contrast, the few 'indigenous minority nationalities' in Tanzania are defined by KIPOC as either pastoralists or hunter-gatherers, who have 'maintained the fabric of their culture': 'They are conspicuously distinct from the rest of the population in dress, language, transhumance systems of resource utilisation and relationship to the environment. Pastoral and hunter-gatherer peoples persevered, through passive resistance, to hold on to their indigenous lifestyles, traditions and cultures.' Although stigmatised by the dominant culture as 'static, rigid [and] hostile to cultural interaction and exchange', these indigenous cultures have in fact never been 'irrationally opposed to economic development nor uncompromising in dealing with external interests and forces.' In reality, these people have been 'left out of the development process', especially in terms of the allocation of resources to social services and economic infrastructure. The documents and brochures of other pastoralist NGOs echoed this rhetoric of culture, power, citizenship and rights.

Parkipuny and other Maasai were remarkably successful in establishing themselves as key players in the transnational indigenous rights movement. At the four annual meetings of the UN Permanent Forum that I attended in 2003, 2004, 2005 and 2007, as well as the UN Working Group meeting that I attended in Geneva in 2004, between ten and fifteen Maasai delegates from Kenya and Tanzania participated as well. Several were regular attendees at the UN meetings and well-known to the other indigenous activists from the US, Asia, Latin America, and elsewhere. Lucy Mulenkei, for example, a Kenyan Maasai journalist, was president of the African Indigenous Women's Caucus and co-chair of the Indigenous Caucus. Adam ole Mwarabu, an IlParakuyo Maasai from Tanzania who had participated in a six-month UN training programme for indigenous activists in Geneva, aggressively networked with other activists, donors and advocates to publicise his grievances against the Tanzanian state and seek financial and logistical support for his NGO. Mary Simat, a long-time Maasai activist from Kenya, was the Deputy Chairperson of the Indigenous Peoples of Africa Coordinating Committee (IPACC), and presented regular statements to the floor in the open sessions. A few Maasai were attending the meetings for the first time. They relied on the experienced activists to introduce them to other delegates, help them formulate and present statements, and navigate the bureaucracy and logistics of the UN meeting. All of the Maasai (and other African activists) whom

I met represented NGOs in their home countries. Most quickly proffered business cards and offered to exchange emails, while others circulated flyers, pamphlets, copies of their formal statements and colorful brochures.

In addition to their leadership roles, the visibility and recognition of Maasai as indigenous people at the UN was clearly marked in several ways. For example, when Ole Henrik Magga, a Saami from Norway, and Member of the Permanent Forum, was elected to chair the 2004 Permanent Forum, he opened the first session by displaying a beaded Maasai *rungu* (carved short stick) to all the delegates. 'Since the last Forum,' he announced, 'I was able to visit East Africa, especially with Maasai. They gave me this beaded *rungu*. I feel I have the inspiration to guide you through the work we have to do.'

All of the activists that I spoke to acknowledged that one benefit of their success at gaining substantial international visibility and recognition as an 'indigenous people' was a tremendous flow of resources from international donors. In effect, international recognition enabled them to circumvent the Tanzanian state to access substantial resources for social and economic development initiatives such as water, education, health services and livestock restocking. For instance, in addition to sponsoring endless workshops, training sessions and meetings for NGO leaders, Danida spent almost $5 million on a livestock development project in Ngorongoro, working through the auspices of a Maasai NGO; the African Wildlife Foundation (with funding from USAID), and Cordaid (an Irish donor) have channelled millions of dollars through another Maasai NGO to create Wildlife Management Areas (WMAs) and promote an array of conservation and income-generating activities for men and women. HIVOS and NOVIB (two Norwegian donors) worked with another Maasai NGO to support water projects, women's income-generating projects and several land rights claims.

Despite their success at attaining visibility in the international indigenous rights movement and the lucrative attention of international donors in the 1990s, most Maasai activists have consciously distanced themselves from the international movement over the past few years. Instead, they have opted to focus their advocacy efforts at the national level, shifted the discursive terms of engagement from 'indigenous rights' to 'pastoralist livelihoods', and started calling themselves civil society organisations (CSOs) instead of NGOs.

There are five key reasons for this shift. First, they responded to the vehement hostility of the Tanzanian government over the widespread international recognition and acceptance of Maasai claims to 'being indigenous'. The government of Tanzania, like almost all African governments, refused to recognise the existence of 'indigenous peoples' within its borders, claiming instead that all Africans were indigenous. It was suspicious of the very terms of Maasai mobilisation, especially the unsettling fusion of assertions of cultural difference with demands for collective rights. By organising around the identity claims of 'being indigenous', premised in part on their ethnicity, Maasai NGOs revitalised ethnic identifications, challenging democratic liberalism's championing of individual rights and the responsibilities of 'citizens' with their claims of collective grievances and rights. The government, however, wary of appearing to endorse 'ethnic favouritism', equated political organising along ethnic lines with 'tribalism', and feared that such ethnic mobilisation could strengthen political opposition, produce economic and political instability, or even foster violence. In the face of active government hostility to political claims based on indigenous rights, Maasai and other pastoralist activists had to resort to increasingly confrontational strategies. In response, the government banned some organisations outright and severely limited the activities of others.

Thus a key reason for shifting to discourses about pastoralist livelihoods was to seek less confrontational approaches to influence government policies and practices. According to an activist whom I will call Samuel, 'Before, we had lots of court cases against the government ... but they were not very fruitful.'[9] Samuel is trained as a lawyer and now heads a pastoralist organisation. Initially, he was a strong proponent of indigenous rights and became an active member of OIPA, the Organisation of Indigenous Peoples of Africa. But in recent years, Samuel has all but abandoned the rhetoric of indigenous rights for the language of pastoralist livelihoods. As he explained, 'the language of indigenous has strong political connotations, while the language of pastoralism is about development.' He continued:

Initially we thought we could change our present situation by engaging in the international struggle, but we have learned that we can't neglect the national struggle. For a number of years we tried to use reporting to the UN system, working with international advocacy groups, and so forth, but those efforts did not have a big impact. So in the past three to four years we have reflected on our struggle and made some changes.

Samuel has been a key player in the new emphasis on engaging the Tanzanian government, using his training and skills as a lawyer to read, decipher, communicate and critique the voluminous policy documents and draft policy proposals produced by the government as it tries to quickly transform key policies and laws to accommodate and facilitate neoliberal reforms. Just in the past few years, Tanzania has 'reformed' its livestock policy (to increase productivity and offtake through the settlement of pastoralists and creation of ranches), land policy (allowing full ownership and sale, including by foreign investors), local government (to decentralise funding and authority), and created a new policy to formalise the informal sector – MKURABITA – which was designed and implemented by Hernando De Soto's Institute for Liberty and Democracy based in Peru. The Tanzanian government has, however, tried to temper the social and economic pain of these reforms by simultaneously sponsoring national policies such as Vision 2025 and MKUKUTA (related to international programmes such as the Millennium Development Goals) to reduce poverty and promote development (albeit within a neoliberal paradigm of individual initiative, private capital, and personal investment). As such, the government has had to pay attention to demands for development by pastoralist activists, however much its vision of 'livestock development' differed from pastoralist visions of 'livelihood security and development'.

Second, as Samuel's comments also suggest, not all the activists found the UN meetings and other international workshops and conferences productive. As one Maasai woman commented to me over coffee at the 2004 Permanent Forum, 'I find that nothing real takes place here. It is a waste of time. These people come as representatives, but I wonder who they really represent. Probably just a few people. They come here, say a few words, but what really happens?' Both experienced and first-time delegates expressed deep frustration over the formalistic procedures at the UN; the limited spaces for dialogue, debate and discussion with other activists; and the glacial pace and Byzantine processes for instituting changes in international and national policies. As another Maasai activist complained to me in response to a question about her experience at a workshop the night before, sponsored by IFAD, WIPO and the ILO; 'It was OK. There was lots of writing. I wonder what all that writing accomplishes? There are lots of policies, but what really happens on the ground?'

Third, pastoralist organisations were maturing, in part because of their international experiences, opportunities and affiliations, but also because of increasing self-awareness and acknowledgment about their own failures and weaknesses. Many were concerned about competition and jealousies among themselves, a lack of accountability to their constituencies, their ongoing inability to inform and influence government policies and programmes and their unhealthy dependence on donor funds and agendas (Hodgson 2002b). Moreover, they were frustrated by the limited impact of their international involvement on their national struggles. Drawing on lessons learned from the international indigenous rights movement about advocacy, alliance-building, and strategies for political engagement, they debated how to reform themselves and build a 'more positive relationship' with the Tanzanian government. Over the past few years, the two coordinating organisations, PINGOs Forum (Pastoralist Indigenous Non-Governmental Organisations Forum) and TAPHGO (Tanzania Pastoralists and Hunter Gatherers Organisation), have sponsored workshops for their member organisations on such topics as advocacy training and responding to the livestock policy; offered smaller training workshops on the new village land law and other relevant laws and policies; created a Tanzanian Pastoralist Parliamentary Group comprised of MPs from the pastoralist districts to discuss relevant issues; lobbied ministers, MPs, and other state officers; sponsored research on such issues as the livestock trade to influence policy initiatives; participated in an annual exhibit of civil society organisations in Dodoma, the state capital; and more. Activists were quick to mention what they perceived as their biggest success to date, which was to convince the government to revise its initial draft of the MKUKUTA, the most recent poverty reduction strategy, to include a commitment to 'promote pastoralism as a sustainable livelihood'. But everyone recognised the formidable challenges to translating that rhetoric into realities, especially once the newly elected President Kikwete and his prime minister, Edward Lowassa, launched an aggressive media campaign immediately after they took office that denounced the destructive and outdated practices of nomadic pastoralists, demanded that they be settled, and made plans to 'ensure that livestock keepers are turned into skilled farmers.'[10] As Kikwete wondered, echoing long-standing stereotypes, 'How do we change the mindset of a nomadic livestock keeper from considering large herds for prestige to that of an important economic resource?'[11]

Fourth, the maturation of pastoralist organisations reflected the growing strength of what calls itself 'civil society' in Tanzania, by which activists themselves mean organised, non-state actors who have the political freedom to comment on, criticise and challenge government policies and practices.[12] Long-time activist organisations like the Tanzania Gender Networking Programme and coalitions of civil society organisations (CSOs), such as the Policy Forum, draw on the expanded range of media options (television, radio, billboards) to pressure the government and expand critical awareness among their constituencies of their rights and responsibilities as citizens. Pastoralist organisations reframed themselves as CSOs in part to align themselves with these prominent civil society coalitions, as well as to distance themselves from increasing questions and suspicions about the accountability, financial transparency and representativeness of NGOs.

Finally, the Tanzanian government has also changed in recent years. Now it slowly and somewhat grudgingly encourages the 'participation' of its citizens in policy-making, under pressure from a strengthening coalition of progressive civil society organisations and the watchful gaze of international proponents of 'democracy'. But some members of the government, especially the 'old guard' who were in power during the days of CCM, are still sensitive to criticism, reluctant to engage representatives of civil society and dismissive of Maasai. When a highly respected Maasai activist presented a list of suggested revisions to the proposed livestock policy to a senior government official, prepared for months by a Task Force of pastoralist activists and others, the official was furious. 'Who are you,' he demanded, 'to criticise government policy?' With his usual calm, the activist responded: 'Well, first of all, I am a citizen of Tanzania. And second of all, I am a representative of over 100 pastoralist CSOs...'

For these and other reasons, according to Samuel, 'now we focus on building alliances with the nation, not with international actors.' As he explained, 'one problem with "indigenous" is that everyone who hears it thinks "Maasai", so it worked at the national level to limit rather than expand our possible alliances and collaborations.' Emphasising 'pastoralist livelihoods' enables organisations to link with non-Maasai pastoralist communities such as Barabaig, and increasingly agro-pastoralist communities as well. Although Maasai leaders still dominate the movement, most are careful to reach out to and include non-Maasai pastoralists in their organisations, deliberations and advocacy. Hunter-gatherers, however, now occupy an even more liminal position – while their histories of marginalisation were acknowledged in the discourse of indigeneity, their issues are generally sidelined in debates over pastoralist livelihoods. Nonetheless, almost all agree that the government has been much more willing to listen to claims made in the interests of 'pastoralist livelihoods' than 'indigenous rights'.

But not everyone supports a complete abandonment of involvement in international campaigns for indigenous rights. A few activists continue to attend the UN Working Group and Permanent Forum meetings, court indigenous rights advocacy groups, and mourn what they see as a neglect of cultural and social issues in the 'pastoralist livelihoods' debates.[13] As Parkipuny complained to me, 'when you just say 'pastoralists and hunter-gatherers' you lose your connection with a big global movement. I think this is a weakness.'

Moreover, like all such discourses and positionings, the term 'pastoralist livelihoods' raises challenges and concerns of its own. Who, at a time of increasing diversification into agriculture, mining and wage employment is really a 'pastoralist' any more? Is there a shared, positive vision of 'pastoralist livelihoods' that activists can articulate to government to counter the enduring negative stereotypes that still inform state policies and interventions? Is pastoralism even viable as a secure livelihood any more, given the rapid neoliberal economic transformations currently underway?

So what does this overview of shifting Maasai political strategies tell us about cosmopolitics, especially about the relationships among civil society, transnational advocacy and the nation-state?

First, in contrast to those like Appadurai (1996) who portend the demise of the nation-state, the Maasai case points to the continuing relevance of the nation-state in shaping political possibilities and positionings in such inherently cosmopolitan endeavors as transnational activism. International recognition of the merits of a people's struggle for rights and resources does not necessarily, or even easily, translate into national recognition. It can, on occasion, even backfire, buttressing rather than bridging government hostility. Faced with a series of failed confrontations, the rapid imposition of neoliberal reforms and the seeming ineffectiveness of international recognition of their plight for their national struggles, pastoralist activists decided to change the terms of political debate. Repositioning themselves from 'indigenous peoples' to 'pastoralists', from a demand for 'rights' to a demand for secure 'livelihoods', and from NGOs to CSOs has enabled them to establish a more productive working relationship with the state.

Second, despite their recent decision to distance themselves from the international indigenous peoples' movement, Maasai and other pastoralist activists benefited in significant ways from their involvement. Many like Parkipuny and Samuel were able to see and learn from the larger patterns of structural similarities between their situation and that of aborigines, Native Americans, and other indigenous peoples, especially about the possible range of relationships between indigenous peoples and nation-states. As Niezen (2003) argues, adopting the term 'indigenous' itself marks a transcendence over the narrow concerns of 'ethnicity', at the same time that it is predicated on those same ethnic concerns. By imagining a different kind of community that is at once located within states but connected beyond states, a bifurcated belonging that articulates the local and global, Maasai also learned new ways to belong to and act within the nation.[14] One could argue, in fact, that their success and support from the international indigenous peoples' movement helped them to transform themselves from 'subjects' to 'citizens' within the wider nation-state (cf. Mamdani 1996); instead of withdrawing in frustrated anger, they now draw on their 'rights' as citizens to demand justice and change. They learned from the comparative experiences of other indigenous peoples how to lobby and advocate the state and how to build strategic alliances among themselves and with other Tanzanians.

These lessons affirm the dynamic relationship between cosmopolitan political projects such as the indigenous peoples' movement and the nation-states in which participants are inevitably located. 'Cosmopolitics', according to Robbins (1998: 12), points to a 'domain of contested politics' located 'both within and beyond the nation ... that is inhabited by a variety of cosmopolitanisms.' Grounding our analysis of 'this newly dynamic space of gushingly unrestrained sentiments, pieties, and urgencies' (Robbins 1998: 9) in the specific social and historical dynamics of its emergence at a certain time, in a certain place, for certain reasons, helps us to understand its appeal, possible dangers and consequences. Given the enduring centrality of the nation-state to neoliberal economic transformations, which must 'reform' the entire state apparatus to make it welcoming for capitalist investment, increased productivity and profit-making, and individual initiative and success, it should come as little surprise that states like Tanzania forcefully oppose the demands for collective rights and restitution for historical grievances made by indigenous peoples within its borders. The resulting shift to a discourse of 'pastoralist livelihoods' could perhaps be understood as a 'sell-out' of sorts to government pressure, a concession to neoliberal demands to talk only in the terms of development and economics. Perhaps. But it might be more useful to think about it as a politically pragmatic decision made in light of perceived risks and benefits. The irony, of course, is that Maasai and other pastoralists in Tanzania have abandoned their demand for recognition as indigenous peoples at the same time that the African Commission on Human and Peoples' Rights has now recognised the viability and legitimacy of such claims for certain African peoples.[15] Thus the shift from 'indigenous rights' to 'pastoralist livelihoods' is only the latest move in an ongoing dynamic of political struggle, of positionings and repositionings, set within complex shifting fields of power within and beyond but always including the nation-state.

Notes

1. The research and writing of this chapter, which is part of a larger book project, has been supported by the John Simon Guggenheim Foundation, American Council of Learned Societies, Fulbright-Hays, National Endowment for the Humanities, Center for Advanced Study in the Behavioral Sciences, and Rutgers University Competitive Fellowship Leave Program. I am grateful to the many people in Tanzania who have shared their lives and words with me, to Pnina Werbner for inviting me to reflect on my findings through the prism of cosmopolitics, to Dick Werbner for reading the paper in my absence at the ASA, and to numerous friends and colleagues who have commented on earlier (and sometimes very different) drafts. Several small sections of the chapter are drawn from Hodgson 1999 and 2002b.
2. My use of 'positionings' draws on Tania Murray Li's (2000) elaboration of Stuart Hall's ideas of 'positioning' and 'articulation' to analyse indigenous politics in Indonesia. See Hodgson (2002a) for more explication.
3. For reflection on the ethics and politics of my own positioning as an anthropologist studying these issues, see Hodgson 1999, 2002a.
4. The history of Maasai relationships with the colonial state are documented in Hodgson 2001.
5. Moreover, there were also radical changes in the priorities and practices of multilateral institutions and other development donors. During the 1990s, most shifted resources away from nation-states in favour of 'local' NGOs and community-based organisations that were presumed to be more effective in reaching the 'grassroots' (Bebbington and Riddell 1997; Edwards and Hulme 1992, 1995; Fowler 1995). For useful studies of neoliberalism, see Harvey (2005) and Ferguson (2006).

6. These excerpts and all others are based on interviews I conducted with Parkipuny in 2005 and 2006 in Tanzania.

7. Maasai claims to being indigenous, like those of most other African and Asian groups, are not based on claims about being 'first peoples' as such. Rather, they argue that there are significant structural similarities between their treatment by colonial and postcolonial states and those of indigenous peoples in former settler colonies like North America and New Zealand (Hodgson 2002a, 2002b).

8. Within Tanzania, there is the Pastoralist Indigenous Non-Governmental Organisations Forum (PINGOs Forum) and Tanzania Pastoralists and Hunters Gatherers Organisation (TAPHGO) and within East Africa there is the Maa Council. The broader pan-African networks include the Indigenous Peoples of Africa Coordinating Committee (IPACC), Organisation of Indigenous Peoples of Africa (OIPA), and the African Indigenous Women's Organisation (AIWO).

9. These excerpts are based on interviews that I conducted with 'Samuel' in 2005 and 2006.

10. 'Call to modernise livestock keeping', *Daily News*, 19 January 2006, p. 1.

11. 'Leaders call for "special zones" to spur economy', *Guardian*, 17 March 2006, p. 2.

12. I do not have the space here to address the long debates in political science, anthropology and other disciplines about the boundaries and definitions of civil society, the degree to which it is in fact distinct from the state, and the role of transnational donors in fostering and promoting certain factions of civil society – as they did with NGOs – to influence national policies. All of these issues are relevant and analysed in the larger book project.

13. The case of Maasai in Kenya provides an interesting contrast that I cannot explore here. They have continued to maintain active involvement with the international indigenous rights movement, and convert that recognition into some national political leverage and gains. But they also lack the strong coalition of pastoralist organisations present in Tanzania. One possible difference is the vastly different history of how ethnicity has been deployed in national politics in Kenya in contrast to Tanzania.

14. Similar in some ways to the 'cosmopolitan ethnicity' described by Werbner (2002) for Kalanga elites in Botswana.

15. See, for example, the *Report of the African Commission's Working Group of Experts on Indigenous Populations/Communities*, which was commissioned by, submitted to and adopted by the African Commission on Human and Peoples' Rights, in accordance with the 'Resolution on the Rights of Indigenous Populations/Communities in Africa.'

References

Appadurai, Arjun (1996), *Modernity at Large: Cultural Dimensions of Globalization*, Minneapolis: University of Minnesota.

Appiah, Kwame Anthony (1997), 'Cosmopolitan Patriots', *Critical Inquiry* 23: 617–639.

—— (2005), *The Ethics of Identity*, Princeton: Princeton University Press.

Bebbington, Anthony and Roger Riddell (1997), 'Heavy Hands, Hidden Hands, Holding Hands? Donors, Intermediary NGOs and Civil Society Organisations', in David Hulme and Michael Edwards (eds), *NGOs, States and Donors: Too Close for Comfort?* New York: St Martin's Press, pp. 107–27.

Breckenridge, Carol A., Sheldon Pollock, Homi K. Bhabha, Dipesh Chakrabarty (eds) (2002), *Cosmopolitanism*, Durham: Duke University Press.

Brockington, Dan (2002), *Fortress Conservation: The Preservation of Mkomazi Game Reserve, Tanzania*, Oxford: James Currey.

Cameron, Greg (2004), 'The Globalization of Indigenous Rights in Tanzanian Pastoralist NGOs', in Alan Bicker, Paul Sillitoe and Johan Pottier (eds), *Development of Local Knowledge: New Approaches to Issues in Natural Resource Management, Conservation, and Agriculture*, London: Routledge, pp. 135–63.

Cheah, Pheng and Bruce Robbins (eds) (1998), *Cosmopolitics: Thinking and Feeling beyond the Nation*, Minneapolis: University of Minnesota Press.

Edwards, Michael and David Hulme (1992), *Making a Difference: NGOs and Development in a Changing World*, London: Earthscan.

—— (eds) (1995), *NGO Performance and Accountability: Beyond the Magic Bullet*, London: Earthscan.

Ferguson, James (2006), *Global Shadows: Africa in the Neoliberal World Order*, Durham: Duke University Press.

Fowler, Alan (1995), 'NGOs and the Globalization of Social Welfare: Perspectives from East Africa', in Joseph Semboja amd Ole Therkildsen (eds), *Service Provision Under Stress in East Africa*, Copenhagen: Centre for Development Research, pp. 51–69.

Harvey, David (2005), *A Brief History of Neoliberalism*, Oxford: Oxford University Press.

Hodgson, Dorothy L. (1999), 'Critical Interventions: Dilemmas of Accountability in Contemporary Ethnographic Research', *Identities: Global Studies in Culture and Power* 6 (2–3): 201–24.

—— (2001), *Once Intrepid Warriors: Gender, Ethnicity and the Cultural Politics of Maasai Development*, Bloomington: Indiana University Press.

—— (2002a), 'Introduction: Comparative Perspectives on the Indigenous Rights Movement in Africa and the Americas', *American Anthropologist* 104 (4): 1037–49.

—— (2002b), 'Precarious Alliances: The Cultural Politics and Structural Pre-dicaments of the Indigenous Rights Movement in Tanzania', *American Anthropologist* 104 (4): 1086–97.

Hodgson, Dorothy L. and Richard Schroeder (2002), 'Dilemmas of Counter-mapping Community Resources in Tanzania', *Development and Change* 33 (1): 79–100.

Igoe, Jim (2000), *Ethnicity, Civil Society, and the Tanzanian Pastoral NGO Movement: The Continuities and Discontinuities of Liberalized Development*, PhD Thesis, Department of Anthropology, Boston University.

—— (2003), 'Scaling up Civil Society: Donor Money, NGOs and the Pastoralist Land Rights Movement in Tanzania', *Development and Change* 34 (5): 863–85.

—— (2004), *Conservation and Globalization: A Study of National Parks and Indigenous Communities from East Africa to South Dakota*, Belmont CA: Thomson/Wadsworth.

—— (2006), 'Becoming Indigenous Peoples: Difference, Inequality, and the Globalization of East African Identity Politics', *African Affairs* 105 (420): 399–420.

KIPOC (1990), *The Constitution*, Document no. 1. Photocopy, Tanzania.

—— (1991), *The Foundational Program: Background, Profile of Activities and Budget*, Principal Document no.2. Photocopy, Tanzania.

Lane, Charles. R. (1996), *Pastures Lost: Barabaig Economy, Resource Tenure, and the Alienation of their Land in Tanzania*, Nairobi: Initiatives Publishers.

Li, Tania Murray (2000), 'Articulating Indigenous Identity in Indonesia: Resource Politics and the Tribal Slot', *Comparative Studies in Society and History* 42 (1): 149–79.

Madsen, Andrew (2000), *The Hadzabe of Tanzania. Land and Human Rights for a Hunter-Gatherer Community*, IWGIA Document 98, Copenhagen: IWGIA.

Mamdani, Mahmood (1996), *Citizen and Subject: Contemporary Africa and the Legacy of Late Colonialism*, Princeton: Princeton University Press.

Neumann, Roderick P. (1995), 'Local Challenges to Global Agendas: Conservation, Economic Liberalization and the Pastoralists' Rights Movement in Tanzania', *Antipode* 27 (4): 363–82.

Niezen, Ronald (2003), *The Origins of Indigenism: Human Rights and the Politics of Identity*, Berkeley: University of California Press.

Parkipuny, Moringe ole (1989), 'The Human Rights Situation of Indigenous Peoples in Africa', *Fourth World Journal* 4 (1): 1–4.

Robbins, Bruce (1998), 'Introduction Part I: Actually Existing Cosmopolitanism', in Pheng Cheah and Bruce Robbins (eds), *Cosmopolitics: Thinking and Feeling beyond the Nation*, Minneapolis: University of Minnesota Press, pp. 1–19.

Schneider, Leander (2006), 'The Maasai's New Clothes: A Developmentalist Modernity and its Exclusions', *Africa Today* 53 (1): 100–31.

Shivji, Issa G. (2006), *Let the People Speak: Tanzania Down the Road to Neo-Liberalism*, Dakar: CODESRIA.

United Nations (2007), *Draft Declaration on the Rights of Indigenous Peoples*, United Nations Document A/61/L.67.

Werbner, Richard (2002), 'Cosmopolitan Ethnicity, Entrepreneurship and the Nation: Minority Elites in Botswana', *Journal of Southern African Studies* 28 (4): 731–53.

Section IV
Vernacular Cosmopolitans, Cosmopolitan National Spaces

–12–

Cosmopolitan Nations, National Cosmopolitans

Richard Fardon

Conviviality Begins at Home: A Ceremony

During a return visit to Ganye[1] (capital of the chiefdom of the same name in Adamawa, Nigeria's easternmost middle-belt state on its border with Cameroon), one of the main topics of daily conversation among Chamba, the majority population, was the precise date their reigning traditional chief (the *Gangwari* of Ganye) would formally receive his First Class Staff of Office from the Lamido of Adamawa, a Fulani.[2] Along with two other non-Fulani[3] chiefs, the Bachama *Hama* of Numan, and the Bata *Hama* of Demsa, the *Gangwari* of Ganye had seen his chiefdom elevated from second-class to first-class status by the Governor of Adamawa State in December 2004. His would be the last of the three ratification ceremonies to be held.

An installation ceremony is a complex and expensive undertaking: invitations must be sent in ample time to be certain the most important dignitaries, Cameroonian as well as Nigerian, may be present; accommodation and food has to be prepared, ceremonial spaces upgraded, and a variety of what the programme calls 'cultural dances' arranged for the entertainment of the distinguished visitors. All this demanded an organising committee well in excess of a hundred people. The dignitaries must be seated according to fine gradations of precedence – the most important at the front – in rows under an awning sheltered from the sun, on one side of a large plaza (Gangwari Square in Ganye), the other three sides of which would be lined by the throng of standing spectators. Before and after the big day, a variety of publications need to be put in hand: a full-colour programme, with a history of the kingdom, biography of the *Gangwari*, order of events and portraits of the main protagonists; and a souvenir brochure and calendar, with more portraits of the main actors, sponsored pages from well-wishers that also emphasise their own contributions to the chiefdom as elected representatives or officials, as well as a photographic record of the events on the day of the 'Official Presentation of First Class Staff of Office'.

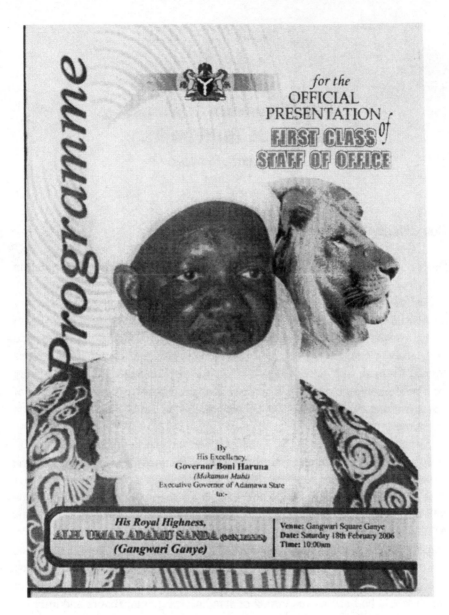

Figure 12.1 Gangwari Presentation. Courtesy of HRH Alh. Umar A. Sanda

Continuing in this vein would add another account to many writings that have explored the modernity of invented tradition, and the prominent role played by neo-traditional chiefs in the politics of contemporary West African nation states. Given the subject of our volume, however, I need to start where such analyses typically end. Readers have become accustomed to such, only superficially, paradoxical counterposings of modernity and tradition. Tradition is important to contemporary ethnic identities in several ways: it gives identities expression and value, making them presently comprehensible and worthwhile both to their members and to outsiders; and this expression is also instrumental in the more narrowly immediate sense of facilitating an interlacing of political interests at local and national levels. Ethnicities cannot be conjured out of nothing: the past of any identity has to be expressed in its present. Hence, it is not just unparadoxical but inevitable that such events are appeals to tradition in urgently contemporary contexts. Taking this as given, my interest here concerns the relation between another two apparently counterposed terms: intensely rooted identity (simultaneously modern *and* traditional) and cosmopolitanism. Can one come to the second through the first, or are they necessarily antithetical? And how does globalisation enter this picture?

One of the several reasons given by the chief for the delay in seeking a date for his installation ceremony from the Governor concerned the poor quality of mobile telephone service in his capital. Ganye was served by Mtel, the mobile telephone subsidiary of the Nigerian statal provider Nitel, but intermittently and with an unreliability to be relied upon. Mtel never seemed to work after dark, something local opinion, whether with technical insight I cannot judge, attributed to the evening boosting from a nearby relay station of the signal of the Adamawa Broadcasting Corporation, the only TV channel available locally without satellite subscription. In a few days during my visit, Glo, by consensus Nigeria's most dynamic provider of Global Systems of Mobile Communications (GSMC), had their mast up and running: there was a brisk business for SIM card salesmen as people either switched, or added, this more expensive but also more reliable provider, and the Chief of Ganye sought a date for his installation ceremony, confident that his visitors would not be rendered incommunicado from their pressing concerns elsewhere in Nigeria, which is also to say, confident that his own capital would not strike these visitors as a 'bush' (or might I say an uncosmopolitan?) place.

Despite an immense oil income during several postcolonial decades (or because of it, in the view of those who argue that mineral wealth may be a curse for developing economies), Nigeria's infrastructure has grown very unevenly; and Ganye's is in some respects, for instance roads, not much better than it was thirty years ago. In fairness, it should be said that particular roads have been upgraded, but 'no condition', as the tried and tested Nigerian idiom has it, 'is permanent': tarred but unmaintained roads soon become less motorable than they were in the first place. The mobile communications industry has been an exception to the hesitant trend in other sectors:[4] Nigeria is touted as home to the world's fastest growing mobile communications industry. Five years after the onset of deregulation in 2001, when Nigeria apparently had 450,000 functioning land lines (and quite what, or when, 'functioning' means in this context is open to argument), mobile telephone ownership had risen to sixteen million. Glo alone claimed to have attracted five million subscribers in the two years to January 2006, and Ganye was among 30 towns connected to the Glo network during just two weeks at the beginning of that year.[5] As any visitor to West Africa pre- and post-GSMC will attest, the difference this technology has made to people's notions of accessibility, punctuality and communicability has been unprecedented, as if some sections of the population had been waiting for the technology that would let them, when it suited their purposes, get off what Anglophone West Africans call 'African time' for particular purposes. The attitude may not persist, but it is anticipated not just that mobile phones will be switched on, but that answering them will take precedence over whatever else is in hand. Not only can some matters, particularly those involving trusted interlocutors, now be transacted virtually, but arrangements that once took weeks to make as messages were sent back and forth by pedestrian, or at best motorised, word of mouth can now be made in minutes. Hence, returning to our subject, an event can now follow hard on the heels of its date being chosen.

There was a second reason for the *Gangwari*'s delay in asking that a date be fixed for his installation. Despite its remoteness from Nigerian centres of power, Ganye chiefdom happens to include the homes of two of Nigeria's most powerful men: Vice-President Abubakar Atiku, and the influential politician and business magnate, Bamanga Tukur, son of the Fulani who presided over Chamba administration from the mid-1930s to mid-1950s. Although neither of these men's fathers was Chamba, both have been given titles on *Gangwari*'s traditional council. It would have been unthinkable to fix the date of the installation before ensuring the presence of the Nigerian Vice-President as guest of honour, and the Vice-President's diary was filled well ahead of time, not least thanks to the wrangle over the constitution, and the limitation of any presidency to two terms of office between himself and President Obasanjo, which had preoccupied Nigerian news media. National electoral politics and Global Satellite Mobile Communications, souvenir brochures and cultural dances, these are just a few of the considerations bearing upon the public celebration of a first-class staff of office, itself of course a colonial introduction.

The internal diversity of contemporary African states has most often been discussed in terms of its deviance from European, or European settler, norms. Top-down discussions of African statehood typically begin from the fact that contemporary state boundaries were imposed by European fiat with only the most occasional attention to pre-existing ethnic resemblances. The step from this truth to the view that most of Africa's state problems stem from the heterogeneity of their populations is sometimes made too quickly. Somalia and Rwanda have not been advertisements for the virtues of a closer fit either between state and pre-existing nation, or between postcolonial and precolonial state boundaries. For their part, investigators looking at matters from the bottom-up have been struck by the consolidation under colonial and postcolonial governments of whatever ethnic identity they have been studying, and they have provided numerous excellent case studies showing how present identities have been teased from past resemblances under conditions conducive to this way of envisaging collective claims on state resources. Fewer studies have analysed the multi-ethnic, and usually multi-faith, national cultures emergent from the interplay of ethnicities defining themselves in some respects contrapuntally, that is to say playing on the terms of their differences from other ethnicities within the nation. Counterpoint has involved a high degree of stereotyping of more or less familiar others, and occasionally it has led to extreme violence. However, it has not been demonstrated that, relative to their internal diversity, African states have been more prone to violence than the history of consolidating nation states globally might lead us to anticipate. More or less lasting accommodations have been reached between diverse elements; pluralistic habits of language use have been arrived at practically, and sometimes recognised post hoc in planning documents; access to media has been shared. From all of this, a variety of majority and minority practices and opinions have crystallised. While ethnicity is prominent, these are not simply ethnic cultures; they involve considerations of social standing, wealth, education, region and religion. Rather than being stable and easy to define, they tend to be called forth in relation to particular issues and events. By being called forth often, and with reasonable reliability, a set of practices and opinions becomes more visible, which in turn may encourage emulation and adherence, or opposition, or schism, or all three simultaneously. This complexity is particularly challenging for the resource-poor minorities, whose main asset may consist in their ability to put on a show of public solidarity.

Very few Chamba from Ganye chiefdom live outside Nigeria; slightly more have either travelled abroad (particularly for pilgrimage to Mecca or Jerusalem) or studied abroad. However, Nigeria is a big and populous place. No one is sure of its exact population; estimation is made contentious by matters of taxation and election which predictably pull population returns in opposite directions. Another attempt to count the population is imminent but, in the meantime, observers bandy around figures in the region of 120 to 135 million, meaning that Nigerians make up more than half and perhaps as much as two-thirds of all West Africans (depending on various assumptions about which countries are considered West African and what their populations might be). Chamba try to argue up their own numbers to around half a million, most of whom live within Adamawa State, but including communities mixed and scattered in neighbouring Taraba State to the west (not counting Chamba to the east in Cameroon). Leaving aside serious quibbles about the basis of ethnicity, in the roughest of terms Chamba make up between one-third and two-fifths of one per cent of the population of Nigeria. Given this status as one of the country's middling-size minorities (in a smaller West African nation they might have been calling the shots), Chamba can move around a good deal and live in Nigeria's larger cities among people unlike themselves, without ever leaving their country. Unlike international emigration, national migration is very substantial. Poster-sized annual almanacs produced in many of the university and commercial cities of Nigeria line up their Chamba residents: larger photos of dignitaries, placed towards the top and centre, preside over thumbnail portraits of Chamba members of local student or cultural associations. The enthusiastic uptake of computer software supporting photographs and artwork has encouraged far more organisations than previously to produce not just almanacs, but ornate invitations, announcements and condolences, drawing on both national and international ideas of appropriate design.

Most literature on cosmopolitanism assumes that cosmopolitan sentiments are, if not antithetical to, then certainly in tension with the nationalism, or 'beyond' the nation (Cheah and Robbins 1998; Archibugi 2003). This strikes me as privileging a particular experience of the nation, pre-eminently that of Europe's language majorities and their settler societies. Particularly if you belong to a minority ethnic group nationally, a cosmopolitan sensibility, in so far as the term is understood to apply to a capacity to reach beyond cultural difference – and not only the cultural differences of people outside your own nation – is necessary to feel any sense of belonging to your own nationalist project. Yet cosmopolitanism is usually presented as transcendent of nationalism, an aspiration to internationalism or transnationalism. Like many such, this argument rests uncomfortably on the assumption and implicit narrative it claims to refute. Nations did not become diverse only through receiving culturally distinctive immigrants; in a loose sense, all were cosmopolitan at their inception and some did not, or have not yet, undergone the nation-building processes which for a time effaced some of the differences within older, mainly European, states. Even discounting immigration from other countries, Nigeria is in this sense a cosmopolitan nation. The proliferation of almanacs strikes me as a slight, but nevertheless interesting, imaginative representation of Chamba in the enormous nation to which they belong: successful or aspirational in these distant places, but claiming ethnic loyalty and pride. *Pen leuka be nokin Samba*, or 'I am proud to be Chamba', as the bumper sticker of the Chamba Progressive Union, Jos Chapter, proclaims bilingually.[6]

Members of the Progressive Union (and of other Cultural Associations) in major Nigerian towns display their ethnic pride for the same reason that the Chamba of Ganye prove their modernity: they have been, in their own eyes – which reflect the views of some Nigerian majorities – disparaged and marginalised. Becoming more cosmopolitan involves a coming to terms with the evaluation of differences within the nation, particularly between themselves and their principle contrapuntal

Figure 12.2 Chamba Progressive Union bumper sticker. Courtesy Steve Simon Samleukenni

other (the Fulani) but also with other majorities. Doing this requires them also to address the differences, especially those between Muslims and Christians, which potentially threaten their own peace.

This leads me to some misgivings about the proposal that cosmopolitanism might serve as a defining trope of anthropology as a discipline (see Rapport 2006). Cosmopolitanism, it seems to me, is no less a loaded focus in the twenty-first century than ethnic authenticity was in the twentieth century. Belonging to a national state dominated by a few regional majorities (matters of power and culture, rather than just numbers), Chamba need to appear both authentic and modern. But this is a reflection of weakness as much as strength: they know that others in the nation-state exercise more cultural clout than they do (over language policy, education, broadcasting, national spectacles, and so forth), and that the same people are in all likelihood better connected than they are in cosmopolitan terms (both nationally and internationally). Chamba, in turn, exercise more power and are better connected than some micro-minorities. Their ethnic identity provides the most important ground of their encapsulation within the nation-state: as individual voters they count for very little, even during civilian transitions between regimes. Consciousness of this ethnic identity has grown alongside the kinds of cosmopolitanism that are products of technological globalisation (mobile telephones and computer graphics, above, being instances).

When I first visited Ganye in 1976, only a small fraction of the elite, who were all older than me, spoke some English (the official Nigerian language), and my Chamba was the more serviceable medium of communication for many of our relations. Now many people younger than me, including women, very few of whom spoke English in 1976, speak English much better than I speak Chamba. They learnt it at school from an early age, and employed that language-learning to get educated, listen to the radio, read English-language Nigerian newspapers, communicate with travellers (including some Nigerians, like Igbo, who may not have learnt Hausa), and so on. Even more Chamba speak very serviceable Hausa (the northern Nigerian national language); again, more than when I visited first. Fewer, however, speak Fulfulde, the language of the old Adamawa Emirate. This simply corresponds to Hausa's cultural dominance in northern Nigeria. Matters could have been different, as is evident from the dominance of Fulfulde in those parts of the Adamawa Emirate (including Chamba populations) that now belong to Cameroon. My (not systematically tested) hunch is that fewer Chamba nowadays speak the languages of their non-Fulani neighbours than was once the case.[7] Most Chamba, Verre, Mumuye, Bachama, or Koma have the option of speaking to one another in Hausa or English.

Do these changing linguistic and, one could demonstrate also, cultural capacities imply that people are becoming more cosmopolitan in outlook, or are they simply being connected more closely to global concerns and adjusting their behaviour and alliances to try to prosper?

Encapsulation and Identity – History

Chamba have been confronted with efforts, serially, to incorporate them into a Fulani Muslim empire, a German empire, a British colonial mandate and trusteeship, and a succession of independent Nigerian governments, both military- and civilian-run (and the two are not mutually exclusive in practice). It has fallen largely to Chamba elites to try to derive value of different kinds (economic, political, symbolic) from their relations with others whose identities (more properly, trajectories of identity, since flux has been the rule) differ from their own. We might like to call these efforts cosmopolitanisation to add moral mission to what the Africanist literature generally calls ethnic brokerage or suchlike. Benefits have percolated to non-elite Chamba to the extent that they have been able to curb elite self-interest (by pressing moral or material claims on them). It would be premature and dangerous for Chamba of the Ganye paramountcy to start relying too much on the kindness of the strangers who make up their huge and diverse national state. Their historic experience has been of degrees of marginality in terms of rights granted, and peripherality in terms of access to them: these degrees, as everywhere, varied with status, but even the best-connected have been far from secure in their relative privilege.

Several writers have suggested phases in globalisation as the extension and overall connectivity of its technologies have deepened (e.g. Mignolo 2002: 157 – 'a set of designs to manage the world'). They write about this, as it were, from the world's point of view. The ethnographer's contribution is made distinctive by reversing the optic, to ask how the wider world seems to those becoming caught up increasingly within it. Although I do not pursue it here, this approach would be just as germane to looking at the 'packaging' of the world for the information-rich (Calhoun 2003: 107). I want, very briefly, to provide a context to local globalisation in the last quarter millennium for the Chamba case, and to ask how this might be related to the extension of their projects for 'conviviality' (Mignolo 2002).[8]

In the mid-eighteenth century most Chamba[9] would have lived in sizeable chiefdoms around the mid-point of what is now the Nigeria-Cameroon border. Their immediate neighbours were much like themselves, and the suppositions about the world they shared allowed a lively trade in cults and cult performances, alongside ties based on co-residence, clan- and ethnic-based relations of privileged insult, intermarriage, and so forth. Chamba were usually self-sufficient in staple foods, although there are indications of droughts in the second half of the eighteenth century. Apart from such small stock as chickens, goats and sheep, Chamba may have kept dwarf cattle and ponies. In these respects, their communities were probably self-sufficient too. Their cosmology – a grand term I use because it resonates with the likely limits of their cosmopolitanism at that time – predicated a distant creator god and an array of more locally rooted and more immediate powers: an underworld from which the dead affected the lives of the living, forces of the wild including malevolent animals, witches, seers and shape-changers. Technologies of offering, ordeal, and cultic performance allied to the expulsion or killing of people who posed supernatural dangers to the community (whether or not they intended to do so) provided a degree of control over these immediately present, super-human powers, and there were also means of reparation for human damage (by theft, killing, adultery, and so forth). God was invoked but did not receive sacrifice.

Chamba would have been aware of various types of people unlike themselves: to the north they presumably knew of the powerful Muslim empire of Bornu, and they would have been familiar with predominantly Hausa traders whose routes crossed Chambaland. Fulani graziers with their herds of zebu cattle and smallstock also traversed Chambaland on seasonal migrations and, in all probability, some settled in small villages. To the south, Chamba may have heard of European traders far away at the coast who brought trade goods and collected slaves. The epicentre of the European slave trade had been moving towards the area due south of Chamba. However, Chamba probably sensed the power of both the Europeans and the Kanuri of Bornu only indirectly, while the Fulani herders were vulnerable and so acted as clients. The most immediate social experience would have been small in scale and extension, but minutely differentiated in terms of kin, clan, ethnicity, dialect and language, and rooted super-human powers. In short, Chamba individuals and groups were themselves at the centre of complex social landscapes of difference.

Richard Fardon

The nineteenth century saw this situation change entirely. Chambaland was largely overrun by the easternmost emirate of the Sokoto Caliphate – at the beginning of the twentieth century the most populous political entity in Africa. Numerous Chamba Leko-speaking chiefdoms disappeared as their members set off south and south-west to escape Fulani domination and to profit from the disruptions of Fulani state-building. Other Chamba retreated into the hills and mountains that nullified the advantages of Fulani cavalry. Those left in the plains had to find some kind of, doubtless changing, *modus vivendi* with the ascendant Fulani powers in whose eyes they were, more often than not, pagans and slaves and racially inferior. In the course of a century, those Chamba who did not emigrate entirely found their status changed – in very crude terms – from being at the centre of their own universe to living on the margins of a Muslim and, in terms of its dominant stratum, ethnically Fulani state to which they were significant only as a resource. A minority of Chamba clients were able to derive value from this wider world, but only at the cost of collusion and exploitation of their fellow Chamba. Early Chamba experience of Islam was as a religion of ethnically distinct conquerors: chiefs who allied with this outside power were often required, at least nominally, to become Muslims. Hence, Islam (in Chamba, praying to, or literally 'greeting or showing respect to God') was seen as an aspect of Fulani identity (to become Muslim was to 'become Fulani'). A further century has done little to dissipate the legacy of rancour and distrust to which this gave rise between Chamba and Fulani as categories, and among Chamba themselves (though not, it needs to be added, always to the exclusion of cordial relations between some Chamba and Fulani as individuals).

Conquest of the Sokoto Caliphate by European imperial powers did not immediately make a substantial change to relations between Chamba and Fulani. Whatever their principled views on the topic, all three European powers involved (Britain, Germany and France) had little option other than to resort to indirect rule through Fulani chiefs. The Europeans found Chamba in the state to which the Fulani consigned them and this, allied to the Europeans' own perceptions of relative superiority among Africans, meant that early colonial rule was experienced by Chamba as at best a rearrangement, at worst a reinforcement, of Fulani dominance. It was not until the inter-war period that the British seriously addressed dismantling an administration that used Fulani intermediaries to deal with Chamba communities, and began to replace it with territorially and ethnically based local administrative units with headmen drawn from the majority ethnic group. The development of an ethnically based administration, drawing in small-scale on those same assumptions (of language, culture, shared history, and continuous identity, as arguments for autonomy) that underlay nationalist arguments,[10] coincided with intensification of two other globalising influences.

Most of Chambaland was missionised relatively late, Lutheran Protestants (initially a New Zealand couple, later Norwegians) arriving from the mid-1920s, and Irish Roman Catholics a couple of decades later. The absence of Anglican, or indeed English, missionaries created a distance between European colonial power and its associated religions that had not been the case for the Fulani Emirate and Islam in the nineteenth century. Simultaneously, conversion to Islam (which had scarcely occurred beyond nominal chiefly conversions during the nineteenth-century jihads) increased. Historic Chamba religion remained predominant for the first half of the twentieth century but declined thereafter, its performances becoming largely folkloristic by the end of the century (albeit some of its presuppositions, notably concerning witchcraft, continued to be entertained). Chamba religious affiliations were set upon a path that is still obvious: whether Chamba Christians are Lutheran Protestant or Roman Catholics may be predicted with a high degree of accuracy on the basis of their present or historic family residence: western Chamba tend to be Protestants, and eastern and southern Chamba are predominantly Catholics, a distribution that follows from the division of Chambaland between missionary interests on the Nigerian side of the border. Muslims are found all over Chambaland, but they especially predominate where no Christian mission was established. So far, other churches have remained very minor players and, according to local testimony, are largely confined to Ganye town where their congregations are predominantly non-Chamba.

The late colonial period[11] thus introduced Chamba to a set of assumptions concerning identity, autonomy and self-government, shared by both colonial and national regimes, as well as to the two major religious currents of Nigeria. The combination did not sit all that easily. Nigeria's religious geography is complex looked at in all its details, but a fundamental tension between a North that looks across the Sahara desert to the Muslim world, and a South which looks across the Atlantic to the Christian world, has centuries of precedent behind it (and is shared by many larger coastal states of West Africa). A campaign to Islamise northern Nigeria was waged in the first decade of independence. More recently, the activities of religious fundamentalists in both camps, and the contest between the Nigerian Constitution and Shariah Law have served to exacerbate tensions (Paden 2005; Ostien, Nasir and Kogelmann 2005). Chamba in Ganye hold strongly, though it is difficult to know how anyone might check their assertions, that they are evenly split between Muslims and Christians. The predominance of either religion would upset a delicate balance because, over and above these religious differences, which are common within families, there is a general insistence that where politics is concerned they are all Chamba and have to stick together. This would be a less sweeping commitment were it not also remarked frequently that in Nigeria everything is politics.

It was not until the British were close to leaving the Trust Territory that a further concerted effort was made to address the problems of Chamba administration. During the 1930s a Subordinate Native Authority had been stitched together that consisted of a few Chamba chiefdoms which had survived the nineteenth century, and a swath of smaller communities in the plains between the two major mountain ranges that border what is now the Ganye chiefdom to the west and east. Chamba and Fulani had become more mixed in this central plain than elsewhere, and the entire area was constituted as a single district headed by a Fulani who also acted as Wakilin Chamba (he was the father of the prominent businessman and politician mentioned earlier), effectively presiding over the Chamba Native Authority as a whole.

By the mid-1950s discontent against what they portrayed as Fulani domination was given voice by young Chamba Protestants. Largely as a result of their having raised the profile of the problem, the British moved the administrative centre of the Chamba Native Authority from Jada, a place founded by Fulani incomers, a few miles south to Ganye, which is said to have been the site of a small market but was otherwise hardly populated.

In 1961, the Northern Trust Territory joined Nigeria, which had gained independence the previous year, and a block of offices was built in Ganye ('The Native Authority Offices. A gift of the people of the United Kingdom to the people of

Figure 12.3 Native Authority Offices Plaque. Photograph Richard Fardon

Chamba'; two textually equivalent 'peoples' related through gift exchange as the plaque commemorating their opening that year avows).

Control over local administration there would become a focus of a Chamba/ Fulani rivalry that took a variety of forms: writing petitions, seeking offices of the different kinds that local administration seemed to have an inexhaustible capacity to generate, and occasional violence.

In 1967, the Fulani scored a symbolic victory when they petitioned success-fully for the Chamba Native Authority to be renamed Ganye Native Authority. A rotational presidency of the Native Authority Council was brought in at the same time, so that the District Heads, Chamba and Fulani, took turns to preside over meetings. However, an eruption of violence in 1971, precipitated by disputed successions in two districts, revealed the inadequacy of this arrangement. In response to what became known as the 'Leko riots', named after the Chamba of one administrative area (Leko District) taking direct action against the installation of a Fulani District Head on the retirement of his Chamba predecessor, the State Governor set up a Commission of Enquiry. It was the recommendation of the enquiry that a paramount chiefship be created in Ganye. A complex election process was set in train, and a forty-year-old, Catholic-educated Muslim, an ex-teacher and veterinary officer, was approved as Chief (*Sarkin*, Hausa) of Ganye in 1972, formally receiving his Third-Class Staff of Office two years later. This was upgraded to a Second-Class Staff in 1982, and ceremonially bestowed the following year. On his death in 2000, his son was elected his successor and, although the position remains officially elective, it will become increasingly difficult to disentangle the resources of the chiefship from those of the family that has now held that office for more than 30 years.

Since its creation, the chiefship has been one of the few constants of Chamba organisation, though it also has not gone uncontested, notably by Fulani petitioners variously demanding (in English): the removal of the incumbent, the division of the chiefdom, or for the chief to be prevented from titling himself *Gangwari* and be obliged to revert to the Hausa title *Sarkin*, on the basis that use of a Chamba term is discriminatory against future Fulani candidates. All of these petitions, according to Chamba in Ganye, have needed to be refuted actively because Fulani are better connected than Chamba at statal and federal levels of government, and who knows what might come to pass otherwise – for everything, recall, is politics.

While the chiefship has been a constant for a large part of the 45 years since the Chamba joined an independent Nigeria, other administrative and electoral arrangements have changed with a frequency that precludes summary here. The country has lurched between civilian and military regimes, often accompanied by creation of states: their number currently stands at 36 (Chamba have successively belonged to Sardauna Province, North-Eastern State, Gongola State and Adamawa

State). Native Authorities have become Local Government Authorities, and these have been created and dissolved, sub-divided and redrawn with little respite. This volatility has been more than matched by the creation and suppression of political parties that have managed both to be new and to have recognisable antecedents in past parties. And every time the political game has been redefined, Chamba have not had a choice whether to participate, both to protect their position vis-à-vis the Fulani, and because political office has been the most common, in fact for Chamba almost sole, route to personal wealth. Each change has required a refashioning of networks of influence, an undertaking that demands the investment of time, as well as the raising and expenditure of financial resources. This process has been not simply repeated but inflated: most simply in monetary terms, but also in the numbers of states, local government areas, special development areas, and chiefdoms, and hence the number and rank of their elected and appointed political functionaries (notably, therefore, excepting those state employees most practically involved in the provision of welfare, education and physical infrastructure).

Chamba have been both citizens and subjects for much of the past four-and-a-half decades, at least when military governments have not held electoral processes entirely in abeyance. Because the Christians predominated among the first Chamba to be educated, there was a tendency for them also to predominate among those elected to offices. All occupants of 'traditional' offices are expected to be Muslims, and there are well-known cases of Christians having converted to Islam shortly before being appointed to some rung of the chiefdom's administration. Christian and Muslim interests have to be kept in some kind of balance in the interests of Chamba retaining ethnic solidarity. Seen from this perspective, there are not two systems of government but only one that happens to operate through two related branches with slightly different protocols, and the more durable of these, which seems capable of surviving transitions between national regimes, is called 'traditional' although it is actually a postcolonial introduction in an invented, syncretised traditional idiom. Moreover, it is not clear that one part of the system is more responsive or representative than the other. The Paramount Chief has to emerge from an electoral process, and he surrounds himself with a Council drawn representatively from those considered successful and influential in the chiefdom. In appointing District Heads (all 18 of whom currently have the honorific title Alhaji, indicating pilgrimage to Mecca), he has to gauge what will be acceptable to those they govern, and he knows that the precedents are plentiful for unpopular appointees to destabilise their own communities.

It is a moot point whether the elected officials are more accountable than the Paramount Chief. Quite how particular candidates for election emerge as such is often unclear to those invited to vote for them, who are left to assume some behind-the-scenes stitch-up. Arguments about ethnic turn-taking are widely imputed and surface explicitly as arguments for candidates. When one political party is ascendant, which is the present case, the candidate for that party inevitably emerges with a popular mandate. Hence the obscure process of candidate selection is more important than the more public process of election, as people are well aware. Federal and statal representatives are likely to spend much of their time respectively in the federal and statal capitals (Yola and Abuja); even local councillors may not always be accessible to their electorates, particularly if they combine elected office with a job elsewhere in the country. When there is a crisis, it is to the Chief that people turn for leadership and reconciliation.[12]

Chamba are politically more experienced than they were 30 years ago, but so are Nigerians generally. Their language repertoires have changed. Chamba identity has self-consciously been maintained in the face of their division between world religions, which is difficult because Muslim identities have typically been seen as supportive of the Northern Nigerian status quo, while Christian identities have as typically been cast as more radical, particularly those of the Protestants who challenged the British to reform the system of colonial administration they considered biased. The Bachama, another of the people who saw their Chief ascend to first-class paramountcy in 2006, are almost uniformly Lutherans and regard Chamba Muslims as an anomaly among two peoples whose solidarity rests in part on a shared history of resistance to incorporation in the Adamawa Emirate. Does any of this suggest Chamba have become more cosmopolitan in recent decades? Does the question in fact illuminate anything much of this process beyond changes in the fashionable concerns of academics?

Cosmopolitan Sleights

Immigrant minorities in older nation-states are often thought to be more cosmo-politan in outlook than the majority population among whom they live: a minority may have international links not simply with a previous homeland but throughout a diaspora from that homeland; members of the minority may have settled in more or less concentrated areas throughout large parts of their new homeland; their favoured economic niches may draw upon their national and international connections, and upon linguistic and cultural skills that allow them to function in several national contexts; their marriage patterns may both tie them into overs-eas and local networks, as well as predominantly reproducing their own identity through a high rate of endogamy. Granted, few minorities exactly fit all these criteria, we might think of this kind of diasporic minority as an ideal type, and one that many anthropologists would be willing to see as cosmopolitan both in its orientation and in its practices. Leaving aside 'internationalism', all these features might apply equally to encapsulated minorities, particularly those in newer nation-states (such as Nigeria). Chamba, for instance, have a high degree of linkage in their Nigerian diaspora, but most also remain tied to their home places; there is a high degree of multilingualism and, while marriage is predominantly to other Chamba, many who have worked or studied outside their homeland married spouses of different ethnicity. Unlike ideal typical international cosmopolitans, however, Chamba, like other Nigerian minorities, have some local place within the nation-state where they are at home as a majority.

There is an extensive literature on West Africa dealing with home-town associations through which migrants stay in touch with projects at home, and these incorporate international migrants in much the same way as national migrants. Though Nigerian Chamba associations are not particularly active in this regard, the Bali Chamba of the Grassfields of Cameroon (some of whose founders left Chambaland as raiders in the nineteenth century, see Fardon 2006) have extensive associations both in the USA and in the UK which fund projects at home. It was in the town of Bali that I heard the only reference to 'cosmopolitans', using that term, while thinking about the subject of this chapter. This was in a comment made by the local mayor to the effect that 'cosmopolitans' were much appreciated for their financial contribution to their home town, but they had to realise they were not always in the best position to decide local priorities.

Although I do not have space to develop the argument here, Bali demonstrates just how dissimilar two related cases can be. Unlike Ganye, Bali is a precolonial *fondom* (kingdom), related to four other intrusive kingdoms in the Cameroon Grassfields. Its alliances tend to be with other kingdoms in the Anglophone region of Cameroon. Unlike Chamba, the Bali population is almost entirely Christian (though of differing denominations) and, in another striking contrast, customary religion linked to the palace is publicly prominent. The differences between the two places could be developed at length, but are introduced here as a caution against generalisations about the ways that national encapsulation functions.

Finally in this section, I want to remark how it appears to be the case that behaviours judged 'cosmopolitan', on the part of some internationalised minorities, are seen instead as 'extraverted' or 'inauthentic' on the part of African minorities. How far is cosmopolitanism in the eye of the beholder? And does that eye see all cases in the same light? How do beholders know cosmopolitanism when they see it? And, what is their interest in seeing it? I don't mean to pursue an argument that reduces interest in talking about cosmopolitanism to the interests of people who believe themselves to be cosmopolitans. Nevertheless, thinking through the concerns of minority peoples in heterogeneous nations does predispose attention to the effects that majorities and their interests (in different senses of this term) can cause, even, perhaps especially, unwittingly. The 'sleight' of this section's title, according to the dictionary definitions, can have relatively approving senses of skilfulness or cleverness, but these characteristics shade into a knack or trick, and this adroitness in turn spills into morally ambiguous areas of artifice, ruse or cunning. The homophonous verb to 'slight', meaning to take at little value, or betray indifference towards, has no etymological connection with 'sleight', but I cannot help hearing a potential for 'slight' lurking in 'sleight'. What, I wonder, is the effect of an increasing interest in cosmopolitanism on (those rendered thereby) the uncosmopolitans, or the aspirant cosmopolitans? Are the uncosmopolitans for cosmopolitans akin to what the uncivilised used to be in the eyes of those who thought themselves civilised? Because cosmopolitanism classifies (and as Bourdieu might have reminded us, classifies the classifiers), ignoring the vexed issue of its definition serves to naturalise it.

Commentators seem to agree both that they know cosmopolitanism when they see it and that it is very difficult to put a finger on quite how this happens. The editors of two recent collections of papers try different strategies to get around the problem. Stephen Vertovec and Robin Cohen (2002) helpfully disentangle six 'perspectives' on cosmopolitanism, without committing themselves either to the argument that these are perspectives on the same object seen from different vantages, or to the proposition that every aspect of the object thus envisioned might not be called something else chosen from the ample vocabulary of escape from hypertrophied identity categories (transnationalism, globalisation, diaspora, creolisation, hybridity, transculturation...). While grateful for their careful literature review, this reader is left unsure whether they are proposing a polythetic delineation of cosmopolitanism, or listing rather different concerns that simply happen to be included in some uses of the term.

Sheldon Pollock, Homi K. Bhabha, Carol A. Breckenridge and Dipesh Chakrabarty devote the first paragraph of their editorial introduction to explaining why, because cosmopolitanism is yet to come, we do not know what it currently is, and cannot therefore say where it came from. Moreover, it must 'always escape positive and definite specification, precisely because specifying cosmopolitanism positively and definitely is an uncosmopolitan thing to do' (Breckenridge et al. 2002: 1). While wanting to sympathise with a project that wants to be so resolutely non-exclusive, arcane non-definition does threaten to defeat its own inclusive intentions by excluding those who simply lack prior knowledge that would allow them to begin to understand what this undefinable project might be. To be on board the cosmopolitan project, to put it crudely, you have to have been on board already.[13]

Kwame Anthony Appiah's urbane and witty account of cosmopolitan ethics in a 'world of strangers' clearly addresses those already on board. I agree with most that he says, but then my profile closely fits his intended audience. I ought to be part of his 'we'. Appiah argues that cosmopolitanism requires a conversation, inter-preted in broad terms, between those who hold differing values, not so they come to agree on those values, but so they can achieve ways of practical coexistence. Extreme cultural relativism is no help here, since it precludes conversation (2006:

14, 57, 70–1, 85). His definition of cosmopolitanism varies from a minimal commitment to mutual obligation and respect for difference between humans (2006: xv), to a more elaborated commitment to fallibilism (recognising the limits to one's certainties) and pluralism (2006: 144) Throughout he emphasises practices and the facts of a shrinking and culturally interpenetrating world in which being a non-cosmopolitan requires unrelenting vigilance. Cosmopolitanism is a normal condition. We are less different from one another than some like to suggest. Because he draws upon his autobiography, Appiah addresses an (elite) triangular cosmopolitanism (American, British and Asante) which sits within a history of Atlantic globalisation. He might also have asked about Ghanaian conviviality, between coastal, central Akan, and northern peoples who differ widely and have historic antagonisms that so far have been restrained by relatively durable compromise in a half century of postcolonial history.

A philosopher appealing to practice is, as Appiah recognises, in danger of putting himself out of business. His conclusion is called 'kindness to strangers' which echoes Kant. But with a change of preposition might also echo Tennessee Williams's Blanche DuBois in *A Streetcar Named Desire*, who claimed always to have relied on the kindness 'of strangers'. (Blanche, we may also recall, traded favours to strangers for their help, and the devaluation of her favours with age is a large part of the plot of the play.) We may become better cosmopolitans, Appiah concludes, by giving up a sum of money small enough not to trouble most Westerners which will nonetheless be large enough to alleviate basic poverty globally. It sounds like a win-win situation, but what does it make of the world's Blanche DuBoises, those who receive strangers' beneficence? Do they become more cosmopolitan in receiving our handouts? Or, will they be cosmopolitans only once they too give? And, are their problems simply a matter of our wealth? In part they certainly are, but wealth transfer and a regard for both cultural pluralism and every culture's plurality misses the connections between economy, practice and that variable degree of extension in the world we tend to recognise as being cosmopolitan or not. Appealing to practice in this fashion actually avoids most practical conundrums because it is devoid of curiosity about the social circumstances under which conversation occurs. When is it reasonable to anticipate people will embrace fallibilism and pluralism? When, most basically, can they afford to do so?

Anthropologists cannot leave the question of practice in quite such abstract terms as philosophers. We need to reinstate some of the sociologics between the philosophical-cum-cultural and political-cum-policy poles towards which much of the debate on cosmopolitanism tends to gravitate, and which are only apparently reconciled when conclusions about the one (say, policy) are drawn directly from the other (say, partial cultural relativism of some stripe). In order to do these things, we cannot allow the meanings of cosmopolitanism to bend so conveniently, since in recruiting a cosmopolitan 'we' on such various grounds, a non-cosmopolitan or uncosmopolitan 'they' is precipitated as a problematic object, and this implies a solution that asks them all to cross the floor to our cosmopolitan camp. Yet, even in principle, anthropologists know that is not how segmentary political processes work and, in practice, as I argued above, the vagueness of cosmopolitanism's definition has the effect of excluding some people's behaviour more because of the context in which they act than because of what they do.

What would be the potential effects of anthropologists framing their interests in terms of cosmopolitanism? Such a shift would certainly be in the spirit of anthropological *bouleversement*: anthropologists, one conventionally progressive version of disciplinary history tells us, were once predominantly interested in exotic places, now they also work at home; once they worked in few field sites over a career, now some undertake multi-sited fieldwork to triangulate extensive social processes from the outset of their research careers; that is, supposing they still privilege fieldwork, for anthropologists now use all kinds of materials not just to supplement fieldwork but as the primary focus of study. Why not complete the process of uprooting ethnography by making study of cosmopolitans or cosmopolitanism exemplary? Of course, the conventional history has been overstated here for effect (and brevity), and I agree with most of the arguments that have broadened the scope of anthropology. But I worry about their, probably unintended, aggregate effects. By doing one thing, we choose not to do others. In an intellectual landscape that is increasingly inter- and post-disciplinary (a single market place in which barriers to trade have been dismantled), if anthropologists choose to do what other (usually more powerful) disciplines also do, there is little likelihood of those other disciplines interesting themselves in the range of societies that used to be anthropology's hallmark. Hence my worry about 'cosmopolitanism' is not just that it seems to precipitate a category of the uncosmopolitan on grounds that take no account of the social logics of action, but that it may make uncosmopolitan enquiry unattractive to prospective researchers.

Ulrich Beck, presumably without meaning to do so, demonstrates what I have in mind when he writes that, 'Identity denies ambivalence, pins things down and attempts to draw boundaries in a process of cosmopolitanisation that suspends and blurs boundaries. There is a corresponding nostalgia on the part of social scientists (not forgetting anthropologists) for an ordered world of clear boundaries and the associated social categories' (Beck 2002: 81). The scholarship here is careless for one so eminent, but also indicative in its assumption that evidence would be unnecessary: who are these anthropologists nostalgic for clear boundaries and social categories? The guilty go unnamed; as well they might.[14] What is studied has been conflated with how that study takes place. Throughout my career, anthropologists – particularly those who have been read widely – have indeed studied how people essentialise their identities and naturalize their social classifications, but to study

Richard Fardon

such processes is neither to endorse them, nor to bemoan their loss where they have been undermined. Rather than berating forebears, I prefer to take seriously the contrapuntal sense of cosmopolitanism and its antonyms to which Beck also points when he writes that identity 'pin[s] things down' – indeed, how could it be identity if it did not? Even the identity of 'cosmopolitan' has the effect of trying, however evasively, to pin down something that otherwise very different people or practices share. If the idea of cosmopolitanism had no intention to pin anything down, why would commentators worry whether defining cosmopolitanism was itself uncosmopolitan? In reality, pinning down most identities is not so easy; it calls for vigilant and unrelenting work, and this is because the social worlds in which most of us live – not being total institutions – are criss-crossed by currents that both call forth and repudiate essentialised identities. *Pace* Beck, identities have as much to do with the creation of ambivalence as its denial: if there were no identities then what would people be ambivalent about? People with strong local identities, like Chamba in Nigeria, are rendered uncosmopolitan on account of their shared identity, without pausing to ask about the sociologics of that identity: which minimally would have to include the minority position in a multi-ethnic national state of people who nevertheless constitute a local majority, or the internal tensions between faith communities among them that ethnicity has to try, quite self-consciously, to trump.

Peripheral Citizenship in Practice

Most of this chapter has concerned the circumstances local to Chamba communities in Nigeria and Cameroon. So in conclusion I want to broaden my comments from this case to a wider sense of peripheral citizenship and do so in the interest of the project of cosmopolitanism. I appreciate the social sciences' current concern with cosmopolitanism as an attempt to highlight efforts at securing conviviality, including global justice and human rights, made in the face of trajectories of cultural, economic and political differentiation under contexts of globalisation. However, processes of conviviality and differentiation have been concurrent, even mutually entailed, by the wider connections which fostered both. Privileging one as the transcendence of the other, as Beck does, also privileges its proponents, those in a position to propose it. How wide a project of conviviality might be anticipated of peripheral citizens under marginalised circumstances? Cosmopolitans, whether in outlook or in practice, usually need to have resolved their national role in one way or another: either secured their share of the national cake, or given it up as a bad job and invested in the outside. Those who have given up on their nation-states may be economic migrants (from the fabulously rich to the indigent), or illegal aliens and refugees, respectively the flotsam and jetsam of globalisation.

Chamba in Ganye have an unresolved relation to their national state about which they need to be constantly vigilant. The identity underwriting their claims in the sub-national area in which they can construct themselves as a majority is the most cogent argument they have for their national position. Chamba neotraditionalism in ethnicity and in chiefship sits in a Nigerian world of ethnic claims, and Chamba anticipate that others will have similar identities to underpin their rights. The assertion of ethnicity is simultaneously a claim to statal and federal resources; in this sense, ethnicity involves a commitment to the national state as quartermaster. 'Traditional' chiefship must both participate in this agonistic jousting and stand slightly to one side of it, rising above sectional struggles and persisting beyond the party interests that are their vehicle.

Ethnicity, most fundamentally for Chamba, and at least for the present, trumps religion: the more confessional identities have become polarised (and this process has been accelerated by the globalising projects of both Christians and Muslims), the more Chamba have been inclined to play down religious differences. Quite how resilient this ethnicising response to religious polarisation will remain is difficult to predict. There is ambivalence among some Chamba about an ethnic project that subordinates religious differences – particularly if one confessional identity seems regularly disadvantaged by it. Clearly, this fragile play of circumstances is not reducible to the kind of antinomian contest between cosmopolitanisation and the essentialisation of identities that Ulrich Beck suggests as a master process. Indeed, such a formulation would entirely fail to recognise the difficulties of constructing ethnic conviviality in a 'cosmopolitan' yet religiously riven nation. Granted the dangers inherent in an ethnic project, it would still be unjust to portray those struggling to contain religious polarisation and contest historic marginality simply as obstacles to cosmopolitanisation because their sole instrument for doing this involved identity politics.

Advocates of cosmopolitanism seek to make the world a better place. To argue that humans are a single species, that cultures are not essences, that loyalties may be complex, that responsibilities for one another do not end at national boundaries, and so forth. Who, among those addressed, would argue? But who is addressed? And under what circumstances are those addressed in a position to concur? Ethnographers have been the main specialists in the knowledge economy asking – on the basis of experience – how this all looks from the other end of the telescope. Without such investigations, cosmopolitanism risks being, by sleight not by intention, another way of excluding and disparaging others. The 'traditionalism' of marginalised ethnic subjects in Nigeria results from processes of globalisation and from currents of cosmopolitanisation as they are played out nationally and experienced locally through divisive world religious affiliations and the opportunities for hegemony offered to majorities by universal 'democratic' processes. Cultural relativism is untenable as a presupposition of cosmopolitanism, as Kwame Anthony Appiah argues, not just because extreme relativism would mean people had nothing to say to one another, but because cultured lives are *already* relative to one another historically and presently (Kahn 2003: 411). While the philosophical argument is unimpeachable in principle, it is irrelevant to the world as it exists. Worse, arguments about cultural relativism, produce a Manichaean outlook. Here I want to return to Appiah's advocacy of cosmopolitan charity in conclusion.

The year 2005 witnessed a series of, what I applaud as having been, genuinely cosmopolitan initiatives. The publication of *Our Common Interest: Report of the Commission for Africa* in March that year was a landmark event, its impact reinforced by Bob Geldof's initiatives as author, television documentary-maker and concertmaster. It in no way diminishes this effort to use it as an example of the desire both to be deferential towards cultural difference and remain appalled by some of the behaviour carried out in the name of identities defined culturally. This shows up in the *Report* as a fretful switching between singular and plural, adding and removing the qualification 'African':

> Different cultures manifest their ideas of political and economic freedom in very different ways. For this reason the Commission decided to consider the issue of culture before embarking on political and economic analysis. By culture we are talking about far more than literature, music, dance, art, sculpture, theatre, film and sport. All of these, of course, are for any social group part of its shared joy in the business of being alive. But culture is more than the arts. It is about shared patterns of identity. It is about how social values are transmitted and individuals are made to be part of a society. Culture is how the past interacts with the future. (Commission for Africa 2005: 30)

> One commonly held fallacy about culture is that it is the expression of unchanging tradition. Those who hold this view usually see African cultures as regressive and tribal and therefore inimical to development. African culture, they often say, is an irrational force that generates inertia and economic backwardness. This is contrary to the evidence. History shows African cultures to have been tremendously adaptive, absorbing a wide range of outside influences, and impositions, as well as finding ways to survive often difficult natural, environmental and social conditions. (Commission for Africa 2005: 31)

These summarised thoughts (and their expansion in pp. 121–32 of the *Report*'s main text) are clearly meant well; their respect for cultural difference, and emphasis on the need for dialogue (which I have not quoted) would presumably make them cosmopolitan in Kwame Anthony Appiah's terms. But like many propositions about culture, they quickly become perplexing. In the first paragraph, cultures are taken as foundational realities: able to 'manifest their ideas of political and economic freedom'; being 'about shared patterns of identity'; being 'how the past interacts with the future'. But, this version of African cultures does indeed lend itself to being construed in terms of a multiplicity of ethnic possessions, particularly when, out of proper deference to the immense variety of African societies, the *Report* insists on pluralising 'cultures'. As Sir Bob puts it succinctly in his own book, 'Talking about tribalism makes Africans sound backward' (Geldof 2005: 235), yet the Commission does choose to start with cultures when talking about Africa.

The second paragraph I quoted tackles this point head on, refuting unnamed critics and arguing that African cultures have simultaneously absorbed outside influences (outside what one wonders?) while finding ways to survive a variety of difficult conditions. Is it not people who survive difficulties? Or is this a variation on the selfish gene: people being the medium through which cultures survive? This begins to sound more essentialist than the notion it was designed to refute. In terms of the likely impact of the Commission for Africa's report, I don't believe that the sort of confusions about the notion of culture likely to be picked up by a nit-picking academic matter much. The incoherence is not the authors' fault but symptomatic of the ambivalent role played by the ambitious idea of culture itself.

My detailed ethnographic example has worked some well-worn themes in the recent ethnography of Africa: that the invention of tradition involves a mixture of self-conscious motivations in addition to the taken-for-grantedness of some aspects of the past; that the increasing prominence of chiefship in contemporary Africa responds to present as well as past politics; that the apparent distinction between citizens and subjects in African societies is largely chimerical: for where both chiefs and elected representatives are found, their activities will have been interlaced in all manner of complicated ways. The social logics of identification have to be understood in terms of such factors and not, in the terms of the *Report of the Commission for Africa*, as a prior state of culture somehow expressing itself through people's values, however much this understanding is founded in a liberal sense of cultural relativism. Chamba emphasis on their ethnic identity, the importance they attribute to their paramount chiefship, their attempts to play down religious divisions among themselves while living in a country that is increasingly becoming polarised on religious grounds, developed in a context of political and economic peripherality. Identity is the vehicle of their interest in belonging to the culturally diverse and unequal national state that is contemporary, cosmopolitan Nigeria.

Philosophical and policy arguments about cosmopolitanism per se, different though they may seem – and indeed are – in many ways, share a tendency to talk about cultures in ways that dislocate them from their social and political contexts. That they tend to ignore the social grounds of their own enunciation should, therefore, not come as a surprise. Social anthropologists may play a role in identifying the social logics of projects of conviviality of ethnographic subjects, whether these subjects are distinguished philosophers and sociologists, or politicians in the 'West', or peripheral citizens and subjects of African states. Current discussions of cosmopolitanism, I have suggested, remain indebted to their roots in European assumptions about the role of cultural homogeneity in the nation (the same assumptions that were exported to settler colonies in the Americas, Antipodes and parts of Africa with the imposition for longer or shorter periods of systems of racial segregation for indigenous or enslaved peoples). West Africa hardly saw settler colonialism. Its racial segregation was restricted to small groups of agents of colonialism (administrative, commercial, religious, and so forth) who were themselves not of single purpose. West Africa's efforts to actualise nation-states (created neither by local domination, on the model of European states, nor by immigrant domination, on the model of settler colonies) involve forms of national cosmopolitanism that are unprecedented in their complexity.

Notes

1. I carried out research in this area regularly between 1976 and 1990 but had not returned between then and a month-long visit in January 2006. I am grateful for small grants from the Central Research Fund of the University of London and the School of Oriental and African Studies which assisted my passage. An even briefer revisit to the *fondom* of Bali Nyonga in Cameroon at the turn of 2004–5 furnishes a very brief comparative observation later in this chapter.
2. In the event this happened on 18 February 2006, a couple of weeks after I had returned home. Strictly, installation is by the Governor, but local discussion tends to present the relationship as one involving traditional rulers rather than transient political figures.
3. I use Fulani rather than Fulbe in this chapter since all my references are to Fulani in Nigeria where this version of the ethnic term is in use.
4. Radio has been another exception thanks to a similar combination of deregulation, technological innovation and potential profitability (though the profits are less readily harvested from users in this case). In thinking about language policy, broadcasting and now majority/minority relations in African states, I am indebted to many years of collaboration with my SOAS colleague Graham Furniss (see, Fardon and Furniss 1994, 2000).

5. These figures are from www.mobileafrica.net and need to be treated with some caution: all Nigerian mobile telephone services are 'pre-pay' or 'pay as you go', and telephone numbers for which no credit is received have their right to receive calls blocked after a period that varies between providers. Where service is patchy, phone users who rely on remaining connected need more than one handset, or a handset adapted to take multiple SIM cards. This reasoning suggests there are likely to be fewer telephone users than there are telephone numbers. Against this, individuals' phones are rarely denied to needful kin or friends who have no phone of their own.

6. Jos, which once had a reputation as a peaceful middle-belt city, has become increasingly fractious in the past decade, especially in relations between predominantly Christian locals and Muslim, predominantly Hausa, incomers. A bumper sticker proclaiming Chamba identity might also be a passport out of the blood-lettings these have visited on one another (on this, see Higazi 2007).

7. With the single exception of Chamba Leko in Nigeria, who usually have a functional grasp of Chamba Daka, the majority Chamba language. Chambaness overrides language difference, but at the cost of Chamba Leko learning the majority Chamba language.

8. Although ideally it would be even-handed to do so, it is impossible, in the current state of our knowledge, to characterise a Chamba half millennium corresponding to the creation of the northern circum-Atlantic part of the world system.

9. I ask the reader to hear, because it would be unreadable if I wrote it on each occurrence that, given the recent crystallisation of current ethnic identities, by 'Chamba' I mean the people who would be Chamba by the time of twentieth-century written records.

10. These assumptions also underlay an emergent sense of the person with the consequence that the self-evidence of ethnic identity received corroborative echoes both from the encompassing nationalist process and from the en-compassed making of modern, ethnic and national subjects, who were also members of salvationist religions.

11. Itself a retarded affair because Ganye Chamba were in the Mandated and later Trust Territories created from German Kamerun, hence outside the main thrust of colonial development.

12. This was very evident during protests against police brutality that occurred during my visit in January 2006 and eventuated in a contingent of Nigeria's unloved Mobile Police being sent into Ganye.

13. I moderate my own erstwhile enthusiasm for polythetic definitions in this context: polythetic definition illuminates the use of complex terms in an

ethnographic sense, but this may be less insightful for those who are not users and hence cannot perform the auto-ethnography required.

14. While not wanting to leave myself open to the charge I just levelled at the eminent professor, neither do I want to clutter this chapter with references to an elderly literature some of which I surveyed twenty years ago (Fardon 1987).

References

Appiah, Kwame Anthony (2006), *Cosmopolitanism: Ethics in a World of Strangers*, New York/London: W.W. Norton.

Archibugi, Daniele (ed.) (2003), *Debating Cosmopolitics*, London and New York: Verso.

Beck, Ulrich (2002), 'The Cosmopolitan Perspective: Sociology in the Second Age of Modernity,' in Steven Vertovec and Robin Cohen (eds), *Conceiving Cosmopolitanism: Theory, Context, and Practice*, Oxford: Oxford University Press, pp. 61–85.

Breckenridge, Carol A., Sheldon Pollock, Homi K. Bhabha and Dipesh Chakrabarty (eds) (2002), *Cosmopolitanism*, Durham/London: Duke University Press.

Calhoun, Craig (2003), 'The Class Consciousness of Frequent Travellers: Towards a Critique of Actually Existing Cosmopolitanisms', in Daniele Archibugi (ed.), *Debating Cosmopolitics*, London: Verso, pp. 86–116.

Cheah, Pheng and Bruce Robbins (eds) (1998), *Cosmopolitics: Thinking and Feeling beyond the Nation*, Minneapolis: University of Minnesota Press.

Commission for Africa (2005), *Our Common Interest: Report of the Commission for Africa*, London: Commission for Africa.

Fardon, Richard (1987), 'African Ethnogenesis: Limits to the Comparability of Ethnic Phenomena,' in Ladislav Holy (ed.), *Comparative Anthropology*, Oxford: Blackwell, pp. 168–88.

—— (2006), *Lela in Bali: History through Ceremony in Cameroon*, Oxford: Berghahn, Cameroon Studies 7.

Fardon, Richard and Graham Furniss (eds) (1994), *African Languages, Development and the State*, London: Routledge, EIDOS Series.

—— (2000), *African Broadcast Culture: Radio in Transition*, Oxford: James Currey; Westport, Connecticut: Praeger; Harare: Baobab; Cape Town: David Philip.

Geldof, Bob (2005), *Geldof in Africa*, London: Century.

Higazi, Adam (2007), 'Violence urbaine et politique à Jos (Nigeria), de la période colonial aux élections de 2007', *Politique Africaine* (Special Issue, *Le Nigeria sous Obasanjo: violences et démocratie*, June) 106: 69–91.

Kahn, Joel (2003), 'Anthropology as Cosmopolitan Practice?', *Anthropological Theory* 3 (4): 403–15.

Mignolo, Walter D. (2002), 'The Many Faces of Cosmo-polis: Border Thinking and Critical Cosmopolitanism,' in Carol A. Breckenridge, Sheldon Pollock, Homi K. Bhabha and Dipesh Chakrabarty (eds), *Cosmopolitanism*, Durham: Duke University Press, pp. 157–88.

Ostien, Philip, Jamila M. Nasir and Franz Kogelmann (2005), *Comparative Perspectives on Shari'ah in Nigeria*, Ibadan: Spectrum Books.

Paden, John N. (2005) *Muslim Civic Cultures and Conflict Resolution: The Challenge of Democratic Federalism in Nigeria*, Washington DC: Brookings Institution Press.

Rapport, Nigel (2006), 'Anthropology as Cosmopolitan Study', *Anthropology Today* February 22(1): 23.

Vertovec, Steven and Robin Cohen (eds) (2002), *Conceiving Cosmopolitanism: Theory, Context, and Practice*, Oxford/New York: Oxford University Press.

13

Other Cosmopolitans in the Making of the Modern Malay World[1]
Joel S. Kahn

Introduction

This chapter explores the cosmopolitan possibilities inherent in existing processes of identity formation and systems of 'co-responsibility'[2] mainly among Malay-speaking Muslim peoples in parts of insular and peninsular Southeast Asia.[3] The issues at stake are not mainly theoretical ones but emerge in the concrete social context of a 'translocal'[4] arena that I call the modern Malay World, a term used here to refer to a fairly extensive region encompassing the relatively sparsely populated areas of intensive commercial exploitation by large number of immigrant peoples from the region, other parts of Asia (notably China and South Asia) and Europe. This arena encompasses the frontiers and borderlands both of the older Malay World and of the colonial and postcolonial states that formed across the region in the modern period. The discussion that follows focuses largely on one part of this modern Malay World, namely, peninsular Malaya. However, the analysis is premised on the assumption that, like the borderlands and frontier regions that are the sites of many of the ongoing ethno-religious conflicts in insular and peninsular Southeast Asia (for example in southern Thailand, the southern Philippines, West Kalimantan, the Moluccas, West Papua (Irian) and parts of Sulawesi), peninsular Malaya is best understood in the context of processes of state formation, nation-building, ethnogenesis, migration, religious reform and commercialisation that have taken place across the region as a whole.

Like other studies of identity formation in transnational contexts, mine is situated within the problematic of what Fine has called 'the new or actually existing cosmopolitanism' (Fine 2003). Interested in the possibility of new kinds of integrative/intercultural practice in a world that is perceived to have fallen victim to ethno-religious conflict and violence, the new cosmopolitans have proposed various revisions of the classical cosmopolitan synthesis. Of particular interest here are the new approaches to the question of the relationship between ethno-national identities and co-responsibilities on the one hand, and the cosmopolitan commitment to ethical and political universalism, on the other. Are the two mutually exclusive, or can they somehow be reconciled? Like others who have pursued these questions, I have been particularly interested in the potential impact of travel and specifically (trans)migration on the formation of new cosmopolitan sensibilities.

Migrants have constituted a significant proportion of the inhabitants of this Malay World since at least the latter decades of the nineteenth century. Many of these might accurately be labelled *trans*-migrant both because they have continued to move back and forth between homeland and frontier and because they have maintained ties with the places from which they came as well as solidarities with fellow migrants from these homelands. However, these peoples have come from a diversity of homelands in older centres of population in insular and peninsular Southeast Asia as well as farther afield, and do not therefore imagine themselves in their totality as a single people dispersed from a original homeland. The translocal 'community' of the modern Malay world, in addition to wage labourers brought from Java and different parts of British India to work on European plantations, also included large numbers of independent merchants, entrepreneurs, land speculators, smugglers, artisans and cash croppers. Unlike the peoples who are the object of much of the current discussion of transmigration, however, the dominant form of movement among them is not and never was mainly to or from the West, but instead to outlying and frontier regions in Sumatra, Borneo, southern Siam, the Mekong Delta and the southern Philippines and even, for those who moved for religious enlightenment, education and pilgrimage, the Middle East. Significantly, then, while the modern Malay World may be a product of globalising forces, these forces – economic, political, religious and cultural – did not emanate solely from the West.

The frontier and border regions that constitute this modern Malay World have thus been home to an extremely diverse population from the latter years of the nineteenth century. Places like peninsular Malaya, southern Siam/Thailand, the southern Philippines, the Mekong Delta, parts of Indonesian Borneo (Kalimantan) and Sumatra became sites of an incredible mix of languages, cultures, 'races' and religions, in large part a consequence of the very high rates of immigration and transmigration discussed above. These regions have also been home to adherents of all of the major world religions, as well as numerous 'indigenous', 'animist' and syncretic belief systems. Moreover this incredible diversity of peoples has been engaged in intensive interaction with each other. In different parts of this world indigenous or aboriginal peoples, local and immigrant 'Malays', Tais, Viet/ Kinh, Tagalog-speaking and other Filipinos, Chinese, Indians, Arabs, Europeans (Dutch, Spanish, Portuguese, French, English) and Americans (to name only the largest groups represented)[5] have interacted, intermarried, engaged in commercial transaction, and became caught up in modern state and nation building projects.

These political projects did not suddenly appear fully formed on the achievement of formal independence and the nationalist movements' rise to power. On the contrary, they have their origins in forms of colonial governance which were themselves aimed at the 'nationalisation' and 'pluralisation' of colonial societies (see Kahn, 2006). The communalist form of rule that characterises postcolonial Malaysia (sometimes labelled 'consociational'), rests atop, and depends for its legitimacy on, a society divided firmly along racial-cum-ethnic lines (Furnivall's 'plural society'). This mode of governance doubtless has its immediate origin in Malay elite opposition to a last-minute plan of the British to grant independence only to a government prepared to guarantee universal citizenship to all the residents of the peninsula, under the so-called Malayan Union proposals (see Harper 1996). Up to that point, however, British rule had itself fostered ethnic pluralism – that is, the rigid classification of all Malayans into a very limited number of racial-cum-ethnic 'communities', relationships among which were managed by, and only by, the state. This came along with a reasonable expectation that there would always be special protection of the rights of one of these communities, the so-called indigenous Malays.

With some exceptions, relations among Malaysia's three main ethnic 'communities' – the Malays, Chinese and Indians – have been more or less peaceful although tensions, particularly between Malays and Chinese, have periodically become apparent. Once was during the so-called Emergency when British forces fought against the Malayan Communist Party; another during a period of Malay-Chinese tensions, when Singapore briefly joined the Federation. A third moment of tension arose in Kuala Lumpur in 1969, when a significant loss of the Malay vote by the politically dominant UMNO (United Malays Nationalist Organisation) to the opposition PMIP (Pan-Malay Islamic Party) seemed to threaten Malay electoral dominance.

It is by no means certain that the credit for such interethnic accommodation can be entirely attributed to the successful management of ethnic relations by the state itself, although state officials are quick to claim the credit for it. Often astonishing rates of economic development, particularly from the mid-1980s, along with the prevalence of popular forms of cosmopolitan practice that I describe below, may have had more to do with Malaysia's ability to avoid the excesses of communal conflict and violence that have characterised similar circumstances in other parts of the world. Nonetheless, the relative (although certainly not Kant's perpetual) peace that characterises interethnic relations in postcolonial Malaysia, at least until recently, when the challenge of a new form of Islamism has changed the rules of the game, cannot be denied.

By contrast to Malaysia, particular zones within what I am calling the modern Malay World – notably southern Thailand and the Philippines, as well as different parts of 'outer island' Indonesia (in Kalimantan, Sumatra, Sulawesi, the Moluccas, West Papua) – are, or until recently have been, sites of intense ethno-religious conflict and violence, hence making the concerns of the new cosmopolitans especially urgent in these contexts. It is not so much the potential for clashes between nation-states, Kant's concern, as that between a diversity of ethno-religious communities, including national ones, that has been of primary concern to observers of this Malay World.

This concern seems peculiarly apt in the contemporary Malaysian context where the proponents of two competing visions, both of which may be plausibly deemed cosmopolitan in the classical sense, are locked in an intense contest for, among other things, the authority to regulate the public spaces where Malaysia's 'racially', ethnically and religiously diverse citizenry meet, interact, worship, conduct business and contend for political power. On the one hand, there are the self-styled secularists, liberals, modernists or moderates who, as the labels suggest, agitate for a form of universal citizenship and for culturally (and religiously) neutral public spaces within which citizens may participate freely regardless of sexual, ethnic or religious persuasion. On the other hand, there are proponents of what can be called the new Malaysian Islam whose power and authority have been boosted by almost three decades of Islamic 'revival' in the country.[6]

If the connections between Kantian cosmopolitanism and the principles of so-called 'good governance' advocated by the former are relatively straightforward,[7] that the new Malaysian Islam can also be deemed cosmopolitan in this sense may be more contentious, since there is a tendency these days to cast Islamic resurgence in a fundamentalist, traditionalist or even medievalist mould.[8] There are, however, features of contemporary Islamic belief and practice in Malaysia that give credibility to the cosmopolitan label, at the same time as they provoke some considerable anxiety not only in many non-Muslim Malaysians but in many self-styled modernist, liberal or moderate Muslims as well. These include the tremendous appeal of new Muslim organisations and projects to a younger generation hostile to all existing forms of social, political, intellectual and religious authority; the rejection of theological and legal tradition that follows from a commitment to the right of believers to make their own religious interpretations (*ijtihad*) based on their own reading the 'true' sources of the religion, i.e. the Koran and the Hadith; the aspirational character of the new Muslim sensibility which encompasses the view that economic success, the accumulation of wealth and consumption are not only not contrary to Islam but are positively enjoined by it; the keenness with which Muslims, and Muslim activists in particular, seek to make use of 'newly available media technologies [which] impinge on and possibly transform existing practices of mediation between the divine and the human world'; the emergence among Malaysian Muslims of new, delocalised community imaginations beyond 'the space of the ethnic group or nation', including a rather deterritorialised vision of an Islamic state; the tendency of Muslims to adopt hostile attitudes towards all kinds of cultural and artistic practice – including or even especially Malay cultural practices – that are deemed traditional; and, most notably for the concerns of this chapter, the desire of Muslim activists to engage not so much with 'politics in a more narrow sense' but with the project of producing a public culture that is deemed 'more Islamic'.[9] It is particularly this last aim, of Islamising the public spaces within which Malay and non-Malay, Muslim and non-Muslim, interact – a goal that many Muslims and non-Muslims alike understand in terms of the project of building a more Islamic state – that serves to distinguish the present project of Malaysian Muslims from that of proponents of the kind of statist Islam that was developed in the colonial period.[10] 'Islamic state' for many new Muslims is not necessarily conceived in terms of a territorially-based institutional apparatus of the same sort as existing nation states. For many it may instead imply merely a kind of Islamised state of affairs, although in striving to reach this goal the new Muslim manifests an eagerness for policing and surveillance using any means at his disposal, including the powers of the existing state (and, in rare circumstances, violence) which he may otherwise deride.[11]

Contrary, therefore, to those who see in this revival evidence of the rise of fund-amentalist traditionalism – some even speak of the return of 'medieval' religious outlooks – the new Malaysian Muslim is global in outlook, hostile to tradition in all its guises, universalising in aspiration, favourably disposed towards entre-preneurship, the accumulation of wealth and conspicuous consumption, and generally very comfortable with the latest technology. And because the religion is being conceived in universalistic/global terms, those behind the latest wave of Islamic reform may and do have ambitions beyond the championing of the rights of any particular ethnic group. Instead they aspire to establish what they take to be a genuinely universal Islamic 'state' in which the principles governing or regulating the spaces of interaction between Malaysia's multiplicity of ethnic and religious groups would be religious rather than ethnicised or secular. This aspiration to the universal on the part of those intent on the Islamisation of Malaysian society raises the question, therefore, of whether this new 'globalised' Islam might constitute an alternative to so-called Western and/or secular forms of cosmopolitan governance, the terms of the coalition among the diverse groups which make up national (or world) society being now somehow derived from the universal principles of Islam itself.

This is not to say that the new Islam in Malaysia is necessarily a progressive and inclusive force. To be sure it may have positive implications for its advocacy of social justice and its stated opposition to neoimperialism, cronyism and corruption and the sexual exploitation of women. Its global outlook together with its opposition to racial and ethno-national exclusion (which it labels *assabiya*)[12] may further support a view of the new Islam as more inclusive than existing communitarian ideologies, something suggested by one not unsympathetic observer in another context (Roy 2004).

On the other hand, many Malaysians do not see the new Islam as either cosmopolitan or inclusive because of its dedication to the suppression of what they take to be basic artistic, intellectual, personal, religious and sexual freedoms. Moreover, its impact certainly seems uneven. Apart from critical intellectuals, women's rights activists, artists and adherents of religions other than Islam, it may well be disadvantaged and otherwise marginalised Muslims (including especially non-Malay Muslims) who are more likely to be subjected to the attentions of the religious police than wealthier, particularly Malay, Muslims, who appear able to violate the new and stringent Islamic moral codes with a certain degree of impunity.

There are a number of reasons why this kind of universalising movement for religious reform may be transforming, but not actually doing away with, the ethnic and racial exclusions that operate at all levels of Malaysian society. Firstly, although all ethnic Malays are, by (constitutional) definition, Muslims, not all Muslims are Malay. As a consequence although Islamisation has at least the potential to create new solidarities that cut across the main ethnic divisions, at the same time, it contributes to a heightened awareness of the boundary between Muslims and non-Muslims. Secondly, because the process is being driven by those whose wish to reform existing Islamic belief and practice, Islamisation also has the potential to generate schisms among Muslims themselves – between those judged more or less pious or faithful to the 'true' tenets of (originary) Islam.[13] Thirdly, like a classical 'Western' universalist who sees in the world of human difference evidence of a kind of evolutionary ladder of peoples who are more or less capable of mature human reason (see Kahn 2001), the new global Muslim is prone to see in the differences among Malays (particularly between rural peasants and urban middle-class Malays) or between Malay and non-Malay Muslims evidence of a kind of historical insufficiency on the part of others who are constantly adjudged 'backward' or 'traditional' in their levels of religious enlightenment (Sloane 1999). And of course there is also a strong belief among many new Muslims in the existence of gender-based differences in the capacity for religious rationality which leads many of Malaysia's new Muslims to a view of a naturally based religious hierarchy between men and women.

If, then, the new global Islam is to be deemed cosmopolitan – and there are numerous parallels between Islamic and 'Western' universalisms that support such a conclusion – then, like classical Western so-called normative cosmopolitanism, it may generate its own exclusions.[14] And this, in turn, raises the question of whether liberalism or secularism or modernism, on the one hand, and Islamic universalism, on the other, are indeed the only real alternatives to the problem of finding properly cosmopolitan modes of social and political integration in a place like Malaysia. It is at this point that the debates among new cosmopolitans over the possibilities of grounded cosmopolitanism become especially pertinent to the Malaysian situation.

Grounding Cosmopolitanism

There is a supremely ironic moment early in the 1955 Malay-language film *Penarik Beca* (Trishaw Driver), although it is difficult to tell whether or not the film's star and director, the great P. Ramlee, intended it entirely as such. The moment serves to frame the apparent contradiction between essentialising ethnonationalist narratives of Malayness, on the one hand, and the presence of a plurality of ethnic groups in a soon-to-be independent Malaya, on the other, providing at the same time a way of thinking about the possibility of cosmopolitan harmony in an ethnically divided society.

The moment occurs during the scene that establishes the character of Ghazali, the villain and chief enemy of Amran, the film's hero, played by Ramlee himself. The scene works to institute an opposition between a pure, authentic Malay culture, on the one hand, and a Western or cosmopolitan sensibility, on the other. By linking villainy to Western cultural contamination, it presents an argument in favour of privileging the former over the latter, the film as a result offering a plea for the decolonisation of Malay culture. Ironically, however, this case for a purified Malay culture is being made in a vehicle (a film) that is an artefact of Western origin, and of an industry at the core of which was a multi-ethnic alliance of Chinese capitalists, Indian directors, and Malay actors.

The scene is set in a cabaret-cum-night club, the *Melati Joget*, where Ghazali and his friends are seen dancing a cha-cha with the hostesses. The music ends and Ghazali returns to his table and calls for another dance, this time a samba. However, one of the performers stands up to announce that the next act will instead be an 'exhibition' of *Inang Baru* to be performed by five male and five female dancers and a female lead singer backed by a small Malay orchestra. Before the exhibition is allowed to proceed, Ghazali shouts out his displeasure, insisting again on a samba. However, he is politely rebuffed and the exhibition goes ahead, much to the delight of the rest of the audience (although when the camera pans to Ghazali he is still looking angry and disgruntled).

When the *Inang* performance finishes, the band then strikes up a *Joget*, a faster Malay dance which, together with the *Inang*, formed the staple musical diet of those who flocked to the public stages staffed by dance hostesses in the large entertainment parks of Singapore, Penang and Kuala Lumpur in the postwar period (Mohd Anis Md Nor 1993: 2). When patrons get up to dance the *Joget*, Ghazali, still protesting, storms out angrily. In the subsequent scene of deserted streets outside the cabaret, Ghazali spots the heroine, Azizah, returning from a night out at the pictures with friends. Ghazali and his friends molest Azizah. She is rescued from their clutches by Amran, the trishaw driver, who appears on the scene and, having seen off Ghazali and his friends, takes Azizah to her home, marking the start of a romance that unfolds during the rest of the film.

This short scene stages an interesting argument about the nature and value of Malay culture. The dispute between Ghazali and the performers can – and was doubtless intended to be – interpreted as evidence of a conflict between Western musical and dance styles and authentically Malay ones. In this sense, the Ramlee film expresses the kinds of anticolonial and communal-national sensibilities that were reaching something of a high-water mark just when Ramlee, a Penang-born musician and singer of Sumatran descent, arrived on the Singapore scene to work for the Shaw Brothers film studio (Kahn 2006).

Nevertheless, familiarity with the conditions under which the film was made and the multicultural character of its audience accounts for a first level of irony, one that would have been fairly evident to the film's makers and audience alike. For although on the surface the film makes a case for Malay cultural authenticity, this particular film, and indeed most of the rest of the Ramlee oeuvre, is also the product of an interethnic coalition. The project of Malay cultural decolonisation, to which Ramlee's work was contributing, was being pushed along by a film industry controlled by Chinese capital and marketing networks, and with directors – many of whom had come from India, with influences from contemporary film-makers in Hollywood, Japan and India – who were under pressure from Malay nationalist intellectuals to produce suitable Malay language films. Moreover, by all accounts the Ramlee films were consumed by an enthusiastic audience of Chinese, Indians, Malays and Indonesians. While on the surface this particular version of the Malay nationalist narrative appears to suppress the pluralistic character of society in British Malaya, at another level its production would have been impossible without the harmonious cooperation of all the main ethnic groups that together made up that plural society. As such the film might be said to have provided a model for successful interracial relations that prefigures how these might operate in the postcolonial period. Indeed the so-called consociational model of governance carried forward into the postcolonial period was based on rather similar principles of interracial cooperation on the part of the political elites of each of Malaysia's constituent 'racial' communities.

Ramlee's cultural practice, therefore, appears to lend support to a view shared by many new cosmopolitans that, not only is there no necessary contradiction between cosmopolitan sensibilities on the one hand and ethnicity, cultural particularism and nationalism on the other, but that in fact cosmopolitan practice may always be 'grounded' or 'rooted' in the experiences of particular 'ethnic' groups.[15]

Does such a revision of classical cosmopolitan thinking actually offer a resolution of the cosmopolitan dilemma? On the face of things the argument that cosmopolitanism may be grounded or rooted in the historical, social, cultural and political circumstances of particular groups of social actors is an attractive one. Indeed one might want to go so far as to suggest that cosmopolitan practice may always and inevitably be inflected by the particular 'cultural' circumstances which give rise to it. Kant's critics have argued that even his own formulation of cosmopolitan right was 'grounded' in a particular set of 'cultural' presuppositions – masculinist, white, middle class – of what constitutes mature human reason.[16]

However, to say that cosmopolitanism must always be assessed as grounded practice may not be to say very much at all. It is by now a truism to argue that all social discourse and practice is inflected by the particular historical and cultural circumstances within which it takes place. If Kantian cosmopolitanism is no less 'grounded' in particular historical and cultural circumstances than any other, then surely 'groundedness' does not serve to distinguish between the intercultural sensibilities and practices of elites and masses. To speak, moreover, of a cosmopolitanism grounded or rooted in Malayness in this sense is to ignore a key aspect of the cosmopolitan project as classically conceived, and that is what is sometimes called its 'openness to the other'. This is perhaps at best a partial if not rather misleading way to describe classical cosmopolitanism's universalising, culture-transforming aspiration. Communities or their cultural forms may of course be said to be more or less tolerant of cultural difference. But to label this tolerance cosmopolitan is, I think, to miss the desire of those committed to cosmopolitan goals – not just to tolerate others but in fact to transform their own culture to such an extent that the division between us and them, between self and other, is bridged if not effaced altogether. In other words, cosmopolitanism in the strict sense can be seen as the aspiration to escape rather than embrace culture.

Malay Culture: Authenticity v Hybridity

I have spoken of the irony in the fact that the Malay nationalistic images that circulate in the films of the revered Malay actor and director P. Ramlee were in fact the product of a 'cosmopolitan' Malayan film industry involving representatives of all of Malaya's main ethnic groups. Yet there are problems with labelling such practices cosmopolitan. Can we speak of a grounded cosmopolitanism without falling back on essentialist notions of culture and without negating the universalising, culture-transforming aspirations of the classical cosmopolitan project?

A clue as to what such an alternative might look like is found, again, in the Ramlee film. For there is a deeper irony in the fact that a model for Malayan multiracialism based on an alliance among a diversity of culturally distinctive communities was being presented in a film that marked the directoral debut of P. Ramlee. In a film so concerned with advocating the decolonisation of Malay culture and celebrating Malay cultural authenticity, no pure or authentic Malay culture can be found. As the cultural practice of P. Ramlee himself clearly demonstrates, Malay musical and dance culture has never been anything but hybrid and continually in flux. If Ramlee's music and Ramlee's choreography is to be considered quintessentially Malay, as many of his admirers – and sometimes Ramlee himself – maintained (Ramlee 1971), then notions of Malay musical or choreographic authenticity must be completely abandoned. Malay music and dance have always been marked by borrowing and hybridisation, practices at which Ramlee was himself highly adept and with which he was entirely comfortable.

Inang and *Joget*, presented in the film as examples of authentic Malay musical and dance tradition, were themselves products of such hybridising practices, deriving as they did from older traditions of music and dance that were indigenised from Arabian sources, and subjected in turn to further outside influences – Portuguese, Latin and North American.[17] It seems particularly ironic, then, that *Inang* and *Joget* were being presented as indigenous alternatives to the cha-cha and the samba in the scene from *Penarik Beca*.

This is not to suggest, as some have, that this 'hybridity' is, on its own, cause for celebration. Establishing the hybrid character of Malay culture is not the same as establishing a cosmopolitan sensibility.[18] On the contrary, it is entirely possible to suppress hybrid origins in a narrative based on the presupposition of indigenous origins and cultural authenticity. This was precisely the case of the concept of Malayness that was developed in nationalist discourse from the 1920s when the meanings of *Melayu* were essentialised as they become directly tied to particular 'national' territories and spaces within them (Arrifin 1993; Milner 1995; Kahn 2006). Does this mean, however, that Malayness cannot provide a grounding for cosmopolitan practice and that we must abandon all notions of an embedded cosmopolitanism?

It is of course possible to read Kant's work as providing a philosophical grounding for forms of governance imposed by nation-states or international institutions to guarantee the rule of law and the principles of good governance based on universalistic principles. However, Kant may also be seen to be arguing instead for a different vision of a kind of grounded cosmopolitan practice, understood as practice towards 'coalition in a cosmopolitan society,' which may arise as much from culturally and historically embedded human individuals and groups who already exist successively side by side,' who cannot avoid 'constantly offending one another' and yet who recognise also that they 'cannot do without associating peacefully' (Kant 1974: 190–1). Is relative peace (certainly a better term than Kant's 'perpetual peace'), where it occurs, always the result of the creation of a deculturalised, secular public space by nation-states or confederations of states? Hardly. Instead a certain cosmopolitanism governs the practices of localised individuals and institutions, everyday social interaction between individuals and groups, popular cultural activities and forms of religious worship, patterns of economic interaction and cooperation, and the informal institutions of local governance in many different parts of the world. In other words, at the level of the popular[19] something like genuine cosmopolitan practice may take place, even though it may be 'contaminated' by the particularities of time, place and culture. This leads to a rather different understanding of the nature of cosmopolitan practice and how we assess that practice in the modern world, one which is both grounded and particularistic in origin, but universalising and culture-transforming in aspiration and effect.

As the critics of universalism have pointed out, the quest to transcend hetero-geneity or to build new communities away from the coordinates of bounded entities (whether imagined as national, ethnic, regional, or primordial) can never be genuinely culture-free. From this perspective universalising projects are inevitably also inflected by or captive to particularistic assumptions and tendencies, both because they emerge in particular historical and cultural circum-stances, and because when adopted by real people they become embedded, integrated, 'grounded' or 'indigenised' in particular cultures. All 'actually existing' universalisms are, so the argument goes, particularistic at the same time.

And yet to draw attention only to the particularlistic dimensions of universalism fails to come to grips with both the culturally disembedding aspirations of univers-alising projects and practices and their culture-transformative potential. To treat the will to universalise as just another kind of cultural essentialism is to fail to explain the culturally disembedding aims of would-be universalists. At the same time, to insist that universalism is inevitably embedded or indigenised within particular cultures is to fail to recognise the extent to which universalistic projects generate change in existing cultural values and assumptions. Projects and movements that aspire to the universal are not always best thought of as resulting only in a state of temporary cultural liminality or as short-lived 'rituals of rebellion' that will inevitably give way under the re-embedding forces of culture and tradition. If and when universalising tendencies are reabsorbed the result is not necessarily a return to the *status quo ante*. We need, in other words, to find ways of recognising that cosmopolitan practices will inevitably be both 'essentialising' and 'disembedding' at the same time.

This way of conceptualising cosmopolitan practice recalls Ernesto Laclau's critical approach to the universal. Modern societies, he maintains, are characterised by increasing fragmentation and a consequential escalation of communitarian demands, which are at the same time 'supplemented by discourses of *rights* ... which are asserted as valid independently of any context.' Are 'these two movements,' asks Laclau *'ultimately* compatible?' It would seem that they are not. However, if such competing communitarianisms are not compatible, then can we argue, again with Laclau, that this incompatibility might nonetheless be positive in so far 'as it opens the terrain for a variety of negotiations and a plurality of language games which are necessary for the constitution of public spaces in the societies in which we live?' (Ernesto Laclau in Butler, Laclau and Žižek, 2000: 7). The development of such 'language games' and 'public spaces' in a place like Malaysia suggests where we might look for the cosmopolitan possibilities in a social order characterised by competing universalisms.

From Peranakan Spaces to a Peranakan Malayness

In the Southeast Asian context, there has been a fairly long convention of distinguishing between the hybridised or creolised cultures of so-called *peranakan* (literally, locally born) Chinese and Indians from those of recent immigrants, on the one hand, and 'indigenous' Malays, on the other. However, speaking metaphorically, all who have resided in Malaysia are at least a little bit *peranakan*. Everyone has to one degree or another had to adapt linguistically and in a myriad of other even quite small ways to life as it is lived in the region. There are in fact no cultural beliefs and practices that are not hybrid. This is most clearly manifest in linguistic practice where, along with multilingualism, linguistic hybridisation of one kind or another affects all the languages spoken on the Peninsula. Questions of language standardisation and the establishment of national languages and mother tongues may exercise members of state educational bureaucracies and intellectual elites. Yet where are the linguistically and culturally pure practices in places like Malaysia and Singapore today? In fact, there are almost as many differentiated modes of language use and combinations of vocabulary and speech patterns of the various dialects of Malay, Chinese, Indian, and even English, as there are so-called native speakers of these languages. All are hybridised in one way or another. Even foreign birth is no guarantee of cultural purity. On setting foot in peninsular Malaya, even the foreign-born are immediately drawn into what remain distinctly localised modes and patterns of speech, conduct, social interaction, cuisine, leisure, and the like.

Far from being an exception to this rule, Malayness is a perfect illustration of it. As the example of Malay musical and dance culture suggests, hybridity exists at the heart of Malay culture and the Malay community, not just at its borders. Far from being the product of late-twentieth-century processes of cultural deterritorialisation, hybridisation actually preceded the rise of a nationalist ideology that sought to unite blood and soil. Malay was, in other words, a 'translocal' identity before it was a national one.

Although it will doubtless scandalise Malay cultural purists to suggest it, surely Malay culture, at least as it has evolved over the last century, is the ultimate *peranakan* culture. This is literally the case for the descendants born in Peninsular

Malaya of the large numbers of other Malays who came to the Peninsula from the late nineteenth century onwards from insular Southeast Asia. Although they were never called *peranakan*, the term is entirely appropriate to describe them. If, moreover, the meaning of *peranakan* is pushed beyond its literal meaning, to take in connotations of hybridity and cultural flux, then Malayness might be described as *peranakan* culture par excellence.

There certainly have been times when Malayness did seem to define not so much an identity in the ethno-nationalist sense, but a broad arena for interaction among a diversity of peoples in Peninsular Malaya and beyond. As I have argued elsewhere, in these interactions *Melayu* was not so much an identity as a way of describing the interstitial linguistic, economic, political and cultural spaces within which locally born and immigrant peoples interacted. One did not have to *be* Malay – indeed the very idea of Malayness as a permanent, fixed identity made little sense in such circumstances.

In the late 1940s some so-called radical Malay nationalists were making out a case for a national identity based on a similarly fluid and hybridised sense of Malayness. Such an identity was particular to local circumstance but sufficiently broad to include all locally born Malayans. There were even Malay activists and intellectuals prepared to accept non-Muslims into the Malay fold provided that in other respects they accepted local linguistic and cultural codes. Such a self-conscious hybridity, one can argue, characterised both the practice and convictions of many Singapore-based Malay journalists, writers and artists up to the mid-1950s, a development that was later suppressed through the implanting of the far more exclusive national narrative associated with UMNO hegemony.

Even today, this other, cosmopolitan Malayness operates at all levels of society both in Malaysia and in a much broader 'transnational' Malay World – a space across which merchants, entrepreneurs and religious reformers continue to travel, as they have been doing since the late nineteenth century, in search of commercial opportunity and religious knowledge or to evangelise. In the case of Muslim reformers this meant the pursuit of the Islamic obligation of *jihad*, whether interpreted as the duty to engage in missionising (*dakwah*) or in a more violent interpretation of the obligation.

This combination of economic, political and religious circumstances has generated, and continues to generate, the 'spontaneous transmigration' of Malay-speaking Muslim peoples along with immigrants from China, India, the Middle East and Europe into outlying areas of what is now Indonesia (especially Kalimantan), the Philippines, Cambodia and Vietnam (particularly Saigon and the Mekong Delta), and into border regions between Indonesia and Malaysia, Malaysia and Thailand, Malaysia and the Philippines, and so on. 'Malay' entrepreneurs and traders are now heavily involved in the commercial networks associated with the transborder trade in designer label and other textiles produced in factories in

Indochina and marketed across the region from Vietnam to Cambodia, Thailand, Malaysia and Indonesia, to give just one example of the forms taken by this commercially-inspired transmigration in the present.

This modern Malay World also encompasses spaces for interaction but, more importantly, for shared sentiments and practices across what is, at least in Malaysia itself, a hardening ethno-religious divide. Levels of interaction do not necessarily provide the best measure of the extent of such popular cosmopolitan practice. Interaction can, after all, be governed by exclusionary sensibilities, just as non-interaction may not preclude the recognition of shared attitudes and experiences. But the preservation of the peace quite clearly extends beyond the narrow circle of political, economic and cultural elites. Instead, it relies on the presence not of a single, culturally neutral public space but of a myriad of spaces and language games that together may be labelled *peranakan* Malay. In contemporary Malaysia and Singapore such spaces and language games are found in the fields of popular and youth culture; movements for cultural heritage; around academic institutions; in particular shopping centres and, interestingly, Western fast-food outlets; in popular shrines visited by people of diverse formal religious association; in the arts; in the *mamak* (Indian Muslim) foodstalls favoured by working-class Malays, Indians and Chinese;[20] in some of the NGOs that have flourished in recent years; even to some extent in the *reformasi* movement. One must not exaggerate the significance of such spaces. It is clear that they do not, at least in present circumstances, constitute the basis for an alternative counter-hegemonic narrative, universalising in intent, of the sort envisaged by Laclau.

Social transformations in Malaysia over the past 20 to 30 years have acted in different ways to destabilise the entrenched ethno-nationalist narrative of Malay peoplehood and the system of consociational governance with which it has been associated. In its place, universalising global 'Islam' and 'Western 'secularism' compete for the job of regulating the spaces of interaction between Malays and non-Malays, Muslims and non-Muslims. While both may justifiably lay claim to the mantle of classical cosmopolitanism, both also manifest the authoritarian and exclusionary tendencies inherent in modernist universalism in all its guises. The purpose of this chapter has been to show, using some of the insights provided by the new cosmopolitans, that an alternative more cosmopolitan future may already be prefigured in the social practices associated with an inclusive and hybrid Malayness that serves to govern social interaction in many parts of the modern Malay world. It remains to be seen whether they will continue to do so in the future.

Notes

1. This is a revised version of a paper originally delivered at the ASA Conference on Cosmopolitanism held at Keele University in April 2006. I would like to thank Pnina Werbner both for inviting me to attend the conference and for her suggestions on how the paper might be revised for publication.
2. The term is borrowed from Pnina Werbner (Werbner 2002: 121).
3. Ongoing research on Malaysia and the Malay World has been generously supported over the years by grants from the Australian Research Council. Some results of that research appear in a recent monograph (Kahn 2006), and the material in the body of this chapter is drawn from that. I would like to express my gratitude to the Asia Research Institute at the National University of Singapore, and particularly to its director, Professor Anthony Reid, for a visiting fellowship in 2004 during which much of the background work for the monograph was done.
4. I am using this term, rather than 'transnational' or 'global', for two reasons. Firstly, strictly speaking, 'transnational' would be an anachronistic label for a population that was 'translocal' before it was national. Secondly, I want to avoid the radical national–transnational distinction that appears in much of the current literature. National identities, although envisioned within national territories, do not arise automatically out of pre-existing, localised cultures, and for this reason cannot be so neatly distinguished from other translocal identifications.
5. As I have already suggested, many of these labels are problematic for the early period since they have acquired their contemporary meanings largely through their constitution in modern, nationalist discourse in the twentieth century
6. I use the term 'revival' here – although the accuracy of the term has been debated – to describe the processes of social Islamisation that have proceeded apace since the since the 1970s, when a plethora of Muslim evangelical (*dakwah*) organisations sprang up across the country, and those 'of the Islamist [sic] tendency began to impose a new definition of Malay identity which conflated it with Islam and being Muslim' so that Islam was 'elevated (via a number of discursive strategies and narrative devices) to the status of a transcendental signifier … that escapes the play of meaning/signification so as to create a closed and totalised discourse that forecloses any possibility of alternative interpretations/readings of the past.' One consequence of the revival has been that 'Malaysia's history has become a highly contested discursive terrain where the struggle to define Malay history and Malayness itself [is] fought' (Noor 2004b: 3). There is by now a very large critical literature on various aspects of Malaysia's Islamic revival. See, for example, Noor (2003, 2004a,

b), Hussin Muthalib (1993), Kamarulziam (1999), Lee and Ackerman (1997, 2002), Muzaffar (1987), Nagata (1984), Othman (1998), Sloane (1999) and Weiss (2004).

7. The argument that the problematic of good governance represents a resurrection of the central themes of Kantian cosmopolitanism is made most elegantly by Anthony Pagden (see Pagden 1998).

8. Recently, and rather surprisingly given that he recognises that the majority of contemporary so-called Muslim 'neofundamentalists' (Roy 2004) oppose violence and the individualistic interpretation of *jihad* that goes with it, Appiah has described this version of reformist Islam as 'counter-cosmopolitan' (Appiah 2006, especially pp. 138–40).

9. It is noteworthy that a rather similar constellation of features has been reported for developments in Islam in other parts of the world, including or even especially for locally born children of Muslim immigrants in Western Europe (see Roy 2004). Moreover, much of what has been observed in the new Islam in Malaysia has also been reported of other world religions. It is surely no accident, for example, that in describing some aspects of Malaysian Islam above, I have been able to quote directly from a paper summarising the activities of Pentecostal-Charismatic churches in Africa over the last couple of decades (Meyer 2004: especially pp. 461, 466). In describing these developments, both Roy and Meyer have occasion to speak of the emergence of new 'globalised' religious forms and identities, although it needs to be stressed that this 'globe' is not the same as the one imagined by those who speak of globalisation in (neoliberal) economic terms or in terms of the spread of a global culture of rights. Both uses speak to processes of de-territorialisation, de-nationlisation and de-culturation, but the globe looks a very different one to the new 'globalised Muslim'.

10. For the links between colonialism, modernisation and the development of statist Islam in Malaysia, see Yegar (1979) and Kahn (2006).

11. Although there are women among the new Muslim activists in Malaysia, the use of the male personal pronoun is deliberate here.

12. Literally tribal loyalty, but used more broadly to refer to nationalism and racism (Roy 2004: 245).

13. See Ricklefs (1979) for an illuminating discussion of the way in which earlier waves of Islamic reform in Southeast Asia actually resulted in greatly increased levels of fragmentation among Muslims themselves.

14. It is important to note in this regard that advocates of this new Malaysian Islam accuse their self-styled 'liberal' or 'secular' opponents precisely of 'excluding' Muslims in advocating that Malaysia be governed by a set of values of 'Western' origin. For the critique of Kantian cosmopolitanism as exclusionary despite its universalistic aspirations, see, for example, Mendes

(1992), Waters (1994), Hermann (1997), Harvey (2000) and Melville (2002). Such criticisms cannot be dismissed as mere anachronisms. An important new study of Kant shows that at least a version of the feminist critique was made by contemporaries of Kant and hence would have been familiar to him (see Zammito 2002). For the argument that universalism is always informed at the same time by particular cultural assumptions about human nature, see Kahn (2001).

15. See Appiah (2005, 2006), Fine (2003), P. Werbner (2002), R. Werbner (2002).

16. See Note 13 above.

17. For an important study of the 'cosmopolitan' history of Malay dance and of Ramlee's own adaptations of Malay dance to the demands of the cinema, see Mohd Anis Md Nor (1993). A discussion of the variety of foreign influences on Ramlee's music is found in Lockard (1997). One Malaysian musician and composer with whom I discussed Ramlee's music in the late 1990s informed me that there was absolutely nothing local, indigenous or uniquely Malay about the compositions themselves. Be that as it may, on listening to his music we can have no doubts that it is Malay, which says something important about the differences between Malay *culture*, on the one hand, and Malay *identity*, on the other.

18. For similar criticisms of the widespread tendency on the part of cultural theorists to equate hybridity with cosmopolitanism, see Friedman (1999) and Werbner (2002).

19. Popular is used here in a distinctive sense to distinguish this kind of practice from both exemplary or high modernism and so-called subaltern consciousness (see Kahn 2001).

20. I have relied for some of this on ongoing research by myself and others. Particularly important have been the findings of researchers like Sumit Mandal and Khoo Geik Cheng, much of it still unpublished.

References

Appiah, Kwame Anthony (2005), *The Ethics of Identity*, Princeton: Princeton University Press.

—— (2006), *Cosmopolitanism: Ethics in a World of Strangers*, New York/ London: W.W. Norton.

Butler, Judith, Laclau, Ernesto and Žižek, Slavoj (2000), *Contingency, Hegemony, Universality*, London/New York: Verso.

Fine, Robert (2003), 'Taking the "Ism" out of Cosmopolitanism: An Essay in Reconstruction', *European Journal of Social Theory* 6 (4): 451–70.

Friedman, Jonathan (1999), 'The Hybridization of Roots and the Abhorence of the Bush', in Mike Featherstone and Scott Lash (eds), *Spaces of Culture: City-Nation-World*, London/Thousand Oaks/New Delhi: Sage, pp. 230–56.

Harper, Timothy N. (1996), *The End of Empire and the Making of Malaya*, Cambridge: Cambridge University Press.

Harvey, David (2000), 'Cosmopolitanism and the Banality of Geographical Evils', *Public Culture* 12 (2): 529–64.

Hermann, Barbara (1997), 'Could it be Worth Thinking about Kant on Sex and Marriage?', in Louise Anthony and Charlotte Witt (eds) *A Mind of One's Own*, Boulder CO: Westview.

Hussin Mutalib (1993), *Islam in Malaysia: From Revivalism to Islamic State*, Singapore: Singapore University Press, pp. 53–72.

Kahn, Joel S. (2001), *Modernity and Exclusion*, New York/London: Sage.

—— (2006), *Other Malays: Nationalism and Cosmopolitanism in the Modern Malay World*, Singapore: Singapore University Press.

Kamarulnizam Anbdullah (1999), 'National Security and Malay Unity: The Issue of Radical Religious Elements in Malaysia', *Contemporary Southeast Asia* 21 (2): 261–87.

Kant, Immanuel (1974), *Anthropology from a Pragmatic Point of View* (translated, with introduction and notes by Mary J. Gregor), The Hague: Martinus Nijhoff.

Lee, Raymond L.M. and Susan E. Ackerman (1997), *Sacred Tensions: Modernity and Religious Transformation in Malaysia*, Columbia SC: University of South Carolina Press.

—— (2002), *The Challenge of Religion after Modernity: Beyond Disenchantment*, Aldershot: Ashgate.

Lockard, Craig A. (1997), *Dance of Life: Popular Music and Politics in Southeast Asia*, Honolulu: University of Hawaii Press.

Melville, Peter (2002), 'Kant's Dinner Party: Anthropology from a Foucauldian Point of View', *Mosaic* 35 (2): 93–109.

Mendes, Susan (1992), 'Kant: "An Honest but Narrow-Minded Bourgeois?"', in Howard Williams (ed.) *Essays on Kant's Political Philosophy*, Chicago IL: University of Chicago Press, pp. 166–90.

Meyer, Birgit (2004), 'Christianity in Africa: From African Independent to Pentecostal-Charismatic Churches', *Annual Review of Anthropology* 33: 447–74.

Milner, Anthony C. (1995), *The Invention of Politics in Colonial Malaya: Contesting Nationalism and the expansion of the Public Sphere*, Cambridge: Cambridge University Press.

Mohd Anis Md Nor (1993), *Zapin: Folk Dance of the Malay World*, Singapore: Oxford University Press.

Muzaffar, Chandra (1987), *Islamic Resurgence in Malaysia*, Petaling Jaya, Selangor: Penerbit Fajar Bakti.

Nagata, Judith A. (1984), *The Reflowering of Malaysian Islam: Modern Religious Radicals and their Roots*, Vancouver: University of British Columbia Press.

Noor, Farish A. (2003), 'Blood, Sweat and Jihad: the radicalization of the political discourse of the Pan-Malayan Islamic Party (PAS) from 1982 onwards', *Contemporary Southeast Asia* 25 (2): 200–233.

—— (2004a), 'The Challenges and Prospects for "Progressive Islam" in Southeast Asia: Reclaiming the Faith in the Age of George Bush and Osama ben Laden', *ICIP Journal* 1 (1): 1–30.

—— (2004b), 'The One-Dimensional Malay: The Homogenisation of Malay Identity in the Revisionist Writing of History in Malaysia', (http://phuakl.tripod.com/eTHOUGHT/onedimension.doc, accessed 29 March 2004).

Omar, Ariffin (1993), *Bangsa Melayu: Malay Concepts of Democracy and Community, 1945–1950*, Kuala Lumpur/New York: Oxford University Press.

Othman, Norani (1998), 'Islamization and Modernization in Malaysia: Competing Cultural Reassertions and Women's Identity in a Changing Society', in Rick Wilford and Robert L. Miller, *Women, Ethnicity and Nationalism: The Politics of Transition*, London/New York: Routledge, pp. 170–91.

Pagden, Anthony (1998), 'The Genesis of "Governance" and Enlightenment Conceptions of the Cosmopolitan World Order', *International Social Science Journal* 50 (155): 7–15.

Ramlee, P. (1971), 'Chara-chara Meninggikan Mutu dan Mempoerkayakan Muzik Jenis Asli dan Tradisional Malaysia Demi Kepentingan Negara', in Proceedings of Kongres Kebudayaan Kebangsaan (Seminar Seni Muzik), 16–20 August 1971 (unpublished manuscript), Za'aba Collection, University of Malaya library.

Rickleffs, Merle C. (1979), 'Six Centuries of Islamization in Java', in Nehemia Levtzion (ed.), *Conversion to Islam*, New York: Holmes & Meier, pp. 100–28.

—— (2004), *Globalised Islam: the Search for a New Ummah*, New York: Columbia University Press.

Sloane, Patricia (1999), *Islam, Modernity and Entrepreneurship among the Malays*, Basingstoke: Macmillan and NY: St Martin's Press.

Waters, Kristin (1994), 'Women in Kantian Ethics: A Failure of Universality', in Bat-Ami Bar On (ed.), *Modern Engendering*, Albany: SUNY Press, pp. 117–25.

Weiss, Meredith L. (2004), 'The Changing shape of Islamic Politics in Malaysia', *Journal of East Asian Studies* 4 (1): 139–74.

Werbner, Pnina (2002), 'The Place Which is Diaspora: Citizenship, Religion and Gender in the Making of Chaordic Transnationalism', *Journal of Ethnic and Migration Studies* 28 (1): 119–33.

Werbner, Richard (2002), 'Cosmopolitan Ethnicity. Entrepreneurship and the Nation: Minority Elites in Botswana', *Journal of Southern African Studies* 28 (4): 731–53.

Yegar, Moshe (1979), *Islam and Islamic Institutions in British Malaya: Policy and Implementation*, Jerusalem: Magnes Press/Hebrew University.

Zammito, John H. (2002), *Kant, Herder, and the Birth of Anthropology*, Chicago: University of Chicago Press.

14

On Cosmpolitanism and (Vernacular) Democratic Creativity: Or, There Never Was a West

David Graeber

At the tail-end of the eighteenth century those who called themselves democrats were, according to John Markoff, 'likely to be very suspicious of parliaments, downright hostile to competitive political parties, critical of secret ballots, uninterested or even opposed to women's suffrage, and sometimes tolerant of slavery' (1999: 661) – hardly surprising, for those who wished to revive something along the lines of ancient Athens.

At the time, outright democrats – men like Tom Paine, for instance – were considered a tiny minority of rabble-rousers even within revolutionary regimes.[1] Things only began to change in the first half of the next century. In the United States, as the franchise widened in the first decades of the nineteenth century, and politicians were increasingly forced to seek the votes of small farmers and urban labourers, some began to adopt the term. Andrew Jackson led the way. He started referring to himself as a democrat in the 1820s; within twenty years, almost all political parties, not just populists but even the most conservative, began to follow suit. In France, socialists began calling for 'democracy' in the 1830s, with similar results: within ten or fifteen years, the term was being used by even moderate and conservative republicans forced to compete with them for the popular vote (Dupuis-Deris 1999, 2004). The same period saw a dramatic reappraisal of Athens, which – again starting in the 1820s – began to be represented as embodying a noble ideal of public participation, rather than a nightmare of violent crowd psychology (Saxonhouse 1993). This is not, however, because anyone, at this point, was endorsing Athenian-style direct democracy, even on the local level. (In fact, one rather imagines it was precisely this fact that made the rehabilitation of Athens possible.) For the most part, politicians simply began substituting the word 'democracy' for 'republic', without any change in meaning. Myself, I suspect the new positive appraisal of Athens had more to do with popular fascination with events in Greece at the time than anything else: specifically, the war of independence against the Ottoman Empire between 1821 and 1829. It was hard not to see it as a modern replay of the clash between the Persian Empire and Greek city states narrated by Herodotus, a kind of founding text of the opposition between freedom-loving Europe and the despotic East. And of course changing one's frame of reference from Thucydides to Herodotus could only do Athens' image good.

When novelists like Victor Hugo and poets like Walt Whitman began touting democracy as a beautiful ideal – as they began to do soon after – they were not, however, referring to word games on the part of elites but the broader popular sentiment that caused small farmers and urban labourers to look with favour on the term to begin with – even back when the political elite was still largely using it as a term of abuse. The 'democratic ideal', in other words, did not emerge from the Western literary-philosophical tradition. It was, rather, imposed on it. In fact, the notion that democracy was a distinctly 'Western' ideal only came much later. For most of the nineteenth century, when Europeans defined themselves against 'the East' or 'the Orient', they did so precisely as 'Europeans' – not 'Westerners'.[2] With few exceptions, 'the West' referred to the Americas, considered lands as crude and uncivilised as the East was considered overly refined and decadent. It was only in the 1890s, when Europeans began to see the United States as part of the same coequal civilisation, that many started using the term in its current sense (GoGwilt 1995; Lewis and Wigen 1997: 49–62). Huntington's 'Western civilisation' comes even later: this notion was first developed in American universities in the years following World War I (Federici 1995: 67).[3] Over the course of the twentieth century, the concept of 'Western civilisation' proved perfectly tailored for an age that saw the gradual dissolution of colonial empires, since it managed to lump together the former colonial metropoles with their wealthiest and most powerful settler colonies while, at the same time, insisting on their shared moral and intellectual superiority, and abandoning any notion that they necessarily had a responsibility to 'civilise' anybody else. The peculiar tension evident in phrases like 'Western science', 'Western freedoms' or 'Western consumer goods' – do these reflect universal truths that all human beings should recognise? or are they the products of one tradition among many? – would appear to stem directly from the ambiguities of the historical moment. The resulting formulation is, as I've noted, so riddled with contradictions that it is hard to see how it could have arisen except to fill a very particular historical need.

If you examine these terms more closely, however, it becomes obvious that all these 'Western' objects are the products of endless entanglements. 'Western science' was patched together out of discoveries made on many continents, and is now largely produced by non-Westerners. 'Western consumer goods' were always drawn from materials taken from all over the world, many explicitly imitated Asian products, and nowadays, most are produced in China. The same, I think, can be said of 'Western freedoms'.

A World Systemic Perspective

In debates about the origins of capitalism, one of the main bones of contention is whether capitalism – or, alternately, industrial capitalism – emerged primarily within European societies, or whether it can only be understood in the context of a larger world-system connecting Europe and its possessions, markets and sources of labour overseas. It is possible to have the argument, I think, because so many capitalist forms began so early – many could be said to already be present, at least in embryonic form, at the very dawn of European expansion. This can hardly be said for democracy. Even if one is willing to follow the by-now accepted convention and identify republican forms of government with that word, democracy only emerges within centres of empire like England and France, and colonies like the United States, after the Atlantic system had existed for almost 300 years.

Giovanni Arrighi, Iftikhar Ahmad and Min-wen Shih (1997) have produced what is to my mind one of the more interesting responses to Huntington's famous argument that democracy, like other liberal values, is an exclusive property of Western civilisation. One of the most telling points: it was at exactly the same time as European powers came to start thinking of themselves as 'democratic' – in the 1830s, '40s and '50s – that those same powers began pursuing an intentional policy of supporting reactionary elites against those pushing for anything remotely resembling democratic reforms overseas. Great Britain was particularly flagrant in this regard: whether in its support for the Ottoman Empire against the rebellion of Egyptian governor Muhammed Ali after the Balta Limani Treaty of 1838, or in its support for the Qing imperial forces against the Taiping rebellion after the Nanjing Treaty of 1842. In either case, Britain first found some excuse to launch a military attack on one of the great Asian *ancien régimes*, defeated it militarily and imposed a commercially advantageous treaty; then, almost immediately upon doing so, swung around to prop that same regime up against political rebels who clearly were closer to their own supposed 'Western' values than the regime itself. (In the first case, this took the form of a rebellion aiming to turn Egypt into something more like a modern nation-state, in the second, an egalitarian Christian movement calling for universal brotherhood.) After the Great Rebellion of 1857 in India, Britain began employing the same strategy in her own colonies, self-consciously propping up 'landed magnates and the petty rulers of 'native states' within its own Indian empire' (ibid.: 34). All of this was buttressed on the intellectual level by the development around the same time of Orientalist theories that argued that in Asia such authoritarian regimes were inevitable, and democratising movements were unnatural or did not exist.[4]

Huntington's claim that Western civilisation is the bearer of a heritage of liberalism, constitutionalism, human rights, equality, liberty, the rule of law, democracy, free markets, and other similarly attractive ideals – all of which are said to have permeated other civilisations only superficially – rings false to anyone familiar with the Western record in Asia in the so-called age of nation-states. In this long list of ideals, it is hard to find a single one that was not denied in part or full by the leading Western powers of the epoch in their dealings either with the peoples they subjected to direct colonial rule or with the governments over which they sought to establish suzerainty. And conversely, it is just as hard to find a single one of those ideals that was not upheld by movements of national liberation in their struggle against the Western powers. In upholding these ideals, however, non-Western peoples and governments invariably combined them with ideals derived from their own civilisations in those spheres in which they had little to learn from the West. (Arrighi, Ahmad and Shih 1997: 25)

Actually, I think one could go much further. Opposition to European expansion in much of the world, even quite early on, appears to have been carried out in the name of 'Western values' that the Europeans in question did not yet even have. Engseng Ho (2004: 222–4), for example, draws our attention to the first known articulation of the notion of jihad against Europeans in the Indian Ocean, a book called 'Gift of the Jihad Warriors in Matters Regarding the Portuguese', written in 1574 by an Arab jurist named Zayn al-Din al Malibari, and addressed to the Muslim sultan of the Deccan state of Bijapur. In it, the author makes a case that it is justified to wage war against the Portuguese, demonstrating as he did so how they destroyed a tolerant, pluralistic society in which Muslims, Hindus, Christians and Jews had always managed to coexist.

In the Muslim trading ecumene of the Indian Ocean, some of the values elaborated by Huntiington – a certain notion of liberty, a certain constitutionalism,[5] very explicit ideas about freedom of trade and the rule of law – had long been widely cherished. Others, such as religious tolerance, were simply assumed – though in some cases they appear to have become values as a result of Europeans coming onto the scene – if only by point of contrast. My real point is that one simply cannot put any of these values down to the one particular moral, intellectual or cultural tradition. They arise, for better or worse, from exactly this sort of interaction.

I also want to make another point though. We are dealing with the work of a Muslim jurist, writing a book addressed to a South Indian king. The values of tolerance and mutual accommodation he wishes to defend – actually, these are our terms, he himself speaks of 'kindness' – might have emerged from a complex intercultural space, outside the authority of any overarching state power, and they might have only crystallised as values in the face of those who wished to destroy that space. Yet in order to write about them, to justify their defence, he was forced to deal with states and frame his argument in terms of a single literary-philosophical tradition: in this case, the legal tradition of Sunni Islam. There was an act of reincorporation. There inevitably must be, once one re-enters the world of state power and textual authority. And when later authors write about such ideas, they tend to represent matters as if the ideals emerged from that tradition, rather than from the spaces in between.

So do historians. In a way, it is almost inevitable that they should, considering the nature of their source material. They are, after all, primarily students of textual traditions, and information about the spaces in between is often very difficult to come by. What's more, they are – at least when dealing with the 'Western tradition' – writing, in large part, within the same literary tradition as their sources. This is what makes the real origins of democratic ideals – especially the popular enthusiasm for ideas of liberty and popular sovereignty that obliged politicians to adopt the term 'democracy' to begin with – so difficult to reconstruct.

The 'Influence Debate'

In 1977, Donald Grinde, an historian of the Iroquois confederacy (and himself a Native American and member of AIM, the American Indian Movement) wrote an essay proposing that certain elements of the US constitution – particularly its federal structure – were inspired in part by the League of Six Nations. He expanded on the argument in the 1980s with another historian, David Johansen (Grinde 1977; Grinde and Johansen 1991) suggesting that, in a larger sense, what we now would consider America's democratic spirit was partly inspired by the example of Native Americans.

Some of the specific evidence they assembled was quite compelling. The idea of forming some sort of federation of colonies was indeed proposed by an Onondaga ambassador named Canassatego, exhausted by having to negotiate with so many separate colonies during negotiations over the Lancaster Treaty in 1744. The image he used to demonstrate the strength of union – a bundle of six arrows – still appears on the Seal of the Union of the United States (the number was later increased to thirteen). Ben Franklin, present at the event, took up the idea and promoted it widely through his printing house over the next decade, and in 1754 his efforts came to fruition with a conference in Albany, New York – with representatives of the Six Nations in attendance – that drew up what came to be known as the Albany Plan of Union. The plan was ultimately rejected both by British authorities and colonial parliaments, but it was clearly an important first step. More importantly, perhaps, proponents of what has come to be known as the 'influence theory' argued that the values of egalitarianism and personal freedom that marked so many Eastern Woodlands societies served as a broader inspiration for the equality and liberty promoted by colonial rebels. When Boston patriots triggered their revolution by dressing up as Mohawks and dumping British tea into the harbour, they were making a self-conscious statement of their model for individual liberty.

That Iroquois federal institutions might have had some influence on the US constitution was considered a completely unremarkable notion in the nineteenth century when it was occasionally proposed, but when it began to get attention again in the 1980s, it set off a political maelstrom. Many Native Americans strongly endorsed the idea, Congress passed a bill acknowledging it; all sorts of right-wing commentators immediately pounced on it as an example of the worst sort of political correctness. At the same time, though, the argument met immediate and quite virulent opposition both from professional historians, considered authorities on the Constitution, and from anthropological experts on the Iroquois.

The actual debate ended up turning almost entirely on whether one could prove a direct relation between Iroquois institutions and the thinking of the framers of the constitution. Payne (1997), for example, noted that some New England colonists were discussing federal schemes before they were even aware of the League's existence; in a larger sense, opponents argued that proponents of the 'influence theory', as it came to be known, had essentially cooked the books by picking out every existing passage in the writings of colonial politicians that praised Iroquoian institutions, while ignoring hundreds of texts in which those same politicians denounced the Iroquois, and Indians in general, as ignorant murdering savages. Their opponents, they said, left the reader with the impression that explicit, textual proof of an Iroquoian influence on the Constitution existed, and this was simply not the case. Even the Indians present at constitutional conventions appear to have been there, officially, to state grievances, not to offer advice. Invariably, when colonial politicians discussed the origins of their ideas, they invoked Classical, Biblical or European examples: the book of Judges, the Achaean League, the Swiss Confederacy, the United Provinces of the Netherlands. Proponents of the influence theory, in turn, replied that this kind of linear thinking was simplistic: no one was claiming the Six Nations were the only or even primary model for American federalism, just one of many elements that went into the mix – and considering that it was the only functioning example of a federal system of which the colonists had any direct experience, to insist it had no influence whatever was simply bizarre. Here, they certainly had a point. Indeed some of the objections to the 'influence theory' raised by anthropologists seem so peculiar – for example, Elisabeth Tooker's objection (1988) that since the League worked by consensus and reserved an important place for women, and the US constitution used a majority system and only allowed men to vote, the one could not possibly have served as inspiration for the other; or Dean Snow's remark (1994: 154) that such claims 'muddle and denigrate the subtle and remarkable features of Iroquois government.' One can only conclude that Native American activist Vine Deloria was right to suggest much of this was simply an effort by scholars to protect what they considered their turf – a knee-jerk defence of intellectual property rights (in Johansen 1998: 82).

In other quarters, the proprietary reaction is much clearer. 'This myth isn't just silly, it's destructive,' wrote one contributor to *The New Republic*. 'Obviously Western civilisation, beginning in Greece, had provided models of government much closer to the hearts of the Founding Fathers than this one. There was nothing to be gained by looking to the New World for inspiration' (Newman 1998: 18). If one is speaking of the immediate perceptions of many of the United States' 'founding fathers', this may well be true. But if we are trying to understand the Iroquois influence on American *democracy*, then matters look quite different. As we've seen, the Framers did indeed identify with the classical tradition, but they were hostile to democracy for that very reason. They identified democracy with untrammelled liberty and equality, and insofar as they were aware of Indian customs at all most were likely to see them as objectionable for precisely the same reasons.

If one re-examines some of the mooted passages, this is precisely what one finds. John Adams, remember, had argued in his Defence of the Constitution that egalitarian societies do not exist; political power in every human society is divided between the monarchical, aristocratic, and democratic elements. He wrote that the Indians resembled the ancient Germans in that 'the democratical branch, in particular, is so determined, that real sovereignty resided in the body of the people,' but all three managed to convince themselves they were really the ones in charge. This he said worked well enough when one was dealing with populations scattered over a wide territory with no real concentrations of wealth, but, as the Goths found when they conquered the Roman empire, it could only lead to confusion, instability, and strife as soon as such populations became more settled and had significant resources to administer (Adams 1797: 296, see Levy 1996: 598, Payne 1997: 618). His observations are typical. Madison, even Jefferson, tended to describe Indians much as did John Locke, as exemplars of an individual liberty untrammelled by any form of state or systematic coercion – a condition made possible by the fact that Indian societies were not marked by significant divisions of property. They considered Native institutions obviously inappropriate for a society such as their own, that did.[6]

Still, Enlightenment theory notwithstanding, nations are not really created by the acts of wise lawgivers. Neither is democracy invented in texts, even if we are forced to rely on texts to divine its history. Actually, the men who wrote the constitution were not only for the most part wealthy landowners; few had a great deal of experience in sitting down to make decisions with a group of equals – at least, until they became involved in colonial congresses. Democratic practices tend to first get hammered out in places far from the purview of such men, and if one sets out in search for which of their contemporaries had the most hands-on

David Graeber

experience in such matters, the results are sometimes startling. One of the leading contemporary historians of European democracy, John Markoff, in an essay called 'Where and When Was Democracy Invented?', remarks, at one point, very much in passing:

> [T]hat leadership could derive from the consent of the led, rather than be bestowed by higher authority, would have been a likely experience of the crews of pirate vessels in the early modern Atlantic world. Pirate crews not only elected their captains, but were familiar with countervailing power (in the forms of the quartermaster and ship's council) and contractual relations of individual and collectivity (in the form of written ship's articles specifying shares of booty and rates of compensation for on-the-job injury). (Markoff 1999: 673n62)

As a matter of fact, the typical organisation of eighteenth century pirate ships, as reconstructed by historians like Marcus Rediker (2004: 60–82), appears to have been remarkably democratic. Captains were not only elected, they usually functioned much like Native American war chiefs. Granted total power during chase or combat, they were otherwise treated like ordinary crewmen. Those ships whose captains were granted more general powers also insisted on the crew's right to remove them at any time for cowardice, cruelty, or any other reason. In every case, ultimate power rested in a general assembly, that often ruled on even the most minor matters, always, apparently, by majority show of hands.

All this might seem less surprising if one considers the pirates' origins. Pirates were generally mutineers, sailors often originally pressed into service against their will in port towns across the Atlantic, who had mutinied against tyrannical captains and 'declared war against the whole world'. They often became classic social bandits, wreaking vengeance against captains who abused their crews, and releasing or even rewarding those against whom they found no complaints. The make-up of crews was often extraordinarily heterogeneous. 'Black Sam Bellamy's crew of 1717 was "a Mix'd Multitude of all Country's," including British, French, Dutch, Spanish, Swedish, Native American, African American, and two dozen Africans who had been liberated from a slave ship' (Rediker 2004: 53). In other words, we are dealing with a collection of people in which there was likely to be at least some first-hand knowledge of a very wide range of directly democratic institutions, ranging from Swedish *things* to African village assemblies to Native American councils such as those from which the League of Six Nations itself developed, suddenly finding themselves forced to improvise some mode of self-government in the complete absence of any state. It was the perfect intercultural space of experiment. In fact, there was likely to be no more conducive ground for the development of new democratic institutions anywhere in the Atlantic world at the time.

I bring this up for two reasons. One is the obvious one. We have no evidence that democratic practices developed on Atlantic pirate ships in the early part of the eighteenth century had any influence, direct or indirect, on the evolution of democratic constitutions sixty or seventy years later. Nor could we. While accounts of pirates and their adventures circulated widely, having much the same popular appeal as they do today, they would be about the very last influence that a French, English, or colonial gentleman would ever have been willing to acknowledge. This is not to say that pirate practices were likely to have influenced democratic constitutions. Only that we would not know if they did. One can hardly imagine things would be too different with those they ordinarily referred to as 'the American savages'.

The other reason is that frontier societies in the Americas were probably more similar to pirate ships than we would be given to imagine. They might not have been as densely populated, or in as immediate need of constant cooperation, but they were spaces of intercultural improvisation, largely outside of the purview of states. Colin Calloway (1997; cf. Axtell 1985) has documented just how entangled the societies of settlers and natives often were, with settlers adopting Indian crops, clothes, medicines, customs, and styles of warfare, trading, often living side by side, sometimes intermarrying, and most of all, the endless fears among the leaders of colonial communities and military units that their subordinates were absorbing Indian attitudes of equality and individual liberty. At the same time as New England Puritan minister Cotton Mather, for example, was inveighing against pirates as a blaspheming scourge of mankind, he was also complaining that fellow colonists had begun to imitate Indian customs of child-rearing (for example, by abandoning corporal punishment), and increasingly forgetting the principles of proper discipline and 'severity' in the governance of families for the 'foolish indulgence' typical of Indians – whether in relations between masters and servants, men and women, or old and young (Calloway 1997: 192).[7] This was true most of all in communities, often made up of escaped slaves and servants who 'became Indians' outside the control of colonial governments entirely (Sakolsky and Koehnline 1993), or island enclaves of what Linebaugh (1991) has called 'the Atlantic proletariat', the motley collection of freedmen, sailors, ships whores, renegades, Antinomians and rebels who developed in the port cities of the North Atlantic world before the emergence of modern racism, and from whom much of the democratic impulse of the American – and other – revolutions seems to have first emerged. But it was true for ordinary settlers as well. The irony is that this was the real argument of Bruce Johansen's book 'Forgotten Founders' (1982), that first kicked off the 'influence debate' – an argument that largely ended up getting lost in all the sound and fury about the constitution: that ordinary Englishmen and Frenchmen settled in the colonies only began to think of themselves as 'Americans', as a new sort of freedom-loving people, when they began to see themselves as more like Indians. And that this sense was inspired not primarily by the sort of romanticisation at a distance one might encounter in texts by Montesquieu or even Jefferson, but rather, by the actual experience of living in frontier societies that were essentially as Calloway puts it, 'amalgams'. The colonists who came to America were in a unique situation: having fled the hierarchy and conformism of Europe, they found themselves face to face with an indigenous population far more dedicated to principles of equality and individualism than they had hitherto been able to imagine. They proceeded to exterminate them, even at the same time as they found themselves becoming like them, adopting many of their customs, mores and attitudes.

Crucially, during this period the Five (later Six) Nations were something of an amalgam as well. Originally a collection of groups that had made a kind of contractual agreement with one another to create a way of mediating disputes and making peace, they became, during their period of expansion in the seventeenth century, an extraordinary jumble of peoples, with large proportions of the population war captives adopted into Iroquois families to replace family members who were dead. Missionaries in those days often complained that it was difficult to preach to Seneca in their own languages, because a majority were not completely fluent in it (Quain 1937). Even during the eighteenth century, for instance, while Canassatego was an Onondaga sachem, the other main negotiator with the colonists, Swatane (called Schickallemy) was actually French – or, at least, born to French parents in what's now Canada. On all sides, then, borders were blurred. We are dealing with a graded succession of spaces of democratic improvisation, from the Puritan communities of New England, with their town councils, to frontier communities, to the Iroquois themselves.

Traditions as Acts of Endless Refoundation

Thinking about the relation of cosmopolitanism and democracy, my particular concern has been to consider where democratic innovation – that is, the creation of new forms of egalitarian political decision-making – tends to come from. It seems to me that the most likely place to look for it is in what I refer to as 'cosmopolitan spaces', situations where people of a wide variety of backgrounds and drawing on a variety of traditions find themselves obliged to improvise some mode of collective governance outside the effective supervision of the state.

Democratic *practice*, whether defined as procedures of egalitarian decision-making, or government by public discussion, tends to emerge from situations in which communities of one sort or another manage their own affairs outside the purview of the state. The absence of state power means the absence of any systematic mechanism of coercion to enforce decisions; this tends to result either in some form of consensus process, or, at least in the case of essentially military formations like Greek hoplites or pirate ships, a system of majority voting (since in such cases the results, if it did come down to a contest of force, are readily apparent). Democratic innovation, and the emergence of what might be called democratic values, has a tendency to spring from what I call zones of cultural improvisation, usually also outside of the control of states, in which diverse sorts of people with different traditions and experiences are obliged to figure out some way to get on with one another. The creation of European colonial empires after 1492 had the indirect effect of creating many such cosmopolitan spaces along its fringes. Frontier communities whether in Madagascar or Medieval Iceland, pirate ships, Indian Ocean trading communities, Native American confederations on the edge of European expansion, could all be taken as examples. Obviously, such societies do not necessarily produce democracy. They might well produce forms of brutal tyranny. Often there is a mix of both. Nonetheless, this is where new democratic forms are most likely to come from.

All of this has very little to do with the great literary-philosophical traditions that tend to be seen as the pillars of great civilisations: indeed, with few exceptions, those traditions are explicitly hostile to democratic procedures and the sort of people that employ them. Governing elites, in turn, have tended either to ignore these forms, or to try to stomp them out.

At a certain point in time, however, first in the core states of the Atlantic system – notably England and France, the two that had the largest colonies in North America – this began to change. The creation of that system had been heralded by such unprecedented destruction that it allowed endless new improvisational spaces for the emerging 'Atlantic proletariat'; states, under pressure from social movements, began to institute reforms; eventually, those working the elite literary tradition started seeking precedents for them. The result was the creation of representative systems modelled on the Roman Republic that then were later redubbed, under popular pressure, 'democracies' and traced to Athens.

Actually, I would suggest that this process of democratic recuperation and refoundation was typical of a broader process that probably marks any civilisational tradition, but was then entering a phase of critical intensity. As European states expanded and the Atlantic system came to encompass the world, all sorts of global influences appear to have coalesced in European capitals, and to have been reabsorbed within the tradition that eventually came to be known as 'Western'. The actual genealogy of the elements that came together in the modern state, for example, is probably impossible to reconstruct – if only because the very process of recuperation tends to scrub away the more exotic elements in written accounts. Historians, who tend to rely almost exclusively on texts and pride themselves on exacting standards of evidence, therefore often end up, as they did with the Iroquois influence theory, feeling it their professional responsibility to act as if

David Graeber

new ideas really do emerge from within textual traditions. Let me throw out two
examples:

- *African fetishism and the idea of the social contract.* The Atlantic system
of course began to take form in West Africa even before Columbus sailed to
America. In a fascinating series of essays, William Pietz (1985, 1987, 1988)
has described the life of the resulting coastal enclaves where Venetian, Dutch,
Portuguese, and every other variety of European merchant and adventurer
cohabited with African merchants and adventurers speaking dozens of different
languages, a mix of Muslim, Catholic, Protestant, and a variety of ancestral
religions. Trade within these enclaves was regulated by objects the Europeans
came to refer to as 'fetishes', and Pietz does much to elaborate the European
merchants' theories of value and materiality to which this notion ultimately
gave rise. More interesting perhaps is the African perspective. Insofar as it
can be reconstructed, it appears strikingly similar to the kind of social contract
theories developed by men like Thomas Hobbes in Europe at the same time
(MacGaffey 1994; Graeber 2005). Essentially, fetishes were created by a series
of contracting parties who wished to enter into ongoing economic relations
with one another, and were accompanied by agreements on property rights and
the rules of exchange; those violating them were to be destroyed by the objects'
power. In other words, just as in Hobbes, social relations are created when a
group of men agree to create a sovereign power to threaten them with violence
if they fail to respect their property rights and contractual obligations. There
are even later African texts praising the fetish as preventing a war of all against
all. Unfortunately, it is completely impossible to find evidence that Hobbes was
aware of any of this: he grew up in a merchant's house, lived most of his life
in port towns and very likely had met traders familiar with such customs; but
his political works contain no references to the African continent whatsoever,
other than one or two references to Classical Greek sources.
- *China and the European nation-state.* Over the course of the Early Modern
period, European elites gradually conceived the ideal of governments that
ruled over uniform populations, speaking the same language, under a uniform
system of law and administration, and eventually, too, that this system should
be administered by an meritocratic elite whose training should consist largely in
the study of literary classics in that nation's vernacular language. The odd thing
is that nothing approaching a precedent for a state of this sort existed anywhere
in previous European history, though it almost exactly corresponded to the
system Europeans believed to hold sway (and which to a large extent, did hold
sway) in Imperial China.[8] Is there evidence for a Chinese 'influence theory'? In
this case, there is a good deal. The prestige of the Chinese government evidently
being higher, in the eyes of European philosophers, than African merchants,

-292-

some such influences could be acknowledged. From Liebniz's famous remark that the Chinese should really be sending missionaries to Europe rather than the other way around, to the work of Montesquieu and Voltaire, one sees a succession of political philosophers extolling Chinese institutions. In addition there was a popular fascination with Chinese art, gardens, fashions and moral philosophy (Lovejoy 1955) at exactly the time that Absolutism took form – only to fade away in the nineteenth century once China had become the object of European imperial expansion. Obviously, none of this constitutes proof that the modern nation state is in any way of Chinese inspiration, but considering the nature of the literary traditions we're dealing with, even if it were true, this would be about as much proof as we could ever expect to get.

So is the modern nation-state really a Chinese model of administration, adopted to channel and control democratic impulses derived largely from the influence of Native American societies and the pressures of the Atlantic proletariat, that ultimately came to be justified by a social contract theory derived from Africa? Probably this would be wildly overstating things. Still, it seems naïve indeed to assume it was simply a coincidence that democratic ideals of statecraft first emerged during a period in which the Atlantic powers were at the centre of vast global empires and an endless confluence of knowledge and influences, or that they eventually developed the theory that those ideals sprang instead exclusively from their own 'Western' civilisation – despite the fact that during the period in which Europeans had not been at the centre of global empires they had developed nothing of the kind.

Finally, I think it is important to emphasise that this process of recuperation is by no means limited to Europe. In fact, one of the striking things is how quickly most everyone else in the world began playing the same game. To some degree, as the example of al-Malibari suggests, it was probably happening in other parts of the world even before it began happening in Europe. Of course, overseas movements only started using the word 'democracy' much later – but even in the Atlantic world, that term only came into common usage around the middle of the nineteenth century. It was also around the middle of the nineteenth century – just as European powers began recuperating notions of democracy for their own tradition – when Britain led the way in a very self-conscious policy of suppressing anything that looked like it might even have the potential to become a democratic, popular, movement overseas. The ultimate response, in much of the colonial world, was to begin playing the exact same game. Opponents to colonial rule scoured their own literary-philosophical traditions for parallels to ancient Athens, along with examining traditional communal decision-making forms in their hinterlands. Material wasn't hard to find. As Steve Muhlenberger and Phil Payne (1993; cf. Baechler 1985), for example, have documented, if one simply defines it as decision-making by public discussion, 'democracy' is a fairly common phenomenon; examples can be found even under states and empires, if only, usually, in those places or domains of human activity in which the rulers of states and empires took little interest. Greek historians writing about India, for example, bore witness to any number of polities they considered worthy of the name. Between 1911 and 1918, a number of Indian historians (K.P. Jayaswal, D.R. Bhandarkar, R.C. Majumdar)[9] began examining some of these sources, not only Greek accounts of Alexander's campaigns but also early Buddhist documents in Pali and early Hindu vocabularies and works of political theory. They discovered dozens of local equivalents to fifth century Athens on South Asian soil: cities and political confederations in which all men formally classified as warriors – which in some cases meant a very large proportion of adult males – were expected to make important decisions collectively, through public deliberation in communal assemblies. The literary sources of the time were almost as hostile to popular rule as Greek literary sources,[10] but until around 400 AD at least, such polities definitely existed, and some of the deliberative mechanisms they employed continued to be employed, in everything from the governance of Buddhist monasteries to craft guilds, until the present day. It is possible, then, to say that the Indian, or even Hindu, tradition was always inherently democratic, and this became a strong argument for those seeking independence or self-rule.

These historians clearly overstated their case. After independence came the inevitable backlash. Historians began to point out that these 'clan republics' were very limited democracies at best: the overwhelming majority of the population – women, slaves, those defined as outsiders – were completely disenfranchised. Of course all this was true of Athens as well, and historians have pointed that out at length too. But it seems to me questions of authenticity are, at best, of secondary importance. Such traditions are always largely fabrications. To some degree that's what traditions are: the continual process of their own fabrication. The point is that in every case, what we have are political elites – or would-be political elites – identifying with a tradition of democracy in order to validate essentially republican forms of government; also, that not only was democracy not the special invention of 'the West', neither was this process of recuperation and refoundation. True, elites in India started playing the game some 60 years later than those in England and France, but historically, this is not a particularly long period of time. Rather than seeing Indian, or Malagasy, or Tswana, or Maya claims to being part of an inherently democratic tradition as an attempt to ape the West, it seems to me, we are looking at different aspects of the same planetary process: a crystallisation of long-standing democratic practices in the formation of a global system, in which ideas were flying back and forth in all directions, and the gradual, usually grudging, adoption of some of these ideas (and, occasionally, practices) by ruling elites.

Contemporary Parallels

Our habit of framing everything in terms of 'Western' ideologies, or 'Western' discourse (and then arguing over whether these are good or evil) tends to blind us, I think, to the actual historical dynamics at play – and certainly hobbles any ability to assess their real political implications. Let me choose just one example here: the Zapatista rebellion in Chiapas that began in 1994, and some of the scholarly arguments that have swirled around it.

The Zapatista base is made up of speakers of a variety of Maya languages – Tzeltal, Tojalobal, Ch'ol, Tzotzil, Mam – originally from communities tradition-ally allowed a certain degree of self-governance (largely so they could function as indigenous labour reserves for ranches and plantations located elsewhere), who had formed new, largely multi-ethnic, communities in newly opened lands in the Lacandon (Collier 1999; Ross 2000, Rus, Hernandez and Mattiace 2003). In other words, a perfect example of what I've been calling spaces of democratic improvisation: a jumbled amalgam of people, most with at least some initial experience of methods of communal self-governance, that found themselves in new communities outside the immediate supervision of the state. They were, too, at the fulcrum of a global play of influences, absorbing ideas from everywhere; they also, by their own example, had an enormous impact on social movements across the planet. The first Zapatista *encuentro* in 1996, for example, eventually led to the formation of an international network, People's Global Action (PGA) based on principles of autonomy, horizontality and direct democracy, stretching from India to Brazil. It was PGA, in turn, that put out the original call for the famous actions against the WTO meetings in Seattle in November 1999. The central principles of Zapatismo – the rejection of vanguardism, the emphasis on creating viable alternatives in one's own community as a way of subverting the logic of global capital – has had an enormous influence on participants in social movements that in some cases are at best vaguely aware of the Zapatistas them-selves and have certainly never heard of PGA. No doubt the growth of the Internet and global communications have allowed the process to proceed much faster than ever before, and allowed for more formal, explicit alliances, but I doubt this sort of ramifying effect is in any way unprecedented. In fact I suspect it represents a very common historical pattern.

Our accustomed terms of analysis and, even more, of debate, tend to make all this very difficult to see. This is true even of those who are nothing if not sympathetic. Let me take as an example an author whose position is in many ways quite close to my own. In a book called *Cosmopolitanism* (2002), literary theorist Walter Mignolo writes a response to an essay by Slavoj Žižek that argues that those on the Left need to temper their critiques of Eurocentrism in order to embrace democracy, since this is, he argues, 'the true European legacy from ancient Greece onward' (1998: 1009). A remarkable statement in and of itself, of course. Mignolo's response is to examine the cosmopolitanism of Vittoro and Kant (that Žižek praises), showing just how much their ideas took shape within, and indeed presumed, the brutal violence of European colonial empires. He then invokes Zapatista calls for democracy as a counter-example:

> The Zapatistas have used the word democracy, although it has a different meaning for them than it has for the Mexican government. Democracy for the Zapatistas is not conceptualised in terms of European political philosophy but in terms of Maya social organisation based on reciprocity, communal (instead of individual) values, the value of wisdom rather than epistemology, and so forth... The Zapatistas have no choice but to use the word that political hegemony imposed, though using that word does not mean bending to its mono-logic interpretation. Once democracy is singled out by the Zapatistas, it becomes a connector through which liberal concepts of democracy and indigenous concepts of reciprocity and community social organisation for the common good must come to terms. (Mignolo 2002: 180)

Mignolo calls this 'border thinking'. He suggests it might be taken as a model for how to come up with a healthy, 'critical cosmopolitanism', as opposed to the Eurocentric variety represented by Kant, or Žižek. It is an appealing idea. The problem though, it seems to me, is that in doing so, Mignolo himself ends up falling into a more modest version of the very essentialising discourse he's trying to escape.

First of all, to say 'the Zapatistas have no choice but to use the word [demo-cracy]' is simply untrue. Of course they have a choice. Other indigenous-based groups have made very different choices, and insist their own traditions of egal-itarian decision-making as having nothing to do with democracy.[11] The Zapatista decision to embrace the term, it seems to me, was more than anything else a decision to reject anything that smacked of a politics of identity, and to appeal for allies, in Mexico and elsewhere, among those interested in a broader conversation about forms of self-organisation – in much the same way as they also sought to begin a conversation with those interested in re-examining the meaning of the word 'revolution'. Second of all, and even more serious, Mignolo falls into the same trap as so many who invoke 'the West': comparing Western theory with indigenous practice. Just like an anthropologist who compares concepts derived from observing the way people act as 'dividuals' in India or Papua New Guinea with some philosopher's conception of 'the Western individual' (rather than from, say, the way people act in a church in Florence or New Jersey), he contrasts democracy as 'conceptualised in terms of European political philosophy' with democracy as it emerges in 'Maya social organisation.' But in fact, Zapatismo is not simply an emanation of traditional Maya practices. Its origins, rather, have to be sought in a prolonged confrontation between those practices and, among other things, the ideas of local Maya intellectuals (many, presumably, not entirely unfamiliar with the work of Kant), liberation theologists (who drew inspiration from prophetic texts written in ancient Judea), and mestizo revolutionaries (who drew inspiration from the works of Chairman Mao, from China). Democracy, in turn, did not emerge from anybody's discourse. It is as if simply taking the Western literary tradition as one's starting point – even for purposes of critique – means authors like Mignolo always somehow end up trapped inside it.

In reality, the 'word that political hegemony imposed' is in this case itself a fractured compromise. If it weren't, we would not have a Greek word originally coined to describe a form of communal self-governance applied to representative republics to begin with. It is exactly this contradiction the Zapatistas were seizing on. In fact, the contradiction seems impossible to get rid of. Liberal theorists (e.g. Sartori 1987: 279) do occasionally evince a desire to brush aside Athenian democracy entirely, to declare it irrelevant and be done with it, but for ideological purposes, such a move would be simply inadmissible. After all, without Athens, there would be no way to claim that 'the Western tradition' had anything inherently democratic about it. We would be left tracing back our political ideals to the totalitarian musings of Plato or, if not, perhaps compelled to admit there's really no such thing as 'the West'. In effect, liberal theorists have boxed themselves into a corner. Obviously, the Zapatistas are hardly the first revolutionaries to have seized on this contradiction, but their doing so found an unusually powerful resonance – this time, in part, because this is a moment of a profound crisis of the state.

The Impossible Marriage

In its essence, I think, the contradiction is not simply one of language. It reflects something deeper. For the last 200 years, democrats have been trying to graft ideals of popular self-governance onto the coercive apparatus of the state. In the end, the project is simply unworkable. States cannot, by their nature, ever truly be democratised. They are, after all, basically ways of organising violence. The American Federalists were being quite realistic when they argued that democracy is inconsistent with a society based on inequalities of wealth, since, in order to protect wealth, one needs an apparatus of coercion to keep down the very 'mob' that democracy would empower. Athens was a unique case in this respect because it was, in effect, transitional: there were certainly inequalities of wealth, even, arguably, a ruling class, but there was virtually no formal apparatus of coercion. Hence there is no consensus among scholars whether it can really be considered a state at all.

It is precisely when one considers the problem of the modern state's monopoly of coercive force that the whole pretence of democracy dissolves into a welter of contradictions. For example: while modern elites have largely put aside the earlier discourse of the 'mob' as a murderous 'great beast', the same imagery still pops back, in almost exactly the form it had in the sixteenth century the moment anyone proposes democratising some aspect of the apparatus of coercion. In the US, for example, advocates of the 'fully informed jury movement', who point out that the Constitution actually allows juries to decide on questions of law, not just of evidence, are regularly denounced in the media as wishing to go back to the days of lynchings and 'mob rule'. It is no coincidence that the United States, a country that still prides itself on its democratic spirit, has also led the world in mythologising, even deifying, its police.

Francis Dupuis-Deri (2002) has coined the term 'political agoraphobia' to refer to the suspicion of public deliberation and decision-making that runs through the Western tradition, just as much in the works of Constant, Sieyés, or Madison as in Plato or Aristotle. I would add that even the most impressive accomplishments of the liberal state, its most genuinely democratic elements – for instance, its guarantees on freedom of speech and freedom of assembly – are premised on it. It is only once it becomes absolutely clear that public speech and assembly is no longer, can no longer be, the medium of political decision-making, but at best an attempt to criticise, influence or make suggestions to political decision-makers, that they can be treated as sacrosanct.

Jurists, meanwhile, have long been aware that the coercive nature of the state ensures that democratic constitutions are founded on a fundamental contradiction. Walter Benjamin (1978) summed it up nicely by pointing out that any legal order that claims a monopoly of the use of violence has to be founded by some power other than itself, which inevitably means, by acts that were illegal according to whatever system of law came before it. The legitimacy of a system of law thus necessarily rests on acts of criminal violence. American and French revolutionaries were, after all, guilty of high treason according to the system of law under which they grew up. Of course, sacred kings from Africa to Nepal have managed to solve this logical conundrum by placing themselves, like God, outside the system. But as political theorists from Agamben to Negri remind us, there is no obvious way for 'the people' to exercise sovereignty in the same way. Either the right-wing solution (constitutional orders are founded by, and can be set aside by, inspired leaders – whether Founding Fathers or Fuhrers – who embody the popular will), or the left-wing solution (constitutional orders gain their legitimacy through popular revolutions) lead to endless practical contradictions. In fact, as sociologist Michael Mann has hinted (1999), much of the slaughter of the twentieth century derives from some version of this problem. The demand to simultaneously create a uniform apparatus of coercion over every piece of land on the surface of the planet, and to maintain the pretence that the legitimacy of these apparatuses derives from 'the people', has led to an endless need to determine who, precisely, 'the people' are supposed to be. Try to solve the problem using the coercive mechanisms themselves and terrible things are likely to happen.

> In all the varied German law courts of the last eighty years – from Weimar to Nazi to communist DDR to the Bundesrepublik – the judges have used the same opening formula: 'In Namen des Volkes', 'In the Name of the People.' American courts prefer the formula 'The Case of the People versus X'. (Mann 1999: 19)

In other words, 'the People' must be evoked as the authority behind the allocation of state violence despite the fact that any suggestion that the proceedings be in any way democratised is likely to be greeted with horror by all concerned. Mann suggests that pragmatic efforts to work out this contradiction, to use the apparatus of violence to identify and constitute a 'people' whom those maintaining that apparatus feel worthy of being the source of their authority, has been responsible for at least 60 million murders in the twentieth century alone.

It is in this context that I might suggest that the anarchist position – that there really is no resolution to this paradox – is really not all that unreasonable. The democratic state was always a contradiction. Globalisation has simply exposed the rotten underpinnings – by creating the need for decision-making structures on a planetary scale where any attempt to maintain the pretence of popular sovereignty, let alone participation, would be obviously absurd. The neoliberal solution of course is to declare the market the only form of public deliberation one really needs, and to restrict the state almost exclusively to its coercive function. In this context, the Zapatista response – to abandon the notion that revolution is a matter of seizing control over the coercive apparatus of the state, and instead proposing to refound democracy in the self-organisation of autonomous communities – makes perfect sense. This is the reason an otherwise obscure insurrection in southern Mexico caused such a sensation in radical circles to begin with. Democracy, then, seems for the moment to be returning to the spaces in which it originated: cosmopolitan spaces – the spaces in between. What forms it will eventually take, if it does manage to detach itself from the mechanisms of systematic violence in which it has been entangled, is something we cannot, at present, predict. But the endless elaboration of new cosmopolitan spaces, and the retreat of states in so many parts of the globe, suggests that there is the potential at least for a vast outpouring of new democratic creativity.

Notes

I'd like to thank Allain Caille, Francis Dupuis-Déris, Magnus Fiskesjo, Andrej Grubacic, Engseng Ho, Bruce Johansen, Sabu Kohso, Brooke Lehman, Lauren

Leve, Christina Moon, Stuart Rockefeller, Marshall Sahlins, Marina Sitrin, Pnina Werbner, and Richard Werbner for their help and contributions to this paper.

1. Thomas Jefferson for example is remembered as the founder of the 'Democrat-Republican Party' but in fact when founded in 1792 it was known simply as the 'Republican' party: the Federalists called its members 'Democrats' as a term of abuse, to associate them with mob rule, though later they came to adopt the term themselves.
2. One reason this is often overlooked is that Hegel was among the first to use the term 'the West' in its modern sense, and Marx often followed him in this. However, this usage was, at the time, extremely unusual.
3. At a time when German intellectuals were already locked in debate about whether they were part of the West at all. Another origin of the idea of 'the West' was in fact from Russian discourse, where Slavophiles defined themselves against it.
4. One should probably throw in a small proviso here: Orientalism allowed colonial powers to make a distinction between rival civilisations, which were seen as hopelessly decadent and corrupt, and 'savages', who insofar as they were not seen as hopelessly racially inferior, could be considered possible objects of a 'civilising mission'. Hence Britain might have largely abandoned attempts to reform Indian institutions in the 1860s, but it took up the exact same rhetoric later in Africa.
5. As Engseng Ho points out to me (personal communication, 7 February 2005), constitutionalism in the Indian Ocean tended to emerge first in ports of trade, where merchants, with or without the help of local rulers, were likely to create systems of commercial law, and written communal rules more generally, by mutual agreement. How it spread inland is an interesting question.
6. One of the most fascinating pieces of evidence produced by the pro-influence theory side is a text from 1775, during the writing of the Articles of Confederation, when colonial representatives negotiating with the Six Nations were willing to represent the entire idea of a colonial union as stemming from Canassatego's suggestion to their 'forefathers' some 30 years before. In other words they were perfectly content to speak of the federation as an Iroquois idea when speaking *to* the Iroquois – despite the fact that, if one simply considers texts written or public statements made by colonial politicians to European or settler audiences at the time, one would not be able to produce evidence they were still unaware that Canassatego had ever existed (Grinde and Johansen 1995: 627).
7. 'Though the first English planters in this country had usually a government and a discipline in their families and had a sufficient severity in it, yet, as if the climate had taught us to Indianise, the relaxation of it is now such that it

is wholly laid aside, and a foolish indulgence to children is become an epi-
demical miscarriage of the country, and like to be attended with many evil
consequences' (Calloway 1997:192).

8. Obviously the Chinese state was profoundly different in some ways as well:
first of all it was a universalistic empire. But Tooker to the contrary, one can
borrow an idea without embracing every element.

9. Rather than pretend to be an expert on early twentieth-century Indian scholarship, which I'm not, I'll just reproduce Muhlenberger's footnote:

> K.P. Jayaswal, Hindu Polity: A Constitutional History of India in Hindu Times
> 2nd and enl. edn. (Bangalore, 1943), published first in article form in 1911–13;
> D.R. Bhandarkar, Lectures on the Ancient History of India on the Period form
> 650 to 325 BC, The Carmichael Lectures, 1918 (Calcutta, 1919); R.C. Majumdar.
> Corporate Life in Ancient India. (original written in 1918; cited here from the 3rd
> edn, Calcutta, 1969, as Corporate Life).

10. I say 'almost' because Early Buddhism was something of an exception. The
Buddha himself appears to have been a supporter of governance by popular
assembly. The Brahmanical tradition though is uniformly hostile. Some of
the first political tracts in India contain advice to kings on how to co-opt and
suppress democratic institutions.

11. The Aymara movement in Bolivia, to select one fairly random example, chose
to reject the word 'democracy' entirely on the grounds that in their people's
historical experience the name has only been used for systems imposed on
them through violence. I am drawing here on a conversation with Nolasco
Mamani (who is, among other things, the Aymara observer at the UN) in
London during the European Social Forum 2004.

References

Adams, John (1797), *Defense of the Constitutions of Government of the United
States of America, against the Attack of M. Turgot in his Letter to Dr. Price*,
dated the twenty-second day of March, 1778. Philadelphia: W. Cobbet.

Arrighi, Giovanni, Iftikhar Ahmad and Miin-wen Shih (1997), 'Beyond Western
Hegemonies', paper presented at the XXI Meeting of the Social Science
History Association, New Orleans, Louisiana, 10–13 October 1996. Available
at: http://fbc.binghamton.edu/gaht5.htm.

Arrighi, Giovanni, Po-Keung Hui, Ho-Fung Hung and Mark Selden (2003),
'Historical Capitalism, East and West,' in Giovanni Arrighi, Takeshi Hamashita
and Mark Selden (eds), *The Resurgence of East Asia: 500, 150, and 50 Year
Perspectives*, London: Routledge, pp. 259–333.

Axtell, James (1985), *The Invasion Within: The Contest of Cultures in Colonial North America*, Oxford: Oxford University Press.

Baechler, Jean (1985), *Démocraties*, Paris: Calmann-Lévy.

Benjamin, Walter (1978), 'Critique of Violence,' in his *Reflections: Essays, Aphorisms, and Autobiographical Writings*, New York: Harcourt Brace Jovanovichl, pp. 277–300.

Calloway, Colin (1997), *New Worlds For All: Indians, Europeans, and the Remaking of Early America*, Baltimore: Johns Hopkins.

Castoriadis, Cornelius (1991), *Philosophy, Politics, Autonomy: Essays in Political Philosophy*, New York: Oxford University Press.

Collier, G. with Quaratiello, E. (1999), *Basta! Land and The Zapatista Rebellion in Chiapas*, revised edn, Oakland: Food First Books.

Dupuis-Déri, Francis (1999), 'L'Esprit anti-démocratique des fondateurs des 'démocraties' modernes,' *Agone*, 22: 95–113.

—— (2002), 'The Struggle Between Political Agoraphobia and Agoraphilia', paper presented at MIT Political Science Workshop.

—— (2004), 'The Political Power of Words: The Birth of Pro-Democratic Discourse in the Nineteenth Century in the United States and Canada', *Political Studies* 52 (1): 118–34.

—— (2005), 'Anarchy in Political Philosophy', *Anarchist Studies* 13 (1): 24–47.

Federici, Silvia (ed.) (1995), *Enduring Western Civilization: The Construction of the Concept of Western Civilization and its 'Others'*, London: Praeger.

Gilroy, Paul (1993), *The Black Atlantic: Modernity and Double Consciousness*, Cambridge: Harvard University Press.

GoGwilt, Chris (1995), 'True West: The Changing Idea of the West from the 1880s to the 1820s', in Sylvia Federici (ed.), *Western Civilization and its 'Others'*, London: Praeger, pp. 37–61.

Graeber, David (2001), *Toward an Anthropological Theory of Value*, New York: Palgrave.

—— (2005), 'Fetishism and Social Creativity, or Fetishes are Gods in Process of Construction', *Anthropological Theory* 5 (4): 407–38.

Grinde, Donald A. (1977), *The Iroquois and the Founding of the American Nation*, San Francisco: Indian Historian Press.

Grinde, Donald A. and Bruce E. Johansen (1991), *Exemplar of Liberty: Native America and the Evolution of Democracy*, Berkeley: University of California Press.

—— (1995), 'Sauce for the Goose: Demand and Definitions for "Proof" Regarding the Iroquois and Democracy', *William and Mary Quarterly* 53 (3): 628–35.

Hammond, Mason (2000), 'The Indo-European Origins of the Concept of a Democratic Society', in Martha Lamber-Karlovsky (ed.), *The Breakout: The Origins of Civilization*, Cambridge MA: Harvard University Press, pp. 57–62.

Ho, Engseng (2004), 'Empire Through Diasporic Eyes: A View From the Other Boat', *Comparative Studies in Society and History* 46 (2): 210–46.

Huntington, Samuel P. (1993), 'The Clash of Civilizations', *Foreign Affairs* 72 (3): 22–48.

—— (1996), 'The West: Unique, Not Universal', *Foreign Affairs* 75 (1): 28–46.

Johansen, Bruce (1982), *Forgotten Founders: How the American Indian Helped Shape Democracy*, Boston: Harvard Common Press.

—— (1998), *Debating Democracy; Native American Legacy of Freedom*, Santa Fe: Clear Light Publishers.

Levy, Philip A. (1996), 'Exemplars of Taking Liberties: The Iroquois Influence Thesis and the Problem of Evidence', *William and Mary Quarterly* 53 (3): 587–604.

Lewis, Martin W. and Kären E. Wigen (1997), *The Myth of Continents: A Critique of Metageography*. Berkeley: University of California Press.

Linebaugh, Peter (1991), *The London Hanged: Crime and Civil Society in the Eighteenth Century*, New York: Allen Lane.

Linebaugh, Peter and Marcus Rediker (2000), *Many-headed Hydra: Sailors, Slaves, Commoners, and the Hidden History of the Revolutionary Atlantic*, Boston: Beacon Press.

Lovejoy, Arthur (1955), 'The Chinese Origin of a Romanticism', in his *Essays in the History of Ideas*, New York: George Braziller, pp. 99–135.

MacGaffey, Wyatt (1994), 'African Objects and the Idea of the Fetish', *RES: Journal of Anthropology and Aesthetics* 25: 123–31.

Manin, Bernard (1994), 'On Legitimacy and Political Deliberation', in Mark Lilla (ed.), *New French Thought: Political Philosophy*, Princeton: Princeton University Press, pp.186–200.

Mann, Michael (1999), 'The Dark Side of Democracy: The Modern Tradition of Ethnic and Political Cleansing', *New Left Review* I/235, May–June: 18–45.

Markoff, John (1995), *Waves of Democracy: Social Movements and Political Change*, Thousand Oaks CA: Pine Forge Press.

—— (1999), 'Where and When Was Democracy Invented?', *Comparative Studies in Society and History* 41 (4): 660–90.

Mignolo, Walter D. (2002), 'The Many Faces of Cosmo-polis: Border Thinking and Critical Cosmopolitanism', in Carol Breckenridge, Sheldon Pollock, Homi Bhabha and Dipesh Chakrabarty (eds), *Cosmoplitanism*, Durham NC: Duke University Press, pp. 157–88.

Muhlenberger, Steven and Phil Paine (1993), 'Democracy's Place in World History', *Journal of World History* 4 (1): 23–45

—— (1997), 'Democracy in Ancient India', *World History of Democracy* site: http://www.nipissingu.ca./department/history/histdem/ (accessed 22 November 2004).

Negri, Antonio (1999), *Insurgencies: Constituent Power and the Modern State*, (trans.) Maurizia Boscagli, Minneapolis: University of Minnesota Press.

Newman, Michael (1998), 'Founding Feathers: The Iroquois and the Constitution', *New Republic* 199 (19): 17–21.

Ober, Josiah (1996), *The Athenian Revolution: Essays on Ancient Greek Democracy and Political Theory*, Princeton NJ: Princeton University Press.

Ostrom, Elinor (1990), *Governing the Commons: The Evolution of Institutions for Collective Action*, Cambridge: Cambridge University Press.

Payne, Samuel B. (1997), 'The Iroquois League, the Articles of the Confederation, and the Constitution', *William and Mary Quarterly* 53 (3): 605–20.

Pietz, William (1985), 'The Problem of the Fetish I', *RES: Journal of Anthropology and Aesthetics* 9: 5–17.

—— (1987), 'The Problem of the Fetish II: The Origin of the Fetish' *RES, Journal of Anthropology and Aesthetics* 13: 23–45.

—— (1988), 'The Problem of the Fetish IIIa: Bosman's Guinea and the Enlightenment Theory of Fetishism', *RES: Journal of Anthropology and Aesthetics: Journal of Anthropology and Aesthetics* 16: 105–23.

Quain, Buell (1937) 'The Iroquois', in Margaret Mead (ed.), *Cooperation and Competition Among Primitive Peoples*, New York: McGraw Hill, 240–81.

Rediker, Marcus (1981), 'Under the Banner of King Death': The Social World of Anglo-American Pirates, 1716–1726', *William and Mary Quarterly*, 3rd series, 38 (2): 203–27.

—— (1987), *Between the Devil and the Deep Blue Sea: Merchant Seamen, Pirates, and the Anglo-American Maritime World, 1700–1750*, Cambridge: Cambridge University Press.

—— (2004), *Villains of All Nations: Atlantic Pirates in the Golden Age*, Beacon Press: Boston.

Ross, J. (2000), *The War Against Oblivion: The Zapatista Chronicles*, Monroe, Maine: Common Courage Press.

Rus, Jan, Rosalva Aída Hernández Castillo, and Shannan L. Mattiace (2003), *Mayan Lives, Mayan Utopias: The Indigenous Peoples of Chiapas and the Zapatista Rebellion*, Lanham, MD: Rowman and Littlefield.

Sakolsky, Ron and James Koehnline (eds) (1993), *Gone to Croatan: The Origins of North American Dropout Culture*, Brooklyn, NY: Autonomedia.

Sartori, Giovanni (1987), *The Theory of Democracy Revisited*, Chatham NJ: Chatham House.

Saxonhouse, Arlene W. (1993) 'Athenian Democracy: Modern Mythmakers and Ancient Theorists', *PS: Political Science and Politics* 26 (3): 486–90.

Snow, Dean R. (1994), *The Iroquois*, London: Blackwell.

Sousa Santos, Boaventura de (ed.) (2005), *Democratizing Democracy: Beyond the Liberal Democratic Canon*, London: Verso.

Tooker, Elizabeth (1988), 'The United States Constitution and the Iroquois League', *Ethnohistory* 35 (3): 305–36.

—— (1990), 'Rejoinder to Johansen', *Ethnohistory* 37 (3): 291–97.

Trouillot, Michel-Rolph (2003), *Global Transformations: Anthropology and the Modern World*, New York: Palgrave.

Žižek, Slavoj (1998), 'A Leftist Plea for Eurocentrism', *Critical Inquiry* 24: 989–1009.

Section V
Demotic and Working-Class Cosmopolitanisms

–15–

Xenophobia and Xenophilia in South Africa: African Migrants in Cape Town[1]

Owen B. Sichone

'Mwana shenda atasha nyina kunaya ('He who doesn't travel claims his mother is the best cook in the world').

Zambian saying

The New Global Apartheid

A certain type of migrant, the sort that travels without passports or visas, without any particular place to go, making a new life wherever he or she happens to be, challenges the system of global apartheid and claims the right to move freely in defiance of the regime of state borders (erroneously referred to as 'national boundaries'). Such migrants also make it possible for others, who belong to the immobile 97 per cent of the human population that never leaves home, to connect with the world in ways that facilitate cultural, economic and other transfers. Sometimes their impact upon the host population belies their small numbers in dramatic and unpredictable ways. This chapter explores such demotic cosmopolitans and their personal mobility in post-apartheid South Africa. In doing so, it seeks to shift the focus in migration studies from labour migration and refugees to independent 'economic' migrants in order to argue that, despite the best efforts of postcolonial states to tie African people's mobility to labour contracts, some migrants have managed to venture beyond the confines of their nation-states, crafts or levels of education, in order to 'find a place for themselves' wherever they choose. Depending as they do for their success on personal relationships with fellow migrants and with individuals in the host country, these migrants are able to make journeys to unknown destinations which recall the migration myths of old, the sorts of journeys that in Zambian Bemba are referred to as going *iciyeyeye*.

There are, it seems, many ways of being cosmopolitan in a globalising world. While Hannerz (1990) has looked for cosmopolitan attitudes and competencies only among the elites 'wishing to engage with the Other,' Werbner (1999) describes working-class people who are open, and have the skills and experience to manoeuvre in different cultures as competently and effectively as the elites do. In addition, cosmopolitanism demonstrates (ibid.: 34) 'the possibility of belonging to more than one ethnic and cultural localism simultaneously.' And even though cosmopolitanism implies mobility, not all citizens of the world are mobile. Some people live transnationally while remaining rooted at home, waiting for the world to come to them and provide the opportunity for tapping into other human experiences. Indeed, demographers have shown that the great majority of the world's population has never crossed state borders. Modernisation has meant sedentarisation rather than steadily increasing mobility for most Africans, according to Cooper (2001). Even in countries affected by war and famine, internally displaced persons always outnumber international refugees. Thus Cohen's (1997: 162) observation that, 'In the age of globalization, unexpected people turn up in the most unexpected places,' while true, refers to a small minority. This mobile minority is not unique to the present era of globalisation: in Africa, myths of migration are as common as origin/creation myths. Many anthropologists who have worked in Africa have certainly been aware of strangers – like the Ndebele that Colson encountered in Tonga villages, or Banyarwanda that Robertson met in Uganda, not to mention the urban migrants that Lewis, Mayer, Mitchell, Epstein, and many others have studied – and much of what dominant anthropology currently grapples with concerning hybrid cultures and multiple identities was anticipated by colonial-era ethnography.

My interest in the lives of migrants in Cape Town was in part stimulated by newspaper stories on the plight of migrants in South Africa. But rather than look at refugees and asylum seekers, I sought out the free agents whose refugee status is mainly a means of gaining access to government documents, and who might otherwise be called 'economic migrants'. Although driven to migrate by economic and social pressures, such migrants do not leave home to look for a job on a farm or in the mines but set out to attain upward social mobility and create their own niche in the global market – what some migrants refer to as 'finding a place'. This concept is central to the management of shifting, flexible citizenships. As in swidden agriculture, movement is in stages and thus involves straddling sites of declining fertility that have supported life up to now, alongside still-hostile and unknown new sites of higher productivity and future abundance. Shifting citizenship, I argue in this chapter, involves gathering what is available in the new site and staking a claim to civic citizenship there in return for new labour.

In the face of widespread xenophobia towards stranger-newcomers in South Africa, it is remarkable that women more than men in Cape Town seem to be the ones who understand the practice of greeting strangers with gifts of food and, on the third day, to quote Julius Nyerere, giving them the hoe and inviting them to join in the cultivation of the land. Unlike their womenfolk, South African men appear to believe that more strangers means less resources for everyone.

These observations question the xenophobia survey by Crush and Pendleton (2003) that appears to show that there is no statistical difference between the attitudes of men and women or black and white South Africans. While not refuting the SAMP findings,[2] that survey fails to tell the whole story: at the local, micro-level, persons may make choices that contradict their own beliefs and attitudes. The perception of many migrants is that South African men are more xenophobic in practice than women.

Freedom of movement, like the free market, is a concept that the colonial world attempted systematically to undermine. The newly emerging global apartheid arguably generates the same kind of *laager* mentality that sees everyone who is on the other side of the border as an enemy. In South Africa both the new global apartheid and the old colonial legacy combine to create a system that goes against the country's liberal constitution with its Rainbow Nation ideology, framed by the makers of South Africa's miraculous transition from apartheid to liberal democracy.

Even though apartheid as official policy ceased to exist in 1994, when South Africa held its first democratic elections based on universal adult franchise, the colonial legacies still linger on in institutionalised spatial, social and mental divides. The society that separates people from one another despite living together historically for centuries is the unwelcoming land that thousands of immigrants encounter when they arrive in increasing numbers in the New South Africa. As many studies show, they find black and white South Africans generally hostile hosts.

Cape Town: A Cosmopolitan City?

South Africa, and especially Cape Town, is one of the 'most cosmopolitan regions of the world'. The Report of the Global Commission on International Migration (2005: 42) defines global cities as 'highly cosmopolitan urban areas that accommodate large numbers of migrants, allowing them to be well placed to capitalize on new trading, investment and business opportunities opened up by the process of globalization.' Cape Town was such a place centuries before jet travel and the Internet. This is revealed in an early study of the predominantly African township of Langa (Wilson and Mafeje 1963) that showed that Langa's extensive connections with the rest of the city made segregation impossible, even at the height of apartheid urban planning, because the different sections of the city operated within one social and economic system.

Despite having one of the most liberal constitutions in the world, South Africa has acquired a reputation for illiberal, xenophobic and nationalist attitudes and practices in both the state and civil society. Exposing the violence of the police and immigration officials against foreigners (especially foreign Africans) has become the specialisation of many a journalist and scholar, and xenophobia stories are now as frequent as murder and disaster reports. A Cape Town newspaper, for example, dedicated almost its entire 'Current Issues' page to three reports by the same writer on the plight of Nigerians in South Africa. He described how Nigerians must keep receipts for everything they buy because, when raided by police, they could be arrested for not being able to prove that their television, DVD player or microwave oven were not stolen.[3] Such reports tell South African and overseas readers that the manner in which the apartheid state mistreated Africans in the past may even be exceeded by the violent xenophobia that migrants and refugees face today. Thus, for example, black policemen are reportedly more cruel in their treatment of Nigerians than their white counterparts. This goes against the findings of the SAMP surveys which show levels of xenophobia to be evenly distributed in South African society, but confirms the stories I heard from Congolese and East Africans in Cape Town.

It seems to me that to be human (humane) is to be cosmopolitan. The truly isolated and xenophobic society is almost fictitious, but in South African history the hospitality of the host population has tended to be overshadowed by the violence and inhumanity of imperialism, which has over the long period of colonial rule and apartheid left a country with a very divided society.

With the end of official apartheid scholars shifted their research focus from labour migration to forced migration and refugee studies. The global anti-apartheid movement, similarly seeking new challenges, turned its gaze to the protection of human rights generally, and especially the rights of refugees and migrants – those who were being excluded from South Africa's new democratic society.

Cosmopolitanism and Cosmopolitans

Anthropologists like to think that they are privileged citizens of the world because they are able to manoeuvre their way in and out of foreign cultures, but they are not the only ones. The Bemba saying quoted at the head of this chapter suggests that in order to know that your mother is not the best cook in the world you should visit your other relatives, venture further afield and explore places beyond home. Your mother may well be the best cook in the world but unless you have something else to compare to, you will never know. Despite this value attached to travel, migration statistics suggest that only a miniscule proportion of the global population live outside their countries of birth. Thus, according to the Report of the Global Commission on International Migration (2005: 5), 'the number of international migrants has doubled in the past twenty-five years, although as a proportion of the world's total population it remains rather modest, at around three per cent.' Whether this is because they do not wish to travel or because they cannot afford to, we can safely say that for most countries, there has not been an exodus of locals or deluge of foreigners. In South Africa as elsewhere, the number of 'illegal aliens' or undocumented migrants is sensationally raised to more than 20 per cent of the population by security officials, without any evidence to back their claims. Needless to say, such alarmist guesstimates help to create a sense of siege in the local population and to fuel all manner of social conflict.

African migrants thus arrive to a hostile South Africa and need to develop the relevant skills and competencies to survive antagonistic officials, foreign cultures and street violence. Despite this, certain migrants, the sort that travel without passports or visas, without any particular destination, making new lives wherever they happen to be, not only challenge the system of global apartheid which uses the obsolescent regime of state borders ('national boundaries') to keep wealth away from the poverty-stricken. They also make it possible for others, who belong to the immobile 97 per cent of the global population that never leaves home, to connect with the world in ways that facilitate the transfer of culture and economic resources between centres and peripheries. Thirdly, they sometimes impact upon the host population in dramatic and unpredictable ways that belie their small numbers. The case discussed in this chapter celebrates the movement of one mobile African who is not the usual labour migrant or refugee camp fare of most social policy studies. Young men (women and children are also involved) like him are not normally recipients of state, UN agency or NGO humanitarian charity or relief. They enjoy their freedom of movement despite the best efforts of postcolonial and post-imperial states to limit it. What they depend on for their survival are personal relationships with each other and with individuals in the host country.

The numerous mass migrations of pre-colonial Africa provide us with a model – with some idea of how clan, kingdom, territorial and other borders were crossed in the past by people who embarked on one-way journeys to unknown destinations, or what in Zambian Bemba is referred to as *iciyeyeye*. Among policy makers it is still believed that people leave home to seek work as employees. Even the report of the Global Commission on Migration, with its very comprehensive treatment of the phenomenon of migration, nevertheless attaches most attention to labour migrants and their rights. Needless to say, migrants who are not refugees or labourers have little sympathy from the authorities. Nevertheless they do exist. In a song made popular by Alick Nkhata, *Kalindawalo ni mfumu*, the migrant sings: *Napita nkaone njanji ningafe ko saiona*, 'I am off to see the railway line lest I die without setting eyes on it' (*The Alick Nkhata 'Album Shalapo'*, issued on RETRO4CD). This goes beyond the bright lights or rite-of-passage theory of migration, based on pull factors, in that it defines a world in which the freedom of movement is highly valued and this freedom is seriously compromised by the border myths of the tribal authority, colony or modern nation-state. In theory, in the past tribute-paying was voluntary, and not even the martial regimes of the Nguni kingdoms could subject everyone to their rule by force. Subjects could always deprive kings of tribute by going *iciyeye* and not looking back. The modern colonial state fenced in its subjects and could thus rule them whether they liked it or not. In a similar way, state-sanctioned capitalism in South Africa does not free (African) people from feudal immobility but, on the contrary, creates and enforces a system of regulated labour migration where some people die without seeing the railway because they cannot obtain the necessary papers. The following case, however, is of an individual who has refused to be denied his freedom of movement and has become a citizen of the world against many different odds.

The Case of the Somali Nomad

This extended case study of a Somali man's wanderings is not meant to be representative. Rather the aim is to show the skills and resources that are deployed when migrants are away from home. Ishmael had refugee status, was married to a Cape Town woman – and thus welcomed to the city – and was well-established as a street vendor on Durban Road, Mowbray, when Pascal introduced him to me as a fellow East African. During the course of our discussions I provided him with information about refugee rights, visas and international travel, which he used to relocate to Britain. His stories show one thing that my other case studies have confirmed – that even in the most hostile societies, there are always those who take it upon themselves to help others. It would be impossible to travel or do fieldwork were it not for the hospitality that the people we study give to others.

Travels in East Africa

Ishmael's grandfather was a well-to-do businessman in British Somaliland who traded in camels and other livestock. He married a woman from the Ogaden and during the inter-clan wars of the late 1940s (Lewis 1980: 135) lost his entire herd of more than 200 camels. His affines (some people do indeed marry their enemies!) who were from a rival clan, spared his life but took away all his animals. He relocated to the Kenya borderlands with what little property he still had. Ishmael's father, Ahmed, was fourteen when they crossed into Kenya. Ironically East Africans seem to have enjoyed greater freedom of movement before and during the colonial period than they do today. There was no real border at the time as East Africa was all-British territory. The same could be said for other parts of the continent.

At the age of sixteen, Ishmael told me, Ahmed joined the King's African Rifles and was posted to Somaliland where he acted as interpreter for what must have been a Kiswahili-speaking contingent. At the age of eighteen he got married and was transferred to Tanganyika where he worked for five years. When the country became independent, Ahmed left the army and became a trader. The East African units of the King's African Rifles were recruited from all the different British colonies and were deployed on counter insurgency duties in various countries. I did not establish whether Ishmael's father retired or was required to make way for locals, but it seems the Africanisation process was mainly concerned with the replacement of British officers and that other Africans continued to serve as Tanzanian citizens (see Tanzania People's Defence Forces, 1994). Ahmed probably chose to leave the military to start his own business for he did not return to Kenya but remained in Tanzania for a while. Ishmael's claim to Tanzanian citizenship did not become important until much later in his life when he needed to get a Tanzanian passport in order to remain mobile and participate in the global labour market, having lost his Somali citizenship and travel documents in circumstances that will be explained later.

According to Ishmael, after living in Tanzania for a while Ahmed received word from his wife's brother, who had made a fortune trading in the Arab countries, that he wanted his sister to return home to Somalia, as they had not seen each other since she was a young girl. She persuaded Ahmed to sell his business in Tanzania and the family set off to start afresh in their fatherland. When they got to Kenya, however, Ahmed's sister, who was living there, pleaded with him not to leave her alone in Kenya, as they were the last two siblings. 'We must bury each other,' she told him. Much to his wife's displeasure, Ahmed decided not to proceed to Somalia and his family settled in Kenya.

In 1966, secessionist skirmishes broke out on the Kenya borderlands and Kenyan Somalis became suspects in the eyes of their government and of their fellow Kenyan citizens, who considered them a fifth column for the feared Greater Somalia project. Other countries in the Horn of Africa, including Kenya, Ethiopia and Djibouti, were all threatened by the Greater Somalia claims of the regime in Mogadishu, but with the Zambian president Kaunda acting as mediator between Kenya and Somalia, dangerous civil strife was prevented. Even after making peace, however, Kenyan Somalis continued to suffer humiliation at the hands of the Kenyan army, which, according to Ishmael, they have not forgotten.

While he was raising his children as Kenyans, Ishmael told me, Ahmed encouraged them to take their education seriously as a way of giving them a better chance in life, given the decline of pastoralism and because he had seen how other young Kenyans were benefiting from the opportunities presented by independence. Ishmael did not, however, make use of the opportunities and now continually laments not having followed his father's advice. Expelled from one school after another, he squandered the school fees his father gave him on women and mirra, and caused all sorts of problems for his family. Finally, his father gave up and left him to his own devices at the age of eighteen, by which time he had managed to reach up to standard seven in school.

In 1977 Ishmael set off for Somalia to join Siad Barre's army, which was expanding rapidly while the Western Somali Liberation Front was pushing the Ethiopian army out of the Ogaden (Lewis 1994: 223). Ishmael's calculation was that the secondary education he had received in Kenya was enough to earn him a commission in the Somali army. His journey to Mogadishu did not go according to plan, however. By the time he reached Mogadishu his money had run out. The older travelling companion who had kept the money for him appeared to have swindled the inexperienced young traveller. Finding himself in Somalia for the first time in his life and without a penny in his pocket, he was saved by members of his clan who provided for him and gave him enough money to return to Kenya.

Ishmael's life after this took him to Saudi Arabia where he lived for many years. I was not able to discuss what happened to him there except that he earned a lot of money working as a driver but wasted it all on mirra and holidays in Bangkok. His easy life came to a sudden end when he accidentally killed a pedestrian and was imprisoned after failing to pay the $20,000 blood money which the (Islamic) courts demanded. He was rescued from prison by a Saudi prince, the governor of Jeddah, who paid the fines of all poor people in prison to mark a special religious festival. According to Ishmael, the reason why his Isaq clan did not come to his rescue on this occasion was because Ishmael had cut himself off from them when he was living well, and had not been paying his contribution to the clan emergency fund. The elders of the group took this opportunity to show him that it was precisely to cover such contingencies that they collected subscriptions, and to punish him for being a bad example.

When he was released from jail, he could not return to work as his Saudi work permit had expired. His papers appear to have become mixed up during this period for he was deported to or through Eritrea. Using the support of his clan-family in Somalia, he made his way back to Kenya to join his mother and sisters. Returning from Saudi Arabia penniless was embarrassing, so he tried to get back to the Gulf as soon as he could but failed to obtain a passport in Somalia and in Kenya. It was at this point that he decided to use his birth certificate to claim his Tanzanian citizenship.

We shall skip Ishmael's adventures in Tanzania, Zambia, Malawi, Botswana and Mozambique. Suffice it to say that he failed to get a Tanzanian passport but managed to live in the country and engage in cross-border trade, apparently without travel or residence documents. We shall take up his story with his bid to leave South Africa for the USA in 2001.

The role of patrilineal kinship in Somali identity is a crucial one. Not only does it define the place of everybody in relation to others, it also provides an alternative citizenship to that of the nation-state – as Ishmael's experience in many countries repeatedly showed. Somali, and other African migrants in Cape Town, do not exist as individuals but always as holders of various group identities. Any one person has obligations to several other people and loyalties divided between Greater Somalia, different states within the dismembered Greater Somalia, states outside Greater Somalia that they find themselves living in, as well as clans and sub-clans. Full citizenship is thus an ideal never achieved, whether they are in their homeland or in a foreign country. This is not peculiar to the Somali as most Africans have strong loyalties to moral and political communities other than the nation-state. Although Somali are entitled to and obtain the support of the corporate clan network this is not always available and they thus have to develop relationships outside of their clans, learn new languages and adopt a cosmopolitan identity to supplement their Somali nationality.

An Isaq Man in Cape Town

Ishmael did not come to South Africa to stay. His plan was always to travel back to the Middle East, join his brother in Sweden or go to the USA. Nevertheless, he married a Cape Town woman, obtained South African residency and put a good deal of effort into his petty trading. He remained in contact with his family at home in Kenya, where his mother lives, and regularly phoned other members of the family across the world.

One day he told me that the South African authorities had given him a travel document. Earlier, I had informed him that as a resident married to a South African he could if he chose apply for citizenship, which would entitle him to a passport. He had misunderstood me and immediately rushed to the Home Affairs Department to apply for a South African passport. His request had apparently quite confused the officials in the Cape Town office who had phoned to Pretoria for advice. Finally, it was agreed that he could not get a passport but was given a temporary travel document.

He was pleased that it did not refer to him as a refugee. Although he was a South African resident and had never legally been a refugee except in order to facilitate his own movement across borders, it was the most important identity he carried with him after that of being Somali. If he could shed his refugee status in South Africa, his progression to the next phase of his journey to America would be much smoother.

He planned to fly to Guatemala en route to America, via Mexico. He complained about how expensive the ticket his travel agents quoted him was. Apart from that, he was also finding it difficult to obtain a visa. I told him that Guatemala did not seem to me to be a safe route into America and that he might be getting himself into trouble. 'Why do you want to go to Guatemala?' I asked him. He had not really thought it through but clearly had discussed the matter with other Somalis. Someone must have used this route before. 'But why not Canada? At least there are other Somalis there, and you will not have language problems. Who will help you in Guatemala?' He had not really thought about it. 'That is why it is important to talk to educated people, who can tell me what I should do.' What could I tell him? I had never been to that part of the world and he probably knew more about the precarious world of the border jumper than I do. He had already worked out, for example, that the authorities would be easier to bribe in Guatemala than in Mexico. In the end he decided that Canada was a better route into the US than Guatemala.

On Friday, 11 May 2001, I found three desperate messages in my voicemail. Ishmael, whom I believed to be in Pretoria or lying low in Mitchell's Plain to keep out of his ex-wife's way, wanted my help urgently. He phoned again in the evening and told me that the Canadians had responded to his application for a visa and wanted to interview him. What should he do? I had no idea what the Canadian diplomats wanted to ask him. Normally, they want to know that you have a return ticket, a job to return to and enough money to survive while in their country. But being Somali they would obviously be aware of his refugee status and would be determined to ensure he remained a South African problem. At the same time, I knew the Canadians were friendlier towards African immigrants so if he told them the truth they might be willing to take him in.

After a week without hearing from him I wondered if he'd already left. I found Hassan, the young Somali mechanic who was manning the sidewalk cigarette stand, and he told me that Ishmael was still around. As we were waiting for him to come down from his flat, Hassan told me his R200-a-week wages were not adequate for him to support his family in Tanzania. He'd only left his job at Ohan transport in Lusaka because he was misled into thinking he'd get a better job in South Africa. Once he got here he found that employers were asking for college certificates and other documents which he did not have, so he'd given up on getting work and was thinking of moving on. At the time of the interview he had obtained leave from the garage where he worked in order to help Ishmael with his street vending and the idea was that if Ishmael got his visa and left the country, Hassan would take over the cigarette stand on Durban Road.

If Hassan was eager for the older man to leave, Ishmael himself was even more desperate to get out of Cape Town. He told me how the Canadian consular staff asked him straight away if he was not trying to sneak into America. He explained that he just wanted to see the grave of his relative who died there in 1997, and he'd promised his mother that if he ever got enough money he would go, and well, now he had saved enough. But given that he could not tell the consular staff where exactly his relative was buried, he was told that Canada was too big a country for him to embark on such a search with his limited funds, so his visa application was rejected. To add to his misery, his estranged wife had fallen into depression again and was pleading with him for reconciliation. After he'd left her she had fallen onto hard times, even though he'd left her his entire stock of cigarettes and sweets and allowed her to keep the food kiosk that he owned at the Mowbray train station. The quality of her meals had deteriorated and she'd lost customers. Soon she was behind on the R650-rent for the flat. Probably because of this, she sought out the father of her twelve-year old son who was not paying the child maintenance, but soon after they'd appeared in court he was found dead in a ditch where he had apparently drowned after getting drunk.

While she was trying to run the kiosk on her own, working from dawn to dusk, her son, who had stabilised while Ishmael was staying with them (the boy even called him dad), went wild again and was using drugs. Doctors advised that both mother and son should be hospitalised. This the mother refused for fear of losing both her flat and her kiosk. She therefore begged Ishmael to return to live with her and apologised for the trouble she had caused him. She even brought her father to plead her case. Ishmael offered to give her R400 to help with the rent and to arrange for a Somali family to sublet half of the flat so that they could pay part of the rent, but he was completely determined to flee Cape Town. He told his wife that his mother wanted him to go back to Kenya and he would be returning there soon.

All these problems were taking their toll on him. He looked visibly stressed. His main worry was that his wife's sister, who had never liked him, could cause trouble for him by having the authorities strip him of his residency rights. That was why he was so eager to get out of the country before all the various conflicts caught up with him.

What are your options? I asked him. He said he would try Libya and Malta as a final resort. All he wanted was to get out of South Africa. Once he was on foreign soil getting a new set of identity papers would not be difficult. During our conversation he referred to information he had about other Somalis who had tried their luck, with or without success, in different parts of the world and knew how the different countries' immigration regimes functioned.

At Cape Town international airport, corrupt officials were running a racket squeezing bribes out of Africans travelling overseas. They demanded transit and other visas even when they were not required. Travellers anxious to proceed with their journey and not knowing their rights usually paid up. In Kuwait, the immigration authorities had tightened controls at their ports of entry, while the Argentinians would provide easy entry into Europe or America if only he could find a way of getting there.

From his life history I have worked out how he sets out to make his fortune without having a solid project plan. Almost fatalistic in his belief that if luck is on his side he will succeed, he does not worry about arriving penniless in an American city and beginning from scratch to find work. The family is always there to fall back on and his brother in Sweden has sent him money on several occasions to help him out of a fix. He recalled that he'd told his brother in Sweden that he already possessed a visa for America when Ishmael asked him for the air fare, so now that his travel plans had been halted he did not know what to say to him and appeared afraid of being found out by his brother. I advised him to phone and tell him that his visa had fallen through. After all, it had happened to him before.

In the end he made his own plans and successfully entered the UK as an asylum seeker, thereby, I would say, regaining his birthright as a British colonial subject. The last I heard of him in late 2001, he had undergone training as a forklift driver and was working in London.

In many ways Ishmael's case may not be a typical example of a Somali migrant, but he is, in any case, a perfect example of the cosmopolitan postcolonial subject who does not have a college education but is fluent in four languages, has lived in over ten countries on three continents, and, although he is very secure in his Somali ethnicity, he is also Kenyan by choice (of his parents), Tanzanian by birth, South African through marriage, and now, both by accident and by choice, a British resident working to support his family in the Somali diaspora. Our 'lone, culturally promiscuous individual' is not only *not* ever alone, but is cosmopolitan precisely because he is not alone. 'Cosmopolitan spaces and collectivities' are made by people like this, but always in association with others.

Cosmopolitan Hospitality: Women Cosmopolitans

Clearly, there is more than one way to be 'cosmopolitan'. Relatively uneducated, often penniless migrants have the competence to make the same journeys made by anthropologists and other globe-trotting world citizens, and to move in and out of different cultural settings. Unlike anthropologists, they are more likely to be accused of being cosmopolitan in an unpatriotic way, although in the colonial world anthropologists did sometimes get labelled as such – since being cosmopolitan by 'going native' was tantamount to letting the side down. Whether we see cosmopolitanism as 'obligations of justice to non-nationals' or merely being 'marked by diverse cultural influences' (Sypnowich 2005: 56), rather than seeking it among European sophisticates or travellers, in my view we should look to remote African villages and congested urban slums to find the woman who greets the stranger with a tray of food. This woman who has never left home lives her cosmopolitanism by welcoming the world. One does not need to be well-travelled to be a polyglot, polymath or cosmopolitan if one plays host to the world as the women of Cape Town have done since the Mother City was constructed.

Perhaps other women on the trans-Sahara road to Europe, or on the road to Johannesburg, who look after penniless migrants, give them homes, pay for their education and transform them from less than human babblers, *makwerekwere*, into citizens and fellow human beings, qualify on both ethical and cultural accounts. If we want to understand the cosmopolitanism of global justice we may find the answer not in liberal constitutions or UN conventions but in the real lives of the world's a-dollar-a-day multitudes. Many migrants in Cape Town would probably agree with the Congolese refugee who said that, if it were not for the women, we would not make it. I have discussed elsewhere (Sichone 2003: 136–8) the example of two sisters that both married Congolese refugees. Even though these marriages failed, as did Ishmael's, it was the xenophilia of the Capetonian women that allowed foreign migrants to be more than mere labourers. Nava (2002: 93) refers to several authors that have explained the cosmopolitanism of white women who formed relationships with black GIs and West Indian migrants during the war and post-war periods as a form of proto-feminism. There is some cogency in this argument, and we can say similarly that South African women oppose the dehumanisation of the migrant, as well as their own, in such gestures. As Ishmael's case shows, the exchanges that resulted from such relationships involved love as well as conflict, sometimes even violence, but, above all, sharing. Children were born of these unions and new religious practices, modes of dress, cuisines, languages, and even body shapes, were adopted by these women who had never left Cape Town, and the migrants who had travelled thousands of kilometres in search of a new life.

Conclusion: Stay-at-home Cosmopolitans

If Cosmopolitanism is a devotion to the interests of humanity as a whole, then there is nothing more uncosmopolitan than millennial transnational capitalism in its various guises, and its global apartheid project especially. But if to be human is to be cosmopolitan (i.e. to be your brother's keeper), then we will find cosmopolitans in the most unexpected places – not just Parisian cafés, anthropology conferences or gatherings of human rights NGOs.

The South African constitution, modelled as it is on the liberal constitutions of the North Atlantic democracies, repeats the mistake of the colonial powers and limits full humanity to democratic citizenship. Postcolonial subjects that find their freedoms diminished have sought ways of regaining their humanity and staking a claim in a society that seeks to keep them out. It is in this regard that irregular migration is undertaken as a necessary means to freedom and not necessarily to undermine an oppressive regime. In similar vein, those who reach out to the stranded stranger do so, as they have always done, because they must as *abantu* and not necessarily to challenge the state's immigration policies.

The case of Ishmael and his transnational clan and family has been used to demonstrate that strangers are found in remote villages and big cities; that humanity shines through when people take in the stranger and provide care. Equally, on the other hand, xenophobia, as the destructive rejection of the stranger, is most pronounced in the world of the retrenched worker, the men who must blame their unemployability on foreigners and who see themselves in a zero-sum battle for survival. The hospitality of the women, on the other hand, is what makes the mobility of the men humanly possible and reveals different ways of being cosmopolitan.

Inherent in the discriminatory practices of the postcolonial state is the xeno-phobic practice of keeping poor people out, and not the xenophile tradition of recruiting affines, subjects or friends. For Somali people like Ishmael, the well-defined rights, duties, obligations and ascribed roles of the clan-family provide another form of political community that has served them well in times of crisis. Whereas the Somali state created by European colonialism has collapsed completely, Somali society, against all odds, has proved quite resilient. The corpor-atism of the Somali clan is an idea that any member of patrilineal descent systems will be familiar with, though other African migrants have not maintained their clans in the same way. Thus, while agreeing with Norman Long (2000: 199) that new 'imagined communities' have emerged that are increasingly detached from fixed locations or territories, I fear social scientists may have attached too much importance to the phenomenon of global nomads, internally displaced persons and refugees, and forgotten that most people have stayed at home.

What the rising airline and airport traffic statistics do not tell us is that most people 'remain in the country where they are citizens' (Hammar and Tamas 1997:1). Surely, if populations are that stable, remaining within national borders, we should expect old identities to be less prone to destabilization than the notion of the global village suggests. Real existing African villages should continue to provide the mobile citizens of the global village with a source of identity and refuge. That the village has also been destabilised is due to the emergence of the irresponsible state during the 1980s and 1990s that has, on a scale not seen since the days of the slave trade, undermined the ability of people to live decent lives in their own lands, or be welcomed with hospitality when they travel.

In the final analysis, the local experience is more important than the global for human survival, even if the reverse is true for capitalism, which must reproduce itself on a global scale. It is at the local level that cosmopolitanism flourishes, for globally, all we have are unfulfilled UN charters and conventions. Indeed, even people escaping violence and natural disasters are defined as internally displaced persons or refugees, kept under state surveillance until they can be repatriated voluntarily or otherwise.

Notes

1. The research from which this paper is derived was funded by the University Research Committee of the University of Cape Town and the Centre for Scientific Development/National Research Foundation Grant number 15/13/16/0290.The views expressed here do not necessarily reflect those of the NRF or UCT. I am grateful for the research assistance I received from Serge Puatipuati, Mrs Brinkhuis, Issa Nkolomona, David Fuamba, Rachel Adams, and Mrs Miriam Dhlomo in conducting the research, and also to Professor Brokensha and Professor Pendleton for commenting on earlier drafts of this paper. The editor, Pnina Werbner, provided additional readings and made valuable comments on earlier drafts, for which I am grateful. The errors and omissions that remain are my responsibility.

2. The most comprehensive studies of South African xenophobia are in the Southern African Migration Project led by Jonathan Crush which has been monitoring migration policy, patterns and related issues since 1996. http://www.queensu.ca/samp/

3. Yolandi Groenewald 'Desperately seeking status' *Mail & Guardian* 31 March to 6 April 2006, p. 14, or Beauregard Tromp (Independent Foreign Service) 'Tarred with the same dirty brush: years of poisonous xenophobia have made it almost impossible for Nigerians to build a life here', *Cape Argus* Tuesday, 14 March 2006. p. 10. Articles of this nature have been appearing regularly in the local press since the late 1990s; see, for example, 'Job-less Mob Goes on Death Rampage', *Cape Argus*, 4 September 1998, p. 9; 'African Foreigners Terrorized', Tangenu Amupadhi, *Mail and Guardian*, 18–23 December 1998, p. 3; or 'Media Berated for Stoking Xenophobia', Pamela Dube, *Sunday Independent*, 27 February 2000, p. 3.

References

Cohen, Robin (1997), *Global Diasporas: An Introduction*, Seattle: University of Washington Press.

Cooper, Frederick (2001), 'What is the Concept of Globalization Good for? An African Historian's Perspective', *African Affairs* 100 (399): 189–213.

Crush, Jonathan and Wade Pendleton (2003), *Regionalizing Xenophobia? Citizen Attitudes to Immigration and Refugee Policy in Southern Africa*, SAMP Migration Policy Series No 27, Cape Town: IDASA.

Global Commission on International Migration Report (2005), *Migration in an Interconnected World: New Directions for Action*, www.gcim.org.

Hammar, Tomas and Kristaf Tamas (1997), 'Introduction', in Tomas Hammar, Grete Brochmann, Kristof Tamas and Thomas Faist *International Migration, Immobility and Development: Multidisciplinary Perspectives*, Oxford: Berg, pp. 1–19.

Hannerz, Ulf (1990), 'Cosmopolitans and Locals in World Culture', *Theory, Culture and Society* 7 (2–3): 237–51.

Lewis, I.M. (1980), *A Modern History of Somalia: Nation and State in the Horn of Africa*, London: Longman.

—— (1994), *Blood and Bone: The Call of Kinship in Somali Society*, Lawrence-ville NJ: Red Sea Press.

Long, Norman (2000), 'Exploring Local/Global Transformation: A View From Anthropology', in Alberto Arce and Norman Long (eds), *Anthropology, Development, and Modernities: Exploring Discourses, Counter-Tendencies and Violence*, London: Routledge, pp. 184–201.

Nava, Mica (2002), 'Cosmopolitan Modernity. Everyday Imaginaries and the Register of Difference', *Theory, Culture and Society* 19 (1–2): 81–99.

Sichone, Owen (2003), 'Together and Apart: African Refugees and Immigrants in Global Cape Town', in David Chidester, Phillip Dexter and Wilmot James (eds), *What Holds Us Together: Social Cohesion in South Africa*, Cape Town: HSRC Press, pp. 120–40.

Sypnowich, Christine (2005), 'Cosmopolitans, Cosmopolitanism, and Human Flourishing,' in Gillian Brock and H. Brighouse (eds.), *The Political Philosophy of Cosmopolitanism*, Cambridge: Cambridge University Press, pp. 55–74.

Werbner, Pnina (1999) 'Global Pathways: Working-class Cosmopolitans and the Creation of Transnational Ethnic Worlds', *Social Anthropology* 7 (1): 17–35.

Wilson, Monica and Archie Mafeje (1963), *Langa. A Study of Social Groups in an African Township*, Cape Town: Oxford University Press.

–16–

Cosmopolitan Values in a Central Indian Steel Town
Jonathan Parry

The Setting

This chapter focuses on the 'demotic cosmopolitanism' of public sector industrial workers in the central Indian steel town of Bhilai.[1] The Bhilai Steel Plant (BSP), a government undertaking, was constructed in the late 1950s and early 1960s with the fraternal aid of the 'anti-imperialist' Soviet Union on a greenfield site in the 'backward' rural region of Chhattisgarh. An icon of the post-Independence nationalist development project, BSP was intended as a 'beacon' for India's industrial future. It was one of Nehru's 'temples' to modernity. Along with its captive mines, by the mid-1980s it had some 65,000 employees on its direct pay roll. The chill wind of economic liberalisation has since blown and that figure now stands at around 35,000. A majority are provided with quarters in the company township, but a significant proportion lives in the sea of urban sprawl that surrounds it. Surrounding it, too, are hundreds of smaller-scale private sector factories for which the plant provided a magnet. Originally ancillary to BSP, some have grown into substantial concerns that supply a global market.

For reasons discussed in detail elsewhere (Parry 2007), the local peasantry were initially reluctant recruits to the BSP labour force, and the plant and its township were built largely by long-distance migrants drawn from almost every corner of the country. Many put down permanent roots in Bhilai, now proudly described as a 'mini-India' in which people of different regions and religions rub along together in tolerant cosmopolitan amity. Almost the opposite is suggested, however, by stereotypical accounts of the fear and awe with which the local villagers regarded these strangers who flooded the area in the early years of the plant. 'Xenophobia', with its connotations of aggressive and irrational hatred, is perhaps too strong, but many undoubtedly felt swamped and displaced – which is what many literally were. Land from 96 villages was compulsorily purchased to construct the new complex. Whole villages disappeared without trace under industrial plant or township quarters and amenities. Others lost only their arable and wasteland, and their rump residential sites became slum-like labour colonies into which 'foreigners' with other tongues and ways now moved. One expression of the fears and resentments of the local peasantry were recurrent rumours about 'construction' sacrifices on a terrifying scale – sacrifices to get such gargantuan industrial edifices to stand and such awesome machinery to function; sacrifices of which they supposed themselves the most likely victims, nefariously procured by outsiders on behalf of the government (ibid.).

Much has changed since those pioneer days, one instance of which is the cut-throat desperation with which the sons-of-Chhattisgarh-soil now compete for jobs in the plant. That's largely down to the fact that the *regular* BSP workforce (which in non-executive grades is almost exclusively male) has subsequently become an unrivalled aristocracy of local labour, enjoying pay, perks and conditions that make it the envy of all other segments of the so-called 'working class'.[2] As a proportion of the population of the urban area and its rural hinterland, however, 'outsiders' remain greatly over-represented in it. But the plant also employs around 10,000 casual contract workers (including many women) on what are by comparison truly derisory rates of pay, and of these the large majority are locals. Workers in private sector factories are again divided between permanent company employees (a minority, and again almost all male and typically of 'outsider' origin) and temporary contract workers (mostly locals). Apart from these workers in the organised formal sector, there is also a vast reserve army of informal sector labour irregularly employed in jobs related to industry – loading and unloading trucks, sorting scrap and the like.

At the broadest level, then, the Bhilai labouring classes are divided between, on the one hand, relatively privileged workers in the organised formal sector who are employed in fairly large-scale, bureaucratically structured, capital intensive modern factories that are subject to state regulation in the form of employment legislation covering minimum wages, safety procedures, union recognition, and the like; and, on the other hand, those who must glean a precarious living in insecure informal unorganised sector occupations. It's a division that is a direct product of state legislation and policies. Organised sector labour is itself divided between workers in public and private enterprises; and within both of these workforces there is a further crucial distinction between those who are directly employed by the company and who are legally protected against arbitrary dismissal, and a far more vulnerable and less well-remunerated contract labour force. As we will see, a 'cosmopolitan outlook' is very unevenly distributed between these different 'working class' fractions.

Definitions and Propositions

By 'demotic', 'of the people', I mean 'of these labouring classes'. Conventionally opposed to 'hieratic' ('priestly' or 'sacerdotal'), 'demotic' suggests something of the 'secular', with which the cosmopolitanism I describe has some affinity. By 'cosmopolitanism' I mean a significant freedom from local or national prejudices; an openness to, and tolerance of, other ways of life. The claims of one's own to absolute moral authority are relativised. What goes for 'secularism' goes for cosmopolitanism. For the Indian Constitution, secularism is a matter of the even-handed acceptance of all religions, a sense embodied in the etymology of the Hindi neologism for it, *dharamnirpekshta.* Cosmopolitanism is the even-handed tolerance of other life-ways. Both are significantly products of the same historical processes.

The extent to which people are open to other worlds is not only a matter of individual temperament but also of class positioning. My most important ethnographic claim is that different 'working class' fractions are differentially cosmopolitan in outlook. Regular company workers in the *public* sector steel plant are most cosmopolitan. The lives and imaginative horizons of workers in *private* sector factories are more likely to be encapsulated by kinship, caste and regional community; and it is amongst insecure contract workers in the private sector that a localist sons-of-the-soil politics has taken some root. I speak of broad tendencies, difficult to adequately document or properly nuance and qualify in the space at my disposal. One caveat is that these different types of workers are often linked by kinship and neighbourhood ties, and are not discrete groups (cf. Holmström 1984) – though they are increasingly tending to become so (Parry 1999a, 2005).

According to Beck (2002), cosmopolitanism is opposed to nationalism as the 'dialogic imagination' (the ability to internalise the perspectives of others) is opposed to the 'monologic' (which excludes otherness). Though there is nation-alism and nationalism, the common thread is 'the metaphysical essentialism of the nation' that makes all of them antithetical to cosmopolitanism. Though, in a subsequent elaboration of his views, Beck (2006: 61) at one point concedes that 'it is ultimately a mistake to accord too much prominence to the opposition between cosmopolitanism and nationalism', the general thrust of his discussion continues to insist on their incompatibility and that 'the national outlook excludes the cosmopolitan outlook' (ibid.: 31).

Since most cosmopolitans I know in Bhilai are loyal members of the workforce of a *state* enterprise with a special place in the national imagination, I am sceptical. Here nationalism seems to provide the soil in which cosmopolitanism seeds (cf. Turner 2002). A gargantuan nation-building project involved the coordination of a vast and culturally heterogeneous labour force recruited from different regions, religions and castes; and this required of its workers a certain tolerance of, and openness to, other ways of life. Unlike one dominant strand in *contemporary* Hindu nationalism (that associated with the Bharatiya Janata Party, the Rashtriya Swayamsevak Sangh and other constituents of the Sangh Parivar coalition), the

Nehruvian nationalist project never assumed that the nation was, or even should be, characterised by a single hegemonic culture. What it did propose was that regardless of culture each should recognise the other as a fellow citizen. And once a Bengali Brahman has internalised that universalistic value, and begun to regard a Punjabi Untouchable as a member of the same moral community as himself, it is not such a leap to extend that principle to people of other nations. Bhilai was, after all, built with Soviet collaboration, supposedly as testament to the solidarity of two peoples. That memory is still cherished today.

This openness to other worlds is also partly a product of an ideology of 'progress', of the idea that India is treading in the footsteps of, and has something to learn from, other 'more advanced' industrial nations. 'Catching up' is the goal, and that pre-eminently means with the West. 'How far are we behind?' I am often asked; and have learned to suppress a pedagogical instinct to conduct tutorials on the slippery nature of the notion of 'backwardness'. 'Just fourteen years, give or take two or three months,' is the kind of answer expected. 'Cosmopolitanisation' thus has some kinship with 'Westernisation'. But it is not the same. Its world is wider. Many Malayalis and Muslims have done spells in the Gulf; some Bhojpuris in Burma or Thailand. Catholics imagine Lourdes, Shiites Karbala; and some steelworkers speak of the productivity of labour in Japan or Korea.

Notwithstanding the communal bigotry and bloodletting that has blighted the recent history of many (though by no means all) parts of the country, and at the risk of committing the uncosmopolitan sin of essentialism, it might plausibly be claimed that Indians are heirs to a 'tradition' that is tolerant of cultural difference. According to Nandy and collaborators (1997), the increasingly undermined legacy is of a harmonious 'salad bowl' model of community relations in which 'the ingredients retain their distinctiveness, but each ingredient transcends its individuality through the presence of others.' This they contrast with the far less benign 'melting-pot' model, which aims to dissolve differences, and to which 'much of the recent (communal and ethnic) violence in South Asia can be traced' (1997: vi). Beck (2006: 95) deploys precisely this metaphorical contrast in the context of a more generalised discussion (though the source he cites for it, Beck-Gernsheim, comes from closer to home). The American melting-pot model is a product of the fear of being swamped by ethnic difference and 'leads to demands for sameness and uniformity' (ibid.: 52). Its spirit is anti-cosmopolitan (and we are left in no doubt that that is a bad thing to be).

What these enthusiasts for a 'salad bowl' model of the social world suppress, however, is that the ingredients in it have *collective* identities. They are 'ethnic species' of some kind or other. Competition for scarce resources between them is consequently liable to take the form of competition between ascriptively defined groups – at the extreme, of caste wars or ethnic pogroms. The melting-pot model, by contrast, presupposes that these 'primordial' identities will, with time, dissolve, and that it is as formally equal citizens that *individuals* should compete (Parry 1999b). Though there may also be much to worry the moralist in this second alternative, it is far from self-evident that a return to the first is a reliable recipe for human well-being. In many contexts, moreover, these collective identities are in some way hierarchised – 'traditional' India representing only the most elaborated instance. As a system made up of ideologically separate, ranked and yet closely interdependent units, caste clearly requires coexistence with cultural difference; and the well-documented obsession with 'Sanskritisation' clearly implies an openness to other ways and ideas (or to those, at least, of superiors). Rather than being rejected or suppressed, differences are accommodated – but rated as higher or lower. 'In the hierarchical scheme'. as Dumont (1966:191) put it, 'a group's acknowledged differentness whereby it is contrasted with other groups becomes the very principle whereby it is integrated with society. If you eat beef, you must accept being classed among the Untouchables, and on this condition your practice will be tolerated.' It is when the state decrees that Untouchables should have equal rights (of access, for example, to Brahmanic temples) that it immediately comes under pressure to pass legislation aimed at forcibly reforming such practices, and that 'the traditional hierarchical tolerance gives way to a modern mentality' (ibid.: 231) – one that rejects difference.

So does its acceptance of difference make the *'traditional'* caste order cosmopolitan in spirit? Clearly not. Though cosmopolitanism is a fluffy concept, one that we should think about in the plural and resist the temptation to define according to Pollock et al. (2000), those who have worked with it generally agree that it is not just a matter of tolerating differences, but of refusing to *rank* them. Again, we can invoke the authority of Beck (2006: 57): 'Cultural differences are neither arranged in a hierarchy of difference nor subsumed into universalism, but accepted for what they are.' But even in its most exemplary instance there must surely be limits? To suppose otherwise would be to ignore what is perhaps the most fundamental teaching of Durkheimian sociology – that 'not everything in the contract is contractual,' that society is a moral system founded on values. Values mean evaluation, which makes it hard to imagine a social world in which *all* differences are accepted on *equal* terms 'for what they are'. Indeed, it is striking that a strong strand of moral absolutism – with regard, for example, to human rights, gender inequalities or the treatment of minorities – runs right through these social science writings that extol the virtues of the 'cosmopolitan outlook'. Cosmopolitan values, that is to say, are self-limiting, even perhaps somewhat contradictory. The ways of others must be treated with equal respect; but some values are non-negotiable and even the most 'correct' cosmopolitan cannot therefore be expected to regard deviations from them with even-handed neutrality. In short, it is not easy to see how any society could agree to agree that all differences are equally valid. Some must be 'melted'; and though the cosmopolitan world of BSP workers that I describe in what follows retains some of the qualities of the salad bowl, the melting-pot image in which they are muted and softened seems at least as apposite. True, some Malayalis, Muslims and ex-Untouchables know where to buy beef from *sub rosa* sources; but none would consume it openly or expect their Brahman or Jain neighbours to calmly approve.

At one level, and as all this suggests, cosmopolitanism is a matter of conscious ideas, an ideological orientation. At another, however, it is also the product of unconscious forces; and in writing about it there is a danger of sliding rather too smoothly between these two levels – between value and fact, 'ought' and 'is'. In my judgement, Beck (2006) does not entirely avoid it, even if he does seek to carefully distinguish between 'cosmopolitanism' (a philosophical predisposition in relation to 'otherness') and 'cosmopolitanisation' (a set of empirical trends that create practical interdependencies across cultural borders). The brute facts of 'world risk society' – international terrorism, climate change, threats of global pandemics, and so forth – have been powerful agents of the second. And it is as a result of the linkages they create that he finds it possible to speak of 'the growing unreality of the world of nation states' and to claim that 'the human condition has become cosmopolitan'. Unless these interdependencies are embraced and valorised, however, it seems that 'true' cosmopolitanism is absent. When they are coerced, unwilling or merely passively accepted, all we have is a 'deformed' variant of it (ibid.: 2, 20–1). Though Béteille (1994) is more careful to separate his own moral preferences from his analysis of social processes, his distinction between 'secularism' (a matter of values) and 'secularisation' (a product of unconscious forces) strongly prefigures Beck's between 'cosmopolitanism' and 'cosmopolitanisation'.

In both cases, the unconscious force must in some measure promote the conscious value, and both secularism and cosmopolitanism are at least partly a product of structural compulsions of which individuals may only be dimly aware. True, rapid industrialisation may result in interethnic competition and a new assertiveness about what are conceived to be primordial identities. But by assembling a culturally diverse workforce that must cooperate on often dangerous tasks and live as neighbours in a company township, BSP employment has, I believe, encouraged a loosening of the more totalising claims of religion that is a prerequisite for the sort of secular society that Nehru envisioned, and an enlargement of cultural horizons that is the hallmark of the cosmopolitan outlook. Even the unlettered rural migrant acknowledges, moreover, that running a steel plant requires technical competence; and – cynical though he is about the way things are actually done – subscribes to the principle that individual 'merit' is a more rational basis on which to assign jobs than collective identities. Only to the extent that the grip of such identities is relaxed is a cosmopolitan outlook possible.

Friedman (2002, and n.d.) suggests that cosmopolitanism is most salient in periods of strong globalisation. Beck (2002) describes it as 'soaring with the wind of global capital at its back'. BSP still largely produces for a domestic market. Some private-sector factories are significantly geared to export and, in the past few years, a major shareholding in a handful of these has been acquired by global capital. Their workforces, however, tend to be more insular and inward-looking. As I will show, this is not *despite* capitalism (whether global or domestic), but *because* of it – because of the way in which capital recruits labour in order to keep it as cheap and flexible as possible. The segment of the labour force most exposed to global capital flows is least cosmopolitan.

Yet it is management of the *public-sector* Bhilai Steel Plant that has proved more responsive to international pressures – the product of a cosmopolitan sense of interconnectedness and mutual responsibility – to reduce carbon emissions. Private capital has more pressing priorities – to maximise immediate returns and evade constraints that inhibit that goal. Though no doubt prompted by national self-interest (the fear of sanctions against its steel industry in the global market place, for example), it is the *state* that mediates and acts as the agent of cosmopolitan concerns. It is not therefore obvious that 'the national outlook' excludes 'the cosmopolitan outlook', or that the former is 'blind to and obscures the realities of the cosmopolitan age' (Beck 2006: 31). Further, the main means by which the plant has sought to address its environmental impact is highly selective in terms of its effects on 'the working class'. The strategy has consisted in a large increase in unskilled labour-intensive cleaning operations designed to reduce the leakage of noxious gases from the doors of coke-oven batteries and the like. Since BSP is simultaneously under pressure to cheapen its labour in order to maintain its competitive edge on an increasingly globalised market, these are now routinely performed by contract labourers working long hours in the most gruelling and dangerous conditions for pitiful pay. Though Beck rightly observes that the national outlook may mask global inequalities (ibid.: 38–9), cosmopolitan virtue is not always more sensitive to national inequities. In Bhilai, it is in reality the most down-trodden and least cosmopolitan segment of the labour force which is given the life-endangering and poorly remunerated task of slowing the approach of a global ecological disaster, the threat of which is largely created by far-away people who have the resources to widen their horizons and become cosmopolitan.

Short Notes on the Ethnography of Cosmopolitanism in Bhilai

In India, a meaningful measure of social inclusiveness is required of public sector enterprises by legal and bureaucratic fiat. The recruitment procedures that the plant is required to follow make it impossible for any lobby to bias selection *systematically* in favour of one particular regional or religious community, let alone any single caste. In conformity, moreover, with constitutional provisions for 'protective discrimination', there are separate quotas (now amounting to 50 per cent of all recruitment) reserved for candidates from the Scheduled (that is, 'Untouchable') Castes, Scheduled Tribes and Other Backward Classes (Parry 1999a). Whether management likes it or not (they mostly take pride in it), a significant degree of social and cultural heterogeneity is more or less assured by the mix of the local population.

On the three BSP shop floors of which I have first-hand experience, almost every work group reflects it.[3] Each is composed of workers of different regional origins and of 'clean' and 'Untouchable' caste, and most include some of a different religion. In demeanour, they are often startlingly disparate – a local Tribal who during periods of slack spends much of his shift hunting rats; a BSP cricket umpire from south India who engages me in erudite conversation about the English County Championship. Membership of these groups tends to be fairly stable over long periods of time; and the work itself may be dangerous and demands not only cooperation but trust. Some tasks are more arduous and unpleasant than others, and partners rotate them. Even after the down-sizing of the permanent labour force over the past two decades, manning levels remain generous and many teams run their own informal duty rosters that permit them to show up for only half their shift and often not at all. Even so, there are long fallow periods between bouts of productive activity during which there is little to do but socialise. A strong sense of solidarity and fast friendships develop. Regardless of caste, those who work together eat together, shovelling delicacies brought from home onto each other's plates. In this there is sometimes an element of Untouchable bravado, and the Brahmans may silently resent it – but none dares to complain. When they meet at the start of a shift, all shake hands – Hindus and Muslims, officers and men. But none eats or shakes hands with the contract labour that work alongside them.

Not that 'primordial' identities disappear. A certain tenseness about regional identities is expressed in licensed joking about the supposed attributes of this or that group; and regional ethnicity is a major factor in union elections at shop-floor level. The reservations policy that also applies to promotions is a cause of some ill-feeling over caste, though the Scheduled Caste contender fast-tracked over the heads of his peers is generally judged on his merits and resentment against him (if not against the principle) is generally ephemeral. Most striking, however, is the extent to which identity issues are muffled by a robust institutional culture.

The effects of it wash over the perimeter walls. Many work groups run rotating credit societies, 'tour groups' that travel together to spend a few days at some tourist site, and 'dining clubs' that convene to eat meat, booze and banter.

Brahman or Sweeper, entire work groups are generally invited to major life-cycle rituals celebrated by the household. If somebody needs a blood transfusion, his workmates will search out a donor of the right group, and nobody assumes that to be a person of his own caste. But the ethic is wider. When there is a cyclone in Orissa or an earthquake in Maharashtra, and BSP workers are asked to contribute a fraction of their monthly pay to the Prime Minister's Relief Fund, few question the principle of succouring strangers (though plenty complain of intermediary pockets).

The BSP township is divided into sectors, each of which has housing for both managers and workers, and in none of which is there any significant ethnic or religious enclaving. Neighbours are almost certain to have disparate regional origins, and – with only minor exceptions – that is also significantly true in the sprawl that surrounds the township. Regional identities continue to be to some extent marked in terms of diet, dress, the worship of deities and the language of the home. It is in the 'home' rather than the 'world' that distinctions are most manifest, and the maintenance of them is significantly gendered (Parry 2003). But this should not be exaggerated – even in the matter of cuisine over which Indians are culturally programmed to be cautious. Housewives swap preparations and recipes with neighbours, buy (Mother's Pride-style) 'bread' from street hawkers, and succumb to the fashion for packet soup. South Indian snacks (like *dosas* and *idlis*) are prepared in many north Indian homes, and north Indian snacks (like *pakoras*) by Telugus and Malayalis. More and more young women from BSP households bob their hair, possess a pair of jeans, drive a moped and attend karate classes or National Cadet Corps camps.

Especially in the BSP township, and amongst the generation born and raised in Bhilai, a more urban cosmopolitan style has emerged. Most sociability revolves around neighbours, workmates and school fellows who come from different regions. While in the 1970s Malayalam movies played to packed houses, today they are never screened. Once active cultural associations of fellow countrymen are reduced to a rump of old codgers complaining about the younger generation's indifference to their heritage. BSP has a Sports Department that sponsors 'cosmopolitan' games like cricket, boxing and soccer. Some youngsters perform in 'progressive' dramas with the Indian People's Theatre Association (affiliated to the Communist Party of India). Sanjay,[4] a Catholic of Telugu Untouchable origin, plays *tabla* for a mixed group of now semi-professional musicians whose repertoire includes *gazals* (a predominantly Muslim form) and Hindu *bhajans*, and with another ensemble has recently entered '*The Guinness Book*' for the longest non-stop recital on record. The parents of such Sector sophisticates, many themselves unschooled and of rural origin, often find themselves completely bewildered by this new world of birthday parties and cakes, of April Fool's Day japes and Valentine's Day cards, of the Internet and email, that their offspring inhabit.

But not all parents are yokels whose horizons need broadening. Amongst my older friends and acquaintances are BSP workers who are members of the Progessive Writers' Association, enter rose competitions, make animal sculptures out of wire, own Hindi translations of Gorky, and collect every possible species of cactus. One Bengali Brahman friend who joined the plant as an ordinary worker, but rose through the ranks into middle management, has a daughter who worked in a call centre in Delhi answering enquiries about Vietnamese restaurants in Philadelphia and Saab garages in Cincinnati. Her younger sister is employed by a large international NGO and has recently married a Tamil Christian of Tribal origin. An occasional visitor to their house is a now retired man of similar background to their father who is making a study of the (translated) writings of Albert Camus.

It would, of course, be absurd to suggest that the general run of BSP workers are lovers of world literature or experts on exotic plants. Probably more are passionate about booze. Many are content to potter and socialise when they come off shift; and for predictable reasons local Chhattisgarhi workers tend to have less cosmopolitan interests and consumption patterns than 'outsiders'. They are less likely to be adventurous souls. The outsiders are, after all, the self-selected ones who left home; and they tend to be better educated. Many locals, moreover, have fields in the environs, and most have more extensive caste and kinship networks on hand that need to be nurtured. In any event, BSP workers with energy to spare are more likely to devote it to some speculative entrepreneurial moonlighting business made possible by savings from their generous salaries, soft credit from the company and the ample leisure that a job in the plant provides. But the crucial point is that those of a more cosmopolitan cast do not stand out as eccentrically maverick; and in the BSP workforce I am unable to identify the kind of sharp break between 'cosmopolitan' and 'localist' cultural styles that Ferguson (1999) finds amongst Copperbelt miners.

Standard Hindi is the *lingua franca*, though for only a minority of the senior generation of workers is it their mother tongue. Amongst the younger generation, however, many are more comfortable in Hindi than in their regional language and prefer to speak it at home with their siblings, and even sometimes their parents. They are certainly far less likely to be literate in, say, Tamil or Telugu; and this precludes any prospect of white-collar employment in their 'home' state. One former Malayali neighbour of mine was married to a bride from back home. She knew no Hindi and his Malayalam was so rudimentary that during the first year of their marriage they could barely converse.

There is today an almost insatiable appetite for English-medium education. Even in much less affluent fractions of the working class many parents devote a very significant proportion of their meagre resources to sending their sons (more likely than daughters) to private nursery and primary schools that hyperbolically claim to teach in English. BSP runs its own school system, which has significantly higher standards than that of the state government and of most private education. Twelve of its 53 schools are English-medium, and it is a place in one of these that is most desperately sought. From the best of them the results are impressive, and 28 of their students won places in the high achiever's heaven of an Indian Institute of Technology in 2002–3. Even in these flagship company schools, the majority of pupils are the children of ordinary BSP workers, which is to say that they provide a real avenue for significant social mobility (see Parry 2005 for details). The son of a Chhattisgarhi Untouchable friend from the Coke Ovens played chess for the Indian youth team in Spain while he was studying in one of these schools, and is now enrolled in IIT, Bombay. He'll probably be snapped up by Silicon Valley. In a recent discussion with ninth-class students at the most prestigious of these BSP schools, most said they hoped to work in computers and live abroad, and not one aspired to a job in Bhilai or an executive post in the plant.

After every two years, BSP employees are entitled to Leave Travel Concession, which entitles them to reimbursement for first-class train travel for all the family (including dependent parents and siblings) to any destination within India they choose. Many, though their numbers are now diminishing, take their families back to their ancestral villages. Many stay put in Bhilai and lodge bogus bills. But a significant proportion decide to see the world, make a pilgrimage to Kanya Kumari or Kedarnath, visit Delhi or Calcutta, or now – the currently most fashionable destination – even fly to the Andamans. Janaki, an 'Untouchable' BSP schoolteacher of local origin whose illiterate father had been a bullock-drover before becoming a forklift truck operator in the plant, had befriended an itinerant Kashmiri Muslim pedlar whose winter circuit includes Bhilai. She took her family to stay in his village, and came back full of the atrocities perpetrated by the Indian army, and inclined to the view that if Kashmiris want an independent state – or even to join Pakistan – it should be up to them. (Admittedly, however, her cosmopolitan respect for other cultural ways came rather unravelled in the course of her description of the Adamanese aboriginals she fleetingly encountered on her recent visit to the islands). Some BSP workers (but many more managers) have been sent abroad by the plant. Julius Augustine spent a year training in Poland as a rolling operator when the new Plate Mill was about to be commissioned, and was able to worship at the shrine of the Black Madonna of Czestochowa. Despite being at some disadvantage on account of his deafness, Pheku – a local Untouchable – managed to get himself seconded to a Chhattisgarhi folk dance group that BSP's Culture and Recreation Department sent to the Festival of India in Paris. Just a few months back, a small group of my Coke Oven Heating Group friends went, at plant expense, to an international Quality Control Circle convention in Bali, where they stayed in a five-star hotel.

Many 'outsiders' originate from areas that have a considerable history of long-distance migration, both national and international – Malayalis whose grandparents worked in Java or Burma, whose fathers' generation went to Sri Lanka and then shifted to Bhilai, and whose brothers or cousins are now in the Gulf; Gorakhpur Rajputs with kinship networks in Thailand. And I can immediately think of others with a son or a sibling in Australia, Azerbaijan, Britain, Italy, Greece, Saudi Arabia, the United States and Zambia. Though some of those in the pioneer generation went back to their villages of origin on retirement, I estimate that more than half did not. If their sons now leave Bhilai, they are far less likely to return to the rural areas in which their fathers were born than to shift in search of work to some other part of India, or indeed of the world.[5]

The obvious qualification to this picture of a cosmopolitan industrial melting pot is, of course, the persistence of caste endogamy. But while it is true that most marriages continue to be arranged between people from the same caste and region, not everything is quite what it was. Many would prefer to find a spouse for their child who not only meets the traditional criteria but was also raised in Bhilai. Failing that, some parents are prepared to contemplate a match that crosses caste and/or regional boundaries. Uncle-niece and cross-cousin unions have fallen out of favour amongst almost all groups that traditionally favoured them, and there has been a homogenisation – that amounts to a 'Bihari-isation' – of ideas about the prohibited degrees of kinship. Most significant, however, is the growing number of 'love' marriages, the majority of which cross traditional endogamous boundaries. Some parents acquiesce in them with various degrees of grace, but many don't get that opportunity since they are faced with the *fait accompli* of a clandestine elopement.

When Sharada, the younger daughter of the Bengali Brahman friend referred to earlier, insisted on marrying a Tamil Christian she had met as a student, her parents were unhappy and the wider kinship group disapproved. The wedding was to be held in the south, in the church of which the groom's father was the pastor, and Sharada's parents had reluctantly agreed to attend, though none of the rest of the family was proposing to go. Though not his only concern, amongst her father's worries was the family good name in Bhilai. Since I already knew of the engagement and clearly did not regard it as a scandal, one of my visits to the house was used as a convenient pretext to summons one of his most esteemed friends from the plant in order break the still secret news. I shall call this friend Trivedi; he comes from an orthodox cow-belt Brahman background, and I report his reaction here because it seemed to say so much about the spirit of pragmatic tolerance that I would like to be able to capture. As the shocking details gradually unfolded – a boy from 'another community' . . . a Tamil . . . a Christian . . . a 'Tribal' – Trivedi listened with inscrutable patience. But as soon as the tale was told, he launched with measured calm into a couple of parables, both of which concerned the 'misalliances' made by the cherished but self-willed children of other plant colleagues. The first was the story of an only son who had made an inter-caste marriage against his parents' wishes. They had disowned him and rebuffed his later attempts to re-establish contact. Now the boy and his wife were living in the United States, and his ageing parents had not seen him for almost a decade and had never set eyes on their grandchildren. The second story was in conventional terms even more scandalous – of a high caste Hindu girl whose parents had arranged a brilliant (and appropriately endogamous) match for her with a 'wheatish'- complexioned Green Card holder of very 'good family'. But within a week of the wedding – when all the arrangements were in place and all the guests had made travel plans – she had run off with a Muslim boy with whom it transpired she had long been in clandestine love. For a whole year her parents were too ashamed to leave their house; it was as if they had gone into mourning and they would have nothing to do with their daughter. But the boy had turned out well, soon there was a child, the parents allowed themselves to be mollified, and when the young family recently visited Bhilai they held a big gathering to introduce their son-in-law to their friends. 'Which one is better?' Trivedi ended by asking – though he didn't wait for an answer. Parents are stupid to be too stubborn; relationships with children are more important than social conventions, and he did not want to see his friends in mourning.

But Sharada's people are 'outsiders' with other norms; and throughout almost the whole of the local Chhattisgarghi caste hierarchy the marital bond is brittle by wider Indian standards (a point I have documented in detail elsewhere (Parry 2001; see also Parry 2004)). Nearly all primary marriages are arranged within the caste, but a significant proportion of them break down. Both spouses are then likely to contract a secondary union with a partner they have a customary right to choose for themselves. Though this should ideally be a person of their own caste, even in the past this was not always the case. In the urban areas today, such secondary unions are increasingly likely to cross the boundaries of both caste and regional ethnicity. For the peri-urban villages around Bhilai, I estimate that perhaps 15 per cent of all Chhattisgarhi households have a present or previous member who has contracted a union outside their own caste, and of these more than half are between a Chhattisgarhi woman and a man of outsider origin.[6] Though these couples may be shunned by their families, I know many cases in which they are not, and almost none in which they have been subjected to systematic harassment and violence. Nobody can now deprive them of employment or access to services and public amenities, and most neighbours regard it as none of their business.

The large majority – around three-quarters – of Bhilai's population are nominally Hindu. Numerically, Christians (of various denominations) are the most significant religious minority, followed closely by Muslims. There is also a small, but visible, community of Sikhs and a leavening of Jains. Though most of my informants would describe themselves as religious believers, I know many more militant sceptics than zealots. Of the three different contexts in which I have done field research in India,[7] Bhilai is the only one in which I have found it easy to be frank with friends about my own lack of religious faith. The town supports a once active Rationalist Association and a branch of the Andh vishvas Anmoolan Samiti ('Blind-faith Eradication Council') that investigates supposedly supernatural happenings in order to 'prove' their natural causation.

This brings me to what I see as the most crucial evidence for the cosmopolitan character of the town – its comparative communal harmony. Though the Hindu nationalist Bharatiya Janata Party currently forms the Chhattisgarh state government, and there is a steady stream of propaganda against Christian missionisation, in the industrial area around Bhilai the only overt expressions of anti-Christian sentiment I have heard about were of an extremely minor kind. Potentially more explosive Hindu–Muslim tensions are again very low key, and Bhilai has suffered little of the communal savagery that has afflicted so many other Indian industrial centres. In the town's entire history, I know of only one fairly small-scale incident of rioting that appears to have had a communal element, and that was nearly 40 years back.

In 1984, Prime Minister Indira Gandhi was gunned down by her Sikh body-guards, sparking anti-Sikh riots and targeted killings throughout the country. Not in Bhilai. My friend Surinder is a Sikh and one of four brothers. The only one who remains unshorn is the one who has left Bhilai. Surinder himself had dispensed with turban and beard well before Mrs Gandhi was killed, though his (then living) father – a BSP worker – did scrupulously maintain the proper symbols of Sikhism. They lived at that time in a slum area on the wrong side of the tracks outside the BSP township and next to what are known as the Tata Lines, which house a notoriously rough population of workers who, in the early years of the plant's construction, had migrated from the steel town of Jamshedpur in what was then Bihar. In 1984, Surinder's house had the only television in that neighbourhood and, following the assassination, their front room was packed for every news bulletin. Not once, he insists, did he or any other member of the family get the slightest sense of any hostility against them or feel in the least apprehensive.

Regional ethnicity is, in my judgement, a significantly more divisive issue than religion; and the main fault line is between local sons-of-the-Chhattisgarh-soil and 'outsiders'. In large measure, of course, the development of a distinctive Chhattisgarhi identity has been the product of the rapid industrialisation of the region. Before there was any significant contact with outsiders, nobody needed to give it much thought. The main reason for doing so now is that in proportion to their share of the district's population (let alone that of the state), locals believe themselves to be not only under-represented in the aristocracy of BSP labour but also discriminated against in recruitment to it. The first of these claims is true; but – notwithstanding the fact that some managers certainly suppose that locals make less reliable workers – the second is probably not. Local political lobbies are sufficiently powerful to preclude it on any significant scale. A more plausible explanation is that in aggregate their educational levels are lower, while over the years the qualifications required to get a BSP job have been subject to inflation; and that – as I indicated at the outset – in the early years of the plant the local population were extremely reluctant recruits to its labour force. There is much resentment also on the part of the displaced peasantry whose land was requisitioned to build the factory, and who received what they now regard with hindsight as paltry compensation.[8]

It would however be a mistake to exaggerate this sons-of-the-soil sentiment – though were the plant to reduce its labour force further it is easy to imagine it escalating.[9] But, as things stand, BSP remains by far the most dominant employer in town. Its institutional ethos sets the tone for the social life of the whole urban area; and, despite developments in the private sector, that keeps a lid on the open expression of ethnic antagonism.

Even in the best-paying private-sector companies, wage levels are appreciably lower and fringe benefits very much poorer than those enjoyed by BSP employees. The majority of workers are contract labourers liable to retrenchment at any time, and there is a relatively recent history of strikes, closures and lock-outs (discussed in Parry, forthcoming). That makes it prudent for workers to keep a firm foot in the peasant economy; and of a piece with this, they are statistically more likely than their BSP counterparts to return to their home villages when they retire (Parry 2003). They are also more likely to spend their time in Bhilai in a social environment continuous with that from which they have come. In contrast with the social heterogeneity of the BSP work group, they commonly toil alongside kinsmen, caste fellows and co-villagers; and it is through them – and consequently in the same neighbourhoods – that they find somewhere to live in town. The main explanation for this is that in order to evade the labour laws, private-sector employers take on as few direct workers as they can. Most of their labour is at least nominally employed by a 'contractor' – characteristically a skilled former worker in the factory who is given charge of a part of the process and who recruits his own kin or co-villagers to carry it out. Socially, if not spatially, many private-sector workers may hardly leave their villages. A telling contrast is with the commensality of the BSP work group. In private-sector factories, those who work together but are of different caste often eat separately.

A significant proportion of this private-sector contract labour is local, and it is these workers who have become the main constituency for what is by far the most radical union in the region. Though the Chhattisgarh Mukti Morcha ('Liberation Front') pursues a class-based politics, and though the ideology of its now somewhat fragmented leadership is ethnically inclusive, its formerly more regionally heterogeneous rank-and-file membership has over the past decade come to be increasingly dominated by Chhattisgarhis. This is largely because it is they who can best afford to remain loyal. Most have peasant holdings in the vicinity to fall back on during strikes. To combat them, the employers run networks of spies and informers, and sponsor their own 'pocket' union which workers are pressurised to join. Both the informers and the union officials (they are often the same people) are regular company workers, and they are almost invariably outsiders. It is not therefore surprising that amongst the most militant segment of the working class a sons-of-the-soil sentiment has taken root and has begun to find a political voice.

As to informal sector labour at the bottom of the working-class heap, horizons are limited less by hostility to strangers than by limited experience of them and by lack of knowledge of the world from which they come. On the construction sites on which I have recently spent a good deal of time, I have often had the experience of completely bemusing workers when I explain that I come from England. 'Where? Sahib, I am not an educated man. I do not know that place.' And a group of female labourers (*rejas*), with whom I had already spent many days, were genuinely astonished to learn that my home town is even further away than Orissa and that there daughters are not expected to marry as their fathers direct.

Conclusion

What I have tried to suggest, then, is that different segments of the Bhilai 'working class' are markedly different in the degree to which they are cosmopolitan in outlook. Cosmopolitanism and secularism have some affinity in that they both involve a willingness to place in abeyance the hegemonic and totalising claims of one's own religion and culture. Though there is always the possibility of a violent ethnic or communal backlash, there is a certain impetus towards both in the process of rapid industrialisation and in the project of building a nation out of culturally disparate elements. Not only a nation-building project, but any attempt to create a community of moral equals out of significant cultural diversity (and that includes a community that transcends nations), must have something of the melting-pot about it, for it is a priori impossible to imagine a social world in which some kinds of difference are not hierarchised. The spectre of Blimpish chauvinism notwithstanding, cosmopolitanism and nationalism are not necessarily antithetical attitudes. In practice, the state is often the only practical agent there is for giving real effect to measures prompted by cosmopolitan concerns. In the case I have described, a nationalised state industry that was consciously intended to become an icon for the imagination of a new modern India has done a great deal more to foster a cosmopolitan outlook than global capital flows. In fact, it is unregulated capitalism that has here been largely responsible for encouraging a recidivist anti-cosmopolitan retreat into localism through the way in which its quest to maximise profits by making labour as cheap and as flexible as possible has intersected with, and helped to entrench, ethnic divisions in the labour force.

Notes

1. Fieldwork in Bhilai – undertaken between 1993 and 2006 and extending over approximately 26 months – was supported by the Nuffield Foundation, the Economic and Social Research Council and the London School of Economics. I am deeply indebted to Ajay T. G. for invaluable research assistance.
2. This cautious formulation – 'the so-called "working class"' – is intended to signal some serious doubt about whether in this context it is appropriate to speak of *a* working class (in the singular), and about whether the BSP aristocracy of labour has significant interests in common with bottom-of-the-heap informal sector casual labour. If not in the past, there is today a good case for arguing that in terms of the way in which they regard themselves and are regarded by others, and in terms of their economic standing, values and life-styles, BSP workers are now 'middle class'. I explore these issues in a forthcoming paper (Parry, n.d.).
3. In this and the following two paragraphs, I summarise a more detailed discussion of BSP shop-floor culture contained in Parry 1999b.
4. I employ pseudonyms throughout.
5. For a detailed discussion of the issues covered in this paragraph, see Parry 2003.
6. As shown in a previous publication (Parry 2001), the greatest proportion of these inter-caste and inter-regional secondary unions is concentrated in fractions of 'the working class' outside the citadel of secure BSP employment. The main reason for this is that the trend over time has been for the primary marriages of BSP workers of Chhattisgarhi origin to become increasingly stable.
7. A village in the Himachal Pradesh district of Kangra in the second half of the 1960s (reported on in Parry 1979), and in the city of Banaras through the 1970s and 1980s (reported on in Parry 1994).
8. The compensation issue is discussed in more detail in Parry 1999b. In terms of the going market rate at the time, they were in reality treated generously. But a

much larger area was requisitioned than was actually required, and when this was subsequently privatised they saw their plots being sold for many times the amounts they had received for them.

9. Fortunately, there seems no immediate danger of that. The world market for steel has recently been buoyant, and BSP is currently investing to expand its capacity from five to seven million tons per annum, an output it aims to produce on *current* levels of manning.

References

Beck, Ulrich (2002), 'The Cosmopolitan Society and its Enemies'. *Theory, Culture and Society* 19 (1 and 2): 17–44.

—— (2006), *The Cosmopolitan Vision*, Cambridge: Polity Press.

Béteille, André (1994), 'Secularism and the intellectuals'. *Economic and Political Weekly*, 29 (10): 559–66.

Dumont, Louis (1966), *Homo hierarchicus: The Caste System and its Implications*, London: Weidenfeld and Nicolson.

Ferguson, James (1999), *Expectations of Modernity: Myths and Meanings of Urban Life on the Zambian Copperbelt*, Berkeley: University of California Press.

Friedman, Jonathan (2002), 'From Routes to Roots: Tropes for Trippers', *Anthropological Theory* 2 (1): 21–36.

—— (n.d.), 'The Dialectic of Cosmopolitanization and Indigenization in the Contemporary World System: Contradictory Configurations of Class and Culture' (unpublished m.s.).

Holmström, Mark (1984), *Industry and Inequality: The Social Anthropology of Indian Labour*, Cambridge: University Press.

Nandy, Ashis, S. Trivedy, S. Mayaram and A. Yagnik (1997), *Creating a Nationality: The Ramjanmabhumi Movement and the Fear of Self*, Delhi: Oxford University Press.

Parry, Jonathan (1979), *Caste and Kinship in Kangra*, London: Routledge and Kegan Paul.

—— (1994), *Death in Banaras*, Cambridge: University Press.

—— (1999a), 'Two Cheers For Reservation: The Satnamis and the Steel Plant', in Ramachandra Guha and Jonathan P. Parry (eds), *Institutions and Inequalities: Essays in Honour of André Béteille*, Oxford University Press: New Delhi, pp. 129–69.

—— (1999b), 'Lords of Labour: Working and Shirking in Bhilai,' *Contributions to Indian Sociology* (n.s.) 33 (1 and 2): 107–40.

—— (2001), 'Ankalu's Errant Wife: Sex, Marriage and Industry in Contemporary Chhattisgarh', *Modern Asian Studies* 35 (4): 783–820.

—— (2003), 'Nehru's Dream and the Village "Waiting Room": Long Distance Labour Migrants to a Central Indian Steel Town', *Contributions to Indian Sociology* 37 (1 and 2): 217–49.

—— (2004), 'The Marital History of "A Thumb-Impression Man"', in D. Arnold and S. Blackburn (eds), *Telling Lives in India: Biography, Autobiography and Life History*, Bloomington: University of Indiana Press, pp. 281–318.

—— (2005), 'Changing Childhoods in Industrial Chhattisgarh', in R. Chopra and Patricia Jeffery (eds), *Educational Regimes in Contemporary India*, New Delhi/London: Sage Publications, pp 276–98.

—— (2007), 'The Sacrifices of Modernity in a Soviet-built Steel Town in Central India', in Frances Pine and J. Pina-Cabral (eds), *On the Margins of Religion*, Oxford: Berghahn Books, pp. 233–62.

—— (forthcoming), 'Sociological Marxism in Central India: Polanyi, Gramsci and the Case of the Unions', in Chris Hann and Keith Hart (eds), *Market and Society: The Great Transformation Today* (under review).

—— (n.d.), 'The Embourgeoisement of a "Proletarian Vanguard"', (manuscript under revision).

Pollock, Sheldon, Homi K. Bhabha, Carol Breckenridge and Dipesh Chakrabarty (2000), 'Cosmopolitanisms', *Public Culture* 12 (3): 577–89.

Turner, Bryan (2002), 'Cosmopolitan Virtue, Globalization and Patriotism', *Theory, Culture and Society* 19 (1 and 2): 45–63.

Cosmopolitanism, Globalisation and Diaspora[1]
Stuart Hall in Conversation with Pnina Werbner,
March 2006

PW: I want to start by asking something about globalisation, because we talk a lot about globalisation and multiculturalism today but I think that cosmopolitanism is a little bit different from those two concepts, in the sense that it's a vision, some would say a utopian vision – for world citizenship, peace or human rights, but … so how do you see cosmopolitanism today in the world with all its apparently endemic, terrible conflicts, intractable…

SH: Well, I do think I understand cosmopolitanism principally as an ideal, a utopia. I'm not at all sure about 'world citizenship'. What I would say is that nowadays the concept is very closely related to globalisation. We are obliged to talk about the interdependencies across the globe in a planetary way, in which more or less everybody is in the swim of history and connected with one another. Of course, connected in deeply unequal ways – globalisation is a contradictory system, the product of what used to be called 'combined and uneven development'. Outside this uneven and unequal framework, cosmopolitanism is a very limited concept. It can only mean the capacity of certain elites to move around within very limited circles. Once our perspective becomes planetary, and there is a possibility of global citizenship, then cosmopolitanism as a utopia becomes potentially more possible. Of course the actual form that globalisation, – this interconnectedness – has taken, is exactly the opposite. It connects disjunctive histories, the very early and the very late, the too late and the too early, the developed, the developing and the underdeveloped, the colonised and the colonisers, the pre- and the post-colonial, etc. So whereas in the discourse of contemporary globalisation, we speak as though there was one space, one globe, and therefore potentially one citizenship, a universal human morality, the reality is precisely the reverse. Not that the interdependencies don't constitute something new. I think they constitute a profoundly new historical moment. They may even constitute the moment when such a universal vision of belonging is potentially realisable. But the reality of contemporary globalisation – interconnectedness – must be seen as, in fact, a

structure of power, a structure of global power, and therefore of global or transnational inequalities and conflicts rather than the basis of a benign cosmopolitanism.
The differences of power and resources override the interconnectedness. So I see
contemporary globalisation as, realistically, opening not one but two quite different
possibilities simultaneously: a world driven apart into warring differences or one
driven into an overriding sameness and homogenisation, under the hegemony
of those powerful enough to claim to be the universal instance, to represent the
whole of civilisation. So contemporary cosmopolitanism – which, to give it its
proper name, is really the latest phase capitalist modernity operating on a global
scale, poses for me this double perspective.

PW: What you are saying about inequalities is also linked to the fact that we live in
a world of massive transnational movements of refugees and economic migrants
from one place to another. So the next question I was going to ask you has got to
do with diasporas. Diasporas have always been seen as the archetypal, boundary-
crossing strangers, and in that sense they are thought to epitomise cosmopolitanism.
But, on the other hand, diasporas have also been accused of disloyalty to the nation,
of not being rooted anywhere, of not having any commitments, and even these
days of long-distance nationalism without responsibility, as Benedict Anderson
has put it – where they support guns to the IRA, they support Jewish settlers on
the West Bank or Hindu nationalists. So how do you see the role of diasporans in
this globalised, cosmopolitanising world, perhaps?

SH: Before you get to diasporas I would say that we must insist on seeing
globalisation as a deeply contradictory process. I see the tide of the trasnsnational
movement of peoples – driven by civil war, by ethnic cleansing, famine, poverty
and ecological disaster, as well as by the search for economic benefits and a better
life, as a form of 'globalisation from below'. I think it is linked with the systems
of inequality and power, both historical and contemporary, that we talked about
before. And I think, just to put it simply, that there are two ways of life associated
with it. There is a 'cosmopolitanism of the above' – global entrepreneurs following
the pathways of global corporate power and the circuits of global investment and
capital, who can't tell which airport they're in, because they all look the same, and
who have apartments in three continents. This is global cosmopolitanism of a very
limited kind but it is very different from 'cosmopolitanism from below' – people
driven across borders, obliged to uproot themselves from home, place and family,
living in transit camps or climbing on to the backs of lorries or leaky boats or the
bottom of trains and airplanes, to get to somewhere else. Both of them are forms
of globalisation and, in so far as they both interact within the same global sphere,
are deeply interconnected with one another. But they don't constitute the basis of
a 'global citizenship'.

PW: But does cosmopolitanism have to be an elite thing?

SH: No. I'm not saying that it has to be. Historically, there have been many forms of cosmopolitanism. What I am saying is that contemporary forms of globalisation enforce a 'cosmopolitan from below'; it bears down on people who have no choice as to whether or not to become cosmopolitans. They have to learn to live in two countries, to speak a new language and make a life in another place, not by choice but as a condition of survival. They have to acquire the same cosmopolitan skills of adaptation and innovation which an entrepreneur requires – but from a different place. They operate in different markets – illegal markets, black markets, markets in people, the markets for illegal papers and so on. So, culturally, they're living 'in translation' every day of their lives; what has been called elsewhere a 'vernacular cosmopolitanism': not the global life as a reward for status, education or wealth, but the global life as one of the necessities imposed by the disjunctures of modern globalisation. These new settlements are, of course, as a consequence of globalisation from below, diasporas, because they are made up of people from different cultural backgrounds, who have been obliged to live somewhere else but who remain in some deep ways also connected to their homes, cultures and places of origin, and consequently develop what I would call a diasporic form of consciousness and way of life . . . They are what, following the Jamaican anthropologist, David Scott, we should call 'conscripts of global modernity'.

The question then is: what is their position? What is their position in relation to the places they find themselves in, or to the places they came from, and what sense do they make of that experience of displacement and of themselves? Who are they now and where do they belong? This is the identity question, the diasporic dilemma, I'm interested in – identity in the context of the post-colonial era of globalisation and mass migration. How do you make sense of your self, and your life, if this movement between places, cultures, religions, languages, civilisations, histories, times, becomes your lived reality? How can you say, 'This is who I am', and what on earth do you mean by it? What I've tried to say is that this is inevitably the site of what DuBois called 'double consciousness', and of what, somewhat inadvisedly perhaps, I have elsewhere called 'hybridity'. I don't think identity is just a free-floating smorgasbord – you get up today and decide to be whoever you'd like to be: that's just a post-modern fantasy. Identity is always tied to history and place, to time, to narratives, to memory and ideologies. It requires material conditions of existence. You can't just move identity around as you choose. On the other hand, I think identity isn't inscribed, forever, in or transmitted by, the genes. It is socially, historically, culturally constructed. So in that sense, identity is always, to some extent, an open question, always, as they say, 'in process': not because it is entirely self-constructed, a mere self-fashioning of choice, and has no conditions of existence, but because, like meaning itself, it operates *ultimately* in relation to an open horizon, since it cannot be finally fixed. However the disjunctures between globalisation from above and below are resolved will affect what happens to identities in the diasporic conditions of dis-placement which these global process inevitably set in motion. If the prevailing outcome is to homogenise the world globally, militarily, technologically, economically or civilisationally, then of course either people are drawn willy-nilly into the process of assimilation – what in the UK New Labour is offering these days under the misleading title of 'social cohesion'. You can be accepted but only if you become like us. Otherwise, you are driven into the exact opposite alternative, which is to defend yourself against the loss of identity which wholesale assimilation as a strategy entails, and retreat defensively back to where you came from, into that sphere called 'tradition', as if that has remained the same, untouched by history.

PW: And either of those options is not really in a way cosmopolitan.

SH: No, of course not. These are both a retreat from cosmopolitanism, because they are a retreat from or a denial of those 'differences' which are the inevitable consequence of uneven and combined historical development. It polarises 'difference' into unbridgeable extremes. We are all completely different from one another, and the barriers between the differences are insurpassable. Inevitably, as an effect of the resistance to the pressure to assimilate, differences do become more rigid, more entrenched, politicised, emotionally charged and exclusive. The reaction to any variation from this norm of homogeneity is more and more punitive. We start to police those boundaries, to regulate any signs of cultural. mixing. This resistance to change, to history, wherever it comes to predominate, is a form of cultural fundamentalism, a phenomenon by no means restricted to a certain strand within political Islam – indeed perfectly compatible with a certain version of western global modernity.

People who sometimes quote me on identity forget that I've always talked about the possibility that, if we don't move towards the more open horizon pioneered by 'cosmopolitanism from below', we will find ourselves driven either to homogenisation from above or to the retreat into the bunker and the war of all against all.

PW: And you in a way set a kind of aspiration for us in your work, in reaching out, in recognising both difference and the battle for equality as simultaneous struggles. You've come to England from far away, and colonised this country.

SH: That's kind of you. I wish I had. We used to think that difference and equality were mutually exclusive. But I think they are both necessary and set limits for each other. Difference without equality is ultimately the war of all against all. Equality without difference is homogenization.

PW: So the question is – do you feel yourself to be a cosmopolitan?

SH: (Pause) You know, I hesitate every time I use the word. Because a certain view of cosmopolitanism was built into the Enlightenment and Kant's famous question, 'What is Enlightenment?' Kant is the architect of this universalist version of cosmopolitanism. And I resist that kind of cosmopolitanism, not because there weren't enlarging, 'universalising' elements in it, but because, as we know very well, it is a version of cosmopolitanism which represented itself as 'universal' but that universality inevitably became harnessed back to the West. 'We' were the enlightened ones, whose civilizational duty and burden it was to enlighten everybody else – the unenlightened, the non-cosmopolitan. This is the paradox at the heart of the Enlightenment – the particularism of its conception of universality. Inevitably, I'm a sort of child of the Enlightenment, in the sense that I believe in history, sometimes but not often in progress; I'm not religious (though I'm not a militant atheist either), I believe in science (but not scientism), in the rule of law, etc. But I'm not a child of the Enlightenment in the sense that everybody other than 'us' is consigned to what Locke called 'the childhood of Mankind' and only the West and Western civilisation are really the grown-ups. Which is what the Enlightenment, for all its intertest in the 'noble savage', really thought. These days I find myself recruited to many of the Enlightenment aspirations, but I have to remind myself that it never understood difference, never understood that it was underpinned by a particularly Western conception of reason, never came to terms with the supporting ideological underpinning of its 'liberalism', of this particular notion of cosmopolitanism, and of the way the claims to universalism were embedded in a certain form of historical particularity.

So if you ask me, am I a cosmopolitan, I'm not a cosmopolitan in that sense. But I am in the sense that I have never found myself in the position of being tied into identification with the notion of the nation, of nationhood, as the ultimate goal of the political process. I know the tremendous value that the idea of nationhood played, for example, in the moment of decolonisation. It was the driving idea which in a sense enabled us to liberate ourselves from Imperialism, from the degredation and exploitation of colonialism. So I can't undervalue that moment of national liberation but I see everywhere now the limits of nationhood as an all-encompassing point of identification. And it just happens that in my history I have sort-of evaded it because I left the Caribbean at the moment of decolonisation. So I'm not a part of that process when all the hopes were caught up with building the nation. In some sense I regret this, of course. Every diaspora has its regrets. Although you can never go back to the past, you do have a sense of loss of an intimate connection with a history, a landscape, family, tradition, custom – the vernacular. In a sense, this is the fate of all modern people – we have to lose those connections, but we seem to require the myth, the illusion that we are going to go back to them.

So in my history, as it happens, my generation stayed at home and got deeply involved in the struggle for, and writing the history of, the nation. And I wasn't there. I was identified with it but also watching it from afar. But now I see the limits of that vision, when I look back at the Caribbean, and I see that they cannot move any further by trying to resolve their problems within the framework of the nation. Indeed, the nation is being driven by global forces which small nations without great economic resources don't have any leverage on.

When I came to England, I discovered I couldn't be a member of this nation either. Because of my colonial formation I was already displaced. Although I've chosen to live here, and marry into it, I'm not fundamentally part of the self-conception of the British or English nation. So I'm cosmopolitan by default. I have to find my way, like many of us, amongst many attachments, many identifications, none of them self-sufficient or complete. I have to recognise how limited that is. But it's obliged me to maintain what I would call an openness towards the horizon of that which I am not, the experiences I have not had – a sense of one's incompleteness, requiring for my own 'completeness' what is other to it.

Even in this global moment, there are so many experiences we know nothing about. So we can't close everything up around our own narratives. This may be a cosmopolitan moment, but there are other cosmopolitan worlds still to uncover. I don't want to make a fetish of Otherness but universalism only works, not as a state of being but as a constantly shifting horizon towards that point where we, our experience, our history ends, and another history begins; which is adjunct to us, which overlaps with us, which we know part of, but some aspects of which remain ineradicably different from us and which remind us that every positionality, far from, being self-sufficient, can only be fully defined by what it is not, by what is left out or excluded – by its constituitive outside.

I think of Palestine, you know, because although I've never written extensively about it, it's been at the centre of my political thinking for many years, partly through the privilege of my friendship with Edward Said. It's one of the worlds I can't let go of. I don't know it, I've never been there. I look at pictures of the West Bank, I look at the faces of young Palestinians on television, I look at Edward and Jean Mohr's beautiful book *After the Last Sky* – and I think, I know these people because I can identify with their hopes, dilemmas and tribulations. They're not 'my people', but I ought to know them better. I know something of their experience by reading their tragic history. but I ought to know more. I know what it's like to be colonised, to be occupied, excluded, defined by another power, I know what it's like not to be in your home, only to see your from home from a distance, across a barrier. I share so much with them, not despite but because they come from another tradition, another world, another religious universe, another language, another literature. So they're not me – but I'm open in some ways to their existing now in, as part of, my global world. Is that a new kind of cosmopolitanism?

PW: You talked about the people you grew up with, who became the inscribers of the nation in Jamaica, in the Caribbean. Do you think you could be a cosmopolitan at home in Africa or the Caribbean? Do you have to be locked into that national vision or can you also be a cosmopolitan in your own country?

SH: That's a very hard question, and I'm not a good person to answer it because my experience may be too particular to generalise from. One reason is because the Caribbean is by definition cosmopolitan. The original inhabitants – Arawak Indians of the New World – don't exist any longer – they were wiped out by the Spanish conquistadors and by disease within a hundred years of the arrival of Western civilization. So everybody who is there came from somewhere else – the Spanish, the Dutch, the British, the enslaved Africans, the indentured Indians and Pakistanis, the Portugese Jews, the French expelled from Haiti, the Chinese and Lebanese traders ... Everybody comes from somewhere else. This is really the true disaporic society. Perhaps, then, you're sort-of a 'natural' cosmopolitan, and the very distinctiveness of Caribbean culture – what is really indigenous today to the Caribbean – is creolisation, the cultural mix of different elements, which is a kind of 'comopolitanism at home'. Though predominantly a black society, the African presence exists 'in translation' with other cultural elements – it is not African but what 'Africa' has become in the New World.

In what sense, then, can you remain at home and be a cosmopolitan? I think that is difficult. But I think if you understand your history as always a history of movement, migration, conquest, translation, if you don't have some originary conception of your own culture as really, always the same – throbbing away there unchanged since the tribal past – you could become a cosmopolitan at home. If you don't have that originary conception of history, you see the degree to which who you are now and what your society has become, is the result of a long and disrupted process of formation which has been made and remade, and is being remade again by forces which are essentially global, which are external to you in some fundamental way.

But I think this is a different kind of cosmopolitanism from the one which is available to those who've travelled to live permanently in different places, out of choice or as a matter of expanding one's experience. The latter have been obliged to think of themselves not as all 'the same' but as different. They can't have an originary conception of culture because they know their own culture has been transformed, historically. And they see other people like themselves being culturally transformed by new experiences.

I think that, for an anthropologist, my question is: are there then two or three different conceptions of culture? Or is it a fact that culture as such is *always* open to some degree, though cultures change at different paces – Lévi-Strauss divided them into 'hot' and 'cold' societies? And is the real question about those cultures which have remained relatively unchanged over long periods, which have not in recent times been colonized or invaded from outside, not had to absorb large numbers of people, whether they are exempt from my generalization? Won't it turn out that they, too, have been influenced by the outside, aren't self-sufficient, though of course, their sense of movement, of otherness and difference, is bound to be more limited? For those people like me who come from an already diasporic and creolized culture – I'm twice diaspora-ised! – it's easy for me to take on this concept of culture as always to some degree 'unfinished'.

PW: Modern anthropology would say that people, say in Africa, have already had a journey from that theoretically closed culture, which may or may not have once existed. So that they've already been on a journey. And part of that journey they've been on, especially, I suppose, the elite, but even the labour migrants who went into the city to work or whatever, part of their journey has been the making of the nation. And it's within national contours that one has to consider whether you are a cosmopolitan or not. I mean, that would be the question – if you are an African member of an elite, are you going to be a person who just embraces external globalisation, or espouses national homogenisation, or are you going to be somebody who believes in this kind of openness, in the Kantian Enlightenment?

SH: Well, I would agree with all of that. I like that way of thinking about it. They have already been remade by many forces, they are already part of a cosmopolitanising process, so really, it's more a question, not of ideology as such, but of how the culture understands itself – whether there is some impulsion to understand itself as an originary one to which the only really cultural 'progress' would be back towards the original. Or whether it understands itself as inevitably open, and then is working to try to strike a balance between tradition and innovation, between what needs to change, what needs to be let in, let in on what terms, and so on. In a sense, that is the big cultural question of our global times: as soon as the globe is sort of 'one' – not one because it's all the same, but because of the combination of inter-dependencies and the proliferation of differences – how porous should be the borders between cultures, between peoples and histories if they are to retain a sense of identity and specificity? How can they share a space with others who are not like them without demanding that the others become like them? This is 'the multi-cultural question'.

PW: The other side of the question – Can you be a cosmopolitan in your own country? – is can you be a cosmopolitan if you don't have commitments to a place, or people, or maybe even culture? Is it possible to be a cosmopolitan without this rootedness somewhere?

SH: Well, I would have said not. And I'm afraid of the word because sometimes it suggests that. It invokes a kind of cultureless, rootless image of a person who is free-floating, sampling all the cultures, you know, like my global entrepreneurs in the first-class waiting room of some airport, who loves Japanese cooking, a bit of Indian cooking here, French cuisine there. They sample everything, but nothing comes from an understanding of a particular cultural ecology, an attachment to a particular way of handling food, etc. These are the differences that don't make any difference. That doesn't mean you have to eat only one way all the time, but you sort of know what it is like to be attached to a particular cuisine. I think that, without that, the old Marxist jibe, 'rootless cosmopolitan', has some substance. In many ways this is where we encounter an interesting interface with one aspect of liberalism, which exactly thinks that we can only really calculate what individuals are like when we free them from all their attachments. No religion, no culture, nothing but free-floating atoms contracting with one another. I know why this arose – it is part of the Enlightenment desire to free mankind from the burden of tradition. However, I also think this is exactly one of the limitations of liberalism. It's never understood culture. In particular, it's never understood its own culture. This idea of the atomised individual has of course played its role. The idea of the rule of law depends on a certain abstraction of the individual from cultures and particularities, and so does the free exchange of the market. So it does have its value. But liberalism has never understood that it's underpinned by its own culture. There's no liberal democracy that doesn't have roots in a community.

PW: So you always fought your struggles – if they may be called cosmopolitan struggles – from a particular location.

SH: Yes, exactly. I believe in locatedness, in position, attachment, but I believe that these are never singular, never completely determining. Every culture has to be aware of its own 'outside'.

PW: There is a tendency to see cosmopolitans as individual travellers who move around and have, as you say, familiarity with different cultures and tastes, but maybe cosmopolitanism is a collective phenomenon? It's a coming together from many different places potentially to create something new. Maybe even a new culture. So I wondered how you would respond to that question?

SH: I think of it more as a collective phenomenon. I'm interested in certain parts of the world in an earlier period which seemed to have developed a certain kind of cosmopolitanism – the cosmopolitanism of trade. Many of these places are in the Mediterranean or the Middle East, because this was such a point of confluence between Europe and the East. Places like that I think are extremely interesting, because the different cultures don't merge into something entirely new, but they become known as places where many cultures coexist and there are many friendships and marriages across cultural lines. This cosmopolitanism is not driven by the harsh disciplines of the global labour market, of people searching for work, but by markets of a more local kind, with people following different routes, drawn together by the exchange of goods, markets, not The Market as a capitalist abstraction. Places like Beirut or the Lebanon, the Eastern Mediterranean, North Africa or Muslim Spain – places where differences were tolerated, not places of race riots, ethnic cleansing or religious conversion. People had their attachments to particular ways of life, family traditions, and so on. But they were not evangelising societies, they were not trying to recruit people; there was not a crusading vision. These are utopian spots for me. There's a whole history there. Amitav Ghosh has written beautifully about such places. You would have to call them cosmopolitan. I suppose the 'multi-cultural question' is whether Western societies, exposed to the very different circumstances of global capitalism, can ever become 'cosmopolitan' in this vernacular way.

[In the hospital where I go for dialysis] I often sit beside a patient who speaks Russian, and doesn't have a word of English. He's thrilled when I tell him 'Goodbye' in Russian. He's teaching the Filipino nurses Russian phrases and they're teaching him their own language in return. He says to them: 'What are you teaching me?' 'Tagalog, of course', they reply, laughing. He's never heard of it! I think of this man, who is trying desperately to learn English, meanwhile holding on, as an Azerbaijani, to Russian, who can speak only to the Polish woman who is cleaning the ward because Russian is the only means of communication they share, though it is neither of their native languages .... Well, this NHS hospital in central London is a pretty polyglot, cosmopolitan sort of place.

PW: It is remarkable that there are such cosmopolitan sites, like little islands, in the middle of this country where we live.

SH: I think of them as sites rather than societies. It's hard to think of them with a polity, a structure. They are social sites where 'trade-routes' cross.

PW: And one of them is British hospitals in the twenty-first century.

I have one final question to you, which is a serious question but one to which I think to which there isn't a clear answer at the moment. Do you think we should impose cosmopolitan values on other people or places? Should we impose human rights or democracy? Can we impose them?

SH: First of all, I don't know that I would use cosmopolitanism in that way, interchangeably with democracy and human rights. I know that these ideas seem to belong to a common frame. Across the world, democracy is being imposed in the name of modernity, but really as part of a new imperial system. The more democracy is hollowed out in so-called liberal-democracies, the more everybody else is required to have it! People in Iraq or Afghanistan, who have travelled a very different path, historically, and will take a long time to develop a democratic culture which can genuinely underpin democratic institutions, are required to produce it overnight because the Americans need to leave behind a stable state. It also assumes that the forms of democracy in Iraq or Afghanistan will simply replicate Western liberal-democracy. This is not to say that I wouldn't like to see more societies moving towards genuine popular democracy: people developing ways of governing themselves, not being ruled by oligarchies, by elites, by a foreign country or a small political or economic class. In that sense, I think we could do with a lot more of this kind of democracy in this country. There is a genuine problem in the Middle East about the autocratic nature of the governments which have oppressed their people in different ways. But these are exactly the sorts of regimes the West has helped to prop up over the years – an irony not lost on Osama bin Laden. They could do with a good dose of democracy but whether they need it from the muzzle of an AK44 or at the dictate of an armed Hum-Vee is quite another question. I don't think The West can march around the world making people cosmopolitan. On the other hand, the more people can generally begin to hope and aspire in a cosmopolitan way, the less they will be driven to ethnically cleanse people who are not like them, to murder those whom they can't convert, to expel those who won't subscribe to the dominant way of life, etc.

PW: There are countries where almost miraculously, democracy returned, like in Spain, for example, in Poland, in South Africa, partly because of Mandela and de Klerk, so it is possible.

SH: Yes, of course it is possible. But you know, South Africa, in that sense, although it still has many problems to resolve, was extremely lucky that nobody decided to impose anti-apartheid from outside. They managed to do it for themselves, and do it in a way which didn't disable others from joining in, once they'd seen the light. This capacity to constantly enlarge and expand 'the imagined community' is the real ground of a democratic culture: the product of a truly democratic conception of the future. And, though it sounds very individualistic to say so, we know that it couldn't have happened in South Africa without the far-sightedness of people like

Mandela – and even de Klerk! But when things are not leading in that direction, they will take the opposite course: towards the entrenching of differences and the imposition of homogenisation at the barrel of a gun, rather than facilitating the discourse of a critical openness to others.

Which doesn't mean to say a simple-minded relativism – everything that other people do is right. It means saying what you think but being willing to negotiate difference, however difficult and dangerous that turns out to be. In this sense, I'm a child of the Enlightenment. I think one good thing the Enlightenment did understand was that democracy required a big argument, it required an open row, it required a lot of talking, a lot of polemical pamphlets against your opponent, and so on. Not stabbing them in the street. People talk about the stability of democracy but democracy is by definition an open, argumentative, quarrelsome society. It is quarrels that created the enfranchisement of women. Or that gave the majority of people the vote. It's struggles that democratised old aristocratic and industrial capitalist societies, that created the welfare state. All of these advances were strenuously, sometimes bitterly, contested in their time. So the process of democratisation is never an easy passage. Consensus is constructed by the clash between strong positions as to what constitutes the 'good life' – not by some pre-ordained unity.

But translate your question into another: should we then teach cosmopolitan values in schools? Without labelling them as such, I would say yes, a cosmo-politan approach to the discovery of the 'truth'. Of course, all schools are always passing on culture as well as knowledge and scientific understanding. They are transmitting culture. And the more we consciously think about whether we are transmitting the values of critical openness, of respect for but not subservience to difference, of a democratic culture of questioning the orthodoxies, the better. We're in the middle of a debate about whether our schools should become academies, sponsored and to a large extent run by wealthy individuals, private philanthropists and corporate businesess.. I saw the faces of people who have contributed to the next tranche of New Labour's academy strategy in my newspaper yesterday. Will anybody ask the question, why should we be governed by these people, why should a public education system have their priorities imposed on them by the private interests they represent, by people who have no experience or understanding of education? I wouldn't trust them to teach my grandchild to cross the road! But nobody asks that question. So am I in a democratic culture that is really questioning who does and who does not exercise power – which is after all the question with which democracy began? Why should they, because they are very wealthy, have the power to shape the ethos that governs me and my life and the life of my grandchildren to come? I think if we are going to be 'free' to teach Creationism or 'British values' in schools, we ought to be teaching a more cosmopolitan curriculum.

Because Britain has become, whether we like it or not, a kind of proto-cosmopolitan society. Whether or not we are going to get rid of the word 'multiculturalism', we are in effect, irreversibly living in a kind of mixed-up multicultural society. Not one in which the different groups police the differences and patrol the boundaries between them, but a hybrid society of a mixture of cultures and histories, and languages, and traditions, and cuisines, and ways of life. Multiculturalism as a policy goal may be abandoned but 'the multicultural question' – can we find a way of living more equally together without eating one another – will not disappear in a globalising world. Multicultural is what Britain now is, for good or ill, and to have a curriculum which doesn't teach, as one of its underpinning values, a positive view of that kind of cosmopolitan mix, is to sell out the past. Inevitably, we will fall back into ethnic particularism.

PW: So you are a cosmopolitan in your own country, in a way.

SH: That's nice to think, but I am sort of a cosmopolitan without thinking about it.

The following are responses of members of the audience to the viewing of the film of this conversation.

RICHARD WERBNER (Manchester U): Among other things, what intrigued me is the way Stuart wanted us to think of horizons beyond what is actual, to something potential. And this is what I myself view as deeply at the heart of the cosmopolitanism argument, the cosmopolitan question. But one thing, as I listened to him, disturbed me, because I found that I identified too much with him and his kind of experience of being someone who'd left one nation and then had a sense of what had gone on in the nation of origin. And the more I thought about it, I began to worry that the opposition he had between the Ali Baba's Cave sampler, who travels the globe and has a little taste of this and that, and then the cosmopolitan from below, might get in the way of understanding the connection between them, I mean between postcolonial elites and their fellow countrymen. I began wondering how one would see the work that goes on as the people who had to become cosmopolitan willy-nilly, they are still connected to the people who have the luxury of going to different sites in the world with all the comforts that come with it. And having known a cosmopolitan in Africa who kept this organic connection [to his rural ethnic community], I think the challenge for us is not to have too simple an opposition between deracinated, footloose cosmopolitans in the image that would have pleased Stalin, and then the ones that are coming from below and seem to be rooted. So I would say that this is a question to us: how can we think of the connection between them and not only the disjunction between them?

PHIL STENNIGHAM (Keele U): I really enjoyed the discussion, but [there was] one thing about it that really surprised me, which is that all the talk about cosmopolitanism seems to be around the idea that it is a physical phenomenon, people moving around from one place to another, interacting, physically with other people. But it seems to me that there's another whole aspect to this which I guess I would have to call virtual cosmopolitanism, which is being developed through the Internet – the fact is that now, you know, I can sit in Keele and I can be in connection and communication with people all around the world, without actually having to move out of my office. And that seems to me another form that cosmopolitanism can develop, quite apart from the ability to travel or being forced to move. I'm speaking as somebody who grew up in Britain for the first 22 years of my life, and then I went to Canada for 30 years, and then I went to New Zealand, and now I'm back in Britain. And the interesting thing is that the Britain I'm now back in is quite different from the Britain I left 35 years ago. But one of the reasons that it's not quite like when I left, is because of the Internet, and I can now sit in my office and communicate with people all over the world.

PW: Stuart highlighted the difference between the Enlightenment principles of universal rights, and the sense that people have to be located, they do have a culture, they do have an identity that they can defend. I felt that the way Stuart was struggling throughout the film on how to bridge these two different dimensions, and how to think whether cosmopolitanism was an illegitimate word to use to create that bridge – I thought that was a very interesting aspect of the conversation with him. Because I thought that he did go on a kind of journey during the film, so that by the time he reached the end of the film, he had ended up as a cosmopolitan – which he denied, or worried about, at the beginning.

NIGEL RAPPORT (St Andrews U): I wish Stuart would say more about rootless cosmopolitanism and what he saw wrong with it. He referred to a Marxian critique of the term but left it at that. And it seemed to me that he was making a value judgement rather than an analytical judgement about where rootless cosmopolitanism might lead. Because it would seem to me, as a kind of neo-Kantian, to be precisely a route to world peace. And it seemed also to affect what he said earlier about how can one say, this is me, if one lives in-between. This seems to be something that everybody says – that this is me, and we all live in between, in various ways. And he described those kinds of ways of in-betweenness, as those that move and those that don't move, as both living in between in various ways. He claimed that identity isn't a free-floating smorgasbord, but nor is it inscribed in genes. But it's about ideologies and histories and narratives. But those are precisely things that also move between, those aren't fixed in spaces. Narratives and histories and ideologies are things that one can't physically attach, nor can one really cognitively or emotionally attach those things to places. So all this adds up to a query, I suppose (and I wish he was here), because I'd like to press him. It seemed like a conviction that one shouldn't aspire to be rootless. It didn't seem to be an ethnography of his, or an analysis or a theory of his. So I'd like to know more about why we should share his conviction, his value.

PW: I thought that one of the things that Stuart did bring out, linked to your question, Nigel, was the way that he emphasised all the time that there was a problem of inequalities in the world – that there were power inequalities, there were economic inequalities. Maybe, I don't know if that kind of links into your question, because he couldn't get away from the fact that there couldn't be a cosmopolitanism until the problem of inequalities had been resolved.

IAN FAIRWEATHER (Manchester U): It seemed to me that one of the things being struggled with, both in the questions and the answers, was the relationship between cosmopolitan individuals and cosmopolitan cultures, and it came out particularly in the answer to the question, Can you be a cosmopolitan at home? And Stuart Hall described the Caribbean as a place with a cosmopolitan history, a place where culture is created in the mix; and of course another place famous for founding that kind of culture is the United States, another melting-pot culture. But obviously, he wasn't implying that someone coming from there necessarily is a cosmopolitan, despite having that history, or is any more likely to be a cosmopolitan than someone coming from a village with a culture that claims to be unitary for so long. So I think it would be interesting to explore more what is the relationship between coming from a culture that has a cosmopolitan history and being a cosmopolitan individual.

DIEDRE MCKAY (ANU): I was interested when Stuart Hall described himself as an outcome of the Enlightenment, and talked about his belief in history, progress, the rule of law, which I assume is state law, and being secular. And I wanted to think of that as a politics of recognition that we would apply to people who might claim to be cosmopolitan: to what extent recognition by others as cosmopolitan is dependent on a subject being a Western Enlightened, modern subject. If we're talking about people who might be migrating or travelling and engaging with the world in various ways, who don't have a conception of history that we would recognise as modern, aren't people who recognise the rule of state law, may in fact be marginal or in an agonistic relationship with the state which they find themselves in, and are not secular, never have been – where do we end up? I'm sort of concerned that it's only possible to be cosmopolitan as a subject after the modern and after the Enlightenment, that we're talking about a genealogy which then excludes people who then are not caught up in that same genealogy. Do we then have to put them through this process? I was interested in what Hall would have to say about that, because he does ascribe a kind of moral virtue, I think, to being cosmopolitan.

PW: This is something of the tension in the term that he was struggling with as well, I think, because he did talk about cosmopolitanism from below.

KAREN LEONARD (U. of California, Irvine): I was struck by some of the questions that have come back to the film, about the individual versus the collective, or people at home rewriting or writing a national history; and people moving abroad, of course, are also rewriting, remaking the past, as they look to the present, the power configurations of the present, and I thought that this was a very interesting aspect of the interview.

Note

1. See also the film version of this interview: http://www.alanmacfarlane.com/DO/filmshow/Stuart_hall_fast.htm

Index

Index

Schapera, I. 41, 57
Schieffelin, E. 200–1
Schneider, L. 216
Schroeder, R. 217
Schulz, H.L. 167
Scott, D. 347
secular, secularisation, secularism, of
anthropologists 48; anti-feminist
124; cosmopolitan intellectuals 55;
cosmopolitans(ism) 55, 270, 327, 330,
340; in a feature of modernism 96, 126,
266; feminist in SE Asia, 98, 114–16,
119–21, 123, 128; global treaties
119; Indian modernity 327, 330, 340;
in Indonesia 13, 112, 114–15, 116,
119–21, 124–26, 128; in Malaysia 13,
96, 98, 264–66, 274, 276; nationalist,
in Indonesia 112, 114, 119; space 270;
western institution 117, 125, 274; see
also religious
secularists 264
Segev, T. 167
segmentary opposition 56
Seligman, T. 34, 40, 42
Selolwane, O. 61
Seneca 290
Shaw Brothers 264
Shih, M. 283, 284
Shivji, I.G. 216
Siam 262
Sichone, O. 91, 321
Simat, M. 219
Simmel, G. 167, 168
Singapore 268, 274
Sinha, M. 142
Sisters in Islam (SIS), 96, 98–99, 100, 101,
102
Sloane, P. 266, 276n
Snow, D.R. 286
social anthropology, defined, 36–37;
see also anthropology, cosmopolitan
anthropology, fieldwork
social change 118
social contract 292
social field/s 6, 54; unbounded 23; see also
anthropology, community, unit of study
social justice 112, 113, 114, 121, 122, 127,
128; see also gender equity; human rights

social movements 89, 93, 215–16; see
also activism, advocacy, human rights,
indigenous rights
society, defined 54; and part-society 54;
see also community, social field
Solway, J. 190
Somali family/patrilineal clans (Isaq)
316–17, 320, 322; diaspora 320, 322;
migrant, case study 314–20; social
survival 322
Somalia 316; collapse of 322
Somaliland (British) 314, 315
Sons-of-the-soil 326, 327, 338, 339, 340
South Africa 309 passim; apartheid 311;
border crossing 309; 'bright lights'
rite-of-passage theory 313; capitalism
314; citizenship 317; civil society
intolerant 311; colonial rule 312;
corruption 319; dehumanised 321;
fatalism of 320; free agents 310, 322;
hospitality 312; labour migration
regulated 314; languages learnt 317,
320; liberal constitution 311, 321; liberal
democracy 311; loyalty of clan 317;
migration 310 passim; pre-colonial mass
313; predicament of 319; 'Rainbow
Nation' ideology 311; regimes, know-
how of 319; rights of 312; statistics,
global 312, 322; statistics, South Africa
313; subject to xenophobia 312; survival
skills 313; undocumented 'illegal
aliens', irregular 313, 321–22; violence
of police and immigration officers
311–12
spaces, cosmopolitan; see cosmopolitan
spaces
Spain 164; colonial conquest 351; Muslim
354; return to democracy 355
spirit python 209
Stalin, Joseph 176, 357
state Islamic Institutes (Indonesia) 116,
117, 125
state/states 216; African 215, 218;
argument within 54; border regimes 16;
colonial 6, 215, 216, 218, 219, 226n4;
postcolonial 6, 215, 216–17, 218, 219,
220–27; plural 12; resistance to tyranny
173; see also Kenya, nation-states,

Printed in the United Kingdom by
Lightning Source UK Ltd., Milton Keynes
141572UK00001B/19/P